GREEK AND DEMOTIC TEXTS FROM THE ZENON ARCHIVE

TEXT

PAPYROLOGICA LUGDUNO-BATAVA

EDIDIT

VOLUMEN XX A

GREEK AND DEMOTIC TEXTS FROM THE ZENON ARCHIVE

(P. L. Bat. 20)

EDITED UNDER THE GENERAL DIRECTION OF

P.W. PESTMAN

TEXT

LEIDEN — E. J. BRILL — 1980

This book was printed with financial support from the
Netherlands Organization for the Advancement of Pure Research (Z.W.O.)

ISBN 90 04 06113 4
90 04 06114 2

PRINTED IN THE NETHERLANDS

PREFACE

In the immense archive that he built up during his career, Zenon retained relatively few Demotic and Greek-Demotic documents. I had for some time been interested in the latter group of bilingual texts, specifically because they were bilingual. I therefore decided to study and publish them all as a group, when the twelfth International Congress of Papyrology in 1968 gave me a chance to see the original papyri housed in Ann Arbor and New York; and in the following years it proved possible to work upon the papyri that are kept in Florence. In all, editions were prepared of thirteen bilingual receipts; but one swallow does not make a summer, and thirteen texts do not make a book, and so they have remained in store, awaiting an opportunity for publication.

Such an opportunity presented itself in 1975, when the *Leids Universiteitsfonds* offered me a substantial grant for a research project. While working on the bilingual texts, I had realized that the archive is highly inconvenient to consult, and that the publications of the texts are in a state of chaos. I therefore gratefully accepted the grant, proposing, with the help of a large international team, of a kind unparalleled in papyrological studies, to try to put some order in the chaos. The results will be published in the near future as P. L. Bat. 21, *A Guide to the Zenon Archive*.

Soon after embarking upon our work, we discovered that the archive could be made greatly more accessible if a number of texts were reprinted. Thus we have collected together isolated Zenon papyri from editions in which they lay hidden among other texts, for example, from P. Jand., P. S. A. Athen., and even the SB, which proved to contain very few Zenon documents that have not subsequently been republished. In this way we have been able to reduce considerably the number of text editions that need to be consulted when studying the Zenon archive. Moreover, we have reprinted various texts in which so many readings have been improved since the original publications, that these have become virtually unusable. Last, but not least, we have included texts that consist of fragments previously published separately. The archive is now sadly dispersed between many modern collections, and this is true, not only of individual documents, but also of fragments of the same document. The situation is all too well known, and the reconstruction of texts by joining scattered fragments has held a certain fascination for papyrologists. The best illustration is afforded by our no. 32, now nearly complete, which has been reconstructed from four fragments, housed in three countries, and published in different volumes. A fragment in Cairo was published in 1925 as P. Cairo Zen. 1 59.017, and a fragment in New York was published in 1940 as P. Col. Zen. 2 115*g*. A third fragment is in London, and Skeat, having recognized that these three fragments belonged together, in 1974 published them all as P. Lond. 7 1931. Subsequently, however, it was recognized that another New York fragment, published as early as 1940, P. Col. Zen. 2 61, belonged to the same document, and the text now provides us with a new and firm *terminus post quem* for Zenon's return from Palestine to Egypt.

In bringing together all these various kinds of text, our one aim has been to make the archive more accessible. They are printed in the second part of this volume of *Papyrologica Lugduno-Batava,* while the bilingual texts constitute the first part. We judged it appropriate, as we were attempting to reduce the number of editions that need to be consulted, to publish both these groups of Zenon texts in one volume, despite their being of very different types.

As a supplement, we thought it useful to gather together in a third part several texts that do not belong to the Zenon archive, but are closely related to it.

Although, from the very beginning, the texts in the first part were meant to receive a full publication, this was not the intention in the case of the other texts. Originally, it had seemed sufficient simply to reprint each Greek text, and to provide a brief critical apparatus and a translation. However, in many instances this proposed reprinting grew into a more or less complete re-edition of the text. This was mainly for two reasons. In the first place, the individual editors acquired a growing knowledge of the archive in the course of compiling information from and about the archive for publication in P. L. Bat. 21. Secondly, in working together as a team, they were able to discuss among themselves so many problems, that the commentaries on the texts inevitably grew.

Where necessary, plates have been included of as many texts as possible, since we are convinced that a publication of a Greek papyrus is incomplete without a photograph. Moreover, the number of Zenon papyri of which photographs have been published is still so small, that more photographs, even of scraps of papyrus, must prove welcome. We are grateful to the responsible authorities for granting us permission to publish photographs of papyri from their collections and to Dr. Abd el-Qadr Selim for allowing M. Muszynski to collate and photograph the originals of those texts published in this volume that are housed in the Egyptian Museum, Cairo, for generously extending every facility to him in his work, and for granting us permission to reedit them here.

Although with the publication of this work our task is not yet at an end, it is appropriate to thank here all those from Poland, Belgium, England, and the Netherlands who have worked so hard to prepare these texts for publication—and especially Dr. W. J. Tait who undertook the larger share of the work—, Professor Zaki Aly and Professor T. Reekmans who kindly contributed nos. 21 and 62, and of course the *Leids Universiteitsfonds* who made the entire project possible.

March 1977 P. W. Pestman

LIST OF CONTRIBUTORS

Clarysse, W.	17, 18, 30, 33, 38, 41, 46, 54, 57, 61, 63, 76, B, C, E
Muszynski, M. †	21, 27, 37, 42, 43, 44, 55, 60, F
Pestman, P. W.	1-13, A, D
Reekmans, T.	62
Schutgens, Annette	14, 15, 16
Tait, W. J.	19, 20, 25, 26, 28, 29, 32, 34, 35, 36, 38, 40, 45, 47, 48, 50, 52, 53, 58, 59, 64-73, 75
Winnicki, J. K.	22, 23, 24, 31, 39, 49, 51, 56
Zaki Aly	21

It is with deep sorrow that we have learned of the tragic road accident in Upper Egypt which on 12 April 1977 put an untimely end to the promising career of MICHEL MUSZYNSKI before he had even reached his 26th birthday. We have lost in him a dedicated colleague who had devoted much of his inexhaustible energy to the present and forthcoming volumes on the Zenon archive, and who had given us valuable help with various other publications: *ʿnḫ p3j=f bj.*

CONTENTS

LIST OF TEXTS

First part

Ricevute bilingui dell'archivio di Zenon

Second part

Greek texts from the archive of Zenon

---

* We have cancelled n° 74 (P.S.A. Athen. 3) which is to be dated at some time between ca. 183 and 164 B.C.: Parássoglou, *Hellenika* 29 (1976) 47.

Third part

Supplement: Related texts

CONCORDANCES

a. *Previous editions*

P. Baden 6

176 R°	**16**
176 V°	**73**

BGU 6

1297	**D**

BGU 10

1993	**43**
1994	**30**
1995	**41**
1997	**65**
2010	**66**

P. Cairo Zen. 1

59.017	**32**
59.094	**1**
59.102	**7**
59.104	**10**
59.111	**11**

P. Cairo Zen. 2

59.162	**26**
59.169	**28**
59.257	**20**

P. Cairo Zen. 3

59.413	**53**

P. Cairo Zen. 4

59.552	**60**
59.583	**25**
59.615	**34**
59.670	**12**

P. Cairo Zen. 5

59.803	**76 A**

P. Col. Zen. 1

7	**42**
14	**25**
26	**6**
40	**12**
48	**67**

P. Col. Zen. 2

61	**32**
73	**76 B**
78	**38**
114 *j*	**38**
115 *g*	**32**

CPJ 1

3	**59**

P. dem. Zen.

3	**13**
16	**4**
18	**8**
19	**2**
20	**3**
21	**5**
23	**1**
24	**7**
25	**11**

P. Heid. 2

10	**16**

P. Jand. 6

91	**58**
92	**51**

P. Lille 1

1	**A**

P. Lond. 7

1931	**32**
1953, intr.	**55**
1991, intr.	**56**
2019, intr.	**75 b**
2064	**46**

P. Lond. lit.

54	**14**
73	**15**

P. Mich. Zen.

18	**36**
25	**4**

P. Petrie 2

13 (5)	**C**
13 (11)	**B**

SB 1

5796	**F**

SB 3

6762	**21**
6800	**49**
6801 R°	**54**
6801 V°	**61**
6802	**57**
6803	**63**
6807	**28**
7222	**E**

SB 5

7554	**6**
8242	**27**
8244	**56**

SB 6

9565	**38**
9580	**71**

SB 8

9665	**45**
9666	**72**
9667	**60**
9682	**35**
9779	**43**
9780	**41**
9796	**17**
9797	**18**
9798	**19**
9799	**33**

SB 12

10.768	**64**

P. S. A. Athen.

1	**23**
2	**44**
4	**52**

PSI 4

328	**50**
329	**24**
336	**3**
337	**8**
338	**5**
339	**9**
340	**51**
358	**13**
363	**39**
369	**31**
371, note *l.* 8	**75 c**
382, note *l.* 21	**75 d**

PSI 5

484	**29**
489	**22**
496	**48**
506	**2**

PSI 6

624	**64**
638	**37**

639	**38**
663	**42**
681	**55**
PSI 7	
863 *p*	**37**
869	**62**
PSI 9	
1010 A	**5**
1010 B	**3**
1010 C	**8**
1010 D	**13**
1010 E	**2**
1013	**37**
P. Strasb. 4	
228	**46**
P. Strasb. 7	
561	**40**
561, intr.	**75 a**

—

Zaki Aly, Proceedings XIV Int. Congress of Pap. (1975) p. 1-6

no. 1	**47**
no. 2	**67**
no. 3	**68**
no. 4	**69**
no. 5	**70**

b. *Location list*

Ann Arbor (University of Michigan)

Mich. 3199	**4**
3217	**36**

Athens

'Εθνικὸν Μουσεῖον	**56**
Πανεπιστήμιον	**27**
Societas Archeologica	**23, 44, 52**

Berlin (Staatliche Museen)

13.999	**D**
17.278	**65**
17.281	**66**
17.487	**30**
18.088	**43**
18.089	**41**

Cairo (Egyptian Museum)

JdE 44.048	**F**
48.466	**32**
48.542	**1**
48.550	**7**
48.550[a]	**7**
48.552	**10**
48.559	**11**
48.609	**26**
48.616	**28**
48.707	**20**
48.919	**25**
48.942	**53**
53.733	**60**
53.757	**34**
53.781	**12**
— 22-4-33-1	**51**
— 59.803	**76A**
Inv. no. unknown	**36**

Cairo (Egyptian Papyrological Society) ... **47, 67, 68, 69, 70, 71**

Cambridge (Corpus Christi College)

MS. 541	**E**

Florence (Biblioteca Medicea Laurenziana): see list (a) PSI

Giessen (Universitäts-Bibliothek)

Jand. 254	**51**
357	**58**
361	**45**
362	**72**
363	**60**
364	**35**
413 *V°*	**59**

Heidelberg (Universität)

1832	**17**
1834	**18**
1880	**19**
1881	**33**
1891 *R°*	**16**
1891 *V°*	**73**

London (British Library)

534	**C**
539	**B**
1994 B	**46**
2326	**32**
2374 E	**75 b**
2652 A *V°*	**14**
2652 B	**15**
3083	**21**

New York (Columbia University)

Col. 215	**6**
224	**12**
232	**25**
240	**67**
248	**76B**
290	**42**
305[c]	**32**
306[e.3]	**32**
333	**38**
357	**38**

Paris (Sorbonne)

Sorb. 1	**A**
282	**49**
283 *R°*	**54**
283 *V°*	**61**
284	**57**
285	**63**

Strasbourg (Bibliothèque Nationale et Universitaire)

Wiss. Ges. 354	**46**
Strasb. 2484	**40**
2486[a]	**40**
2491[c]	**75 a**

I

RICEVUTE BILINGUI DELL'ARCHIVIO DI ZENON

EDITE DA

P. W. PESTMAN

INTRODUZIONE *

Contenuto

L'archivio in generale

§ 1 *Zenon ed il suo archivio*

Nonostante il gran numero di documenti che l'archivio di Zenon contiene (forse dai 1700 ai 2000 papiri), stranamente ben poco siamo venuti a sapere sull'uomo Zenon e sulla sua vita privata. Non sappiamo né quando è nato, né quando è morto e nemmeno se ha avuto figli o se è mai stato sposato.[1] Tutta l'enorme massa di documenti del suo archivio ci rivela veramente ben poco, tranne che deve essere stato un uomo capace nel suo lavoro e con un cuore buono per tutti coloro che gli chiedevano aiuto (v. ad esempio Suppl. doc. **D**).

Per quanto riguarda la sua vita e carriera,[2] è noto che Zenon, originario di Kaunos (Asia Minore), va come tante altre persone in Egitto, dove entra al servizio del dioiketes Apollonios prima dell'**autunno 261 a.C.** (P. Cairo Zen. 5 59.801). Un anno più tardi (**autunno 260**) Apollonios lo manda in Palestina dove rimarrà fino all'**estate 258** (doc. **32**), fin quando Apollonios non lo richiamerà in Egitto. Nel periodo seguente funge da segretario privato di Apollonios e l'accompagna nei suoi viaggi in Basso Egitto, che sono così numerosi che Apollonios è quasi sempre assente da Alessandria: Ἀπολλώνιομ μὲν συμβαίνει τὸμ πλείω χρόνον διατρίβειν ἐν τῆι χώραι (doc. **51**, 14-15). Se non sono in giro, se ne stanno volontieri in Arsinoe, un villaggio che deve trovarsi sulla costa, non tanto lontano da Alessandria (doc. **36**, 9 n.) e dove, durante l'estate, il clima è forse migliore. Come segretario di Apollonios, Zenon si occupa, tra l'altro, della corrispondenza del suo padrone e colloca molte lettere indirizzate ad Apollonios in un archivio [l'archivio di Apollonios], che Zenon porta poi con sé, per una ragione che mi sfugge, quando lascia il posto di segretario per andare a Philadelphia in *Aprile/Maggio 256*.

* Avevo già pronto il manoscritto sulle ricevute bilingui prima che iniziassimo i lavori preparativi per il resto del presente e per il prossimo volume su Zenon (difatti, i problemi che ho incontrati durante la preparazione del mio manoscritto mi hanno incitato ad iniziare detti lavori). Ho lasciato il manoscritto in gran parte com'era pensando che si possono facilmente trovare ulteriori informazioni nel prossimo volume P. L. Bat. 21.

[1] Cf. A. Świderek, *Zenon fils d'Agréophon de Caunos et sa famille*, Symbolae Taubenschlag, Eos 48.2 (1957) 133-141.

[2] Vedere P. L. Bat. 21. VIII per le date importanti relative alla vita di Zenon.

Nel frattempo il re affida ad Apollonios un terreno di 10.000 arure ($5\frac{1}{4} \times 5\frac{1}{4}$ km.) nel Fayum, la δωρεά vicino a Philadelphia. Questo latifondo è in maggior parte incolto e in **Dicembre 259** Apollonios si reca sul posto per ispezionare questa sua dorea e per decidersi sul progetto delle dighe da costruire e dei canali da scavare (Suppl. doc. **A**).[3] Apollonios dà ordine di iniziare i lavori necessari e già nella stagione seguente (*258/257*) una parte del terreno è in coltivazione (v. doc. **1** e Suppl. doc. **B**). Il **9 Maggio 257** Panakestor [4] arriva sulla dorea (PSI 5 502, 13) con l'incarico, se non erro, di procedere con i lavori di dissodamento del latifondo e di condurli a termine. Un numero assai grande di documenti ci informano sulla dorea e sulle attività di Panakestor in questo periodo, documenti che ci sono pervenuti da tre archivi diversi: dall'archivio dell'architetto Kleon (ritrovato per caso; v. ad esempio Suppl. doc. **B** e **C**), dall'archivio che Zenon tiene, in questo periodo, delle lettere inviate ad Apollonios e a se stesso (e quindi anche delle lettere che Panakestor invia a loro) e infine dall'archivio nel quale Panakestor conserva le lettere che riceve (tra l'altro dagli stessi Apollonios e Zenon) ed altri documenti che riguardano, in un qualche maniera, la gestione della dorea. Quest'ultimo archivio [l'archivio di Panakestor] verrà poi ceduto da Panakestor al suo successore Zenon che l'incorporerà nel suo grande archivio.

Panakestor trova, al suo arrivo sulla dorea, una parte della terra ancora da coltivare e di questa si occupa nella stagione *257/256* (v. ad esempio doc. **2-11**). Ho l'impressione che Panakestor si dedichi con molta energia a questo compito, nonostante ciò che possiamo pensare dalle lettere impazienti di Apollonios che sollecitano Panakestor ad accelerare i lavori affinché si possa ancora profittare della stagione agraria. A quanto pare Panakestor non ha potuto preparare tutta la terra in tempo (doc. **2** n. 9) e le lettere di Apollonios hanno un tono sempre più irritato. Però per Panakestor c'erano tante difficoltà da superare. Tutto gli mancava: soldi per pagare gli operai (P. Cairo Zen. 1 59.124; doc. **2** n. 10), contadini capaci per coltivare la terra (doc. **1** n. 3) e persino l'esperienza necessaria per poter irrigare i campi (Suppl. doc. **C**). Ad ogni modo, pare che Panakestor abbia col tempo potuto risolvere i problemi e, quando viene trasferito a Memphis (doc. **2** n. 14) in **Aprile/Maggio 256**,[5] lascia a Zenon, suo successore, la dorea completamente coltivabile.

Non so per quale motivo Apollonios lascia andare il suo segretario Zenon a Philadelphia incaricandolo della gestione della dorea. C'è chi dice che sia stato per motivo della salute di Zenon, che non gli avrebbe più permesso di viaggiare di continuo e l'avrebbe costretto ad una vita più calma e sedentaria. Può essere vero come non può esserlo, perché sappiamo solo che Zenon è stato ammalato prima di andare a Philadelphia, ma niente di preciso sulla malattia stessa. Comunque sia, Apollonios affida la direzione della

[3] Nelle vicinanze si trovano due altri terreni di 10.000 arure (doc. **38**). Uno di questi, ugualmente incolto, appartiene ad un Greco col nome di Andromakhos, ma l'altro invece, che pare essere coltivato, appartiene ad un certo Panuphis, un Egizio quindi che possiamo annoverare fra i benestanti.

[4] Panakestor è nato in Kalunda non tanto lontano dal paese natale di Zenon, il suo protettore, che l'ha portato con sè dalla Palestina in Egitto (v. P. Cairo Zen. 4 59.579 e P. L. Bat. 21.IV s.v.). Incontriamo Panakestor per la prima volta in Egitto il 5 Ottobre 258 (PSI 6 559 e P. L. Bat. 21.IV s.v.).

[5] Zenon assume la gestione della dorea tra il 25 Aprile (PSI 5 509) ed il 10 Maggio 256 (P. Cairo Zen. 1 59.137). Panakestor si trova a Memphis negli anni 256/255 e 255/254; dopo di che non viene più menzionato nell'archivio.

dorea a Zenon che l'avrà per quasi dieci anni, fino al **248/247**. Zenon stesso dirà più tardi ἐπεστάτησα τῆς ἐμ Φιλαδελφείαι δωρεᾶς ἕως τοῦ λη L, «ho avuto la direzione della dorea in Philadelphia fino all'anno 38» (P. Cairo Zen. 5 59.832, 2-4).[6] La maggior parte dei documenti conservati nell'archivio di Zenon riguarda questo periodo; trattano vari aspetti della gestione della dorea nonché alcuni affari più o meno personali.

Nel *248/247* Zenon si ritira, e di nuovo non so per quale motivo. Non ritorna, come si potrebbe aspettarsi, al suo paese natale né ad Alessandria, ma rimane in campagna, nelle vicinanze della dorea dove, a quanto pare, si trova a suo agio. Continua a ricevere un ὀψώνιον dalla dorea [7] e per il resto vive del reddito delle sue vigne e greggi di capre, pecore e maiali ed i suoi documenti ci parlano di terre affittate e della produzione di vino (ne viene persino rubato dalla sua cantina: PSI 4 396). Però non si ritira interamente dalla vita pubblica. Alcuni documenti accennano ad una sua certa attività giudiziaria. La prova più esplicita è il prostagma C. Ord. Ptol. 27 su un problema processuale che Zenon aveva sottoposto al re (cf. anche la causa di cui tratta il doc. **21** con gli altri documenti relativi).

In questa maniera Zenon mena una vita che è certamente assai più tranquilla di prima. Non sappiamo quando è morto, ma ha goduto almeno 20 anni del ritiro, perché figura ancora in un documento del *14 Febbraio 229* (Suppl. doc. **E**). Supponendo che Zenon non abbia avuto meno di 25-30 anni quando nel 261 è stato inviato da Apollonios in Palestina, ne aveva 29-34 quando ha ricevuto la direzione della dorea, 37-42 quando si è ritirato e 57-62 nell'anno 229, che è forse stato l'ultimo della sua vita.

Rimane ancora un problema: sapere che fine abbia fatto l'archivio.[8] Dopo il suo ritiro nel *248/247*, Zenon continua regolarmente ad usarlo per archiviare i suoi documenti. Però vi è pure un piccolo gruppo di documenti, i quali vanno fino al **244/243** circa e che logicamente non dovrebbero trovarsi in quest'archivio, ma in un altro, quello di Eukles ad esempio, il successore di Zenon (v. doc. **54**, una lettera inviata ad Eukles), oppure nell'archivio di Apollonios (v. doc. **49**, una lettera scritta dallo stesso Eukles al suo segretario Apollonios). Ora è ovvio che queste due lettere citate possono soltanto trovarsi insieme, se insieme erano state archiviate dal predetto Apollonios, nella veste di destinatario (doc. **49**) o di segretario di Eukles (doc. **54**), e mi sembra assai probabile che in questa maniera l'intero gruppo problematico sia andato a finire nelle mani di questo Apollonios, il γραμματεύς di Eukles (P. L. Bat. 21. IX *Prosopography*, Apollonios n. 14). Dall'altra parte, nei documenti di Zenon incontriamo nello stesso periodo un tale che si chiama pure lui Apollonios (loc. cit. *Prosopography*, Apollonios n. 10) ed è un ἀδελφός di Zenon. A suo proposito Reekmans (*Sitométrie*, p. 73 n. 17) scrive che «fut étroitement associé aux activités de Zénon après la confiscation du domaine». Che si tratti qui di due persone diverse? Penso di no. Per quanto mi consta non c'è nessuna ragione per cui il γραμματεύς di Eukles non possa anche essere lo ἀδελφός di Zenon. Il vantaggio di tale identificazione è evidente: d'un colpo il problema dei due archivi trovati insieme sparisce, perché l'ar-

---

[6] Benché la lettura dell'anno 38 non sia sicura in questo documento, l'insieme dell'archivio mi dà l'impressione che Zenon non abbia più avuto la gestione della dorea oltre l'anno 38.

[7] T. Reekmans, *La sitométrie dans les archives de Zénon*, p. 97 n. 157; P. L. Bat. 21.VI, B 18.

[8] Cf. P. L. Bat. 21.VI, A: «Fifth period» e «Sixth period».

chivio del γραμματεύς Apollonios è semplicemente stato incorporato all'archivio di suo *fratello* Zenon.[9]

Qualche anno più tardi, nel **240/239**, Zenon colloca i suoi ultimi documenti personali nell'archivio. Questo è un fatto strano, perché Zenon vivrà ancora almeno dieci anni. Ha evidentemente ceduto l'archivio a qualcun altro e questi, negli anni seguenti, vi ha ancora collocato una decina di documenti.[10] Può darsi che questo Tizio sia stato il «fratello Apollonios» che abbiamo già incontrato nel periodo precedente, ma non sappiamo con quale scopo questo Tizio avrebbe collocato nell'archivio i documenti in questione. Qualche documento pare avere un certo rapporto con Zenon, come la lettera P. Lond. 7 2019 che Zenon ha scritto al νομάρχης Akhoapis, e perciò mi sono chiesto se questo Tizio (Apollonios o un altro) che possiede l'archivio durante gli ultimi anni, non sia forse, ad esempio, un impiegato dell'ufficio del νομάρχης che abbia usato l'archivio, originariamente di Zenon, per archiviarvi dei documenti che gli riguardano.[11]

§ 2 *Greci ed Egizi nell'archivio di Zenon*

Dopo la conquista di Alessandro Magno troviamo in Egitto sostanzialmente due popolazioni: da una parte ci sono gli Egizi indigeni e dall'altra parte gli immigranti stranieri, in maggioranza grecofoni (che verranno designati, in quanto segue, come «Greci»). Queste popolazioni sono talmente diverse — di lingua, cultura, diritto, ecc. — che lo studio dei loro rapporti è veramente affascinante. Anche su questo argomento il ricco archivio di Zenon ci fornisce molte informazioni, che sono inoltre preziose perché concernano un periodo che è ancora relativamente vicino ai primi tempi della conquista.

È un periodo in cui Greci ed Egizi non andavano ancora tanto d'accordo. È noto il caso dell'Egizio che si lamenta del disprezzo che ha sofferto: καταφρονήσας μου ὅτι Αἰγύπτιός εἰμι (P. Yale 46, 13) e difatti, disprezzo viene apertamente dimostrato da un Greco quando, nella famosa enteuxis P. Ent. 79, chiede μή περιιδεῖν με οὕτως ἀλόγως ὑπὸ Αἰγυπτίας ὑβρισμένον Ἕλληνα ὄντα καὶ ξένον, «di non permettere che io sono stato maltrattato così, senza ragioni, da una donna egizia, io che sono un Greco e straniero» (*l.* 9-10). Questo Greco antipatico dice a proposito della donna Αἰγυπτία τις ἧι λέγεται εἶναι ὄνομα Ψενοβάστις (*l.* 4), non sapendo quindi che Psenobastis è un nome maschile. Quando poi dice che loro due hanno avuto un alterco, possiamo essere sicuri che ognuno abbia usato la propria lingua. Non troviamo tali casi estremi nell'archivio di Zenon, ma l'esistenza di una certa qual tensione si rivela in un passo di una lettera (P. Cairo Zen. 4 59.610, 18-22): ὁ δὲ οὐκ ἔφη ἐπιτήδειον εἶναι Αἰγυπτίους δοῦναι νεανίσκους· οὗτοι δὲ παρ' ἡμῖν οὐ μὴ βούλωνται

[9] Questa incorporazione si può spiegare supponendo, ad esempio, che Apollonios sia andato ad aiutare il fratello Zenon e si sia occupato della sua amministrazione e corrispondenza.

L'archivio di Apollonios è probabilmente stato incorporato all'archivio di Zenon al momento in cui Eukles ha ceduto la direzione della dorea a Bion (o poco dopo), cioè nel *244/243* circa.

[10] Visto che Zenon ha ceduto l'archivio è in fondo errato di continuare a chiamarlo «l'archivio di Zenon».

Zenon ha di certo ancora ricevuto documenti personali, durante questi ultimi anni della sua vita. Li avrà collocati in un suo archivio personale, ma niente ci è rimasto di conservato, a meno che il doc. **40** non ne faccia parte.

[11] In questo caso c'è da chiedersi se abbiamo fatto bene a confinare il documento SB 3 7222 (doc. **E**) al Supplemento «Related texts» alla fine del presente volume.

φυλάσσειν, «dice che è inutile dare giovanotti egizi, perché essi non vogliano fare la guardia da noi.»

Dato che la relazione tra Egizi e Greci [12] nell'archivio non è ancora stata fin'ora indagata, non posso far altro qui che segnalarne qualche fenomeno, che mi sembra d'importanza per questa materia complessa e delicata. Se assumiamo — e penso che possiamo tranquillamente farlo — che il nome proprio di una persona è in quest'epoca ancora un indizio assai sicuro della sua nazionalità e provenienza,[13] possiamo trarre alcune informazioni dall'elenco di titoli, di nomi dei titolari, ecc., in P. L. Bat. 21.XV «Official and military titles» e XVI «Trades and occupations».

Non c'è da stupirsi se troviamo nell'*esercito* solo Greci, persone cioè con nomi greci (o per lo meno non-egizi), in qualità di στρατηγός, comandante, ἱππάρχης, ἱππεύς o semplice στρατιώτης. I μάχιμοι, invece, sono Egizi [14] e non fanno parte dell'esercito, mentre nella polizia troviamo Greci accanto ad Egizi in qualità di ἀρχιφυλακίτης, φυλακίτης o φύλαξ.

Nell'*amministrazione civile* ci sono alcune funzioni dove incontriamo soltanto nomi greci: il διοικητής Apollonios, gli ὑποδιοικηταί Diotimos e Nikanor, nonché diversi οἰκονόμοι, πράκτορες, τραπεζῖται, ecc. Dall'altra parte ci sono delle funzioni specificamente indigene dove troviamo soltanto Egizi: ogni κωμογραμματεύς, κώμαρχος e βασιλικὸς γραμματεύς nell'archivio porta un nome egizio. Evidentemente questa parte dell'amministrazione è egizia [15] e funziona come prima della conquista. Significante è soprattutto il fatto che lo strategos in questo periodo non abbia ancora nessuna competenza all'infuori del suo incarico militare.[16]

Per quanto riguarda la *terra* e la spartizione della terra tra gli immigranti e gli indigeni, colpisce il gran numero di κληροῦχοι greci nell'archivio (P. L. Bat. 21.XV Appendice) che possiedono inoltre sovente kleroi di ben 100 arure. Ma questo in sé non ci permette di dedurre che gli immigranti si siano arrichiti alle spalle degli indigeni, prendendo da loro tutte queste arure. Anzi, è ben probabile che la terra dei κληροῦχοι greci fosse terra nuova, come anche le 10.000 arure di Apollonios e di Andromakhos erano terre nuove, laddove le 10.000 arure dell'Egizio Panuphis erano terre coltivate (v. § 1 nota 3 e doc. **38**).

Sulla *dorea* infine troviamo γεωργοί con nomi greci ed egizi. Sembra che gli immigranti e gli indigeni lavorassero insieme la terra (anche se i lavoratori manuali fossero

---

12 V. in generale i numerosi studi di W. PEREMANS.

13 Tuttavia si deve procedere con cautela poiché sappiamo per caso che, un secolo più tardi, alcuni agoranomoi con nomi greci erano in realtà Egizi che portavano, in privato, il proprio nome egizio: P. W. PESTMAN, *L'agoranomie: un avant-poste de l'administration grecque enlevé par les Égyptiens?*, in *Das ptolemäische Ägypten* [Akten des intern. Symposions 27.-29. Sept. 1976 in Berlin, herausgegeben von H. Maehler und V. M. Strocka] (1978) 203-210.

14 Anche Paris è un Αἰγύπτιος: P. L. Bat. 21.IX *Prosopography*, s.v.

15 Cf. la famiglia tebana di Peteharpres (*Prosopographia Ptolemaica* III 7795, 7703 e 7825). Egli stesso era scriba di documenti demotici, già prima della conquista (P. dem. Libbey: E. LÜDDECKENS, *Eheverträge*, Urk. 9); Harmais, un suo figlio, è nel 245 (o prima) *sẖ n Pr-ꜥꜣ* ꜥ.w.s., βασιλικὸς γραμματεύς (P. dem. Louvre 2438, 4: proprietario di una parte della casa K, v. S. R. K. GLANVILLE, Essays and Studies Cook, p. 64 fig. 4) e Phibis, un altro figlio, è nel 280 (o prima) *sẖ pꜣ tš Nw.t*, «scriba del nomos di Thebe» (P. dem. Phil. 10, 3: proprietario dell'altra parte della casa K). I due scribi demotici, poi, Sminis (*Pros. Ptol.* III 7738) e Thotortaios (7745), sono suoi nipoti.

16 «though naturally he would be in a position to exert a considerable influence in local affairs» (SKEAT, P. Lond. 7 1945, 6 n.). Penso che la stessa osservazione valga per Zenon.

sovente, probabilmente, d'origine egizia), ma ci sono naturalmente dei lavori specifici che venivano fatti o dall'uno o dall'altro, come ad esempio la viticoltura veniva curata solamente da ἀμπελουργοί greci. Siccome l'amministrazione della dorea era tenuta in greco, non c'è da stupirsi che vi fossero impiegati scribi greci. Ma vi erano senz'altro pure degli scribi egizi e forse persino in gran numero. La loro presenza era indispensabile per la gestione del latifondo. Per farsi capire dagli indigeni, gli amministratori greci avevano bisogno di Egizi bilingui (anche se sapevano solo un po' di greco) [17] e Zenon ha senz'altro avuto bisogno di un traduttore per poter capire la lettera demotica P. dem. Zen. 17. Dappertutto nell'archivio troviamo tracce della presenza di scribi demotici nell'amministrazione della dorea. Chi guarda, ad esempio, la riproduzione del P. Col. Zen. 1 52 viene subito colpito dall'aspetto demotico della scrittura greca, che sembra decisamente scritta dalla mano di uno scriba demotico. Il doc. **38** è stato scritto da qualcuno che pare conosca meglio la grammatica egizia e che non sa neanche che si usa il simbolo c per indicare la metà di un obolo, non la metà di un'arura. La carta in doc. Suppl. **A** è stata disegnata da un Egizio che l'ha orientata verso il Sud (alla maniera egizia) scrivendovi sopra in demotico i nomi dei punti cardinali. Ed infine colpisce il frequente uso nei conti, registri, ecc. greci dei simboli ⸓, / e ⌒, simboli cioè che derivano dalla ragioneria egizia (doc. **13** nota *o*): la loro frequente presenza nei documenti amministrativi greci, mi sembra provare che molti Egizi erano impiegati nella amministrazione. Pochissimi invece sono i documenti demotici e bilingui ritrovati nell'archivio.

	Documenti demotici
contratti, promesse giurate	P. dem. Zen. 1, 2, 4 + 8, 6, 11 + 12, 13 e 14
ricevuta	P. dem. Zen. 9 + 10
lettere	P. dem. Zen. 7 e 17
conti, registri, ecc.	P. dem. Zen. 15 (verso di PSI 5 546) e 22 (verso di P. Lond. 7 1974 + P. Col. Zen. 1 39)
	Documenti bilingui
ricevute	P. L. Bat. 20 **1-8** e **11-13**
lettera	P. dem. Zen. 5 + P. Cairo Zen. 4 59.566

LE RICEVUTE BILINGUI

§ 3 *Datazione delle ricevute bilingui*

Chi desidera studiare l'archivio di Zenon, viene inevitabilmente confrontato col problema dei tre modi diversi di datare, modi che erano allora contemporaneamente in uso.[18] Troviamo documenti datati secondo l'anno egizio, l'anno finanziario o l'anno macedone, anni che incominciavano con tre giorni diversi e che avevano una durata diversa. Però, anche se per noi è un caos completo, per i contemporanei stessi lo era di meno. Non avevano tanti problemi, perché potevano in genere facilmente capire, in un certo caso, di

[17] Come è noto i Greci stessi non imparavano volontieri la lingua egizia e meno ancora la scrittura demotica che è tanto difficile. Perciò non mi stupirei se l'ἑρμηνεύς Apollonios fosse in realtà un Egizio che avesse cambiato nome (v. nota 13); P. Ryl. 4 563, 8 ci fa vedere che non potevano aver fiducia nella veridicità di questo traduttore (e non sarà stato diverso per i suoi colleghi, temo).

[18] Ne parlerò più a lungo prossimamente (P. L. Bat. 21, capitolo VIII).

che tipo di datazione si trattasse.[19] Penso che erano soltanto confrontati con questo nostro problema quando dovevano convertire una data da un calendario ad un altro, e proprio per ciò Numenios scrive una lettera (P. Ryl. 4 557) a Zenon per chiedere il suo aiuto. Numenios, benché fosse Greco, aveva perso il contatto col calendario macedone perché viveva in campagna, in mezzo agli Egizi; sapeva naturalmente che il compleanno del re veniva festeggiato il 12 Dystros, secondo il calendario macedone, ma ignorava chiaramente il giorno corrispondente secondo il calendario del suo ambiente egizio: καλῶς ἂν οὖν ποιήσαις γράψας ἡμῖν---τίνι ἡμέραι ὡς τῶν Αἰγυπτίων ἡ θυσία ἔσται, «ti prego di scriverci in che giorno, secondo (il calendario) degli Egizi, il sacrificio (per il compleanno del re) avrà luogo.» Zenon faceva ancora in questo momento (Aprile 257) da segretario ad Apollonios ed era certamente in grado di aiutare Numenios, ma qualche anno più tardi si trovava nella stessa situazione di Numenios, quando cioè viveva anche lui in campagna, come dirigente della dorea. Nel suo archivio si trova un papiro con appunti per una petizione, che Zenon doveva (o voleva) datare secondo il calendario macedone. Sapeva il mese macedone, ma non il giorno di quel mese per cui doveva ancora informarsi da qualche parte per esserne sicuro e, per non dimenticarselo, scriveva nei suoi appunti: ἡμέραν προσθεῖναι (P. Col. Zen. 1 54, 41).

Il problema è ben più grande per noi. Sapere quale calendario sia stato usato in un determinato caso è sovente difficile e, qualche volta, persino impossibile.[20] A questo proposito però, le ricevute bilingui ci sono di un aiuto prezioso, perché la parte greca data secondo un'altro calendario della parte demotica. Per poter confrontare queste doppie date e metterle in valore, le ho riunite tutte (compresa la doppia data del doc. **A** pubblicato nel supplemento) nella sinossi qui accanto. Così possiamo constatare a proposito dei doc. **1-8** che l'anno 28 dei testi demotici non può essere altro che l'anno egizio (v. anche il doc. **12**). Per quanto concerne l'anno 29 dei testi greci, ci sono due possibilità: potrebbe essere l'anno finanziario o l'anno macedone, ma nel caso del doc. **13** appare chiaramente che si tratta dell'anno finanziario.[21]

Conviene far notare ancora un piccolo dettaglio. Nel documento **4** (v. nota *a*), le date del testo greco e demotico differiscono di un giorno, probabilmente perché la ricevuta è stata scritta la sera.

§ 4 *Documenti doppi*

a) Un documento è definito doppio quando contiene due volte un medesimo testo, una volta come *scriptura interior* (ossia la parte superiore del documento che veniva arrotolata e sigillata) [22] ed una seconda volta come *scriptura exterior* (ossia la parte inferiore che rimaneva aperta). Il vantaggio di una duplice redazione è che gli interessati possono

---

[19] Come anche noi capiamo facilmente di quale anno si tratta quando riceviamo in Gennaio 197*8* una lettera che porta per isbaglio la data del 1° Gennaio 1977.

[20] Lo stesso problema avrà ovviamente colui che tra qualche anno troverà la lettera menzionata in n. 19.

[21] Penso che tutte le ricevute greche della dorea (per quanto vengano usati mesi egizi) datino secondo l'anno finanziario, tanto più che i registri dove erano iscritte, contavano con anni finanziari.

Fanno eccezione però tre ricevute greche (P. Cairo Zen. 1 59.137-59.139) che menzionano l'anno ed il mese macedone. Queste quietanze sono state scritte in Maggio 256, cioè poco dopo l'arrivo di Zenon sulla dorea, senz'altro da un Greco che era venuto con lui e non si era ancora addattato.

[22] V. le tavole I e XI, doc. **1** e **11**.

sempre consultare il testo (consultandone la *scriptura exterior*), ma non falsificarlo, perché non possono toccare la *scriptura interior*, protetta com'è dai sigilli.

Non era necessario che i due testi di un doppio documento fossero testualmente uguali, bastava che la *scriptura interior* menzionasse l'essenza del testo. Già ai tempi di Zenon l'*interior* è effettivamente qualche volta più breve e in seguito lo diventerà sempre di più. Questo non ha importanza per l'effetto giuridico del documento, come non ha importanza che, soprattutto l'*interior*, contenga spesso errori e correzioni (v. ad esempio doc. **3** e, fuori dell'archivio, SB 8 9841); questo fenomeno è una conseguenza naturale del semplice fatto che l'*interior* veniva scritto prima dell'*exterior* e che serviva qualche volta da brutta copia allo scriba, il quale poi la trascriveva in bella copia: la *scriptura exterior*. Qualche volta però le divergenze tra le due parti sono ben più essenziali: il P. Lond. 7 1963 è una ricevuta per 300 dracme secondo l'*interior*, ma per 200 invece secondo l'*exterior*, come il PSI 4 379 è una ricevuta per 16 e contemporaneamente 17 maiali (v. pure P. Cairo Zen. 5 59.825, 33-34 nota). C'è da chiedersi quale possa ancora essere il valore giuridico di queste ricevute.

Come è noto l'idea della redazione doppia non è egizia. Documenti doppi in demotico sono perciò rari; datano soltanto del terzo secolo (l'ultimo è P. L. Bat. 17 doc. 12: 201 a.C.) e trattano inoltre quasi sempre di rapporti colle autorità greche. Documenti doppi in greco invece sono d'uso comune, non solo in Egitto, ma anche altrove: il contratto doppio P. Cairo Zen. 1 59.003, ad esempio, concerne una vendita (di una giovane schiava) conclusa nel territorio di Tubias in Palestina.

Nell'archivio di Zenon troviamo un gran numero di documenti doppi:[23] contratti, promesse giurate, ricevute, ordini di pagamento, denunzie di reati alle autorità, ecc. La maggior parte di questi documenti è scritta in greco, pochi sono in demotico[24] ed una decina nelle due lingue: le ricevute **1-8** e **11-13**.

b) Tre di queste ricevute bilingui riguardano *l'amministrazione degli affari esterni della dorea*: sono state rilasciate dalle autorità greche dopo aver ricevuto dalla dorea grano (doc. **1**) o ricino (doc. **12** e **13**). Ogni ricevuta è rilasciata da due funzionari (o loro impiegati), uno dei quali pare essere il ricevente, l'altro un suo controllore. Di questi due, nella parte greca il ricevente è sempre menzionato per primo (questa parte è anche quindi la ricevuta vera e propria), nella parte demotica è invece il controllore che viene menzionato per primo (questa parte è il contrassegno). Una ragione speciale, perché questi contrassegni siano stati redatti in demotico, non c'è, penso; è la semplice conseguenza della realtà: quelli che esercitavano il controllo e scrivevano il contrassegno erano degli Egizi: Anosis (doc. **1**), Khaiophis (doc. **12**) e Peteharmais (doc. **13**).

Sinnossi

doc. **1** *ricevente*: il nomarches Damis (tramite Kleitarkhos)
controllore: Diodoros (tramite Andron)[25]
scriba del contrassegno: Anosis (per Andron)

[23] Vedere P. L. Bat. 21. VI, B (5) e, per un elenco delle publicazioni di fotografie di documenti doppi, V 2*b*.

[24] P. dem. Zen. 1, 2, 6, 4 + 8 e 9 + 10.

[25] Se facevano il controllo in nome di Apollonios, come è probabile, era dell'Apollonios nella veste di dioiketes, non in quella di padrone della dorea.

doc. **12** *ricevente*: l'oikonomos Hermolaos (tramite Korragos)
controllore: il basilikos grammateus Horos/Hartephnakhthis (tramite Khaiophis)
scriba del contrassegno: Khaiophis stesso

doc. **13** *ricevente*: l'oikonomos Hermolaos (tramite Korragos)
controllore: il basilikos grammateus Horos/Hartephnakhthis (tramite Khaiophis)
scriba del contrassegno: Peteharmais (per Khaiophis, il suo padrone)

c) Le altre ricevute bilingui riguardano *l'amministrazione degli affari interni della dorea*: sono state rilasciate dai contadini per aver ricevuto, dagli amministratori della dorea, delle scuri (per poter lavorare: doc. **2**) o del denaro — come salario per lavoro alle dighe (doc. **7**, **8** e **11**) e nelle vigne (doc. **3**), o per lavori di dissodamento nei campi della dorea (doc. **4**, **5**, **6**, **9** e **10**).

Questo gruppo di ricevute è del tutto diverso dal gruppo precedente, perché consistono d'una ricevuta e d'una sottoscrizione personale del ricevente (sottoscrizione che è di una natura ben diversa dal contrassegno del controllore sulle ricevute precedenti).

La ricevuta vera e propria è redatta in greca e rilasciata dal contadino ricevente o da un suo rappresentante (doc. **6** e **9**: Hegesias; doc. **8**: Pokas). Come lo faremo notare a proposito del doc. **6** (introduzione, nota 2), il testo greco è stato in alcuni casi chiaramente scritto in due riprese. Si tratta, a quanto pare, di una specie di modulo preparato in anticipo da qualcuno che lo completava poi col nome del ricevente ed altre particolarità. Non sappiamo niente di preciso sulla identità delle persone che hanno scritto e completato questi moduli greci, ma penso che erano delle persone che lavoravano negli uffici della dorea,[26] non solo perché era assai naturale per i contadini di ricorrere, in un caso simile, a una di loro, ma anche perché dubito che al di fuori dell'amministrazione ci fossero tante persone sulla dorea che sapessero scrivere il greco.

La sottoscrizione personale del ricevente, redatta in demotico, si trova sotto il testo greco. Solo in calce del doc. **11** lo spazio era sufficiente per ricevere l'intera sottoscrizione; in altri documenti lo spazio non bastava, cosicché la scrittura demotica continua sul verso. Nel caso del doc. **5** si è persino dovuto scrivere l'intero testo demotico sul verso. Si vede che coloro che preparavano la ricevuta e scrivevano il testo greco non tenevano conto della sottoscrizione. Difatti pare che per la validità della ricevuta non fosse richiesta una sottoscrizione, perché nell'intero archivio non ne ho potuto trovare più di una sola: in calce della ricevuta P. Lond. 7 1963 (che concerne un pagamento effettuato in seguito ad un ordine di pagamento dato da Apollonios) Panakestor scrive di sua propria mano ὁμολογεῖ Πανακέστωρ ἔχειν κατὰ τὸ σύμβολον τοῦτο, «Panakestor riconosce di aver ricevuto conforme a quell'ordine di pagamento.» [27]

Non c'è da stupirsi che i nostri documenti portino in calce della ricevuta greca una sottoscrizione in cui i contadini egizi dichiarano, nella loro propria lingua, di aver ricevuto

[26] Cf. le ricevute P. Cairo Zen. 1 59.137-59.139 che sono state ovviamente scritte da qualcuno che faceva parte del seguito di Zenon (v. qui sopra nota 21).

[27] Diversamente l'editore del testo: «according to this acquittance.» Penso che σύμβολον non significhi qui «ricevuta», ma «ordine di pagamento» e si riferisca al σύμβολον menzionato nel testo (*l*. 10 e 21).

l'ammontare della ricevuta, soprattutto quando quei contadini non capivano il greco o quando avevano ricevuto il pagamento non di persona ma tramite un intermediario (doc. **6**: Hegesias riceve il denaro per Pasis secondo la ricevuta greca, ma la sottoscrizione demotica è dello stesso Pasis; cf. pure doc. **8**). Non so però se quei contadini sapessero scrivere così bene il demotico da poter sottoscrivere personalmente le ricevute: penso che sia più probabile che l'abbiano fatto fare da qualcun altro (salvo forse il segno *sẖ* che potrebbe servire da firma, v. doc. **2** nota *h*). Rimane però un caso problematico,[28] il doc. **11**: perché avrebbe un uomo col nome greco di Nikias (un compatriotta di Zenon, loc. cit. nota 5) sottoscritto in demotico? Lo avrebbe forse fatto fare da uno dei dieci operai a cui il pagamento in oggetto era destinato?

Sinnossi

doc. **2**	ricevente (testo greco)	Harmais
	sottoscrivente (testo demotico)	Harmais
doc. **3**	riceventi	Peteyris, Onnophris, Theophilos
	sottoscriventi	Peteyris, Onnophris, Theophilos
doc. **4**	ricevente	Samoys
	sottoscrivente	Samoys
doc. **5**	riceventi	Phernuthis, Horos
	sottoscrivente	Phernuthis
doc. **6**	ricevente	Hegesias (per Pasis)
	sottoscrivente	Pasis
doc. **7**	riceventi	Phernuthis, Horos
	sottoscrivente	Phernuthis
doc. **8**	ricevente	Pokas (per Horos/Harpaesis)
	sottoscrivente	Horos/Harpaesis
doc. **11**	ricevente	Nikias
	sottoscrivente	Nikias

Cf. i due documenti incompleti (manca la parte inferiore):

doc. **9**	ricevente	Hegesias [= doc. **6**] (per Kleitos)
doc. **10**	ricevente	Samoys [= doc. **4**]

Si fa notare, infine, che le ricevute complete relative all'amministrazione interna della dorea portano sempre una sottoscrizione (demotica) durante il breve periodo che va dal 1º Ottobre al 19 Novembre 257, ma mai dopo.[29]

Ricapitolando, penso che i contadini della dorea si presentavano il giorno del pagamento all'ufficio dell'amministrazione della dorea, dove trovavano un modulo già preparato da chi poi lo completava in loro presenza. Sottoscrivevano quindi il documento (o se lo facevano fare) in demotico, riconoscendo così di aver ricevuto l'ammontare dovuto. Dopo di ché la *scriptura interior* veniva arrotolata, legata e sigillata, sempre ancora alla

[28] Il doc. **9** non è un caso problematico perché non si è sicuri che abbia recato in calce una sottoscrizione demotica, dato che la parte inferiore del documento è sparita.

[29] V. ad esempio le due ricevute rilasciate il 5 e 21 Dicembre 257 (P. Cairo Zen. I 59.115 e 59.116): sono scritte in greco e non recano in calce una sottoscrizione; persino la seconda ricevuta è stata scritta solo in greco, nonostante che sia stata rilasciata dallo stesso Phernuthis che poco prima aveva ancora rilasciato le ricevute bilingui **5** e **7**.

presenza del ricevente che lasciava poi il documento nell'ufficio, dove veniva registrato [30] e archiviato.

d) Sul verso di alcune ricevute (doc. **1-13**) possiamo ancora distinguere delle annotazioni greche che segnalano, ad esempio, la data del pagamento, il nome del ricevente, o l'ammontare pagato.[31] Sono annotazioni che gli amministratori mettevono sui documenti secondo la loro classificazione archivistica ed iscrizione nei registri (il doc. **11** era da iscrivere nel registro dei pagamenti in denaro, ἀργυρικά).

Visto che l'amministratore scriveva l'annotazione sul documento dopo aver arrotolato il papiro, è interessante per noi di rilevare il posto esatto dell'annotazione a papiro srotolato. L'annotazione si trova sempre sul verso, in alcuni casi in calce. Significa che l'amministratore, dopo aver arrotolato e sigillato la *scriptura interior*, ha semplicemente continuato ad arrotolare il papiro. In due casi però si trova nel centro, perché l'amministratore procedeva in un' altra maniera: dopo aver arrotolato la *scriptura interior* dall'alto in basso, arrotolava la *scriptura exterior* nel senso contrario, dal basso in alto[32], finché i due rotolini s'incontravano. Così l'amministratore poteva scrivere l'annotazione del doc. **2** sul rotolino della *scriptura interior* e quella del doc. **3** sul rotolino della *scriptura exterior*.

Sinnossi

l'annotazione si trova *in calce* del verso:

doc. **1** (l'inchiostro è molto sbiadito)

31 L κθ Παῦνι κ̅θ̅.
32 Ἰναρῶτο̣[ς].

doc. **11**

18 Θῶυθ κ̣ε̣.
19 Ἀργυρι(κά).
20 Θῶυτ κ̅ε̅. (altra mano)

doc. **13**

29 L λδ Μεχεὶρ κ̅β̅.
30 Κόρραγος καὶ
31 Χαιῶφις. Κροτῶν(ος) ἀρ(τάβαι) [ρ].

l'annotazione si trova *nel centro* del verso:

doc. **2** (sul verso della *scriptura interior*)

18 Ἁρμάις τοῦ
19 Παχῆτος.

doc. **3** (sul verso della *scriptura exterior*)

23 Ἀμπελουργῶν. ⊢ ε.

---

[30] Il registro in cui queste ricevute sono state iscritte non ci è pervenuto; cf. il registro P. Cairo Zen. 4 59.748 (primavera 256 a.C.) che contiene l'enumerazione di pagamenti (per simili lavori sulla dorea) fatti il giorno 16, probabilmente del mese di Hathyr = 9 Gennaio 256.

[31] Non esistono simili annotazioni in demotico; è anche logico, perché l'intera amministrazione della dorea era greca. Quando l'Edgar scriveva a proposito del nostro doc. **4** «on the verso a demotic docket» (P. Mich. Zen. p. 86) non poteva sapere che si trattava in realtà della fine della sottoscrizione demotica del recto.

[32] Per proteggere la parte della scrittura che si trova sul verso. Vedere SETHE-PARTSCH, *Bürgsch.*, p. 324 per un altro esempio del terzo secolo a.C.

§ 5 *Uso del papiro*

Nel P. Cairo Zen. 4 59.647, 29-31, un amministratore chiede che gli sia mandato il numero considerevole di 100 rotoli di papiro: καλῶς ποιήσεις χάρτας μεταπεμψάμενος ἡμῖν ρ. Difatti, il consumo di papiro dev'essere stato immenso, lo possiamo anche constatare dal P. Col. Zen. 1 4 che contiene un elenco delle quantità di rotoli che erano giornalmente consegnati ai vari amministratori ed agli uffici.

Parte dei rotoli è stata certamente usata nella sua integrità, per lunghi registri, giornali, ecc., ma il nostro archivio non conserva nessun rotolo intero, anzi i pezzi più lunghi misurano solo [33] 163,5 e 159 cm. (P. Lond. 7 1994 e 1995).

Per lettere, ricevute, contratti, invece, gli scribi avevano bisogno di fogli più piccoli e per questo dovevano tagliare i rotoli in pezzi. Si capisce che potevano farlo in due direzioni, in lungo (in modo tale da ricavare da un rotolo alcune *bande* con la stessa lunghezza del rotolo) o in largo (per ottenere alcuni *fogli* con la stessa altezza del rotolo). Per quanto riguarda le nostre ricevute bilingui, dalla classificazione seguente appare che i documenti del tipo I *a* sono *fogli*, quelli del tipo I *b* sono forse pure *fogli*, ma tagliati trasversalmente in due, e quelli del tipo II (colla scrittura trasfibrale) sono forse *bande* tagliate in pezzi.

Classificazione delle ricevute secondo la direzione della scrittura ed il rapporto dei documenti coll'altezza del rotolo

I. la scrittura è perfibrale; il documento è una striscia verticale tagliata dalla

a. altezza totale del rotolo

doc. **1**	33 cm.	(altezza attuale del documento)
doc. **13**	27,8 cm.	(idem)

b. mezza altezza del rotolo

doc. **2**, **7**, **8**	15 cm.	(altezza attuale del documento)
doc. **11**	14,5 cm.	(idem)
doc. **6**	14,2 cm.	(idem)
doc. **5**	13,7 cm.	(idem)
doc. **4**	13,5 cm.	(idem)

II. la scrittura è trasfibrale; il documento è una striscia orizzontale tagliata dalla

a. terza altezza del rotolo

doc. **12**	11,1 cm.	(larghezza attuale del documento)

b. quarta altezza del rotolo

doc. **3**	8 cm.	(larghezza attuale del documento)

[33] Queste dimensioni non sono impressionanti per i demotisti che sono abituati ai grandi papiri che gli scribi demotici usavano, persino per contratti semplici. V. ad esempio G. Botti, *L'archivio demotico da Deir el-Medineh*, specialmente il documento n. 8 che misura oltre 2 metri.

recto del rotolo

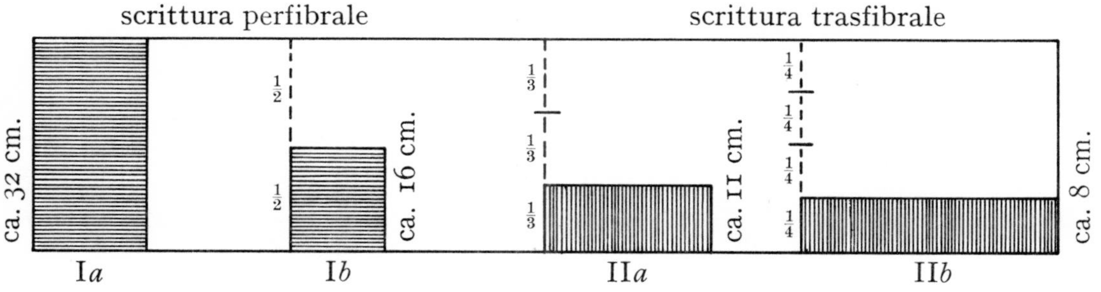

Essendo i singoli fogli di un rotolo attaccati l'uno all'altro per via di una incollatura, gli scribi hanno l'abitudine di scrivere sul papiro in modo tale che il calamo non intoppi contro lo spigolo del foglio successivo, quindi seguono la direzione delle incollature ed è per questo che lo scriba greco usa il rotolo girandolo di 180° in confronto al suo collega egizio:

recto del rotolo

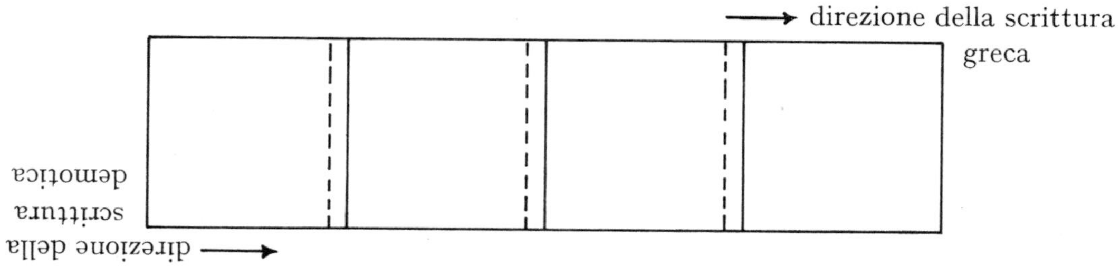

Nel caso di testi bilingui, come le nostre ricevute, c'è quindi da chiedersi quale scrittura segua la direzione delle incollature, quella greca o quella demotica? Logicamente c'è da aspettarsi che sia la scrittura greca (dato il carattere greco delle ricevute) e, in 5 documenti del gruppo I [34] è difatti la scrittura greca, ma invece in un caso, stranamente, è la scrittura demotica (doc. **9**).[35]

[34] Il problema non si pone naturalmente per il gruppo II dove la scrittura è parallela alla incollatura.

[35] Per quanto riguarda il doc. **6**, l'incollatura è irrilevante, perché si trova fuori della parte iscritta del documento.

1

RICEVUTA DI GRANO

Pagamento di imposte

Archivio di Panakestor | A. × L. = 33 × 9 cm. | 20 Agosto 257

P. Cairo Zen. 1 59.094 [Cairo, JdE 48542]. Il testo principale è stato scritto sul recto di una striscia verticale di papiro, tagliata dalla altezza totale di un rotolo [v. l'introduzione § 5]. La scrittura è parallela alle fibre. Vi è, dall'alto in basso, una incollatura; il bordo del foglio sinistro è incollato sopra quello del foglio destro, nella direzione della scrittura greca. Il documento è completo.

Documento doppio [v. l'introduzione § 4]. La scriptura interior è stata arrotolata, sigillata e ritrovata con i tre sigilli [1] intatti (v. tavola I). La scriptura interior contiene un testo greco, quella exterior un testo greco e demotico. Nel verso c'è una notizia in greco di un archivista di Panakestor; si trova dietro la linea 29, ma l'inchiostro è molto sbiadito.

Bibliografia

Testo greco: P. Cairo Zen. I 59.094 (C. C. Edgar, 1925); cf. P. dem. Zen. 23; *testo demotico*: P. dem. Zen. 23 (W. Spiegelberg, 1929); cf. U. Wilcken, Archiv für Papyrusforschung 9 (1930) 239; *fotografia* (del documento colla scriptura interior sigillata): P. Cairo Zen. I, tav. 22 n. 59094 (*l.* 10-30); W. Peremans - J. Vergote, *Papyrologisch Handboek* (1942) tav. VI (accanto alla p. 37).

Contenuto

Si tratta di una ricevuta rilasciata ad Ἰναρῶς Πάιδος Μοιθυμίτης per aver pagato una determinata quantità di grano. Inaros lavora un pezzo di terra di Apollonios, come pure Πᾶσις Πάιτος Μοιθυμίτης, un suo fratello.[2] Provenienti da Meidum, sono venuti a Philadelphia, come tante altre persone,[3] per partecipare alla messa a coltura del terreno nuovamente acquistato da Apollonios (forse verso Dicembre del 259).[4] Una parte di questo terreno era già coltivabile durante la stagione 258/257 (v. ad esempio *l.* 28-29: «quello che si ha fatto crescere in una parte delle terre di Apollonios»). Fatto che è ben noto,[5] ma che si potrebbe facilmente dimenticare per via dell'abbondante materiale che tratta del dissodamento del resto del terreno, eseguito da Panakestor nell'anno seguente 257/256 (v. doc. **2** intr.).

Per poter determinare la natura del pagamento effettuato da Inaros dobbiamo prima vedere chi erano le altre persone menzionate nella ricevuta.

---

[1] «The designs are indistinct: on 1) an object like a palmette; on 2) a pointed curving object; on 3) a bearded head, broken» (C. C. Edgar, P. Cairo Zen. I 59.094, intr.).

[2] P. Mich. Zen. 31, 2-3 (256/255 a.C.).

[3] V. ad esempio P. Lond. 7 1954, 7-8: contadini provenienti dal nomos Heliopolites. Questi scrivono ad Apollonios (Ottobre/Novembre 257) che il lavoro va male perché non c'è nessuno che s'intende della agricoltura: διὰ τὸ μὴ ὑπάρχειν ἄνθρωπον συνετὸν περὶ γεωργίαν. Benché senz'altro esagerata, questa notizia dimostra lo stesso che tra gli immigrati ce n'erano pochi che sapessero coltivare la terra.

[4] È la data del progetto per il ristauro e la costruzione delle dighe e dei canali di un latifondo di Apollonios, probabilmente il suo latifondo vicino a Philadelphia (P. Lille I = Suppl. doc. **A**).

[5] V. ad esempio PSI 5 500 (citato nella introduzione del doc. **2**); la maniera in cui P. Lille I = Suppl. doc. **A** parla del latifondo, fa supporre che non fosse interamente incolto nel Dicembre del 259.

a) *Damis* e *Diodoros*: Δᾶμις Κλέωνος Ἑλένειος e Διόδωρος Ζωπύρου Μάγνης. Figurano insieme, non solo nel nostro documento del 20 Agosto 257, ma anche in una lettera scritta poco prima, il 6 Luglio (PSI 5 500, 3): γράφει μοι Ἀπολλώνιος ... τὴν οἰκοδομίαν εἶναι πρὸς Διόδωρον, τὰ δὲ κατὰ τὴν γῆν πρὸς τοὺς περὶ Δᾶμιν, «Apollonios mi scrive che i lavori di costruzione spettano a Diodoros e tutto quanto riguarda la terra a Damis e ai suoi». E, difatti, alcuni documenti dell'anno 257 ci fanno vedere che Diodoros si è effettivamente occupato per Apollonios dei lavori di costruzione,[6] e Damis della terra.[7] L'anno dopo ritroviamo questi due che assistono, come testimoni, alla redazione dei contratti P. Col. Zen. 1 54 e P. Cairo Zen. 4 59.666, contratti che sono poi affidati alla custodia del Damis che funge da συγγραφοφύλαξ. Questi due contratti ci danno anche una informazione importante sulla posizione dei due uomini, perché Diodoros vi è descritto come uno che appartiene all'ambiente di Apollonios (τῶν περὶ Ἀπολλωνίου τὸν διοικητήν). Tale descrizione manca per Damis, che non si trova quindi al servizio di Apollonios; infatti occupa, forse già in questo momento, il posto di nomarkhes.[8] Tutto questo mi fa supporre che Apollonios quando aveva bisogno, nell'estate del 257, di uomini a cui poter affidare la cura dello svilluppo del suo latifondo, sceglieva Diodoros tra i suoi propri impiegati, per una parte del lavoro, affidando il resto a Damis che, come impiegato dello Stato, si trovava già sul posto. Perciò, per quanto riguarda la nostra ricevuta, rilasciata il 20 Agosto di quell'anno da Damis e Diodoros, non sappiamo se Damis agisca da parte dello Stato o da parte di Apollonios, ma è chiaro che Damis, essendo menzionato per primo, è il vero ricevente e che Diodoros è piuttosto una specie di controllore, e naturalmente di Apollonios, suo padrone.

b) *Kleitarkhos* e *Andron* (*l.* 27): ritroviamo questi due, sempre nello stesso anno 257, in un gruppo di documenti in cui ricevono ordine da Panakestor di pagare del grano, ed effettivamente lo pagano.[9] Andron appare, nel nostro documento, soltanto nella parte demotica, nelle veci di Diodoros che, a suo turno, è menzionato soltanto nella parte greca. Penso che Andron funga da controllore al posto di Diodoros; è possibile che sia il capo della gendarmeria del latifondo, che incontriamo qualche anno più tardi.[10] Kleitarkhos, invece, che agisce da parte di Damis, pare essere il vero ricevente; porta in questo periodo il titolo di ὁ ἐπὶ τοῦ σίτου τεταγμένος [11] ed è attestato qualche anno più tardi come uno di quelli responsabili del granaio, che non vi lasciano entrare il kheiristes Phanesis, mandato da Zenon (P. Mich. Zen. 52, v. doc. **12** nota *g*), ciò che dimostra la sua independenza da Zenon e dal latifondo: difatti nel suo granaio a Philadelphia sono depositati i prodotti del latifondo (insieme ai prodotti, penso, di altre terre nei dintorni); e per questo riceve nel 257 del grano da Inaros, secondo il nostro documento, e per lo stesso fatto fa osservare a Zenon, nel 251, che Herakleides (a quel momento l'amministratore del latifondo) aveva depositato meno di quello che avrebbe dovuto depositare secondo il conto ufficiale del

---

[6] PSI 5 496 = doc. **48**. Si occupava pure di altre cose, specialmente di pagamenti di grano, v. oltre il nostro documento, P. Lond. 7 1953, 31 (con la nota).

[7] P. Lond. 7 1954 e 1955.

[8] P. Lond. 7 1953, 1-2 nota: «Damis was certainly a nomarch in Year 35».

[9] PSI 6 681 = doc. **55**, P. Lond. 7 1953 ed i documenti ivi citati.

[10] 253-250: P. Cairo Zen. 2 59.232, 2; 59.296, 7 e 22; P. Mich. Zen. 85.

[11] P. Cairo Zen. 4 59.788, 44; P. Lond. 7 2172, 17-18; PSI 9 1021.

latifondo,[12] e perciò Kleitarkhos paga, nel 252, per Zenon (cioè dal suo deposito), una certa quantità di ricino alle autorità del Memphites (doc. **13**). Sarà stato per aver reso simili servizi che Kleitarkhos ha ricevuto da Panakestor uno stipendio di 2 oboli al giorno, durante due mesi dell'inverno 257/256.[13]

c) *Anosis*: Ἄνοσις Τοτορχόϊτος (ο Θοτορχῆτος) Σαΐτης. Chi scrive la parte demotica della nostra ricevuta è il famoso Anosis, attestato come κωμογραμματεὺς Φιλαδελφείας fin dall'estate 256 (P. Col. Zen. 1 54); è forse il γραμματεὺς Αἰγύπτιος di cui alcuni contadini si lagnano nell'Ottobre/Novembre del 257 (P. Lond. 7 1954, 6 nota), nel periodo cioè quando era ancora un semplice γεωμέτρης e portava il titolo di ὁ ἐπὶ τῶν χωμάτων κ[ ] τεταγμένος.[14] Lo incontriamo assai sovente nell'archivio, ultimamente in una lettera del 243 in cui Eukles (il successore di Zenon) l'accusa di frode.[15] Il fatto che Anosis figuri tra i testimoni di quattro contratti,[16] prova che sapeva scrivere il suo nome in Greco, ma non so se la sua conoscenza della scrittura greca andasse più in là; infatti non conosco nessun documento greco che sia sicuramente stato scritto dalle sue proprie mani.[17] Il demotico invece, lo sapeva scrivere benissimo.[18] S'indirizza persino in demotico a Zenon (P. dem. Zen. 17), benché sia poco probabile che Zenon, che viene dall'Asia Minore, abbia potuto capirlo.

Ritorniamo ora all'interpretazione del nostro documento. Da quanto precede, ci risultano due possibilità: o si tratta di un pagamento allo Stato o al proprietario Apollonios. Quantunque la prima supposizione sia la più probabile, la soluzione dipende, in primo luogo, dalla parola *dnj* nella *l.* 28 (v. nota *u*). Penso che sia la parola di genere maschile («imposte») e non di genere femminile («parte», «canone»). In questo caso,[19] il grano pagato costituisce le imposte che Inaros deve allo Stato sul prodotto della sua terra nel latifondo di Apollonios, e che paga all'impiegato statale Damis, tramite Kleitarkhos. Un secondo indizio per l'esattezza dell'ipotesi, che si tratti di un pagamento allo Stato, è il fatto che i controllori Diodoros ed Andron confermano il pagamento nella stessa maniera con cui il controllore Khaiophis conferma i pagamenti allo Stato (doc. **12** e **13**), facendo cioè appendere alla ricevuta un contrassegno, una sottoscrizione demotica di un tipo del tutto diverso dalle altre sottoscrizioni appese sotto le ricevute che riguardano gli affari interni del latifondo.

La ricevuta doc. **1**, sebbene rilasciata ad Inaros, è depositata nell'archivio del latifondo, perché costituisce la prova del pagamento avvenuto della tassa dovuta su un terreno, che fa parte del latifondo.

---

[12] V. per questo affare P. Lond. 7 1991, intr. e SB 5 8244 = doc. **56**.

[13] PSI 9 1012; v. doc. **3** intr. nota 6 per l'ammontare della paga giornaliera.

[14] P. Lond. 7 2172, 14-16 (con l'intr.).

[15] P. Col. Zen. 2 88.

[16] P. Cairo Zen. 2 59.173, 59.182; 4 59.666; P. Col. Zen. 1 54.

[17] V. il caso, ormai famoso, del κωμογραμματεύς Petaÿs: H. C. Youtie, *Pétaus, fils de Pétaus, ou le scribe qui ne savait pas écrire*, CdÉ 41 (1966) 127-143.

[18] Doc. **1**; P. dem. Zen. 4, 8 e 17.

[19] Nell'altro caso, il grano pagato costituisce il canone che Inaros deve ad Apollonios, il padrone della terra, e che paga a Damis nella veste di rappresentante di Apollonios. In questo caso però non si capisce perché la ricevuta sia stata depositata nell'archivio del latifondo di Apollonios e non in quello di Inaros.

Trascrizione

recto [tavola I]: scriptura interior

1 Βασιλεύοντος Πτολεμαίου
2 τοῦ Πτολεμαίου Σωτῆρος (ἔτους)
3 κθ [a] μηνὸς Π<α>ῦνι [b] κ̅θ̅. Ὁμολογεῖ [c]
4 Κλείταρχος ὁ παρὰ [d] Δάμιδος
5 καὶ Διόδωρος [e] ἐκ τῆς Ἀπολ`λ´ω-
6 νίου γῆς μεμετρῆσθαι ἀπὸ
7 τῆς ἅλω τῆς Ἰναρῶδος [f] τοῦ
8 Πάιδος [g] Μοιθυμίτου [h] πυ(ροῦ) Συρί(ου) [i]
9 ἀρ(τάβην) α, ἐπιχωρίου [j] κζ c, κρ(ιθῶν) με γ´.[k]

○ ○ ○

scriptura exterior

10 Βασιλεύοντ̣[ος] Π̣τολεμαί-
11 ου τοῦ Πτολεμαίου Σωτῆ-
12 ρος (ἔτους) κθ μηνὸς Παῦνι κ̅θ̅.
13 Ὁμολογεῖ Κλε̣ίταρχος ὁ πα-
14 ρὰ Δάμιδος κα̣ὶ Διόδωρος
15 ἐκ τῆς Ἀπολλωνίου γῆς
16 μεμετρῆσθαι ἀπὸ τῆς
17 ἅλω τῆς Ἰναρῶδος τοῦ
18 Πάιδος Μοιθυμίτου πυ-
19 ροῦ Συρίου ἀρτάβην μίαν,
20 ἐπιχωρίου εἰκοσιεπτὰ
21 ἥμισυ, κριθῶν τεσσαρα-
22 κονταπέντε τρίτον.

23 *ḥ3.t-sp* [l] 28 [a] *ibd-2 šmw sw* 29 *Pr-ʿ3* ʿ.w.s. *Ptlwmjs* ʿ.w.s.
24 *s3 Ptlw⸢mjs* ʿ.w.s.⸣ *p3 ntj nḥm* . [m] *ḏd*
25 *ʿn=w-ṯ3j* [n] *s3 Ḏḥwṱ-i.ir-rḫ* [o] *w3ḥ* [p] *Ir.t-Ḥr-r.r=w* [f] *s3 Pa-ḥi* [g] *p3 rmt Mr-Itm* [h]
26 *⸢ḫ3j⸣ rtb sw n Ḫr* [i] I *sw n Kmj* [j] 27½ *it* 45⅓
27 *(r)* [q] *dr.w(t) 3ntrn* [r] *irm ⸢Glwtrk3s⸣* [s] *p3 rd* [d]
28 *T3ms* [t] *n dnj* [u] *n3.w r.dj=w rd=w ḫn*
29 *dnj* [u] *3ḥ.w 3pw⸢r⸣nis* [v] ---
30 *swṱ* --[--]*.t* [w] . *sḫ ʿn=w-ṯ3j (s3) Ḏḥwṱ-i.ir-rḫ*

verso: [x] annotazione archivistica

31 (Ἔτους) κθ Παῦνι κ̅θ̅.
32 Ἰναρῶτ̣ο̣[ς].

3, 13 ὁμολογεῖ: *l.* ὁμολογοῦσι 18 Πάιδος: corr. da Πάιτος (Muszynski)

recto

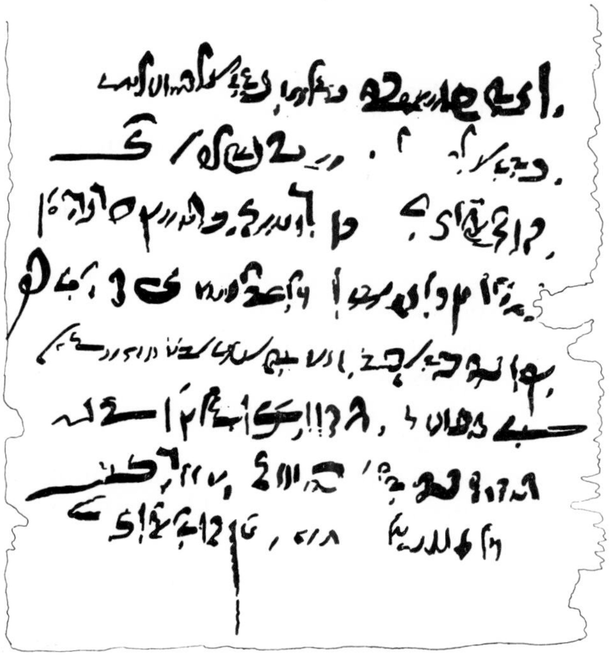

Traduzione

Testo Greco (*l.* 10-22):

Regnante Ptolemaios, figlio di Ptolemaios Soter, anno 29º, il 29 del mese Payni. Kleitarkhos — che (agisce) da parte di Damis — e Diodoros riconoscono di aver misurato per sé dall'aia di Inaros, figlio di Pais, un Moithymites:

una artaba di frumento siriaco, ventisette artabe e mezzo di frumento indigeno e quarantacinque artabe ed un terzo di orzo, provenienti dalla terra di Apollonios.

Testo Demotico (*l.* 23-30):

Anno 28, secondo mese della stagione *šmw*, giorno 29, sotto Faraone Ptolemaios, figlio di Ptolemaios, colui che salva.

Anosis, figlio di Thotorkhes, ha detto:

«Inaros, figlio di Pais, l'uomo da Meidum, ha misurato 1 artaba di frumento di Siria, $27\frac{1}{2}$ artabe di frumento d'Egitto e $45\frac{1}{3}$ artabe di orzo nelle mani di Andron e di Kleitarkhos, il rappresentante di Damis; (grano) che costituisce le imposte per quello che si ha fatto crescere in una parte delle terre di Apollonios - - -».

Anosis, figlio di Thotorkhes, ha scritto.

Testo Greco (*l.* 31-32):

Anno 29, Payni 29. Di Inaros.

Note

a L'anno 29 del testo greco è l'anno finanziario, l'anno 28 del testo demotico quello egizio. Ritroviamo, questa divergenza tra l'anno finanziario e l'anno egizio, nei documenti **2-8** che sono tutti scritti nel periodo antecedente al primo Thoth, giorno in cui incomincerà il 29° anno egizio e che coinciderà coll'anno finanziario (v. l'introduzione § 3).

b Penso che lo scriba abbia scritto πυνι nella *l.* 3: il ν rassomiglia al ν di 'Ιναρῶδος (*l.* 7), ma non voglio escludere la lettura πυινι proposta da Edgar.

c ὁμολογεῖ: ci si aspetterebbe ὁμολογοῦσι. Nell'archivio si riscontra sovente il singolare, invece del plurale, nelle ricevute rilasciate da più di una persona: doc. **3**, **5** e **7** [ὁμολογεῖ invece di ὁμολογοῦσι]; doc. **12** e **13** [ἔχει invece di ἔχουσι].

d ὁ παρά (*l.* 4) = *p3 rd* «il rappresentante» (*l.* 27). Questa locuzione, che ricorre in tutte le ricevute qui pubblicate, designa una persona che ha il diritto di agire per un'altra. L'amministratore del latifondo Panakestor, ad esempio, ha il diritto di agire per Apollonios (doc. **4-10**) perché questi è il suo padrone; ed il funzionario Kleitarkhos ha il diritto di agire per Zenon (doc. **13**) perché questi gli ha dato l'autorizzazione.

e Diodoros non viene menzionato nella parte demotica, dove figura invece Andron (*l.* 27), che è il suo rappresentante.

f 'Ιναρῶς, gen. 'Ιναρῶδος (*l.* 7 e 17) o, meglio, 'Ιναρῶτος (*l.* 32) = *Ir.t-(n)-Ḥr-r.r=w* (*l.* 25).

g Πάις, gen. Πάιδος (*l.* 8), corretto da Πάιτος (*l.* 18) =  cioè probabilmente  *Pa-ḥi* (*l.* 25).

h Μοιθυμίτης (*l.* 8, 18) = *p3 rmt (n) Mr-Itm* «l'uomo di (cioè proveniente da) Meidum» (*l.* 25). Questo villagio si trova nel Memphites (doc. **20**, 8), il nomos da dove provengono tanti di quei contadini che lavorano nel latifondo di Apollonios (cf. Skeat, P. Lond. 7 1936, 2 nota).

i πυρὸς Σύριος (*l.* 8, 18-19) = *sw n Ḫr* «frumento di Siria» (*l.* 26). Edgar ha ragione quando dice, a proposito di questo tipo di frumento: «there is no need to suppose that it had not been grown at Philadelphia» (P. Cairo Zen. 4 p. 171); difatti, nel nostro caso, il testo demotico precisa (*l.* 28-29) che «l'hanno fatto crescere in una parte delle terre di Apollonios». Si tratta di una nuova coltura di grano («a short-seasoned grain»?), introdotta dalla Siria: H. A. Thompson, *Syrian Wheat in Hellenistic Egypt*, Archiv für Papyrusforschung 9 (1930) 207-213; P. Lond. 7 1931 intr.

j πυρὸς ἐπιχώριος (*l.* 9 e 20) = *sw n Kmj* «frumento d'Egitto» (*l.* 26).

k 45 artabe di orzo equivalgono a 27 artabe di frumento, v. Skeat, P. Lond. 7 p. 98-99 («Table of equivalence»).

l *ḥ3.t-sp* o *n ḥ3.t-sp*? La datazione della parte demotica delle nostre ricevute bilingui inizia sovente col gruppo  che si può leggere come *ḥ3.t-sp* o come *n ḥ3.t-sp*; v. Abd el-Halim Nur el-Din e R. L. Vos (P. L. Bat. 19, doc. 42-48 intr.) che considerano questo gruppo, quando si trova all'inizio del testo, come *ḥ3.t-sp*. Non sono interamente convinto che abbiano ragione; nei documenti P. Torino Botti 13 e 14, ad esempio, il gruppo iniziale (scritto nella stessa maniera che verso la fine di quei documenti) mi pare essere *n ḥ3.t-sp*.

m La data viene separata dal resto del testo da un punto, messo sotto la linea. È una specie di interpunzione che si ritrova, dopo la data, nei doc. **2** 14, **6** 15 e **8** 15 e nei doc. **3**, **4** e **6** anche in molti altri luoghi.

n *ʿn=w-ṯ3j* (*l.* 25 e 30), cf.:

 P. dem. Zen. 17, 1 (lo stesso scriba) 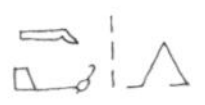

 P. Louvre 7861 V° 2 = Malinine, MDAIK 16 [1958] 223-224 (ieratico anormale; epoca di Amasis) 

La lettura di questo nome raro è sicura, benché si ignori cosa significhi. In greco è reso come Ἄνοσις (o Ἄνοσεις: P. Mich. Zen. 101, 3) o, con un θ invece del σ, come Ἄνοθις.[20] Si ritrova l'alternanza σ/θ con lo stesso *ṯ3j* nel nome proprio *Ṯ3j-n.im=w* = Σαμῶυς o Θαμῶυς (v. doc. **4** nota *b*).

o *Ḏḥwṯ-i.ir-rḫ* (*l.* 25 e 30), scritto più chiaro in P. dem. Zen. 4, 13 ; cf. pure P. dem. Zen. 8, 7 (sempre il nome della stessa persona e scritto da suo figlio) = Τοτορχόις (P. Cairo Zen. 2 59.173, 39; 59.182, 25; P. Col. Zen. 1 54, 28) o Θοτορχῆς (P. Cairo Zen. 4 59.666, 10). Cf. W. Erichsen, *Dem. Lesestücke* II. 2, 233, che distingue *Ḏḥwṯ-(i.)ir-rḫ* = Τοτορχόις da *Ḏḥwṯ-(i.)ir-rḫ-s* = Θοτορχῆς,[21] benché logicamente *-rḫ-s* dovrebbe essere -χοις. Visto che si tratta, nel nostro caso, di una sola persona, penso che siano due forme dello stesso nome e che questi sia da tradurre come «Thot è onnisciente».[22]

p *w3ḥ* N.N. *ḫ3j* (cf. Spiegelberg, *Dem. Grammatik* § 189). Con Spiegelberg (P. dem. Zen. 23) leggo qui *w3ḥ*, benché non mi risulti che ci sia un altro caso simile dove la dichiarazione così incominci.

q (*r*) *dr.w*(*t*): si distinguono il compl. di moto a luogo (con *r*) dal compl. di moto da luogo (con *n*).

r *3ntrn* (*l.* 27): questo personaggio non viene menzionato nella parte greca della ricevuta. Si tratta senz'altro di Ἄνδρων che agisce sovente insieme con Kleitarkhos.

s ⸢*Glwtrk3s*⸣ (*l.* 27) = Κλεὶταρχος (*l.* 4 e 13); cf. doc. **13**, 26 *Gljt3rk3ws*. Per quanto riguarda i segni *rk3*  si noti come la fotografia (tav. I) inganna e che il facsimile (p. 21) è sbagliato. Per il gruppo *k3* v. ad esempio doc. **3** 17 nota *b*.

t *T3ms* (*l.* 28) [la *m* è scritta come nel nome del re Ptolemaios, *l.* 23] = Δᾶμις (*l.* 4 e 14).

u *dnj* ricorre due volte (*l.* 28 e 29) nella stessa frase.

La seconda volta (*l.* 29) si tratta chiaramente della parola *dnj.t* «parte»: *ḫn dnj*(*.t*) *3ḥ.w 3pwrnis* «in una parte delle terre di Apollonios», espressione che ricorre

---

[20] P. Lond. 7 1992, 3; 2061, 16; P. Cairo Zen. 3 59.300, 11 e 12 (qui il θ non è indicato nella trascrizione, ma v. la nota nella editio princeps PSI 4 434; la lettura θ è stata verificata su una fotografia).

[21] V. inoltre W. Spiegelberg, P. dem. Zen., p. 32 (4) e ZÄS 54 (1918) 124-126.

[22] J. Vergote, *De oplossing van een gewichtig probleem*, p. 35: «Thot ist wissend»; l'alternativa è di separare i due nomi, l'uno dall'altro e di tradurre diversamente il nome *Ḏḥwṯ-i.ir-rḫ-s*: «Thot ist es, der ihn kennt».

sovente nelle nostre ricevute bilingui, spesso precisata nel testo greco con l'indicazione del numero delle arure in oggetto (doc. **4-6**) o col nome di chi possiede quella «parte» delle terre di Apollonios (doc. **11**).

Non penso che si tratti nella linea 28 della stessa parola *dnj*(.*t*) «parte» nel senso di «parte della raccolta che il contadino deve al proprietario della terra», cioè «il canone»; cf. *dnj.t nb 3ḥ.w* «landowner's-share» (G. R. Hughes, *Saite Demotic Land Leases*, doc. 6, 6 e 8), perché questo significato di *dnj.t* è finora soltanto attestato dal testo citato, che data inoltre in un periodo ben anteriore. È più probabile quindi che si tratti, nel nostro documento, della parola comune *dnj* «imposte».

v Il nome di Apollonios ricorre sovente nell'archivio, ma è spesso danneggiato. V. però:

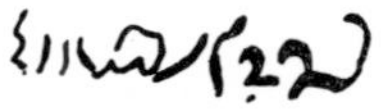
doc. **3** 22

doc. **8** 18

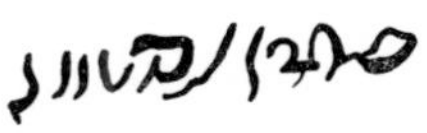
doc. **11** 17

w La parola danneggiata è femminile e indica una costruzione; si aspetta una parola per ἅλως come *ẖt3.t* (Erichsen, *Glossar*, 371).

x Essendo l'inchiostro sul verso molto sbiadito, presento qui il testo com'era letto da Edgar.

2

RICEVUTA DI SCURI

Attrezzi per ξυλοκοπία

Archivio di Panakestor A. × L. = 15 × 8,5 cm. 1 Ottobre 257

PSI 5 506 [Firenze, Biblioteca Medicea Laurenziana]. Il testo principale è stato scritto sul recto, e continua sul verso, di una striscia verticale di papiro, tagliata da un rotolo di mezza altezza [v. l'introduzione § 5]. La scrittura è parallela alle fibre. Vi è, dall'alto in basso, una incollatura; il bordo del foglio sinistro è incollato sopra quello del foglio destro, nella direzione della scrittura greca. Il documento è completo colla eccezione della striscia di papiro che manca a sinistra della scriptura exterior.

Documento doppio [v. l'introduzione § 4]. La scriptura interior è stata originariamente arrotolata e sigillata con un sigillo che è andato perduto. La scriptura interior contiene un testo greco e la scriptura exterior pure; in basso c'è un testo demotico che continua sul verso (dietro le linee 14-15). Sempre sul verso, c'è ancora una notizia in greco di un archivista di Panakestor; si trova dietro le linee 5-6 della scriptura interior ed era quindi originariamente visibile sul lato anteriore del documento, sulla scriptura interior arrotolata, accanto al sigillo, ma ciò solo quando la scriptura interior era arrotolata dall'alto in basso e la scriptura exterior dal basso in alto (e, in questo modo, la scrittura demotica, che si trova sul verso della scriptura exterior, veniva protetta).

Bibliografia

Testo greco: PSI 5 506 (G. VITELLI ed altri, 1917); cf. P. dem. Zen. 19; *testo demotico*: P. dem. Zen. 19 (W. SPIEGELBERG, 1929); cf. PSI 9 1010 E [traduzione] e U. WILCKEN, Archiv für Papyrusforschung 9 (1930) 75; *fotografia*: P. dem. Zen., tav. 9 n. 19 (*l*. 12-17).

Contenuto: ξυλοκοπία

Si tratta di una ricevuta che appartiene al gruppo dei documenti che riguardano l'amministrazione degli *affari interni* del latifondo e più precisamente l'organizzazione del suo dissodamento nell'Ottobre del 257.

Harmais, figlio di Pakhes, riconosce di aver ricevuto da Panakestor, l'amministratore del latifondo, dieci scuri colle quali tagliare la macchia che cresce sulle terre di Apollonios. Scuri, vanghe ed altri attrezzi venivano sovente messi a disposizione dei contadini per il dissodamento; probabilmente venivano dati in prestito.[1] A quanto pare Harmais [2] è un δεκάταρχος (come Horos, doc. **8**, e Nikias, doc. **11**), cioè il capo di un gruppo di dieci operai, che dipendono da lui; il δεκάταρχος è colui che suole ricevere la loro paga dall'amministrazione del latifondo o, come qui, i loro attrezzi.

ξυλοκοπία e ἐμπυρισμός; dissodamento delle terre di Apollonios: documenti **2**, **4**, **5**, **6**, **9** e **10** (1-27 Ottobre 257).

Per rendere coltivabile un terreno incolto bisogna liberarlo dalla macchia e dalle erbacce che vi crescono. Tutto quello che poteva servire — ad esempio per accendere il fuoco in

[1] Cf. PSI 5 488, 17-18: χορηγηθήσεται δὲ ἡμῖν κατὰ τὸ εἰωθὸς σκαφεῖα ἃ πάλιν ἀποκαταστήσομεν.

[2] Deve essere un'altra persona del Harmais di cui tratta PSI 5 488 e che sembra essere un appaltatore importante.

cucina — veniva tagliato (ξυλοκοπία) ed il resto bruciato (ἐμπυρισμός).[3] Questi sono i lavori di dissodamento che Panakestor fa eseguire nel latifondo di Apollonios nell'autunno dell'anno 257, distribuendo delle scuri (doc. **2**) e pagando del denaro ai contadini (doc. **4-6** e **9-10**).[4] Ma un terreno, una volta reso coltivabile, viene facilmente di nuovo invaso dalla macchia (τὴν ἐπιτρέχουσαν κοπάδα),[5] cosicché bisogna di tanto in tanto ripetere la ξυλοκοπία ed il ἐμπυρισμός, lavoro che facevano di preferenza dopo la raccolta (ardendo al momento stesso le stoppie) e prima della nuova stagione.[6] Come tutta questa operazione non fosse senza un certo qual rischio, appare dal rapporto P. Col. Zen. 2 96: ὁ ἐμπυρίσας τὴν χέρσον ἐνεπύρισεν τῶν παρ' ἡμῶν συκᾶς β̅, «chi bruciava la terra incolta, ha bruciato due di quei fichi che crescono da noi».

Per quanto riguarda il latifondo di Apollonios, sappiamo da PSI 5 500 (cf. pure doc. **1**) che una parte delle terre veniva già coltivata durante l'anno agricolo 258/257; il 6 Luglio 257 si scrive a Zenon per rapportargli che il grano è stato raccolto e che le terre coltivate sono state pulite mediante ξυλοκοπία e ἐμπυρισμός.[7] Quel giorno Panakestor si trovava già sul latifondo [8] che doveva dirigere durante l'anno seguente 257/256; aveva a quanto pare l'incarico speciale di rendere coltivabili tutti i terreni che erano ancora incolti. Difatti, nell'Ottobre 257, all'inizio della stagione agraria, spende molto denaro per ξυλοκοπία e ἐμπυρισμός di questi terreni, pagando per ogni arura 2½ dracme (= 15 oboli), tariffa fissa per questi lavori di dissodamento. Le terre così liberate dalla macchia sono pronte in tempo per essere seminate, ma Panakestor non riesce a dissodare tutti i terreni incolti. È noto come ad alcune riprese Apollonios [9] fa pressione su di lui e come Panakestor [10] si lamenta della mancanza di denaro. Nella primavera del 256 fa ancora dissodare alcuni terreni (sempre pagando 2½ dracme per ogni arura),[11] ma la maggioranza dei suoi pagamenti concerne ora i lavori di mantenimento di quelle terre già coltivabili, ciò che gli costa 8 oboli l'arura: 4 oboli per ξυλοκοπία e altrettanto per ἐμπυρισμός,[12] la tariffa fissa per questi lavori di manutenzione. Avrà Panakestor potuto finire il dissodamento di tutti i terreni del latifondo prima del momento [13] in cui veniva chiamato a Memphis come ὁ πρὸς ταῖς ἀποστολαῖς? [14] Penso di sì: dalle lettere di Apollonios capiamo che era del parere che si poteva presto finire il dissodamento; difatti Zenon, che succede a Panakestor come amministratore del latifondo, non ne parla più.

Trascrizione

recto [tavola II]: scriptura interior

1 Βασιλεύοντος Πτολεμαίου
2 τοῦ Πτολεμαίου Σωτῆρος
3 (ἔτους) κθ μηνὸς Μεσορὴ ι̅α̅.
4 Ὁμολογεῖ Ἁρμάις [a] Παχῆτος [b]
5 ἔχειν παρὰ Πανακέστορος
6 ὥστε εἰς τὴν ξυλοκοπίαν
7 πελέκεις [c] δέκα.

○

Per le note 3-14, vedere p. 29.

scriptura exterior

8 Β̣ασιλεύοντος Πτολεμαίου
9 τ̣ο̣ῦ̣ Π̣τολεμαίου Σωτῆρος
10 [(ἔτους)] κ̣θ μ̣ηνὸς Μεσορὴ ια. Ὁμολογεῖ
11 [Ἁ]ρμάι̣ς Π̣α̣χῆτος ἔχειν παρὰ
12 [Π]ανακέστορος ὥστε εἰς τὴν
13 ξυλ̣ο̣κ̣ο̣π̣ί̣α̣ν̣ π̣[ε]λέκεις δέκα.

14 *ḥ3.t-sp* 28 *ibd*-4 *šmw* [d] (*sw*) 11 . *ḏd Ḥr-m-ḥb* [a] *s3* [e] *Pa-*⸢*3ḫ.t*⸣ [b]
15 *n Pngsṯr* [f] *dj=k n=j ḳrb*[*n*] [c]

verso [tavola II]:

16 10 *t3j=f pš* 5 *r* 10 *ꜥn r sf ḫt* [g] *n.im*[*=w*]
17 *ḫn dnj 3ḫ.w 3pwrnis sḫ* [h]

annotazione archivistica

18 Ἁρμάις τοῦ
19 Παχῆτος.

recto

14
15

verso

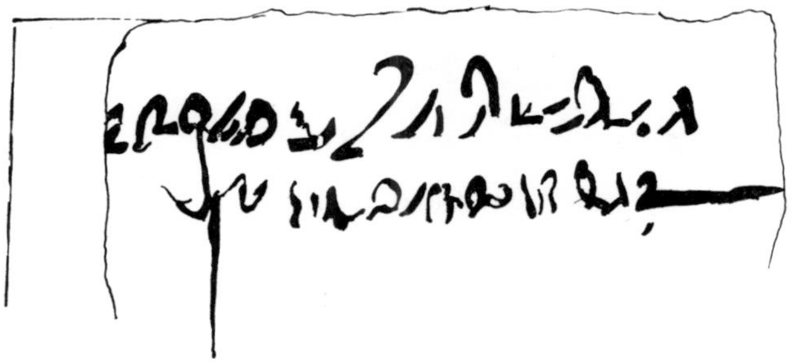

16
17

Traduzione

Testo Greco (*l.* 8-13):

Regnante Ptolemaios, figlio di Ptolemaios Soter, anno 29º, l'11 del mese Mesore. Harmais, figlio di Pakhes, riconosce di aver avuto da Panakestor: dieci scuri destinate per il taglio del legno.

Testo Demotico (*l.* 14-17):

Anno 28, quarto mese della stagione *šmw*, giorno 11.

Harmais, figlio di Pakhes, ha detto a Panakestor:

«Tu hai dato 10 — la sua metà è 5, fa 10 di nuovo — scuri a me per tagliare con esse del legno in una parte delle terre di Apollonios».

Scritto.

Testo Greco (*l.* 18-19):

Harmais, figlio di Pakhes.

Note

a 'Αρμάις (*l.* 4, 11 e 18) = *Ḥr-m-ḥb* (*l.* 14).

b Παχῆς (*l.* 4, 11 e 19) = *Pa-⌜3ḫ.t⌝* (*l.* 14): la seconda parte del nome demotico è mutilo, ma incomincia forse col gruppo .

PREISIGKE, *Namenbuch*, 468 rinvia per Φρὶ Παχῆς (gen. Παχέους) a P. Par. 5 = UPZ 180*a* (che è una specie di bilingue, v. P. dem. Berl. 3116, pubblicato da W. ERICHSEN in Aegyptus 32 [1952] 10-32), ma questo rinvio non ci aiuta per la lettura del nostro nome demotico, perché Preisigke si è sbagliato: Παχέους è in realtà il nominativo invece del genitivo; questo nome corrisponde a *Pa-ḫj* (UPZ 180*a* 14 8 = P. dem. Berl. 3116 6 12).

c πέλεκυς (*l.* 7 e 13) = *ḳrb*[*n*] (*l.* 15), Copto ⲕⲉⲗⲉⲃⲓⲛ «axe, pickaxe» (CRUM, *Coptic Dict.*, 102*b*). La prima lettera della parola demotica è certamente *ḳ*; Spiegelberg la prendeva a torto per una *p* e leggeva *prg*[*s*] che riteneva come una trascrizione del greco.

d Il gruppo *šmw* è scritto molto abbreviato . Cf. doc. **5**, 17 , **6**, 15  e **8**, 15 .

e Penso che il punto che si trova sotto la linea, nello spazio tra i due nomi, sia *s3*.

f Il nome di Πανακέστωρ è scritto *Pngsṯr*, v. ad esempio:

 **2** 15

 **3** 19

 **8** 16

Si notino il gruppo *ṯ*  e la legatura della *r* con il determinativo dei nomi propri stranieri .

g *sf ḫt* (*l.* 16) «tagliare il legno» (cf. ξυλοκοπία):

 **2** 16

 **5** 20

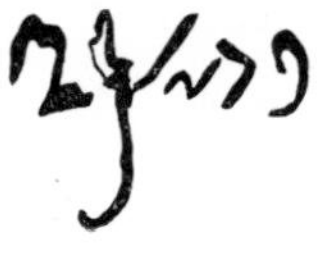 **6** 17

Queste parole, che ritornano ancora, ma mutile, nel doc. **4** 16, sono da trascrivere come

Per il verbo *sf*, v. Wb 3 442.11: *sf*, «etw. abschneiden»; cf. ERICHSEN, *Glossar*, 429: *sfj*, «Schwert, Messer».

Accanto a *sf ḫt* c'è nei documenti **5** e **6** l'espressione *mḥ* (*n*) *sṯ* «bruciare (il legno) con fuoco» (cf. ἐμπυρισμός):

5 20

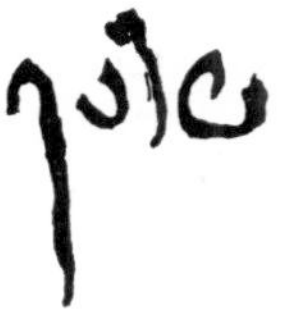

6 17

Note della p. 26.

[3] M. SCHNEBEL, *Die Landwirtschaft im Hellenistischen Ägypten* (1925) 20-24; W. L. WESTERMANN, *Regarding Receipts in the Zenon Archive*, JEA 16 (1930) 24-30.

P. JOUGUET (P. Lille, p. 218) a proposito di ξυλοκοπία: «déboisement s'entendant non seulement des grands arbres, mais encore et surtout des arbrisseaux, buissons et taillis qui empêchent une terre d'être cultivable»; e a proposito di ἐμπυρισμός: «très vraisemblablement l'opération qui consiste à brûler les tiges, branches et brousailles qu'il serait trop difficile ou trop long de couper».

V. per un'epoca anteriore, E. F. WENTE, *Late Ramesside Letters* (1967) 31 n. *ae* e *ag*.

[4] V. inoltre, per lo stesso periodo, Ottobre 257, la ricevuta P. Cairo Zen. 1 59.103 (incompleta; non è da escludere la possibilità che sia stata redatta in due lingue, come le altre ricevute dell'Ottobre 257).

Della primavera dell'anno 256 (Gennaio-Marzo) datano le ricevute per il dissodamento mediante ξυλοκοπία e ἐμπυρισμός: P. Cairo Zen. 1 59.127 e 4 59.550; P. Col. Zen. 1 27 e 28.

[5] P. Cairo Zen. 3 59.517, 8; cf. P. Col. Zen. 1 54, 11: εἰς ξυλοκοπίαν, ἐὰν ἐμπίπτηι κοπάς.

[6] Ottobre: PSI 6 560 (v. nota 7); Novembre: P. Cairo Zen. 3 59.517, «an account of the money spent in wages to workmen who have been engaged to collect the dry sticks from the fields, burn out the old stumps and cut down the brushwood. These operations lasted from the 25th of Thoth to the 9th of Phaophi, after which the workmen were turned on to irrigate the land thus cleared».

[7] Ma non tutte le terre coltivate: in Ottobre 257 (PSI 6 560) Panakestor deve ancora pagare per la manutenzione di terre coltivate durante l'anno 258/257: εἰς ξυλοκοπίαν καὶ ἐμπυρισμὸν τῆς περυσινῆς; i lavori sono stati eseguiti da un gran numero di operai che ricevono, ciascuno, 2 dracme, ciò che corrisponde a 16 giorni di lavoro (la paga giornaliera degli operai è, per questo tipo di lavoro, ¾ obolo: P. Cairo Zen. 3 59.517, 4).

[8] PSI 5 502, una lettera scritta da Panakestor il 7 Luglio 257.

[9] P. Cairo Zen. 5 59.816 (26 Dicembre 257), 3 59.387 (Gennaio 256).

[10] PSI 5 499 (fine Febbraio 256); ma cf. la lettera di Artemidoros a Panakestor (P. Cairo Zen. 5 59.816, 10-12): «I have also told Zenon and Artemidoros of Memphis, as Apollonios ordered me, that they are to supply you with as much copper as you need for this work. Arrange therefore to get it, for it will be given to you» (26 Dicembre 257).

[11] V. i documenti citati nota 4.

[12] 21 Dicembre 257-27 Gennaio 256: P. Cairo Zen. 1 59.116-59.118; 4 59.549; P. Col. Zen. 1 22-24; PSI 4 323; cf. il conto P. Cairo Zen. 4 59.748 (16 Hathyr [? v. *l.* 2 e 45-46] = 9 Gennaio 256).

[13] Probabilmente verso la fine di Aprile del 256.

[14] P. Lond. 7 1963 (Luglio/Agosto 256): «Superintendent of dispatches (consignments of goods destined to be sent down river from Memphis)», cf. SKEAT, P. Lond. 7 p. 55 n. 5-6.

e queste parole sono da trascrivere come

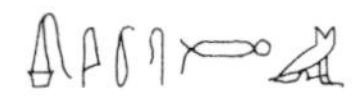

Per *mḥ* (o *mẖ*), v. Erichsen, *Glossar*, 173 e 177: «brennen», «verbrennen»; Wb 2 31.8: *m3ẖ* «verbrennen durch Feuer (mit *n*)»; Crum, *Coptic Dict.* 210: ⲙⲟⲩϩ «burn». Questo verbo può essere transitivo (come nei nostri documenti) e intransitivo: *tw=f mḥ=f n stj*[.*t*] «egli faceva in modo tale che (il papiro) bruciava con fuoco» (Setne I 4 4).

Nel documento **2** *r sf ẖt n.im=w* «per tagliare con esse (cioè con le scuri) del legno» corrisponde a ὥστε εἰς τὴν ξυλοκοπίαν; negli altri documenti citati si legge *b3k* (*n*) *sf ẖt* «il lavoro di tagliare il legno» (ξυλοκοπία) o *b3k* (*n*) *sf ẖt mḥ sṯ* «il lavoro di tagliare il legno e di bruciar(lo) con fuoco» (ξυλοκοπία e ἐμπυρισμός): gli scribi demotici hanno cercato di rendere i sostantivi greci mediante la perifrasi *b3k* (*n*) + infinitivo, «il lavoro di ...»; si ritrova la stessa costruzione nei documenti **7** 17 e **8** 17: *b3k* (*n*) *ṯ3j nb*, «il lavoro di prendere naubia (per le dighe)».

h Normalmente i documenti demotici finiscono con il verbo *sẖ* e l'indicazione dello scriba (v. doc. **1**, **12** e **13**). Alla fine dei documenti **2-8** e **11** manca però il nome dello scriba, come ad esempio pure alla fine del giuramento O. Leid. Nur el-Din 317 e P. Tur. Botti 34 B + C, del contratto P. Tur. 2144 (copia di P. Berl. 3101), della denunzia P. Fitzhugh D 2 (*l.* 20; JEA 58 [1972] tav. XLIV, accanto a p. 256).

In alcuni dei nostri documenti quel segno *sẖ* isolato scende molto in basso, in doc. **3** persino cinque centimetri. Data l'improbabilità che in tutti questi casi il contadino abbia scritto personalmente l'intero testo demotico, non mi stupirei se di sua propria mano non ci sia che quel segno *sẖ*, che fungerebbe così da firma.

3

RICEVUTA DI DENARO

Salario di tre viticoltori

Archivio di Panakestor A. × L. = 21,5 × 8 cm. 2 Ottobre 257

PSI 4 336 [Firenze, Biblioteca Medicea Laurenziana]. Il testo principale è stato scritto sul recto, e continua sul verso, di una striscia orizzontale di papiro, tagliata da un rotolo di quarta altezza [v. l'introduzione § 5]. La scrittura corre trasversalmente alle fibre. Vi è una incollatura orizzontale sotto la *l.* 7, nello spazio bianco tra la scriptura exterior e interior; una seconda incollatura si trova all'estremità inferiore del documento. Il documento è quasi completo. Vi è una macchia d'inchiostro sopra la prima lettera della *l.* 8.

Documento doppio [v. l'introduzione § 4]. La scriptura interior è stata originariamente arrotolata e sigillata con tre sigilli che ci sono stati conservati.[1] La scriptura interior contiene un testo greco e la scriptura exterior pure; in basso c'è un testo demotico che continua sul verso (dietro la *l.* 20). Sempre sul verso, c'è ancora una notizia in greco di un archivista di Panakestor; si trova dietro la linea 9 della scriptura exterior ed era quindi visibile sul lato anteriore del documento, sulla scriptura exterior arrotolata, ma ciò solo quando la scriptura interior era arrotolata dall'alto in basso e la scriptura exterior dal basso in alto (e, in questo modo, la scrittura demotica, che si trova sul verso della scriptura exterior, veniva protetta).

Il testo greco è pieno di errori; nel testo demotico si notano molti punti d'interpunzione, messi sotto la linea.

Bibliografia

Testo greco: PSI 4 336 (G. Vitelli ed altri, 1917); cf. P. dem. Zen. 20; *testo demotico*: P. dem. Zen. 20 (W. Spiegelberg, 1929); cf. PSI 9 1010 B [traduzione] e U. Wilcken, Archiv für Papyrusforschung 9 (1930) 75; *fotografia*: P. dem. Zen., tav. 9 n. 20 (*l.* 15-21).

Contenuto

Si tratta di una ricevuta che appartiene al gruppo dei documenti che riguardano l'amministrazione degli *affari interni* del latifondo e della sua coltivazione.

Tre persone — Peteyris, Onnophris e Theophilos — giardinieri (κηπουρός, *k3m*) o più precisamente, viticoltori, riconoscono di aver ricevuto da Panakestor, l'amministratore del latifondo, una somma di 5 dracme = 2½ kite, cioè il loro stipendio di 20 giorni. Il testo demotico specifica che questo periodo di 20 giorni va dall' 11 al 30 Mesore = 1-20 Ottobre 257. Visto che la ricevuta è rilasciata il 2 Ottobre, tratta chiaramente di un pagamento anticipato. Questa informazione, fornita dal testo demotico, è preziosa, tanto più che il testo greco non accenna neanche, che il lavoro pagato, è ancora da fare.

Il testo demotico fa inoltre vedere che il lavoro si svolgerà in quella parte del latifondo di Apollonios dove si trovano delle terre alte e secche, in quella parte cioè dove ci sono le vigne.[2] Com'è noto Apollonios destinava un gran pezzo del suo latifondo alla viticoltura e

[1] PSI 4 336, intr.: «La parte superiore del documento ... era arrotolata, legata con triplice legatura di fibre di papiro, e suggellata con tre suggelli (che si conservano).»

[2] V. per la viticoltura in Egitto M. Schnebel, *Die Landwirtschaft im Hellenistischen Ägypten* (1925) 239-281 e per la viticoltura nel latifondo di Apollonios Claire Préaux, *Les Grecs en Égypte*

faceva portare per piantarvi delle viti in gran quantità. Anche Zenon possedeva privatamente nelle vicinanze una vigna, e così pure altre persone. Pare che la regione fosse idonea per la viticoltura e che i Greci ne profittassero per aumentare la produzione del vino e per migliorarne la qualità. Sui vari stadi della coltivazione siamo assai ben informati; possediamo persino una agenda di Zenon su questo argomento.[3] I lavori veri e propri incominciavano in Gennaio [4] col taglio rigenerativo della vita e finivano colla vendemmia in Luglio. Nel periodo seguente, da Luglio a Gennaio, vi era poco da fare nelle vigne, eccetto nel mese di Ottobre, quando si doveva preparare la terra. Forse proprio per l'esecuzione di tali lavori i tre viticoltori del nostro documento ricevono pagamento nel mese di Ottobre.[5]

La somma di 5 dracme = 30 oboli che ricevono, corrisponde ad una paga giornaliera di $\frac{1}{2}$ obolo, circa la metà della paga normale.[6] Riceveranno forse il resto alla fine del periodo di venti giorni?

I tre viticoltori si chiamano: Peteyris figlio di Kolluthes, Onnophris figlio di Hethpheus, e Theophilos figlio di *Tim3ḳrts*. Due di questi sono quindi di origine egizia, e ciò è notevole essendo la maggior parte dei viticoltori di Apollonios di origine straniera.[7] È difficile sapere, se queste persone figurino in altri documenti dell'archivio. I nomi di Onnophris e Theophilos sono assai frequenti, ma conviene far notare il κηπουρός Onnophris che lavora quattro anni più tardi nell'oliveto (P. Mich. Zen. 45, 26) e lo ἀμπελουργός Theophilos che incassa, una decina di anni più tardi, una somma di denaro per lavori di diserbatura (fatti, a quanto pare, da 15 operai suoi durante alcuni giorni consecutivi; P. Col. Zen. 2 77 verso).

Trascrizione

recto [tavola III]: scriptura interior

Βασιλεύοντος Πτολεμαίου
τοῦ Πτολεμαίου Σωτῆρος
(ἔτους) κθ μηνὸς Μεσορὴ $\overline{\iota\beta}$. Ὁμολογεῖ
Πετεῦρις [a] Κολλούθου [b] καὶ Ὀννώ-
φρει [c] Ἑφθεῦτος [d] καὶ Θεοφίλωι

d'après les archives de Zénon (1947) 22-26 e HÉLÈNE CADELL, *La viticulture scientifique dans les archives de Zénon*: *PSI 624* (Aegyptus 49 [1969] 105-120) = doc. **64**; per μόσχευμα, v. doc. **26**, nota *l.* 2.

[3] PSI 6 624 (v. la fine della nota precedente) = doc. **64**.

[4] Gennaio è anche il mese adatto per piantare la vite: ὥρα φυτεύειν ἐστὶ τὴν ἄμπελον καὶ τὴν ἐλάαν καὶ τὰ λοιπὰ μοσχεύματα scrive Apollonios il 7 Gennaio, promettendo di inviare a Zenon «altre talee di vite», ἀμπέλινα μοσχεύματα πλείονα (P. Cairo Zen. 2 59.159). Difatti, nei primi anni della storia del latifondo, i documenti parlano sovente di spedizioni, in Gennaio o Febbraio, di μοσχεύματα, «barbate» o «talee di vite (che hanno messe le barbe, le radici)», v. ad esempio doc. **26**.

[5] Ho l'impressione che nel 257 non vi crescevano ancora delle viti e che si trattava quindi della preparazione della terra per poter piantarvi poi le barbate che Panakestor riceverà in Gennaio o Febbraio (v. ad esempio PSI 5 499).

[6] La paga giornaliera di contadini ecc., era normalmente un obolo (T. REEKMANS, *The Ptolemaic Copper Inflation*, Studia Hellenistica 7 [1951] 107), quella degli scribi 1-1$\frac{1}{2}$ obolo (eccetto lo scriba Diodoros che riceveva 3 oboli: P. Col. Zen. 1 p. 114-115), e quella del Kleitarkhos, ὁ ἐπὶ τοῦ σίτου τεταγμένος (doc. **1** e **13**) 2 oboli (PSI 9 1012; 16 Gennaio 256). È interessante paragonare queste paghe con l'ammontare di 60 oboli che Panakestor stesso incassa al giorno nell'estate 256 (dopo il suo trasferimento a Memphis: P. Lond. 7 1963).

[7] C. C. EDGAR, P. Cairo Zen. 3 59.329, nota 1: «The vineyards were worked chiefly by Greeks, though we also find Jews and Syrians employed in the same business».

6 κηπουροῖς [e] οὖσι γ̄ <ἔχειν ὀψώνιον> [f] τῆς (εἰκοσ)ημ(ερίας)
7 τοῦ Μεσορὴ (δραχμὰς) ε.

○ ○ ○

scriptura exterior

8 Βασιλεύοντος Πτολεμαί[ου]
9 τοῦ Πτολεμαίου Σωτῆ[ρος]
10 (ἔτους) κθ μηνὸς Μεσορὴ ιβ̄.
11 Ὁμολογεῖ Πετεῦρις Κολλού[θου]
12 καὶ Ὀννῶφρις Ἑ`θ´φεῦτος κα[ὶ]
13 Θεόφιλος κηπουροί{ς} ὄντε[ς γ̄ <ἔχειν>]
14 `ὀψώνιον´ τῆς (εἰκοσ)ημ(ερίας) τοῦ Μεσορ[ὴ]
15 δραχμὰς πέντε.

16 *ḥ3.t-sp* 28 *ibd*-4 *šmw* [g] (*sw*) 12 . *ḏd k3m* [e] *p3 k3m* [h]
17 *ḳ3j . P3-dj-Ḥr* [a] *s3 K3rḏ* [b] . *ḥn*ʿ *mj-nn* [i] *Wn-nfr* [c] *s3* [j] *Ḥtp.w* [d]
18 . *ḥn*ʿ *mj-nn Ṯwprs* [k] *s3 Tim3ḳrts* [l] *r* [m] *s* 3
19 *n . Pngsṯr . dj=k n=n*
20 *ḳt* 2½ *t3j=f pš ḳt* 1¼ *ḳt* 2½ ʿ*n n* [n] *p3 ḥbs* [f]
21 *ibd*-4 *šmw* (*sw*) 11 *r sw* ʿ*rḳj r hrw* 20 . *m-ḫn* [o] *dnj n3* [p] *3ḥ.w*

verso [tavola III]:

22 *ḳ3j . 3pwrnis sḫ*

annotazione archivistica

23 Ἀμπελουργῶν.[e] (Δραχμαὶ) ε.

3 ὁμολογεῖ: *l.* ὁμολογοῦσι 4-5 Ὀννώφρει: *l.* Ὀννῶφρις 5 Ἑφθεῦτος: *l.* Ἑθφεῦτος; Θεοφίλωι: *l.* Θεόφιλος 6 κηπουροῖς οὖσι: *l.* κηπουροὶ ὄντες; (εἰκοσ)ημ(ερίας): Pap. κ̄ ημ̄  11 ὁμολογεῖ: *l.* ὁμολογοῦσι 12 Ἑ`θ´φεῦτος: Pap.  14 (εἰκοσ)ημ(ερίας): Pap. κ̄ ημ̄ 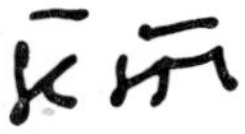

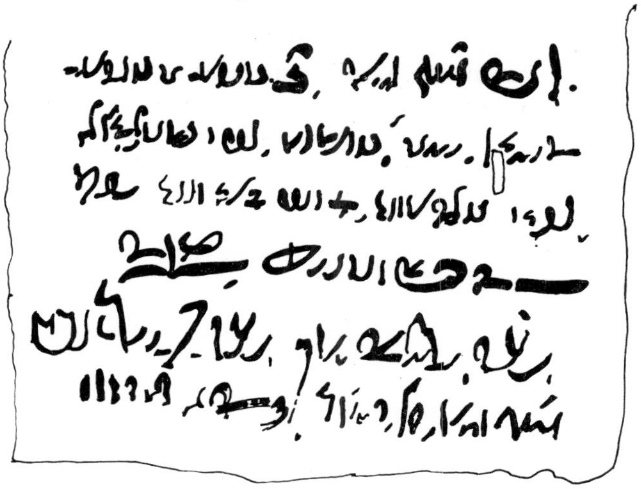

recto

16

17

18

19

20

21

verso

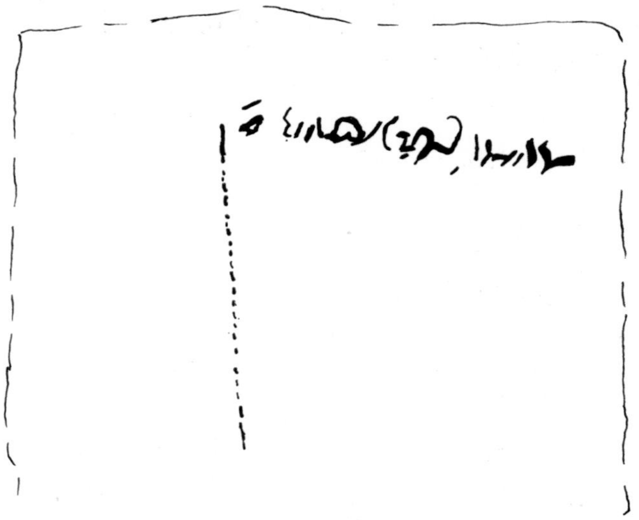

22

Traduzione

Testo Greco (*l.* 8-15):

Regnante Ptolemaios, figlio di Ptolemaios Soter, anno 29º, il 12 del mese Mesore. I giardinieri Peteyris, figlio di Kolluthes, e Onnophris, figlio di Hethpheus, e Theophilos — essendo 3 (persone) — riconoscono di aver avuto:

cinque dracme, lo stipendio per il periodo di venti giorni del (mese) Mesore.

Testo Demotico (*l.* 16-22):

Anno 28, quarto mese della stagione *šmw*, giorno 12.

Il giardiniere del giardino alto Peteyris, figlio di Kolluthes, e idem Onnophris, figlio di Hethpheus, e idem Theophilos, figlio di *Tim3ḳrts* — essendo 3 persone — hanno detto a Panakestor:

«Tu hai dato a noi $2\frac{1}{2}$ kite — la sua metà è $1\frac{1}{4}$ kite, (fa) $2\frac{1}{2}$ kite di nuovo — come (il denaro per) il vestimento, per il quarto mese della stagione *šmw*, dal giorno 11 all'ultimo giorno, fanno 20 giorni (di lavoro) in una parte delle terre alte di Apollonios».

Scritto.

Testo Greco (*l.* 23):

Di viticoltori.

5 dracme.

Note

a Πετεῦρις = *P3-dj-Ḥr* (*l.* 17).

b Κολλούθης [var. Κολλύθης, P. Cairo Zen. 2 59.292, 253, 417] = *K3rḏ* (*l.* 17), scritto col gruppo 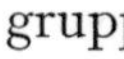 (v. *k3m, l.* 16) invece del segno *ḳ* o *g* che sembra più comune; cf. W. Spiegelberg, *Eigennamen*, p. 18* n. 121*a* e W. E. Crum, *Coptic Dictionary*, 104*b* **ⲕⲉⲗⲗⲟϫ** «buffalo». Nei papiri greci si riscontra Κολλούθης accanto a Κολλοῦθος; la desinenza -ης è attestata nell'archivio di Zenon (cf. ad esempio Κολλούθης, P. Cairo Zen. 2 59.245, 1) e la desinenza -ος sembra essere romana (E. Mayser, *Grammatik* I. 2 [1938] p. 49).

c Ὀννῶφρις = *Wn-nfr* (*l.* 17).

d Ἑθφεῦς [var. Ἑτφεῦς (P. Cairo Zen. 2 59.182, 3), Ἁτφεῦς (P. Cairo Zen. 3 59.329, 15)] = *Ḥtp.w*, J. Vergote, *Oplossing van een gewichtig probleem*, p. 29: «Die, welche gnädig sind».

Ἑφθεῦς (*l.* 5) è senz'altro un errore per Ἑθφεῦς; lo scriba l'ha corretto nella *l.* 12, ma il *Namenbuch* di Preisigke menziona ancora l'ortografia sbagliata (e persino una etimologia sbagliata: il cosidetto «variante» Φθεῦς corrisponde a *P3-ḏw*).

e κηπουρός «giardiniere» (*l.* 6 e 13) o, più preciso, ἀμπελουργός «viticoltore» (*l.* 23) = *k3m* «giardiniere» (*l.* 16): *k3m p3 k3m* «giardiniere del giardino (o della vigna, v. nota *h*)».

f ὀψώνιον appare nei documenti accanto a σιτομετρία (v. ad esempio P. Lond. 7 2061, 11-12); la prima parola indica lo stipendio pagato in denaro, la seconda lo stipendio pagato in natura (grano o pane, v. T. Reekmans, *La sitométrie dans les Archives de Zénon*).

ḥbs (*l.* 20) «vestimento» corrisponde a ὀψώνιον e porta perciò qualche volta il determinativo «argento, denaro» (Pestman, *Marriage*, 145, 1). Ignoro quale è l'origine di questo significato della parola *ḥbs* «vestimento» ma penso che bisogna cercarla nel periodo precedente quando non si usava ancora del denaro come moneta. Accanto a *ḥbs* = ὀψώνιον si trova la parola *ʿḳ* «pane» (cf. σιτομετρία); le parole *ʿḳ ḥbs* indicano insieme l'alimentazione che un marito deve alla moglie (Pestman, *Marriage*, 145-150) e la parola *ḥbs* da sola la paga (μισθός) di soldati: μισθοφόρος = *rmt iw=f šp ḥbs* «uomo che riceve vestimento», v. per la lettura di questo titolo l'articolo di S. Vleeming nel P. L. Bat. 23 (in corso di stampa).

g Una parte del principio della parola *šmw* (*l.* 16) e della fine del nome *Ṯwprs* (*l.* 18) si trova su una fibra a metà staccata (v. tav. III), ma rimessa a posto sul nostro facsimile. V. la tavola 9 nella pubblicazione di Spiegelberg per la posizione originale della fibra. Il danno è causato dal fatto che era impossibile, per via dei sigilli, di premere il vetro contro il papiro cosicché non è ben fissato.

h *p3 k3m* «il giardino»; che si tratta in realtà di una vigna, lo prova l'annotazione archivistica sul verso (*l.* 23) dove i nostri «giardinieri» sono chiamati «viticoltori». In Pathyris si trova una vigna, ἀμπελών = *3ḥ 3ll*, che viene designata pure come *k3m* (Pestman, P. L. Bat. 14 [1965] 84 n. 247 e 249).

i *mj-nn* (*l.* 17 e 18) indica la ripetizione di qualche cosa che precede (v. gli esempi citati da Pestman, OMRO 44 [1963] 14) e in questo caso la ripetizione del titolo *k3m p3 k3m ḳ3j* «giardiniere del giardino alto».

j La lineetta curva sotto il determinativo del nome *Wn-nfr* sta per *s3*. Si ritrova *s3* in questa notevole posizione in altri documenti dello stesso gruppo: **4** 14; **5** 17; **8** 15; cf. la posizione simile della *=f* di *Ḏ'j=f* (doc. **12** nota *c*).

k *Ṯwprs* (v. nota *g*) = Θεόφιλος (*l.* 5 e 13); il determinativo è uguale a quello del nome di Apollonios e non indica l'origine straniera.

l *Tim3ḳrts*: la lettura delle lettere *im3* non è interamente sicura, ma non vedo nessuna alternativa (la lettura *s*, ad esempio, in vece di *im*, è impossibile per via della grafia della *s* in Panakestor, *l.* 19). Si ignora come questa persona si chiamasse in greco.

m *r s* 3 = ὄντες $\bar{\gamma}$ (*l.* 13, cf. *l.* 6) e *r hrw* 20 (*l.* 21); questa *r* è generalmente considerata come una grafia di *ir/irj n*.

n *n*, a meno che il segno faccia parte del gruppo *'n* che precede.

o *m-ẖn*: la *m* antica non ricorre negli altri documenti di questo gruppo. Difatti, solo di rado si riscontra questa *m* in demotico (eccetto nei casi di *m-b3ḥ* e *m-s3*). Per *m-ẖn* Spiegelberg (*Dem. Grammatik*, p. 142 nota 2) cita tre istanze.

p *n3 3ḥ.w*: nella indicazione delle terre di Apollonios, l'articolo si usa soltanto nella espressione *n3 3ḥ.w ḳ3j*.

4

RICEVUTA DI DENARO

Salario per ξυλοκοπία e ἐμπυρισμός

Archivio di Panakestor A. × L. = 13,5 × 11 cm. 12 Ottobre 257

P. Mich. Zen. 25 [Ann Arbor, Michigan University Library, Inv. No. 3199]. Il testo è stato scritto sul recto, e continua sul verso, di una striscia verticale di papiro, tagliata da un rotolo di mezza altezza [v. l'introduzione § 5]. La scrittura è parallela alle fibre. Vi è, dall'alto in basso, una incollatura; il bordo del foglio sinistro è incollato sopra quello del foglio destro nella direzione della scrittura greca. Il documento è quasi completo.

Documento doppio [v. l'introduzione § 4]. La scriptura interior è stata originariamente arrotolata e sigillata con un sigillo che ci è rimasto conservato.[1] La scriptura interior contiene un testo greco e la scriptura exterior pure; in basso un testo demotico che continua sul verso (dietro la *l.* 15). Il documento è una specie di modulo: una parte del testo greco e l'intero testo demotico sono stati aggiunti più tardi. Lo spazio disponibile non bastava però per tutto il testo demotico, cosicché lo scriba è stato costretto a scrivere sul verso l'ultima linea.

I segni demotici sul verso sono quasi indistinguibili, anche sull'originale. Si notano alcuni punti, messi sotto la linea, che servono da interpunzione.

Bibliografia

Testo greco: P. Mich. Zen. 25 (C. C. Edgar, 1931); cf. P. dem. Zen. 16; *testo demotico*: P. dem. Zen. 16 (W. Spiegelberg, 1929); cf. P. Mich. Zen. 25 [traduzione]; *fotografia*: P. dem. Zen., tav. 8 n. 16 (*l.* 11-16).

Contenuto: ξυλοκοπία e ἐμπυρισμός [v. doc. **2**, introduzione].

Si tratta di una ricevuta che appartiene al gruppo dei documenti che riguardano l'amministrazione degli *affari interni* del latifondo e più precisamente l'organizzazione del suo dissodamento nell'Ottobre del 257.

Samoys, figlio di Amenneus, riconosce di aver ricevuto da Panakestor, l'amministratore del latifondo, una somma di $2\frac{1}{2}$ dracme = $1\frac{1}{4}$ kite per la pulizia di una arura. Quindici giorni dopo riceverà altre 10 dracme per lo stesso tipo di lavoro (doc. **10**).

Samoys è uno di quei contadini che lavorano sui terreni incolti di Apollonios per renderli coltivabili tagliando la macchia che vi cresce e bruciando gli sterpi. Ora c'è da chiedersi se lui ed i suoi compagni Phernuthis e Horos (doc. **5**), Pasis (doc. **6**) e Kleitos (doc. **9**) facciano quel lavoro personalmente (eventualmente aiutati da parenti) o se incarichino altre persone di farlo.[2] Qualche volta viene specificato che un certo pagamento, fatto bensì a qualcuno, è in realtà il salario di altre persone, operai, schiavi ecc. Logica-

[1] «The clay sealing is preserved. It is an impression of an Egyptian seal, probably a scarab, representing Ptah squatting to left on a basket; above his knees an indistinct cartouche, perhaps Men-kheper-Re; in the field a □ and at the top some indistinct lines» (P. Mich. Zen. p. 85-86).

[2] Le dieci scuri che Harmais riceve per tagliare la macchia (doc. **2**) sono probabilmente destinate per tali persone.

mente la destinazione del denaro viene specificata nei casi dove quel denaro non è destinato per il ricevente stesso, e penso che sia stato di regola lo specificarla.[3] Se questo è vero, significa che negli altri casi il denaro era destinato per i riceventi stessi, come ad esempio, per il Samoys del nostro documento. Lui ed i suoi compagni facevano quindi, probabilmente, loro stessi il lavoro del taglio della macchia e quello della bruciatura degli sterpi.

Il lavoro dei tagliatori della macchia era pagato secondo la tariffa fissa di 2½ dracme = 15 oboli per arura, ciò che corrisponde a 15 giorni di lavoro circa, perché la paga media giornaliera era un obolo (v. doc. **3**, intr.). Il nostro Samoys riceve in due riprese del denaro per il taglio della macchia: la prima volta una somma di 15 oboli (doc. **4**) e la seconda un'altra somma, 15 giorni più tardi (doc. **10**). A quanto pare, il pagamento del doc. **4** era quindi un pagamento anticipato, per il lavoro che Samoys doveva fare durante i quindici giorni seguenti. Samoys — e probabilmente pure i suoi compagni — si trovano in conclusione nella stessa situazione dei viticoltori del doc. **3** che erano, anche loro, pagati anticipatamente.

Trascrizione

recto [tavola IV]: scriptura interior

1 [Β]ạσιλεύοντος Πτολẹμαίου τοῦ
2 Π̣τọλ̣ẹμạίου Σωτῆ̣ρ̣[ο]ς̣ (ἔτους) κθ̣
3 Μ̣ε[σο]ρὴ κγ̅.[a] Ὁμολογεῖ vacat
4 Σ̣αμῶ⟦υτι⟧<υ>\`ς´ [b] Ἀμεννέως [c] vacat
5 [ἔ]χ̣ειν παρὰ Πανακέστορος τοῦ παρ'
6 Ἀπολλωνίου εἰς ξυ̣λοκοπίαν καὶ ἐμπυρισμὸν
7 ἀρού(ρας) α (δραχμὰς) β (τριώβολον)

○

scriptura exterior

8 Βασιλεύο̣ντος Πτολεμαίου τοῦ Πτο-
9 λεμαίου Σωτῆρος (ἔτους) κθ Μεσορὴ κγ̅.
10 Ὁμολογεῖ Σαμῶυς Ἀμεννέως
11 ἔχειν παρὰ Πανακέστορος τοῦ παρ'
12 Ἀπολλωνίου εἰς ξυλοκοπίαν καὶ
13 ἐμπυρισμὸν ἀρού(ρας) α (δραχμὰς) δύο τριώβολον.

14 *ḥ3.t-sp* 28 *ibd*-4 *šmw* [d] (*sw*) 22 [a] *ḏd Ṯ3j-n.im=w* [b] *s3* [e] *Imn-iw* [c] *n Pngsṭr*
15 *dj=k n=j ḥḏ ḳt* 1¼ *t3j=f pš* . *ḥḏ ḳt* $\frac{1}{2}$ $\frac{1}{10}$ $\frac{1}{60}$ $\frac{1}{120}$. *ḥḏ ḳt* 1¼ *ʿn*

verso [tavola V]:

16 *b3k* ⌜*sf ẖt* [f] *ẖn dnj*⌝ *3ḥ.w* . *3pwrnjs* . *sẖ*

[3] V. però l'introduzione del doc. **5**.

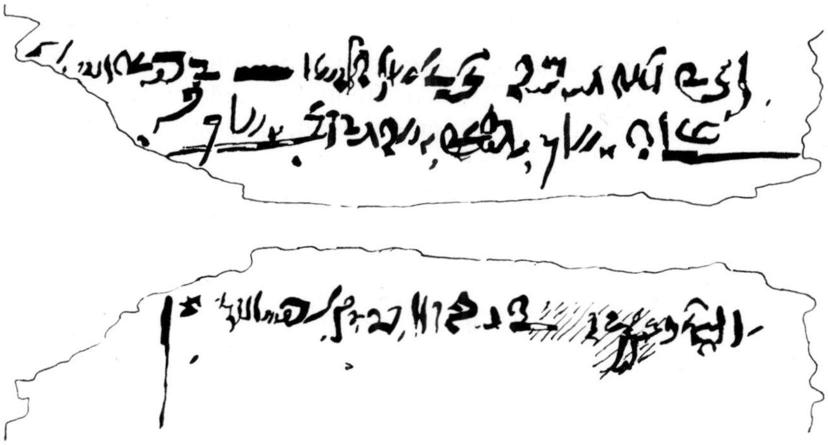

recto

14

15

verso

16

Traduzione

Testo Greco (*l.* 8-13):

Regnante Ptolemaios, figlio di Ptolemaios Soter, anno 29°, Mesore 23.
Samoys, figlio di Amenneus, riconosce di aver avuto da Panakestor, che (agisce) da parte di Apollonios:
due dracme e tre oboli per il taglio del legno e la bruciatura di 1 arura.

Testo Demotico (*l.* 14-16):

Anno 28, quarto mese della stagione *šmw*, giorno 22.
Samoys, figlio di Amenneus, ha detto a Panakestor:
«Tu hai dato a me $1\frac{1}{4}$ kite d'argento — la sua metà è $\frac{1}{2}$ $\frac{1}{10}$ $\frac{1}{60}$ $\frac{1}{120}$ kite d'argento, (fa) $1\frac{1}{4}$ kite d'argento di nuovo — (per il) lavoro di tagliare il legno in una parte delle terre di Apollonios».
Scritto.

Note

a Secondo il testo greco (*l.* 3 e 9), la ricevuta sarebbe stata scritta il *23* di Mesore invece, secondo il testo demotico (*l.* 14), il *22*. Edgar (P. Mich. Zen. p. 86 nota 2-3) dice a proposito di questa divergenza: «Mesore 22 is probably a mistake of the scribe». Non è necessario però di ricorrere alla supposizione di un errore, perché i giorni greci non coincidono interamente con i giorni egizi: per i Greci un giorno incomincia la sera, al tramonto e per gli Egizi la mattina dopo, allo spuntar del sole. Il 23 Mesore del testo greco del nostro documento incomincia quindi la sera del 12 Ottobre ed il 22 Mesore del testo demotico dura fin all'alba del 13 Ottobre. Suppongo perciò che la nostra ricevuta sia stata rilasciata la sera del 12 Ottobre, alla fine della giornata di lavoro.

b Σαμῶυς (var. Θαμῶυς)[4] = *Ṯ3j-n.im=w* (*l.* 14; cf. doc. **6**), un nome teoforo nel quale il nome del dio in oggetto va sottinteso: «(Dio N.N.) ha preso loro (cioè i nemici,

[4] PSI 5 532, 1.

demoni)» oppure «Che (dio N.N.) prenda loro». La forma piena è, per quanto mi consta, non attestata in greco, ma alcuni esempi si trovano in H. RANKE, *Die ägyptischen Personennamen* I, p. 387-388): con Amon (*Ṯ3j-Imn-n.im=w*), Khonsu (*Ṯ3j-Ḫnsw-n.im=w*) ed altri dei. V. inoltre W. SPIEGELBERG, ZÄS 64 (1929) 84 e J. VERGOTE, *De oplossing van een gewichtig probleem*, p. 15.

Nella *l.* 4 del nostro documento lo scriba aveva originariamente scritto il dativo Σαμώυτι invece del nominativo Σαμῶυς. Correggendo l'errore ha cancellato per isbaglio l'υ.

c ᾿Αμεννεύς = *Imn-iw* (*l.* 14) «Amon è venuto»; per altri nomi formati con Dio N.N. + *iw* v. J. VERGOTE, *De oplossing van een gewichtig probleem*, p. 26-27 [si noti a proposito della sua osservazione (p. 26, 7) che il nostro documento bilingue dà ragione a Ranke].

d La macchia nera al di sopra *šmw* è un buco nel papiro.

e *s3*: scritto contro il piede del determinativo della parola precedente (v. doc. **3** nota *j*).

f V. doc. **2** nota *g* per le parole *b3k sf ḫt* = ξυλοκοπία; l'espressione demotica per ἐμπυρισμός (*l.* 6 e 13) = *b3k mḥ sṯ* manca.

5

RICEVUTA DI DENARO

Salario per ξυλοκοπία e ἐμπυρισμός

Archivio di Panakestor A. × L. = 13,7 × 8 cm. 13 Ottobre 257

PSI 4 338 [Firenze, Biblioteca Medicea Laurenziana]. Il testo è stato scritto sul recto, e continua sul verso, di una striscia verticale di papiro, tagliata da un rotolo di mezza altezza [v. l'introduzione § 5]. La scrittura è parallela alle fibre. Vi è, dall'alto in basso, una incollatura; il bordo del foglio sinistro è incollato sopra quello del foglio destro, nella direzione della scrittura greca. Il documento è un po' danneggiato; dal verso, una parte del bordo incollato, è sparita. Sotto l'α di Ποκᾶτος (*l.* 12) c'è una macchia d'inchiostro.

Documento doppio [v. l'introduzione § 4]. La scriptura interior è stata originariamente arrotolata e sigillata con un sigillo che è andato perduto. La scriptura interior contiene un testo greco e la scriptura exterior pure; l'intero testo demotico si trova sul verso della scriptura exterior (dietro *l.* 13-16). Il documento è una specie di modulo: una parte del testo greco e l'intero testo demotico sono stati aggiunti più tardi, quello demotico sul verso, perché sul recto non c'era più spazio.

La scrittura demotica è assai danneggiata ed i singoli segni sono difficili da riconoscere, anche sull'originale; la mano sembra essere quella del doc. **8**.

Bibliografia

Testo greco: PSI 4 338 (G. Vitelli ed altri, 1917); cf. P. dem. Zen. 21; *testo demotico*: P. dem. Zen. 21 (W. Spiegelberg, 1929); cf. PSI 9 1010 A [traduzione] e U. Wilcken, Archiv für Papyrusforschung 9 (1930) 75; *fotografia*: P. dem. Zen., tav. 9 n. 21 (*l.* 17-21).

Contenuto: ξυλοκοπία e ἐμπυρισμός [v. doc. **2**, introduzione].

Si tratta di una ricevuta che appartiene al gruppo dei documenti che riguardano l'amministrazione degli *affari interni* del latifondo e più precisamente l'organizzazione del suo dissodamento nell'Ottobre del 257.

Pher(e)nuthis ed il suo compagno Horos riconoscono di aver ricevuto da Panakestor, l'amministratore del latifondo, una somma di $12\frac{1}{2}$ dracme = $6\frac{1}{4}$ kite per la pulizia di 5 arure. Le stesse persone ricevono, lo stesso giorno, altre 14 dracme per lavoro alle dighe (doc. **7**) e compaiono insieme in una lista della paga del latifondo (P. Cairo Zen. 4 59.788, 52). L'ammontare totale che ricevono il 13 Ottobre è molto alto: $12\frac{1}{2}$ dracme (doc. **5**) e 14 dracme (doc. **7**), cioè in tutto $26\frac{1}{2}$ dracme o 159 oboli, corrispondenti a 159 giorni di lavoro (la paga giornaliera per il lavoro alle dighe è un obolo, v. doc. **11**). Di qui si può dedurre che Pher(e)nuthis e Horos facevano fare almeno una parte del lavoro da un gruppo di operai.

Dei due compagni, Pher(e)nuthis è, a quanto pare, colui che si occupa della parte amministrativa dei loro lavori: è lui a far redigere il testo demotico delle ricevute **5** e **7** e la ricevuta P. Cairo Zen. 1 59.116 (21 Dicembre dello stesso anno 257): ("Ετους) κθ Φαῶφι κζ. Ἔχει Φερνοῦθις εἰς κάθαρσιν τῆς κοπάδος ἀρου(ρῶν) ϛ ἀν(ὰ) (τετρώβολον) (γίνονται) (δραχμαὶ) δ. Faccio notare che su quest'ultima ricevuta non figura più la sottoscrizione demotica, che ritroviamo soltanto in Ottobre su tali ricevute rilasciate dai contadini.

Trascrizione

recto [tavola IV]: scriptura interior

1 Βασιλεύοντος Πτολεμαίου τοῦ
2 Πτολεμαίου <Σωτῆρος> (ἔτους) κθ Μεσορὴ κ̄γ̄.
3 Ὁμολογεῖ Φε̣ρ̣νοῦθ̣[ις [a] Παῶτ]ος [b]
4 καὶ Ὧρος Π̣ο̣κᾶ̣τος [c] vacat
5 ἔχειν παρὰ Πανακέστορος
6 τ̣ο̣ῦ̣ π̣α̣ρ̣’ Ἀ̣π̣ολλων̣ί̣ο̣υ̣ ε̣ἰ̣ς̣
7 ξυλ[οκ]οπίαν καὶ ἐ[μπυρισμὸν]
8 ἀρου(ρῶν) ε (δραχμὰς) ιβ (τριώβολον).

○

scriptura exterior

9 Βα̣σ̣ι̣λ̣ε̣ύ̣ο̣ντ̣ο̣ς Πτολεμαίο̣υ̣
10 τοῦ Πτολεμαίου Σωτῆρος (ἔτους) κθ
11 Μεσορὴ κ̄γ̄. Ὁμολογεῖ Φερνοῦθις
12 Παῶτ̣ο̣ς καὶ Ὧρος Ποκᾶτος
13 ἔχειν παρὰ Πανακέστορ̣ο̣ς τοῦ̣
14 παρ’ Ἀπολλωνίου εἰς ξ̣υ̣λ̣ο̣-
15 κοπίαν καὶ ἐμπυρισ[μὸν ἀρου(ρῶν) ε]
16 (δραχμὰς) δεκαδύο τριώβολον.

verso [tavola V]:

17 *ḥ3.t-sp* 28 *ibd*-4 *šmw* [d] (*sw*) 23 ⌜*ḏd*⌝ *P3-(i.)ir-ntr* [a] *s3* [e] *Pa-ḥr* [b]
18 *n Pngsṯ[r]* [f] *dj=k n=j ḳt* 6$\frac{1}{4}$
19 *t3j=f pš ḳt* 3 $\frac{1}{10}$ $\frac{1}{60}$ $\frac{1}{[20]}$ [*ḳt*] 6$\frac{1}{4}$ *ʿn b3k*
20 *sf ẖt mḥ sṯ* [g] ⌜*ẖn*⌝ *dnj 3ḥ.w 3pwrns* [h]
21 *sẖ*

3, 11 ὁμολογεῖ: *l.* ὁμολογοῦσι

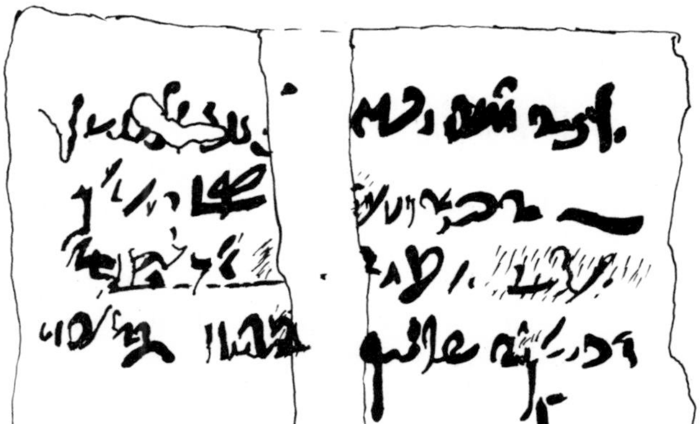

verso

17

18

19

20

21

Traduzione

Testo Greco (*l.* 9-16):

Regnante Ptolemaios, figlio di Ptolemaios Soter, anno 29º, Mesore 23.
Phernuthis, figlio di Paos, e Horos, figlio di Pokas, riconoscono di aver avuto da Panakestor, che (agisce) da parte di Apollonios:
dodici dracme e tre oboli per il taglio del legno e la bruciatura di 5 arure.

Testo Demotico (*l.* 17-21):

Anno 28, quarto mese della stagione *šmw*, giorno 23.
Phernuthis, figlio di Paos, ha detto a Panakestor:
«Tu hai dato a me $6\frac{1}{4}$ kite — la sua metà è $3\frac{1}{10}\frac{1}{60}\frac{1}{120}$ kite, (fa) $6\frac{1}{4}$ kite di nuovo — (per il) lavoro di tagliare il legno e di bruciare con fuoco in una parte delle terre di Apollonios».
Scritto.

Note

a Φερνοῦθις (var. Φερενοῦθις) = *P3-(i.)ir-ntr* (*l.* 17; cf. doc. **7**): «Colui che Dio ha fatto''; v. J. Vergote (*Oplossing van een gewichtig probleem*, p. 40) per questi ed altri nomi di persona formati con la forma relativa *i.ir*.

La lettura *P3-(i.)ir-ntr* mi sembra sicura. In doc. **7** i segni demotici sono quasi illeggibili, ma nel nostro documento il primo gruppo è *p3* (scritto assai grande), il secondo è *ir* (non può essere *rn*), il terzo *ntr* (si noti il piede del segno sotto la lacuna) e l'ultimo è il determinativo divino (la curva sotto la lacuna rappresenta *s3* «figlio di»). Spiegelberg, invece, interpretava questi segni come *P3j*(?)-*rnn.t*(?) ed i segni che seguono come dei determinativi (e non come *s3 Pa-ḥr*), ma la sua interpretazione mi pare impossibile (bisogna tenerselo presente leggendo la notizia di W. Swinnen nella Miscellanea Vergote = Orientalia Lovaniensia Periodica 6-7 [1975-1976] 533).

b Παῶς = *Pa-ḥr* (*l.* 17; cf. doc. **7**). Il nome demotico è leggermente danneggiato; suppongo che il segno *pa*  sia scritto come *pa* in *Ḥr-pa-Is.t* 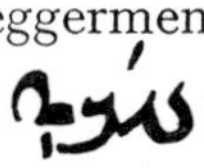 nel doc. **8** (dalla stessa mano); manca però nel nostro documento la parte superiore che è decisiva per la lettura. La parola *ḥr* è stata abbreviata (come nel nome comune *Ḏd-ḥr*, Erichsen, *Glossar*, 317). L'equivalenza Παῶς = *Pa-ḥr* è tra l'altro attestata da P. Ashm. I n. 14, 4 (demotico) + n. 25, 7-8 (greco). Strano che il nome del nostro Paos sia scritto come Παῶις in P. Cairo Zen. 2 59.292, 388.

c Ποκᾶτος, ma Ποκῶτος in doc. **7**. Nella *l.* 12 del nostro documento l'α mi sembra sicuro perché il segno è troppo stretto e, in alto, troppo acuto per essere un ω. Si tratta, in questi due documenti, della stessa persona che si chiama quindi Ποκᾶς o Ποκῶς; il nome Πογᾶς (doc. **8**) è forse un'altra variante dello stesso nome.

d *šmw* è ancor più abbreviato che nel doc. **8** (v. doc. **2** nota *d*), così tanto che Spiegelberg pensava che lo scriba l'avesse dimenticato.

e *s3*: scritto contro il piede (che si trova in lacuna) del determinativo del nome precedente (v. doc. **3** nota *j*).

f *Pngsṱ[r]*: scritto come nel doc. **8**.

g V. doc. **2** nota *g* per le parole *bꜣk sf ẖt mḥ sṱ*.

h *ꜣpwrns*: si legge le lettere *ꜣpw*  dal basso (a destra) in alto (a sinistra); la *p* è assai piccola e la *w* ancora di più.

Alla fine manca il gruppo *j* (per mancanza di spazio?); il determinativo coincide con l'ultimo segno del gruppo *s*.

6

RICEVUTA DI DENARO

Salario per ξυλοκοπία e ἐμπυρισμός

Archivio di Panakestor A. × L. = 14,2 × 10,4 cm. 13 Ottobre 257

P. Col. Zen. 1 26 [New York, Columbia University, Inv. No. 215]. Il testo è stato scritto sul recto, e continua sul verso, di una striscia verticale di papiro, tagliata da un rotolo di mezza altezza [v. l'introduzione § 5]. La scrittura è parallela alle fibre. Vi è, alla estremità sinistra del documento, una incollatura dall'alto in basso; il bordo del foglio destro è incollato sopra quello del foglio sinistro, nella direzione della scrittura demotica. Il documento sembra essere completo, benché il bordo superiore dia l'impressione d'essere stato tagliato colle forbici.

Documento doppio [v. l'introduzione § 4]. La scriptura interior è stata originariamente arrotolata e sigillata con un sigillo che ci è, in parte, rimasto conservato sul verso del documento (v. la fotografia, tav. VII).[1] La scriptura interior contiene un testo greco e la scriptura exterior pure; in basso un testo demotico che continua sul verso (dietro la *l.* 16). Il documento è una specie di modulo; una parte del testo greco e l'intero testo demotico sono stati aggiunti più tardi.[2] Nel testo demotico si notano alcuni punti, messi sotto la linea, che servono da interpunzione.

Bibliografia

Testo greco: W. L. Westermann, JEA 16 (1930) 25-26 = SB 5 7554 [prima edizione]; P. Col. Zen. 1 26 (W. L. Westermann - E. S. Hasenoerl, 1934) [seconda edizione]; senza fotografia; *testo demotico*: W. Spiegelberg, *Der demotische Text des Papyrus Columbia No. 25* [3], Aegyptus 11 (1930-1931) 72-75 [con un facsimile, ma senza trascrizione], cf. P. Col. Zen. 1 26 [traduzione].

Contenuto: ξυλοκοπία e ἐμπυρισμός [v. doc. **2**, introduzione].

Si tratta di una ricevuta che appartiene al gruppo dei documenti che riguardano l'amministrazione degli *affari interni* del latifondo e più precisamente l'organizzazione del suo dissodamento nell'Ottobre del 257.

Pasis, figlio di Samoys, riconosce tramite Hegesias di aver ricevuto da Panakestor, l'amministratore del latifondo, una somma di cinque dracme = $2\frac{1}{2}$ kite per la pulizia di due arure. È impossibile sapere se questa persona figuri altrove nell'archivio; il suo nome è troppo comune, e ricorre persino tra i nomi dei tagliatori della macchia [v. ad esempio il Pasis, padre dei fratelli (?) Pasis e Nekhthoys in P. Cairo Zen. 4 59.748, 14 e 27].

---

[1] «Three-quarters of the clay seal remain; but we cannot interpret the figures of the impression» (P. Col. Zen. 1 p. 75).

[2] Si nota uno spazio bianco alla fine della *l.* 4, poi tra le linee 4 e 5 e alla fine della *l.* 11 (v. la fotografia, tav. VI). Inoltre si nota nella *l.* 3, da Πᾶσις in poi, che l'inchiostro delle lettere è più nero e che i piedi delle lettere scendono più in giù di quelli delle lettere precedenti. Ho l'impressione che lo scriba abbia preparato prima una specie di modulo, lasciando uno spazio libero tra ὁμολογεῖ (*l.* 3 e *l.* 10) e ἔχειν (*l.* 5 e *l.* 12) per scrivervi poi, ad un altro momento, il nome del ricevente. Forse procedeva nella stessa maniera alla fine del testo greco (*l.* 7 e *l.* 14), per quanto riguarda il numero delle arure e l'ammontare delle dracme in oggetto. Questi dati venivano quindi aggiunti più tardi, al momento cioè del pagamento, quando si conosceva il nome, ecc. del ricevente. Nello stesso momento si aggiungeva pure il testo demotico, per il quale lo spazio disponibile non bastava, cosicché lo scriba era costretto di finirlo sul verso del documento.

[3] No. 25: si intende (Inv.) No. 215.

Pasis non si è presentato di persona all'ufficio di pagamento,[4] ma ha incaricato un certo Hegesias di riscuotere il 13 Ottobre il suo salario,[5] lo stesso Hegesias che riscuoterà il 18 Ottobre il salario di Kleitos (doc. **9**).

Trascrizione

recto [tavola VI]: scriptura interior

Βασιλεύοντος Πτολεμαίου τοῦ
Πτολεμαίου Σωτῆρος (ἔτους) κθ Μεσορὴ
κγ. Ὁμολογεῖ Πᾶσις [a] Σαμῴυτος [b]
διὰ Ἡγησίου [c] vacat
ἔχειν παρὰ Πανακέστορος τοῦ
παρ' Ἀπολλωνίου ε̣[ἰ]ς̣ ξυλοκοπίαν
καὶ ἐμπυρισ̣μ[ὸ]ν̣ ἀ̣ρ̣ου(ρῶν) β (δραχμὰς) ε.

○

scriptura exterior

Β̣α̣σιλεύοντος Πτολεμαίου τοῦ Πτο- [d]
λεμαίου Σ[ω]τῆρος (ἔτους) κθ Μεσορὴ κγ.
Ὁμολογεῖ Πᾶσις Σαμώ̣υτος [b] διὰ
Ἡγησίου vacat
ἔχειν παρὰ Πανακέστορος τοῦ
παρ' Ἀπολλωνίου εἰς ξυλοκοπίαν̣
καὶ ἐμπυρισμὸν ἀρου(ρῶν) β (δραχμὰς) πέντε.

ḥ3.t-sp 28 *ibd*-4 *šmw* [e] (*sw*) 23 . *ḏd Pa-sj* [a] *s3 Ṯ3j-n.im=w* [b] . *n Pngs-*
ṯr . *dj=k n=j ḳt* $2\frac{1}{2}$ *t3j=f pš ḳt* $1\frac{1}{4}$ *ḳt* $2\frac{1}{2}$ *ʿn*

verso [tavola VII]:

b3k sf ḫt mḥ sṯ [f] . *ḫn dnj 3ḥ.w* . *3*⌜*pwrn*⌝[*js*] ⌜*sḫ*⌝

14 ἀρου(ρῶν): Pap. 

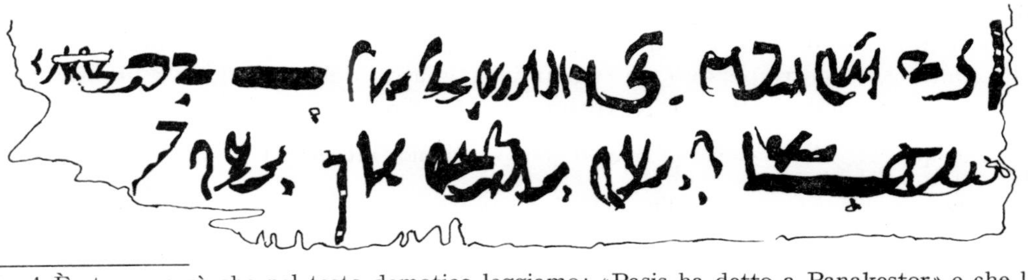

recto
15
16

[4] È strano però che nel testo demotico leggiamo: «Pasis ha detto a Panakestor» e che l'intermediario non vi figuri (e nemmeno nel testo demotico del doc. **8**). Penso che non dobbiamo dare troppa importanza a questo fatto. Non mi sembra necessario di pensare che Pasis fosse personalmente presente al momento in cui si scriveva questo testo demotico (difatti, per quanto riguarda Panakestor, è poco probabile che facesse di persona i pagamenti, come lo pretende il testo demotico) e, anche se Pasis abbia firmato il documento in persona (v. doc. **2** nota *h*), potrà averlo fatto facilmente in un altro momento.

[5] Hegesias non è stato l'unico intermediario a presentarsi il 13 Ottobre all'ufficio di pagamento; in doc. **8** figura come tale un certo Pogas.

verso

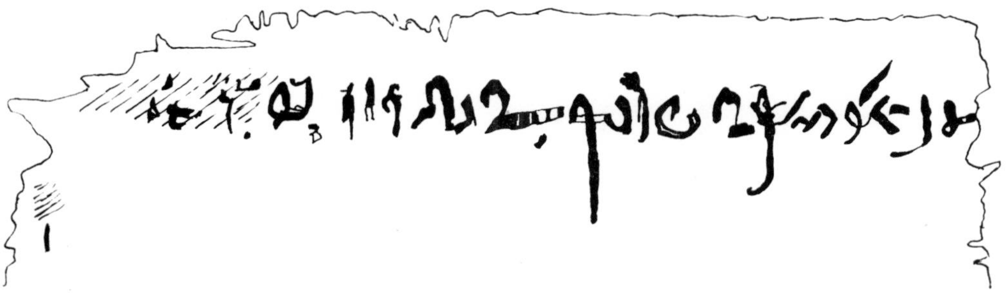

17

Traduzione

Testo Greco (*l.* 8-14):

Regnante Ptolemaios, figlio di Ptolemaios Soter, anno 29°, Mesore 23. Pasis, figlio di Samoys — tramite Hegesias — riconosce di aver avuto da Panakestor, che (agisce) da parte di Apollonios:

5 dracme per il taglio del legno e la bruciatura di 2 arure.

Testo Demotico (*l.* 15-17):

Anno 28, quarto mese della stagione *šmw*, giorno 23. Pasis, figlio di Samoys, ha detto a Panakestor:

«Tu hai dato a me $2\frac{1}{2}$ kite — la sua metà è $1\frac{1}{4}$ kite, (fa) $2\frac{1}{2}$ kite di nuovo — (per il) lavoro di tagliare il legno e di bruciare con fuoco in una parte delle terre di Apollonios». Scritto.

Note

a Πᾶσις = *Pa-sj*, un nome che ricorre frequentemente nell'archivio. De Meulenaere (CdÉ 38 [1963] 215) ha dimostrato, con alcuni esempi, che il nome maschile *Pa-sj* o Πᾶσις/Φᾶσις corrisponde a *P3-dj-Wsir* o Πετοσῖρις «Colui che Osiris ha dato» e che nella stessa maniera il nome femminile *Ta-sj* o Τᾶσις/Θᾶσις corrisponde a *T3-dj-Wsir* o Τετοσῖρις «Colei che Osiris ha data». Questa ultima corrispondenza è ancora confermata dal documento bilingue P. Cairo 10.262 (W. Spiegelberg, P. Cairo II p. 336-337, tav. 146), dove leggiamo *s.ḥm.t T3-r.dj-Wsir ḏd.ṯ n=s Ta-sj* «la donna Tetosiris, chiamata Tasis» (testo demotico) = Τάσιτι (dativo; testo greco). Pasis e Tasis sono quindi vezzeggiativi di Petosiris e Tetosiris.

b Σαμῴυτος [*l.* 3 e 10] (piuttosto che Σαμόυτος), gen. di Σαμῶυς = *Ṯ3j-n.im=w* [*l.* 15], v. doc. **4**, nota *b*.

c Ἡγησίου, gen. di Ἡγησίας (v. P. Col. Zen. I 26, traduzione, = SB 5 7554, indice). Strano che questo stesso nome figuri come Ἡγήσιος nell'indice di P. Col. Zen. e che ambedue le forme siano riportate (sempre per questo stesso testo) in Foraboschi, *Onomasticon alterum*, 121.

d Sopra l'o di Πτο- (*l.* 8) si trova una lineetta obliqua.

e Si noti la maniera in cui la grafia di *šmw* è stata semplificata (doc. **2** nota *d*).

f V. doc. **2** nota *g* per le parole *b3k sf ḫt mḥ sṯ*.

7

RICEVUTA DI DENARO

Salario per lavoro alle dighe

Archivio di Panakestor A. × L. = 15 × 8,5 cm. 13 Ottobre 257
(a) 6 × 6 cm.
(b) 9 × 8,5 cm.

P. Cairo Zen. 1 59.102 [(a) Cairo, JdE 48550*a*; (b) Cairo, JdE 48550]. Il documento ci è pervenuto in due pezzi, che vanno però insieme: una parte del bordo inferiore del frammento (a) si raccorda al bordo superiore del frammento (b). Il testo è stato scritto sul recto di una striscia verticale di papiro, tagliata da un rotolo di mezza altezza [v. l'introduzione § 5]. La scrittura è parallela alle fibre. Il documento è assai danneggiato; dal frammento (a) manca il bordo sinistro e il frammento (b) è pieno di buchi.

Documento doppio [v. l'introduzione § 4]. La scriptura interior è stata originariamente arrotolata e sigillata con un sigillo che è andato perduto. La scriptura interior contiene un testo greco e quella exterior un testo greco e demotico. Lo spazio libero alla fine della linea 4 e tra le linee 11 e 12 sembra indicare che si tratti di una specie di modulo anticipatamente preparato.

Bibliografia

Testo greco: P. Cairo Zen. 1 59.102 (C. C. Edgar, 1925); cf. P. dem. Zen. 24; *testo demotico*: P. dem. Zen. 24 (W. Spiegelberg, 1929); *fotografia*: P. Cairo Zen. 1, tav. 22 n. 59.102 (*l*. 8-18).

Contenuto: lavoro alle dighe

Si tratta di una ricevuta che appartiene al gruppo dei documenti che riguardano l'amministrazione degli *affari interni* del latifondo.

Phernuthis e Horos riconoscono di aver ricevuto da Panakestor, l'amministratore del latifondo, una somma di 14 dracme = 7 kite per lavoro alle dighe. Lo stesso giorno ricevono altre $12\frac{1}{2}$ dracme per la pulizia di 5 arure, cioè, in totale, la somma considerevole di $26\frac{1}{2}$ dracme, probabilmente destinate alla paga di un gruppo di operai (v. doc. **5**).

Lavoro alle dighe, τὰ διαχώματα, *wn wḥm*: documenti **7**, **8** e **11** (13 Ottobre e 19 Novembre 257)

I tre documenti trattano delle dighe del latifondo di Apollonios, o più precisamente delle dighe trasversali (τὰ διαχώματα), di quelle dighe cioè che si trovano nell'interno del latifondo: tre che vanno da Nord a Sud e nove da Est ad Ovest; v. tav. XXIX, il disegno sul P. Lille 1 (= Suppl. doc. **A**).

Notevole è il fatto che ben di rado si parli di dighe nei documenti dell'archivio e che questi documenti trattino per di più quasi mai del latifondo vicino a Philadelphia.[1] Eppure c'erano un costruttore di dighe (Komoapis, l'architetto) [2] e almeno due ἐπὶ τῶν

[1] P. Mich. Zen. 31, 33 e PSI 5 488, ad esempio, riguardano le dighe di un altro latifondo di Apollonios, quello che si trova vicino a Memphis.

[2] P. Lond. 7 2173; cf. P. Cairo Zen. 1 59.109.

χωμάτων τεταγμένοι, «intendenti delle dighe» contemporaneamente al servizio del latifondo [3] nonché alcuni χωματοφύλακες,[4] che dovevano, insieme ai primi, occuparsi delle 16 dighe del latifondo, dighe che raggiungevano una lunghezza totale di ben oltre 82 chilometri. Questa lunghezza la conosciamo per mezzo di un documento che contiene il progetto, fatto per Apollonios nell'autunno del 259, con il piano di lavoro per la costruzione delle dighe e dei canali sul latifondo che egli aveva, a quanto pare, appena acquistato e che doveva mettere a coltura (P. Lille 1 = Suppl. doc. **A**). Vi esisteva già qualche tratto di diga che poteva ancora servire, ma la più grande parte delle dighe era ancora da costruire, ciò che si doveva fare colla terra ricavata dai canali da scavare. Dopo aver esaminato sul posto la situazione, Apollonios ha dato, prima di partire il 1° Gennaio 258, l'ordine di incominciare con la misura del terreno per progettare i canali da scavare e le dighe da costruire. Era un lavoro che si poteva finire in alcuni mesi [5] e che è stato di certo finito prima che la stagione agricola incominciasse, nell'autunno del 258. Quando poi, un anno più tardi, si ha bisogno di denaro per pagare il lavoro alle dighe (P. Cairo Zen. 1 59.073: Maggio/Giugno 257), e si paga poi effettivamente del denaro per tali lavori (doc. **7**, **8** e **11**: Ottobre-Novembre 257), non si tratta più di costruire nuove dighe, ma di mantenere le dighe già esistenti, con lavori quindi che dovevano essere ripetuti ogni anno, come lo accenna sempre lo stesso P. Lille 1 (verso 22-23) = Suppl. doc. **A** (37-38): χωμάτων τῶν ἐν ἔθει ὄντων κατασκευάζεσθαι κατ' ἐνιαυτόν.

Trascrizione

recto [tavola VIII]: scriptura interior

1 [Βασιλεύο]ντος Πτολεμαίου τοῦ
2 [Πτολεμαίο]υ Σωτῆρος (ἔτους) κθ Μεσο-
3 [ρὴ κ̅γ̅. Ὁμο]λογεῖ Φερνοῦθις [a] Παῶ-
4 [τος [b] καὶ Ὧρος] Ποκῶτος [c] vacat
5 [ἔχειν παρὰ] Π̣α̣νακέστορος τοῦ
6 [παρ' Ἀπολλ]ωνίου εἰς τὸ διά-
7 [χωμα [d]] (δραχμὰς) ιδ.

○

scriptura exterior

8 [Β]ασ[ιλεύον]τ̣ο̣ς Πτολ̣εμ̣α̣ίο̣υ̣ τ̣οῦ
9 Π̣[τολεμαί]ο̣υ Σωτῆρος (ἔτους) κθ
10 Μ̣εσ[ορὴ κ̅γ̅]. Ὁμολογεῖ Φερνοῦθ̣ι̣[ς]
11 Π̣αῶτ̣[ο]ς̣ [e] καὶ Ὧ̣ρ[ο]ς̣ Ποκῶτ̣ο̣ς̣
12 ἔχ[ειν παρὰ Π]ανακέ[στ]ο̣ρο̣[ς] τ̣οῦ
13 [παρ' Ἀπολλωνίο]υ̣ εἰς [τὸ δι]ά-
14 χ[ωμα (δραχμὰς) δεκα]τέσσαρας.

3, 10 ὁμολογεῖ: *l.* ὁμολογοῦσι

---

[3] P. Lond. 7 2172, 11-16: Polemarkhos e Anosis (circa quest'ultimo v. doc. **1**, introduzione).
[4] P. Cairo Zen. 2 59.296, 15-16.
[5] P. Lille 1 recto 14 e verso 9 = Suppl. doc. **A**, 14 e 24.

15 *[ḥ3.t-sp]* [f] 28 *ibd-4 šmw (sw)* 23 ⸢*ḏd P3-(i.)ir-ntr* [a] *(s3) Pa-ḥr*⸣ [b] *n*
16 ⸢*Pngsṯr*⸣ *dj=k n=j ḳt* 7 *t3j=f pš ḳt* 3⸢½⸣
17 *ḳt* 7 *ʿn b3k ṯ3j nb ẖn dnj 3ḥ.w*
18 *3pwrnis sẖ*

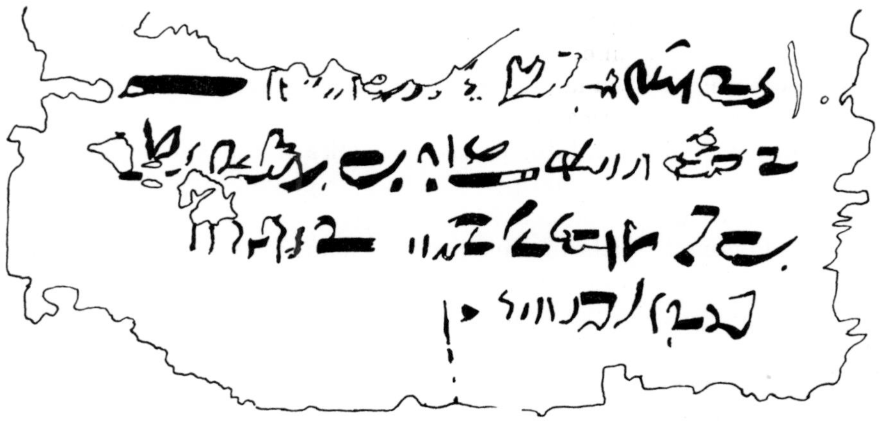

recto
15
16
17
18

Traduzione

Testo Greco (*l.* 8-14):

Regnante Ptolemaios, figlio di Ptolemaios Soter, anno 29°, Mesore 23.
Phernuthis, figlio di Paos, e Horos, figlio di Pokas, riconoscono di aver avuto da Panakestor, che (agisce) da parte di Apollonios:
quattordici dracme per (la manutenzione del)la diga trasversale.

Testo Demotico (*l.* 15-18):

Anno 28, quarto mese della stagione *šmw*, giorno 23.
Phernuthis, figlio di Paos, ha detto a Panakestor:
«Tu hai dato a me 7 kite — la sua metà è 3½ kite, (fa) 7 kite di nuovo — (per il) lavoro di prendere naubia in una parte delle terre di Apollonios».
Scritto.

Note

a Φερνοῦθις (*l.* 3 e 10) = *P3-(i.)ir-ntr* (*l.* 15): v. doc. **5** nota *a*.

b Παῶς (*l.* 3-4 e 11) = *Pa-ḥr* (*l.* 15): v. doc. **5** nota *b*.

c Il nome del padre di Horos è scritto qui Ποκῶς (*l.* 4 e 11), ma Ποκᾶς nel doc. **5** (nota *c*).

d εἰς τὸ διάχωμα [corrisponde a *r wn wḥm* nel documento **11** (nota *d*)]: la parola διάχωμα «diga trasversale» deve indicare una delle dighe che si trovano nell'interno del latifondo (v. la pianta, tavola XXIX) e che «ripetono» (*wḥm*, doc. **11** nota *d*) la grande diga che contorna il latifondo intero.

b3k ṯ3j nb, «il lavoro di prendere ναύβια»: per la perifrasi *b3k (n)* + infinitivo «il lavoro che consiste nel fare qualche cosa» cf. *b3k (n) sf ẖt* «il lavoro che consiste nel tagliare il legno» (doc. **2** nota *g*). Qui il lavoro consiste nel prendere o portare (*ṯ3j*) naubia (*nb*) per la diga trasversale (διάχωμα). La parola *nb*, che corrisponde a ναύβιον,[6] è già attestata nella 18ª dinastia (W. C. Hayes, Ostraka and Name Stones [1942] p. 36-37). Indica una quantità di 8 cubiti cubi e viene soprattutto usata per misurare la terra che serve per la costruzione o la manutenzione delle dighe (v. il documento greco P. Lille 1 = Suppl. doc. **A**); tanto è vero che nei documenti **7** e **8** *nb* indica piuttosto «la terra per le dighe».[7] Il determinativo di *nb* non è chiaro in doc. **7** 17, ma deve essere il gruppo ⸗λ, come nel doc. **8** (nota *f*).

e Le lettere del nome Παῶτος (*l.* 11) sono scritte molto larghe; l'asta del τ si trova subito davanti alla grande lacuna.

f Ciò che sulla fotografia rassomiglia tanto al gruppo *ḥ3.t-sp* è in realtà l'ombra ingannevole di due buchi (che ho indicati sul facsimile).

---

[6] V. l'ostracon bilingue Berl. 1113 (O. Wilcken 1025 + E. Revillout, Revue égyptologique 6 [1891] 11 n. 11).

[7] In questo caso si tratta della manutenzione delle dighe private nell'interno del latifondo; per quanto riguarda le dighe pubbliche, vi era un obbligo (legato alle terre) di partecipare alla loro manutenzione, sia per via di una prestazione obbligatoria di lavoro, sia per via del pagamento di una tassa (ambedue chiamati *nb*).

8

RICEVUTA DI DENARO

Salario per lavoro alle dighe

Archivio di Panakestor A. × L. = 15 × 10 cm. 13 Ottobre 257

PSI 4 337 [Firenze, Biblioteca Medicea Laurenziana]. Il testo è stato scritto sul recto, e continua sul verso, di una striscia verticale di papiro, tagliata da un rotolo di mezza altezza [v. l'introduzione § 5]. Sul recto la scrittura è parallela alle fibre. Il documento è quasi completo.

Documento doppio [v. l'introduzione § 4]. La scriptura interior è stata originariamente arrotolata e sigillata con un sigillo che è andato perduto. La scriptura interior contiene un testo greco e quella exterior pure; in basso c'è un testo demotico che continua sul verso (dietro la linea 16). Lo spazio libero alla fine delle linee 4 e 11 (e tra le linee 4-5 e 11-12) come pure il fatto che non tutto il testo demotico stia sul recto, sembrano indicare che si tratti di un modulo anticipatamente preparato.

La scrittura demotica del doc. **5** è probabilmente della stessa mano.

Bibliografia

Testo greco: PSI 4 337 (G. VITELLI ed altri, 1917); cf. P. dem. Zen. 18; *testo demotico*: P. dem. Zen. 18 (W. SPIEGELBERG, 1929); cf. PSI 9 1010 C [traduzione] e U. WILCKEN, Archiv für Papyrusforschung 9 (1930) 75; *fotografia*: P. dem. Zen., tav. 9 n. 18 (*l.* 11-18).

Contenuto: lavoro alle dighe [doc. **7**, introduzione].

Si tratta di una ricevuta che appartiene al gruppo dei documenti che riguardano l'amministrazione degli *affari interni* del latifondo.

Horos, figlio di Nekhthoys, riconosce di aver ricevuto da Panakestor, l'amministratore del latifondo, una somma di 4 dracme (o 24 oboli) = 2 kite. Horos essendo un δεκάταρχος, cioè capo di un gruppo di dieci operai, riceve, in conseguenza, per ognuno dei suoi uomini 2,4 oboli, almeno se, in questo momento, abbia veramente 10 operai al suo servizio. Lo dubito, perché l'ammontare di 2,4 oboli è strano, visto che la paga giornaliera per il lavoro alle dighe è un obolo (doc. **11**), cosicché 2,4 oboli corrisponderebbero a 2,4 giorni di lavoro.[1]

Horos non si è presentato di persona all'ufficio di pagamento, ma ha incaricato un certo Pogas [2] di riscuotere il denaro, nella stessa maniera in cui lo stesso giorno, Pasis aveva incaricato un'altra persona, Hegesias (doc. **6**).

Una settimana più tardi il nostro Horos riceverà un'altra somma di denaro da Panakestor, secondo la ricevuta PSI 6 560 (un documento doppio). Questa volta riceve la paga per i suoi operai per ξυλοκοπία e ἐμπυρισμός, ma se la riceve di persona o tramite qualcun altro (Pogas, ad esempio), non lo possiamo sapere, perché solo una piccola parte del documento ci è rimasta conservata.

---

[1] Se vi erano però davvero 10 operai, bisogna ammettere che la ricevuta concerne il pagamento di soltanto una parte del loro stipendio.

[2] Forse questo Pogas è un collega di Horos, dato che nel PSI 6 675, 1 + P. Mich. Zen. 113, 3 c'è un determinato Ποκᾶς δεκάταρχος.

Trascrizione

recto [tavola VI]: scriptura interior

1 Βασιλεύοντος Πτολεμαίου τοῦ
2 Πτολεμαίου Σωτῆρος (ἔτους) κθ Μεσορὴ κ̄γ̄.
3 Ὁμολογεῖ Ὧρος [a] Νεχθώυτος [b]
4 δεκάταρχος [c] διὰ Πογᾶτος [d] vacat
5 ἔχειν παρὰ Πανακέστορος τοῦ
6 παρ' Ἀπολλωνίου εἰς [e] τὸ διάχω-
7 μα [f] (δραχμὰς) δ.

○

scriptura exterior

8 Βασιλεύοντ[ος] Πτολεμαίου το[ῦ]
9 Πτολεμαίου Σωτῆρος (ἔτους) κθ Μεσορὴ κ̄γ̄.
10 Ὁμολογεῖ Ὧρος Νεχθώυτος [g]
11 δεκάταρχος διὰ Πογᾶτος vacat
12 ἔχειν παρὰ Πανακέστορος τ̣ο̣ῦ̣
13 παρ' Ἀπολλωνίου εἰς τὸ διά̣χ̣ω̣μ̣α̣
14 (δραχμὰς) τέσσαρας.

15 *ḥ3.t-sp* 28 *ibd*-4 *šmw* [h] (*sw*) 23 . *ḏd Ḥr-pa-Is.t* [a] *s3 Nḫt̯=w* [b] *n*
16 *Pngst̯r* [i] *dj=k n=j ḳt* 2 *t3j=f pš ḳt* 1
17 vacat [j] *ḳt* 2 *ʿn b3k ṯ3j nb* [f] *ẖn dnj 3ḥ.w*

verso [tavola VII]:

18 *3pwrnis sẖ*

2 Σωτῆρος: Pap. ρ

recto

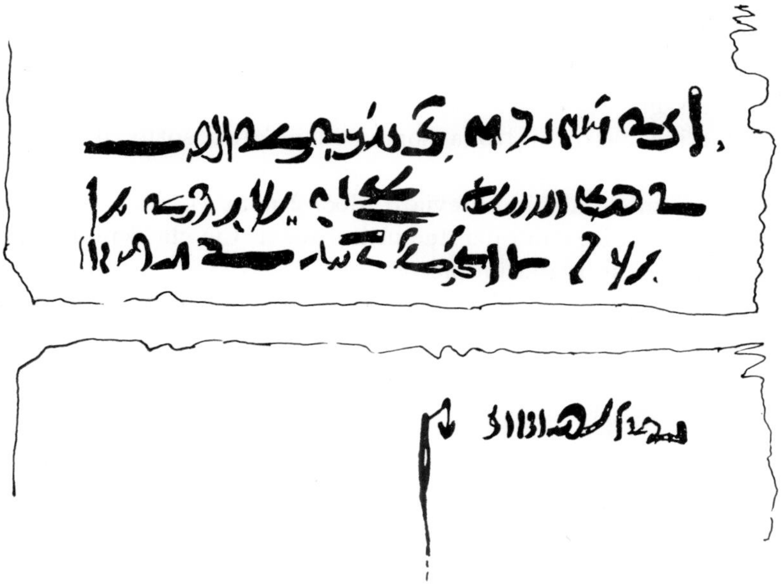

15
16
17

verso

18

Traduzione

Testo Greco (*l.* 8-14):

Regnante Ptolemaios, figlio di Ptolemaios Soter, anno 29°, Mesore 23.
Il dekatarkhos Horos, figlio di Nekhthoys — tramite Pogas — riconosce di aver avuto da Panakestor — che (agisce) da parte di Apollonios:
quattro dracme per (la manutenzione del)la diga trasversale.

Testo Demotico (*l.* 15-18):

Anno 28, quarto mese della stagione *šmw*, giorno 23.
Harpaesis, figlio di Nekhthoys, ha detto a Panakestor:
«Tu hai dato a me 2 kite — la sua metà è 1 kite, (fa) 2 kite di nuovo — (per il) lavoro di prendere naubia in una parte delle terre di Apollonios».
Scritto.

Note

a ῟Ωρος (*l.* 3 e 10) = *Ḥr-pa-Is.t* «Harpaesis» (*l.* 15). Per un altro esempio dell'uso del nome Horos come nome abbreviato, v. il basilikos grammateus Horos = Harteph-nakhthis (doc. **12** nota *d*).

b Νεχθῶυς (*l.* 3 e 10) = *Nḫt=w*  (*l.* 15; penso che l'ultimo segno sia il determinativo), «Che siano forti», J. Vergote, *De oplossing van een gewichtig probleem*, 22.

c Il titolo δεκάταρχος (*l.* 4 e 11) manca nel testo demotico.

d Πογᾶς è forse una variante di Ποκᾶς/Ποκῶς (doc. **5** nota *c*). La lettura διὰ Πογᾶτος (ed. princ.) è esatta, benché a prima vista δι' Ἀμολῆτος sembri possibile.

e L'inchiostro delle lettere ι e ς si è allargato verso l'alto, probabilmente al momento stesso in cui la scriptura interior veniva arrotolata.

f Per le espressioni εἰς τὸ διάχωμα «per (la manutenzione del)la diga trasversale» e *b3k ṯ3j nb* «il lavoro di prendere naubia», v. doc. **7** nota *d*. La parola *nb* è scritta , cioè determinata col segno «casa» accompagnato dal solito tratto diacritico che però tocca il segno seguente.

g Una macchia d'inchiostro si trova sopra, ed un'altra sotto, il tratto orizzontale del'υ.

h *šmw*: scritto in un modo assai abbreviato (doc. **2** nota *d*).

i V. doc. **2** nota *f* per la legatura dei due ultimi segni. Ciò che sembra sulla fotografia un punto sotto la *p*, è in realtà un piccolo buco.

j Ci sarebbe posto nello spazio libero per il segno *r*, ma non c'è la minima traccia d'inchiostro.

9

RICEVUTA DI DENARO

Salario per ξυλοκοπία e ἐμπυρισμός

Archivio di Panakestor | A. × L. = 9,2 × 8,7 cm. | 18 Ottobre 257

PSI 4 339 [Firenze, Biblioteca Medicea Laurenziana]. Il testo è stato scritto sul recto di una striscia verticale di papiro, tagliata da un rotolo di mezza (?) altezza [v. l'introduzione § 5]. La scrittura è parallela alle fibre. Vi è, dall'alto in basso, una incollatura; il bordo del foglio destro è incollato sopra quello del foglio sinistro, nella direzione della scrittura demotica. Al documento manca la parte inferiore (ca. 5 cm.?); per il resto è completo.

Documento doppio [v. l'introduzione § 4]. La scriptura interior è stata originariamente arrotolata e sigillata con un sigillo che è però andato perduto. La scriptura interior contiene un testo greco e la scriptura ẹxterior pure; il testo demotico [1] non ci è rimasto conservato.

Bibliografia

Testo greco: PSI 4 339 (G. Vitelli ed altri, 1917); senza fotografia.

Contenuto: ξυλοκοπία e ἐμπυρισμός [v. doc. **2**, introduzione].

Si tratta di una ricevuta che appartiene al gruppo dei documenti che riguardano l'amministrazione degli *affari interni* del latifondo e più precisamente l'organizzazione del suo dissodamento nell'Ottobre del 257.

Kleitos, figlio di Nikadas, riconosce tramite Hegesias di aver ricevuto da Panakestor, l'amministratore del latifondo, una somma di cinque dracme per la pulizia di due arure. È sorprendente riscontrare qui, tra gli operai che tagliano la legna, un uomo col nome greco di Kleitos, però ve ne sono altri ancora, come ad esempio il Demetrios, figlio di Demeas (P. Cairo Zen. 4 59.748, 40). Questo Kleitos non risulta in nessun altro documento dell'archivio. L'intermediario Hegesias invece, s'incontra ancora, nella stessa veste, nel doc. **6** (13 Ottobre); nei due casi è stato lui a presentarsi al posto di qualcun altro all'ufficio di pagamento di Panakestor.

Trascrizione

recto [tavola II]: scriptura interior

1 Βασιλεύοντος Πτολεμαίου
2 τοῦ Πτολεμαίο[υ] Σωτῆρος
3 (ἔτους) κθ Μεσορὴ $\overline{\kappa\theta}$.[a] Ὁμολογεῖ
4 Κλεῖτος Νικάδους [b] διὰ Ἡγησίου <ἔχειν> [c]
5 παρὰ Πανακέστορος τοῦ

---

[1] Non è certo che la ricevuta abbia portato un testo demotico, ma solo 6 giorni prima lo stesso intermediario Hegesias figurava in una ricevuta bilingue (doc. **6**); inoltre non è del tutto impossibile che il Greco Kleitos abbia fatto fare una dichiarazione demotica (v. Nikias, doc. **11**).

παρ' Ἀπολλωνίου εἰς ξυλο-
κοπίαν καὶ ἐμπυρισμὸν ἀρου(ρῶν) β (δραχμὰς) ε.[d]

○

scriptura exterior

Βασιλεύοντος Πτολεμαίου
τοῦ Πτολεμαίου Σωτῆρος
(ἔτους) κθ Μεσορὴ κθ.[a] Ὁμολογεῖ
Κλεῖτος Ν̣ικάδους διὰ Ἡγησίου <ἔχειν>
[π]α̣ρ̣ὰ Πανακέστορος τοῦ
[παρ' Ἀπολλωνίου - - -]
- - - - - - - - - - - - - - - - - - - -

2 τοῦ: Pap. το  7 ἀρου(ρῶν): Pap. ; (δραχμὰς) ε: Pap. 

Traduzione

Testo Greco (*l.* 1-7):

Regnante Ptolemaios, figlio di Ptolemaios Soter, anno 29°, Mesore 29. Kleitos, figlio di Nikadas — tramite Hegesias — riconosce di aver avuto da Panakestor — che (agisce) da parte di Apollonios:

5 dracme per il taglio del legno e la bruciatura di 2 arure.

Note

a $\overline{\kappa\theta}$ in *l.* 3, ma κθ (senza la lineetta) *l.* 10.

b Νικάδους (invece di Νικάδου), gen. di Νικάδας, v. E. Mayser, *Grammatik griechischen Papyri* I. 2 (1938) § 58.6 (p. 5) Anm. 3. Per il dativo Νικάδαι e l'accusativo Νικάδαν v. ad esempio P. Cairo Zen. 1 59.016, 2 e 5.

c Il verbo ἔχειν manca pure nel doc. **3** che però sembra scritto da un altro scriba.

d ἀρου(ρῶν) β (δραχμὰς) ε: ed. princ. ἀν(ὰ) β ∠ ε.

Addendum. Il presente volume era già in corso di stampa quando è saltata fuori la parte inferiore mancante: P. Jand. inv. 424 (Archiv für Papyrusforschung 26, 1978, 26).

10

RICEVUTA DI DENARO

Salario per ξυλοκοπία e ἐμπυρισμός

Archivio di Panakestor   A. × L. = 10 × 4,2 cm.   27 Ottobre 257

P. Cairo Zen. 1 59.104 [Cairo, JdE 48552]. Il testo è stato scritto sul recto di una striscia verticale di papiro, tagliata da un rotolo di mezza(?) [1] altezza [v. l'introduzione § 5]. La scrittura è parallela alle fibre. Una parte del documento, a sinistra e in basso, è andata perduta.

Documento doppio [v. l'introduzione § 4]. La scriptura interior è stata originariamente arrotolata e sigillata con un sigillo che è però andato perduto. La scriptura interior contiene un testo greco e la scriptura exterior pure; il testo demotico non ci è rimasto conservato.[2] È probabile che si tratti di una specie di modulo e che una parte del testo greco sia stata scritta prima del resto.

Bibliografia

Testo greco: P. Cairo Zen. I 59.104 (C. C. Edgar, 1925); senza fotografia.

Contenuto: ξυλοκοπία e ἐμπυρισμός [v. doc. **2**, introduzione].

Si tratta di una ricevuta che appartiene al gruppo dei documenti che riguardano l'amministrazione degli *affari interni* del latifondo e più precisamente l'organizzazione del suo dissodamento nell'Ottobre del 257.

Samoys, figlio di Amenneus, è uno di quegli operai che lavorano sui terreni incolti di Apollonios per renderli coltivabili tagliando la macchia che vi cresce e bruciando gli sterpi. Ora riconosce di aver ricevuto per questo lavoro dalle mani di Panakestor, l'amministratore del latifondo, una somma di dieci dracme = 60 oboli, che corrispondono alla paga di 60 giorni di lavoro.[3] Quindici giorni prima, Samoys aveva già ricevuto due dracme e tre oboli per lo stesso tipo di lavoro = 15 oboli, corrispondenti a 15 giorni di lavoro (doc. **4**). Dall'insieme dei due documenti possiamo dedurre che i pagamenti per ξυλοκοπία e ἐμπυρισμός erano pagamenti anticipati: dapprima Samoys riceve la paga per 15 giorni di lavoro (doc. **4**) poi, dopo 15 giorni, la paga per altri 60 giorni di lavoro (doc. **10**). Samoys ed i suoi compagni si trovano quindi nella stessa situazione dei viticoltori del doc. **3**, dove, benché il testo greco non lo dica, il testo demotico dimostra che in effetti i viticoltori vengono pagati anticipatamente.

---

[1] L'altezza attuale della striscia è di cm. 10; in basso manca un pezzo con quattro linee di greco e, con ogni probabilità, alcune linee di demotico, cosicché si arriva facilmente ad una altezza originale di 15 cm., cioè mezza altezza di un rotolo.

[2] Supponiamo che la ricevuta porti pure un testo demotico perché Samoys ha rilasciato una ricevuta bilingue quindici giorni prima (doc. **4**).

[3] Il salario di un contadino era 1 obolo al giorno circa (v. doc. **3**, intr. nota 6).

Trascrizione

recto [tavola II]: scriptura interior

[Βασιλεύοντος] Πτολεμαίου τοῦ
[Πτολεμαίου] Σ̣ωτῆρος (ἔτους) κθ
[Θῶυθ [a] β̅. Ὁ]μολογεῖ Σαμῶυς [b]
[Ἀμεννέως] [c] vacat
[ἔχειν παρὰ] Π̣ανακέστορος
[τοῦ παρ' Ἀπ]ολλωνίου εἰς
[ξυλοκοπί]αν καὶ ἐμπυ-
[ρισμὸν ἀρου(ρῶν)] δ̣ (δραχμὰς) ι.

○

scriptura exterior

[Βασιλεύο]ν̣τ̣ο̣ς Πτολεμαίου
[τοῦ Πτ]ολεμαίου Σωτῆρος
[(ἔτους) κθ Θῶυθ] β̅. Ὁμολογεῖ
[Σαμῶυς Ἀμ]εννέως
[ἔχειν παρὰ Παν]ακέστορος
[τοῦ παρ' Ἀπολλωνίου ---]

Traduzione

Testo Greco (*l.* 1-8):

Regnante Ptolemaios, figlio di Ptolemaios Soter, anno 29°, Thoth 2.
Samoys, figlio di Amenneus, riconosce di aver avuto da Panakestor — che (agisce) da parte di Apollonios:
10 dracme per il taglio del legno e la bruciatura di 4 arure.

Note

a Θῶυθ (o Θῶυτ) β̅ = 27 Ottobre (257 a.C.). Il mese è integrato sulla base del nome di Panakestor che si ritrova soltanto nel mese di Ottobre (fine Mesore, principio Thoth) in ricevute come questa.

b Σαμῶυς = *T̠ꜣj-n.im=w*, v. doc. **4** nota *b*.

c Ἀμεννεύς = *Imn-iw*, v. doc. **4** nota *c*. Abbiamo integrato il nome in *l.*4 supponendo che lo scriba abbia lasciato vuota la fine della linea (come, ad esempio, in **4**, 4 e negli altri moduli in cui il nome del ricevente veniva scritto solo piú tardi, v. l'introduzione § 4*c*). Edgar, nella edizione originale, salta la linea in oggetto.

11

RICEVUTA DI DENARO

Salario di dieci operai per lavoro alle dighe

Archivio di Panakestor A. × L. = 14,5 × 6 cm. 19 Novembre 257

P. Cairo Zen. 1 59.111 [Cairo, JdE 48559]. Il testo è stato scritto su una striscia verticale di papiro, tagliata da un rotolo di mezza altezza [v. l'introduzione § 5]. Il testo principale si trova sul recto del papiro; la scrittura è qui parallela alle fibre. Il documento è quasi completo.

Documento doppio [v. l'introduzione § 4]. La scriptura interior è stata arrotolata e sigillata; è stata ritrovata con il sigillo [1] ancora intatto (v. tavola XI). La scriptura interior contiene un testo greco, quella exterior un testo greco e demotico. Sull'altra facciata del foglio ci sono due notizie in greco, l'una (*l.* 18-19) dietro la *l.* 14 e l'altra (*l.* 20) dietro la *l.* 16; più in alto, nel senso opposto, si vede (dietro *l.* 7-9) $\frac{\epsilon}{\epsilon}$.

Bibliografia

Testo greco: P. Cairo Zen. I 59.111 (C. C. Edgar, 1925); cf. P. dem. Zen. 25; *testo demotico*: P. dem. Zen. 25 (W. Spiegelberg, 1929); *fotografia* (del documento colla scriptura interior ancora sigillata): P. Cairo Zen. I, tav. 22 n. 59.111 (*l.* 7-17).

Contenuto: lavoro alle dighe [doc. **7**, introduzione].

Si tratta di una ricevuta che appartiene al gruppo dei documenti che riguardano l'amministrazione degli *affari interni* del latifondo.

Nikias riconosce di aver ricevuto una somma di 10 oboli (o $\frac{5}{3}$ dracme) = $\frac{5}{6}$ kite per dieci operai suoi, un obolo per ciascuno, cioè la paga normale per un giorno di lavoro (doc. **3** intr. nota 6). Nikias possiede un terreno nel latifondo di Apollonios ed è perciò responsabile della manutenzione delle dighe confinanti. Ora fa eseguire da una compagnia [2] di dieci operai i lavori autunnali, lavori che si possono fare, a quanto pare, in una giornata.

Nella stagione 257/256 Nikias riceve, ad alcune riprese, qualche cosa per il suo terreno da parte di Panakestor: il 19 Novembre per il lavoro alle dighe (il nostro documento), nel mese di Novembre/Dicembre per la semina (?, PSI 13 1352) ed il 20 Marzo per la diserbatura (P. Col. Zen. I 25). Non si occupa soltanto del suo terreno, ma anche di bestie da soma [3] ed è perciò, probabilmente, quello stesso Nikias che dirige il trasporto con asini sul latifondo di Apollonios [4] e che riceve durante il mese di Novembre/Dicembre uno stipendio di $1\frac{1}{2}$ obolo al giorno (P. Col. Zen. I 20).[5]

---

[1] «On the clay sealing a female figure looking to right» (C. C. Edgar, P. Cairo Zen. I 59.111, intr.).

[2] V. doc. **2** intr. Non so chi era il capo (δεκάταρχος) di questa compagnia. Penso che Nikias fosse un uomo troppo importante per esserlo e che avesse semplicemente preso a servizio un δεκάταρχος e la sua compagnia per l'esecuzione del lavoro in oggetto.

[3] P. Cairo Zen. 4 59.748, 41-42 (principio 256): εἰς σκαλ(ισμὸν) καὶ εἰς μισθὸν ὑποζυ(γίων) κ.

[4] P. Col. Zen. I 20, introduzione.

[5] V. per Nikias (forse sempre lo stesso) T. Reekmans, *La Sitométrie dans les Archives de Zénon* (1966) 88, n. 102; A. Świderek, *Zenon fils d'Agréophon de Caunos et sa famille*, Eos 48, 2 (1957) 136: «peut-être un cousin de Zenon et sûrement son compatriote».

Trascrizione

recto [tavola XI]: scriptura interior

("Ετους) κθ [a] Θῶυτ κε̅.
Ἔχει Νικίας [b] εἰς τὴν
γῆν ἣν ἔχει [c] εἰς τὰ
διαχώματα [d] εἰς
ἐργάτας ῑ ἀν(ὰ) (ὀβολόν)·
(δραχμὴν) α (τετρώβολον).

○

scriptura exterior

("Ετους) κθ Θῶυτ κε̅.
Ἔχει Νικίας εἰς
τὴν γῆν ἣν ἔχει
[εἰς τὰ] δ̣ι̣αχώμα-
[τα εἰς ἐργ]ά̣τα[ς]
ῑ ἀν(ὰ) (ὀβολόν)· δεκόβολο̣[ν] [e]

ḥ3.t-sp 29 [a] *ibd*-1 *3ẖ.t* (*sw*) 25 *ḏd Nigis* [b]
n Pngsṱr dj=k n=j
ḳt $\frac{2}{3}$ $\frac{1}{6}$ *t3j=f pš ḳt* $\frac{1}{3}$ ⸢$\frac{1}{12}$⸣ [f] *r ḳt* $\frac{2}{3}$ $\frac{1}{6}$ *ʿn r wn*
wḥm [d] *ẖn n3j=n 3ḥ.w* [c] *ẖn*
dnj 3ḥ.w 3pwrnis sẖ

verso [tavola X]: annotazione archivistica

Θῶυθ κ̣ε̣.
Ἀργυρι(κά). [g]
Θῶυτ κε̅.

1, 7 (ἔτους): Pap. 

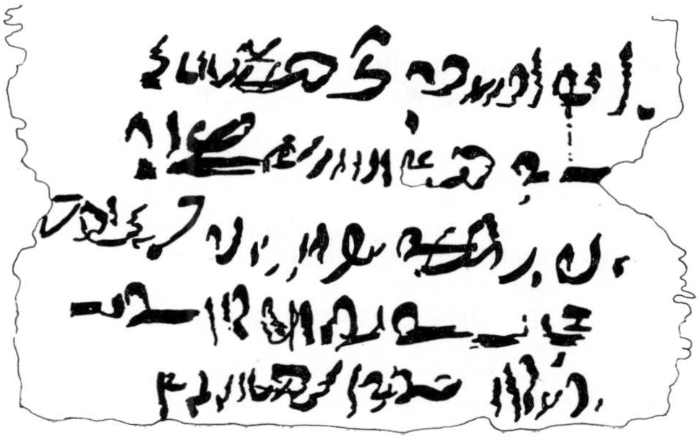

Traduzione

Testo Greco (*l.* 7-12):

Anno 29°, Thoth 25.

Nikias ha avuto per la terra che tiene:

per 10 operai, un obolo ciascuno, (cioè) dieci oboli per (la manutenzione del)le dighe trasversali.

Testo Demotico (*l.* 13-17):

Anno 29, primo mese della stagione *3ḫ.t*, giorno 25.

Nikias ha detto a Panakestor:

«Tu hai dato a me $\frac{2}{3}\frac{1}{6}$ kite — la sua metà è $\frac{1}{3}\frac{1}{12}$ kite, fa $\frac{2}{3}\frac{1}{6}$ kite di nuovo — per (la manutenzione della) diga *wḥm*, nelle nostre terre (che si trovano) in una parte delle terre di Apollonios».

Scritto.

Testo Greco (*l.* 18-20):

Thoth 25. Affari pecuniari.

Thoth 25.

Note

a L'anno 29 del testo greco è finanziario e l'anno 29 del testo demotico, egizio; nel mese di Thoth coincidono.

b Νικίας (*l.* 2 e 8) = *Nigis* (piuttosto di *Ngjs*), *l.* 13.

c τὴν γῆν ἣν ἔχει «la terra che (Nikias) tiene (cioè possiede)»: una parcella del latifondo di Apollonios è stata affidata a Nikias. Il fatto dell'affidamento è indicato pure in una ricevuta rilasciata il mese seguente (PSI 13 1352; Novembre/Dicembre), ma, in un'altra ricevuta, si parla semplicemente di τῆς ἑαυτοῦ γῆς (P. Col. Zen. 1 25; 20 Marzo 256).

Il testo demotico invece parla di *n3j=n 3ḥ.w* «le nostre terre» (*l.* 16) e non accenna neanche al fatto dell'affidamento.

d εἰς τὰ διαχώματα «per le dighe trasversali», cioè per le dighe che si trovano nell'interno del latifondo. L'espressione demotica *r wn wḥm* «per (la) diga che ripete» (*l.* 15-16) deve rendere la stessa idea.

wn «diga», cf. copto ⲟⲩⲁⲛ «dyke» (variante di *tn*, ⲧⲏⲛⲉ, χῶμα, CRUM, *Coptic Dict.* 480*a*); la parola è accompagnata dallo stesso determinativo «grasso» di *ʿm*(*.t*) «argilla» [6] per indicare il materiale con cui la diga è stata fatta. Si riscontra la parola *wn* nel testo demotico della Rosettana, nel passo che descrive in quale maniera il re cinge d'assedio la città ribelle: *3rb=f t3 rs3.t rn=s n sbd wn p3j=s bnr* «egli contornava la detta fortezza con mura e diga, all'esteriore» (*l.* 13) = ἀντικαθίσας χώμασίν τε καὶ τάφροις καὶ τείχεσιν αὐτὴν ἀξιολόγοις περιέλαβεν (*l.* 24, v. ad es. SB 5 8299).[7]

---

[6] Anche la parola *t3 ʿm.t* può significare «la diga»: A. H. GARDINER, *Onomastica* II p. 219 «mud bank»; cf. P. L. Bat. 14 p. 55 n. 73: χῶμα προσαγορευόμενον Τοᾶμε (*t3 ʿm.t*).

[7] Si noti il chiasmo *sbd* / τείχεσιν e *wn* / χώμασιν.

wḥm [8] è da collegare col verbo *wḥm* «ripetere» e si ritrova nel titolo di sacerdoti che «ripetono» *ḥm-ntr wḥm* [9] («Der berichtende Gottesdiener: Berichterstatter und Ausleger eines Gottesurteils an Königs Statt», H. KEES, ZÄS 85 [1960] 138-143). A Pathyris si ritrova *tꜣ wḥm.t*, ora come denominazione di una determinata diga.[10] Penso che si tratti, nei nostri documenti ed in quelli di Pathyris, di dighe interne e che siano chiamate *wḥm* perché «ripetono» una diga più grande.

e δεκόβολο̣[ν]: ci si aspetterebbe δέκ' ὀβολο̣[ύς], «10 oboli» (cf. P. Col. Zen. 1 22, 6: δύ' ὀβολούς e PSI 8 976, 7 δύ' ὀβολῶν).[11] Però la lacuna è assai piccola e sarà per questo che EDGAR (ed. princ.) e LIDDELL-SCOTT-JONES (*Lexicon*, Supplement 1968) hanno accettato la lettura δεκόβολον.

f $\frac{1}{12}$  (*l.* 15): a sinistra manca la parte superiore del gruppo, cf.  (P. dem. Zen. 1 *b*, 8).

g ἀργυρικά (*l.* 19): questa notizia indica che il documento in oggetto tratta di denaro ed è, in conseguenza, da conservare nell'archivio, insieme agli altri documenti sugli affari pecuniari; collo stesso scopo si scrive σιτικά sui documenti che riguardano pagamenti di grano (SKEAT, P. Lond. 7 1953, 34 nota). Nello stesso tempo questa notizia indica in quale giornale il documento veniva iscritto (in quello dei pagamenti di grano) e sotto quale data (insieme agli altri pagamenti fatti il 25 Thoth).

---

[8] Esistono due grafie di *wḥm*, una breve (come nel nostro documento) e una più elaborata, v. PESTMAN-QUAEGEBEUR-VOS, *Recueil de textes démotiques et bilingues*, I p. 99 n. 19. Con ROCCATI (RdÉ 25 [1973] 254-255) trascrivo *wḥm* e non *whm*, benché non voglia escludere la possibilità che *wḥm* — che è attestato fin all'epoca saitica — sia diventato in seguito *whm*.

[9] PESTMAN-QUAEGEBEUR-VOS, *Recueil*, doc. 10, 3.

[10] Questa diga *tꜣ wḥm.t* è menzionata in P. Heid. Kaplony-Heckel 9, 7 e nei testi elencati P. L. Bat. 14 p. 55 n. 73 (dove, però, avevo letto incorrettamente *tꜣ štj.t*: la parola è scritta esattamente come nel testo citato qui sopra: *Recueil*, doc. 10, 3 [vol. I p. 99 n. 19]).

[11] Trascrivo δύ' ὀβολούς e ὀβολῶν, invece di δυοβόλους e δυοβόλων, perché non riesco a spiegarmi il plurale δυόβολοι (per l'ordine delle parole nel primo documento citato v. P. Lond. 7 2017, 17 e 18: δραχμὰς ἑπτὰ τρεῖς ὀβολούς, «7 dracme e 3 oboli»).

12

RICEVUTA DI CHICCHI DI RICINO

Consegna alle autorità del Memphites

Archivio di Zenon	A. × L. = 29,9 × 11,1 cm. (a) 16,4 × 11,1 cm. (b) 13,5 × 11 cm.	12 Settembre 254

(a) **P. Col. Zen. 1 40** [New York, Columbia University, Inv. No. 224]; (b) **P. Cairo Zen. 4 59.670** [Cairo, JdE 53781]. Il documento ci è pervenuto in due pezzi, che vanno però insieme: il bordo inferiore del frammento *a* si raccorda al bordo superiore del frammento *b*. Il testo è stato scritto sul recto di una striscia orizzontale di papiro, tagliata da un rotolo di terza altezza [v. l'introduzione § 5]. La scrittura corre trasversalmente alle fibre. Vi è una incollatura orizzontale sotto la *l.* 13, nello spazio libero tra la scriptura interior e quella exterior. La parte superiore del documento (frammento *a*) è quasi completa; quella inferiore (frammento *b*) è invece molto danneggiata.

Documento doppio [v. l'introduzione § 4]. La scriptura interior è stata originariamente arrotolata e sigillata con un sigillo che si conserva in parte. Questa scriptura interior contiene un testo greco e demotico; sotto la *l.* 13, nel margine sinistro, si vede qualche segno (demotico?). La scriptura exterior contiene soltanto più una parte del testo greco e resti della prima linea demotica; il bordo inferiore del frammento è sparito,[1] portando con sé il testo demotico (nel recto) e l'annotazione archivistica (sempre se si trovasse in calce del verso: v. la posizione dell'annotazione nel verso del doc. **13**, tav. XII).

Il testo demotico è stato scritto da Khaiophis; il testo greco da un'altrà mano.

Bibliografia

(a) *Testo greco*: P. Col. Zen. 1 40 (W. L. Westermann - E. S. Hasenoerl, 1934); senza fotografia; il testo demotico è inedito.
(b) *Testo greco*: P. Cairo Zen. 4 59.670 (C. C. Edgar, 1931); senza fotografia.

Contenuto

Si tratta di una ricevuta che appartiene al gruppo dei documenti che riguardano l'amministrazione degli *affari esterni* del latifondo.

Korragos e Khaiophis — rispettivamente i rappresentanti di Hermolaos e Horos — dichiarano di aver ricevuto da Phanesis, un impiegato di Zenon, la quantità di 100⅔ artabe di chicchi di ricino. Una parte (un σήκωμα) di questi chicchi è messa in un sacco di cuoio (φορω) che viene poi sigillato dall'impiegato di Zenon; servirà da campione (*mn.t*).

I riceventi sono le stesse persone che ritroviamo, due anni più tardi, in una simile ricevuta di ricino (doc. **13**). Sono delle persone assai conosciute: *Hermolaos* è l'oikonomos del Memphites [2] (cioè il funzionario responsabile degli affari economici del nomos) e

[1] Benché l'altezza dei due frammenti messi insieme sia 29,9 cm. (cioè quasi l'altezza normale di un rotolo), il documento può essere stato più alto perché non è tagliato dall'altezza ma dalla larghezza di un rotolo.

[2] Il suo superiore è Athenagoras, probabilmente un hypodioiketes (v. P. Lond. 7 2074, 1, nota), che sta direttamente sotto il dioiketes Apollonios (il padrone di Zenon).

Hermolaos funge anche da oikonomos dell'Aphroditopolites al momento della redazione del nostro documento. V. a proposito di Hermolaos M.-Th. Lenger, CdÉ 23 (1948) 109-121 e specialmente 116-117.

Korragos [3] un suo impiegato; *Horos* (o meglio Hartephnakhthis, nota *d*) è il basilikos grammateus dello stesso Memphites (doc. **13** 25) e *Khaiophis* (nota *c*) un suo impiegato.

I due impiegati Korragos e Khaiophis sono venuti quindi dal Memphites a Philadelphia nell'Arsinoites per cercarvi del ricino. La ragione ci viene spiegata dai cosidetti «Revenue Laws» (una raccolta di misure economiche prese pochi anni prima).[4] A quanto pare l'Arsinoites produceva, tra l'altro, troppo ricino ed il Memphites invece troppo poco. Perciò il governo aveva ordinato ai coltivatori di ricino nell'Arsinoites di consegnare alle autorità del Memphites 2120 artabe da 30 khoinikes = 63.600 khoinikes di ricino pulito (Rev. Laws, col. 72, 11-14), oppure 68.052 di ricino *non* pulito.[5] Zenon paga nel Settembre del 254 (doc. **12**) 100⅔ artabe da 29 khoinikes = 2919⅓ khoinikes di ricino non pulito e 100 artabe da 30 khoinikes = 3000 khoinikes nell'Aprile del 252 (doc. **13**). Penso che sia la quota annuale del latifondo, circa 4,3% cioè della quantità totale stabilita per l'intero nomos.

Dai «Revenue Laws» appare che due funzionari erano responsabili degli affari dell'olio: in primo luogo l'oikonomos (nel nostro caso l'oikonomos del Memphites) eppoi lo ἀντιγραφεύς, una specie di «controllore» (nel nostro caso il basilikos grammateus dello stesso Memphites). Poiché il compito dello ἀντιγραφεύς deve essere il controllare le attività dell'oikonomos, è l'oikonomos colui che fa il lavoro. Difatti, chi scrive a Zenon sulla consegna del ricino, è l'oikonomos Hermolaos (P. Lond. 7 1982, 1-5): [6]

> Ἑρμόλαος Ζήνωνι χαίρειν. . . . Ἀπεστάλκαμεν Κόρραγον παραλαβεῖν τὸν παρὰ σοὶ ὑπάρχοντα κροτῶνα καὶ παρακομίσαι. Καλῶς οὖν ποιήσεις συντάξας μισθώσασθαι αὐτῶι ὑποζύγια ἵνα ἐν τάχει παρακομίσηι.
>
> «Hermolaos saluta Zenon . . . Ho inviato Korragos a prendere il ricino che si trova da te e di portarlo via. Dà ordine, per piacere, di affittare per lui delle bestie da soma, affinché possa portarlo via presto».

L'andamento delle cose è quindi assai chiaro. L'oikonomos Hermolaos scrive dal Memphites una lettera a Zenon per annunciargli l'arrivo di un suo impiegato, Korragos. Questi arriva, accompagnato da un controllore, Khaiophis (un impiegato del basilikos grammateus del Memphites) e probabilmente da qualche altra persona. Zenon fa consegnare a loro la quantità di ricino che il latifondo deve al Memphites e Korragos gli rilascia una ricevuta greca (scritta da uno scriba greco) e sottoscritta in demotico dal controllore

---

[3] V. P. Lond. 7 1982 (citato più avanti) per Korragos, impiegato di Hermolaos. Anche Leon ed il suo fratello Apollonios erano stati un tempo impiegati dello stesso Hermolaos: R. S. Bagnall, *The Toparch Leon and his Archive* (Greek, Roman and Byzantine Studies 15 [1974] 215-220) e M.-Th. Lenger (CdÉ 24 [1949] 108).

[4] B. P. Grenfell, *Revenue Laws of Ptolemy Philadelphus* (1896); J. Bingen, *Papyrus Revenue Laws*, Nouvelle édition du texte (Sammelbuch, Beiheft 1, 1952). Cf. A. S. Hunt - C. C. Edgar, *Select Papyri* II n. 203.

[5] 63.600 + 7% = 68.052; la quantità dovuta veniva aumentata del 7% quando il ricino consegnato non era ancora pulito (Rev. Laws, col. 39, 8-12): peso netto (100%) + 7% = peso lordo (107%); oppure (cf. P. Tebt. 3.2 844, 3-5), 107% — 7% = 100%: ἀρ(τάβαι) φ, (ὧν) [v. per questo segno doc. **13** nota *o*] κάθαρσις ὡς ταῖς ρ ἀρ(τάβαις) ζ (γίνονται) ἀρ(τάβαι) λβ β', καθαροῦ τῶι (τριακοντα)χο(ινίχωι) ἀρ(τάβαι) υξζ γ' «500 art., from which deduct 7 per cent. for loss in cleansing, making 32⅔ art., leaving 467⅓ art. of clean sesame by the 30-choenix measure» (256 a.C.).

[6] Questa lettera è stata scritta il 7 Aprile 252 e concerne il ricino che Zenon consegnerà una settimana più tardi: 14 Aprile 252 (doc. **13**).

Khaiophis. Una parte del ricino viene chiusa in un sacco di cuoio e poi sigillato, come campione, dopo di che Korragos ed i suoi partano, portando con sé il ricino ed il campione, sulle bestie da soma che Zenon aveva per loro affittate.

Trascrizione

recto [tavola IX, *l.* 1-23]: scriptura interior

1 (Ἔτους) [λ]β [a] Ἐπεὶφ κ̅β̅. Ἔχει Κόρραγος [b]
2 ὁ παρὰ Ἑρμολάου [b] καὶ Χαιῶφις [c] ὁ πα-
3 ρὰ Ὥρου [d] βασιλικοῦ γραμματέως [e]
4 παρὰ Φανήσιος [f] χειριστοῦ [g] τοῦ
5 παρὰ Ζήνωνος [b] κροτῶνος [h] ῥυ-
6 παροῦ [i] 'τοῦ ἐκ τοῦ Ἀρσινοίτου', [j] οὗ σήκωμα [k] κατεσφρα-
7 γίσατο ἐν φορω [l] ὁ χειριστής,
8 μέτρωι [m] ἐννεακα<ι>εικοσαχοι-
9 νίκωι [n] ἀρτάβας ἑκατὸν δί-
10 μοιρον.

11 [*ḥ3.t-sp*] ⌜31.⌝*t* [a] *ibd*-3 *šmw* (*sw*) 22 *iw* (*n*) *dr.t Pa-n-Is.t* [f] *p3 rd n Snn rtb tgm* [h] *brbrj* [o]
12 [*n p3*] ⌜*kws*⌝ [m] *n mḥ* [n] 29 100 *irm* [p] $\frac{2}{3}$ *t3j=w pš* 50$\frac{1}{3}$ *r* 100 *irm* $\frac{2}{3}$ *ˁn ntj iw t3j=w mn.t* [q]
13 [*ḏbˁ*] [r] ⌜*ḥn*⌝ 1.*t pwr3* [l] *sh Ḫˁj=f* [c] *p3 rd n Ḥr* [d] *p3 sh* [e] *Pr-ˁ3ˁ.w.s.*

○ ○ ○

scriptura exterior

14 (Ἔτους) λβ Ἐπεὶφ κ̅β̅. Ἔ[χει Κόρραγος]
15 ὁ π̣αρὰ Ἑρμολάου κ̣α̣ὶ̣ [Χαιῶφις]
16 ὁ παρὰ Ὥρου βασιλικοῦ γ[ραμ-]
17 ματέως παρ[ὰ] Φ̣[ανήσιος χει-]
18 ριστ̣οῦ τ̣οῦ πα[ρὰ Ζήνωνος κρο-]
19 τῶνος ῥυπαρ[οῦ τοῦ ἐκ Φιλα-]
20 [δ]ε̣λφείας, οὗ σήκω̣[μα κατε-]
21 σφραγίσατο ἐν φορω ὁ [χειριστής,]
22 μέ[τρωι ἐννεακαιεικοσι-]
23 χο[ινίκωι ἀρτάβας ἑκατὸν]
24 δ̣ί̣[μοιρον.]

---------------tracce di scrittura demotica ---

1, 14 ἔχει: *l.* ἔχουσι 8 -εικοσα-: *l.* -εικοσι-

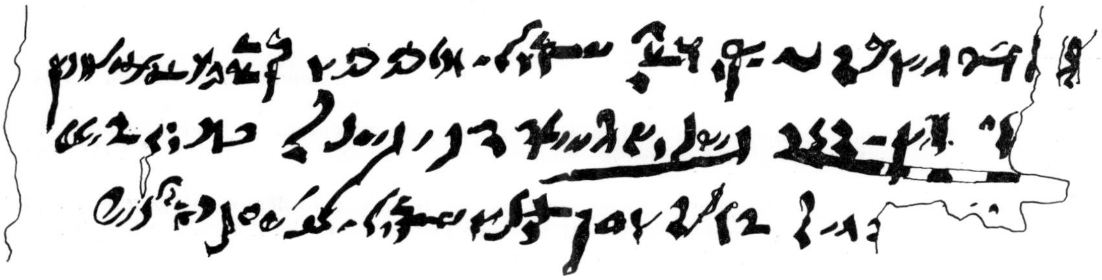

11
12
13

5

Traduzione

Testo Greco (*l.* 1-10):

Anno 32°, Epeiph 22.

Korragos — che (agisce) da parte di Hermolaos — e Khaiophis — che (agisce) da parte di Horos, il basilikos grammateus — hanno avuto dal kheiristes Phanesis, che (agisce) da parte di Zenon:

chicchi di ricino non puliti, provenienti dall'Arsinoites — dei quali il kheiristes ha sigillato in una phoro la quantità di un sekoma — (misurati) con la misura di ventinove khoinikes: cento artabe e due terzi.

Testo Demotico (*l.* 11-13):

Anno 31, terzo mese della stagione *šmw*, giorno 22.

Ricevuti dalla mano di Phanesis, il rappresentante di Zenon:

chicchi di ricino (misurati) con la misura della capacità di ventinove (khoinikes): 100 e $\frac{2}{3}$ artabe — la loro metà è $50\frac{1}{3}$, fa 100 e $\frac{2}{3}$ di nuovo —, (chicchi) il cui campione è stato sigillato in una *pwrꜣ*.

Khaiophis, il rappresentante di Horos, lo scriba di Faraone, ha scritto.

Note

a L'anno 32 del testo greco (*l.* 1 e 14) è finanziario e l'anno 31 del testo demotico (*l.* 11) quello egizio.

Si noti che nella *l.* 11 il gruppo «30» si trova sulla striscia a metà staccata, sul margine destro del documento.

b Per la trascrizione demotica dei nomi greci Korragos, Hermolaos e Zenon, v. doc. **13**.

c Χαιῶφις (*l.* 2 e 15; doc. **13** *l.* 3, 16 e 31) = *Ḫꜥj=f* (*l.* 13; doc. **13**, 28; in ambedue i casi, la *=f* si trova sotto il determinativo divino di *ḫꜥj*, cfr. la posizione del segno *sꜣ*, doc. **3** nota *j*). La *=f* si rapporta, penso, al portatore del nome (e non ad un dio) visto che il nome è determinato con il segno «uomo» invece del segno «dio». Forse si tratta di un'abbreviazione del nome 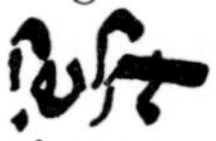 (P. dem. Zen. 4, 2) che leggo come *Ḫꜥj=f-m-ḥb* «Egli è apparso durante la festa».

Il nome *Ḫꜥj=f* = Χαιῶφις è raro; [7] più frequenti sono i nomi del tipo *ḫꜥj* + dio, come *Ḫꜥj-Ḥr* = Χαιῦρις o *Ḫꜥj-Ḥp* = Χαιᾶπις «Horos (o Apis) è apparso».[8]

d Ὧρος (*l.* 3 e 16; doc. **13**, 3 e 16) = *Ḥr* (*l.* 13) = *Ḥr-tꜣj=f-nḫt* (doc. **13**, 25), i.e. Ἁρτοφνάχθης (Foraboschi, *Onomasticon*, s.v.). Il nome «Horos» è anche un nome

[7] Il nome Χαιῶφις ricorre solo in tre altri documenti dell'archivio di Zenon (P. Cairo Zen. 3 59.346, 10; 4 59.782 *b*, 145; P. Lond. 7 2155) e poi in P. Ryl. 2 72, intr. (v. Preisigke, *Namenbuch*) e P. Tebt. 3.2 851, 64. Questi documenti vengono tutti dal Fayum, ma anche a Memphis e a Siut si incontra *Ḫꜥj=f* (P. dem. Brux. 3, 4; ASA 17, 5-20; Thompson, *Family Archive*, tav. XV [verso VI 12], XVIII e XIX [A, 7]).

[8] J. Vergote, *Oplossing van een gewichtig probleem*, 14. Il dizionario demotico (Erichsen, 351) menziona, per isbaglio, *Ḫꜥj=f-Rꜥ* invece di *ꜥnḫ-Pꜣ-Rꜥ* come l'equivalente del nome Χαπρῆς (che forse non esiste neanche, v. Clarysse, CdÉ 48 [1973] 326-328).

abbreviato nel doc. **8** dove Ὦρος corrisponde a *Ḥr-pa-Is.t*, i.e. Ἁρπαῆσις (altri esempi in P. Cairo Zen. 2 indice p. 182; v. pure *Ḥr* = *Ḥr-pa-Kmj*, G. R. Hughes, Studies Wilson, 47-48, *l.* 2, nota).

e βασιλικὸς γραμματεύς (*l.* 3 e 16; doc. **13**, 3 e 16) = *sẖ Pr-ʿ3* ʿ.w.s. «scriba di Faraone» (*l.* 13; doc. **13**, 25), un titolo generale che indica qualsiasi impiegato del Re (P. L. Bat. 19, doc. 1 nota *i*), ma in questo caso, come sovente, l'alto impiegato del nomos: *sẖ Pr-ʿ3* ʿ.w.s. *n p3 tš Mn-nfr* «scriba di Faraone del Memphites».

f Φανῆσις (*l.* 4 e 17), var. Πανῆσις = *Pa-n-Is.t*  (*l.* 11). In greco e in demotico figura in questo nome la notevole *n* che sembra caratteristica per questo nome del Fayum; altrove si incontra la forma Παῆσις = *Pa-Is.t*. Visto che *pa* sta per *p3 n* «colui di», la forma *Pa-Is.t* (cioè *P3-n-Is.t*) è normale e si traduce («Colui di Isis»): la forma *Pa-n-Is.t* (cioè *P3-n-n-Is.t*) invece è anormale e non si traduce.

Spiegelberg (ZÄS 54 [1918] 104 nota 5) considera P(h)anesis come la forma antica del nome, dove la *n* si conserva (*pan-* = *p3 n*), e Paesis come la forma più recente, dove la *n* è sparita. Questa interpretazione del nome P(h)anesis non mi soddisfa, perché ci si aspetterebbe P(h)*e*nesis invece di P(h)*a*nesis. Sarebbe strano che questo nome fosse stato l'unico a conservare la *n* antica, perché nello stesso ambiente i nomi con la forma recente *pa-* abbondano; nel doc. **8** si riscontra persino la forma *Pa-Is.t* (senza la *n*!) nel nome proprio *Ḥr-pa-Is.t*.

Mi pare quindi impossibile considerare P(h)anesis come una semplice variante di Paesis. Penso che si tratti di due nomi diversi e che *Pa-n-Is.t* sia una grafia non etimologica di un altro nome, anche se non so quale sia quel nome.

g Un χειριστής è una specie di amministratore.[9] La natura esatta del suo incarico è difficile da stabilire ed il testo demotico non ci aiuta perché il titolo non vi è menzionato.

Nell'archivio di Zenon il titolo denota sovente quegli amministratori che si occupano di provviste (semente, grano, olio di ricino, ἄρακος, ecc.), ne comperano per Zenon (P. Col. Zen. 1 51) e per Apollonios (SB 5 8242 = doc. **27**), controllano la loro imbarcazione (P. Corn. 3, 18) ed il loro trasporto (PSI 5 537). Pare che il loro incarico vero e proprio sia di controllare le provviste che escono dai magazzini e di cui sono responsabili. Per questo preciso scopo Zenon manda il nostro Phanesis al θησαυρός di Philadelphia nell'Aprile del 251 (o 250), dove non viene ammesso dalle autorità (tra l'altro il Kleitarkhos e lo Anosis, menzionati nel doc. **1**), che preferiscono a lui un certo Stotoetis (P. Mich. Zen. 52).[10] Il nostro Phanesis ed il suo collega Stotoetis non vanno molto d'accordo e si capisce quindi che piacere Phanesis abbia provato quando ha potuto rapportare a Zenon che Stotoetis ed i suoi non erano presenti sul lavoro, e che la gente aveva chiesto a lui di venire a farlo (PSI 6 603).

[9] Liddell-Scott, *Greek-English Lexicon*: «manager, administrator»; Claire Préaux (CdÉ 28 [1953] 111): «le titre de χειριστής s'applique ... au personnel de différents services et notamment des banques». La «Prosopographia Ptolemaica» cita nel capitolo «Administration financière de la chôra», par. 9 (numeri 1442-1454) oltre il nostro Phanesis (a torto, v. nota 10) due persone che sono χειριστὴς τραπέζης ed uno che è χειριστὴς ἐπιστάτου φυλακιτῶν.

[10] Phanesis non è quindi un impiegato statale. È adetto all'amministrazione del latifondo e agisce da parte di Zenon (doc. **12** 4-5).

h Il ricino (κίκι o κροτών) è una pianta con semi (κροτών), da cui si estrae l'olio di ricino (κίκι).

κίκι è una parola egizia, probabilmente *k3k3*, dem. *g'g'*; v. H. von Deines - H. Grapow, *Wörterbuch der ägyptischen Drogennamen*, 526-527; E. Bresciani, Studi Classici e Orientali 19/20 (1970/1971) 365. La parola κίκι non solo denota l'olio di ricino, ma anche la pianta stessa (PSI 5 500, 5: κίκιος φυτεία).

κροτών invece è una parola greca (per l'accento, v. Liddell-Scott, *Greek-English Lexicon*). I semi di ricino venivano chiamati così per via della loro somiglianza con l'insetto κροτών, la zecca. Qualche volta la parola κροτών denota la pianta: φυτεία τοῦ κροτῶνος (PSI 5 499, 5).

In demotico, la parola *tgm* «ricino» è usata indifferentemente per indicare la pianta, il seme e l'olio (v. gli esempi citati da Erichsen, *Glossar*, 662).[11] Nei documenti **12** e **13** la parola *tgm* viene precisata da *brbrj(.t)* «chicco» (v. nota *o*): messe insieme rendono esattamente κροτών «chicco (o seme) di ricino».

Il ricino è una pianta eccezionale.[12] Si può piantarla, a quanto pare, in ogni stagione; [13] cresce velocemente e può diventare alta come un albero; il chicco è molto velenoso, ma l'olio che se ne estrae è medicinale. Nell'Egitto antico si adoperava l'olio di ricino in primo luogo nelle lampade ad olio,[14] ma anche per ungere il corpo, per fare del sapone [15] e persino per preparare del pane; adesso è solo più usato come olio purgativo e industriale.

i ῥυπαρός «sporco, non pulito»; il contrario di καθαρός (v. ad esempio P. Col. Zen. 2 113, 31-35). Liddell-Scott, *Greek-English Lexicon*, menziona sub voce ῥυπαρός «filthy, dirty» il nostro documento dicendo (nel par. 4): «κροτὼν ῥυπαρός probably = ἀδειγμάτιστος» (cioè «without a sample»); [16] questa supposizione è impossibile perché, dalla parte demotica del testo, sappiamo che vi era bensì un campione.

C'è da chiedersi in che stato questi chicchi di ricino «non puliti» si trovino. Il testo demotico non ci aiuta perché non ne parla, ma nei cosidetti «Revenue Laws» [17] leggiamo che i chicchi consegnati devono essere puliti e pronti per la spremitura o, se non sono puliti, almeno vagliati (col. 39, 8-12). Penso che i nostri chicchi, vagliati ma non puliti, siano dei chicchi che si trovino ancora nelle loro capsule e che la nozione ῥυπαρός sia resa in demotico dalle parole *r* (per *iw*) *p3j=w stḥ ḥn=w* «mentre le loro capsule si trovano (ancora) tra loro» (doc. **13**, 12 e 26, nota *m*).

---

[11] Bisogna cancellarvi però l'esempio *tgm ḳrtns*, v. nota *o*.

[12] V. ad esempio M. Schnebel, *Die Landwirtschaft im hellenistischen Ägypten*, 200-201; B. Porten, *Archives from Elephantine*, 92-93 e per l'archivio di Zenon, Skeat, P. Lond. 7 2061, 7 nota.

[13] La stagione la più adatta sembra però essere la primavera (v. Skeat, citato nota 12). Difatti, nell'anno famoso 257/256 in cui Panakestor non riesce nell'autunno a preparare in tempo le terre di Apollonios per la coltivazione del grano, procede, nella primavera, alla piantagione di ricino.

[14] P. Cornell 1 e P. Col. Zen. 1 37, 24 trattano di olio di ricino distribuito a chi deve lavorare la notte: panettieri, scribi (v. doc. **4** nota *a* in fine), ecc. Cf. A. E. Samuel, *Illumination by Castor Oil*, BASP 1 [1963/1964] 32-38.

[15] C. C. Edgar, P. Cairo Zen. 3 59.304 intr.: «castor-oil . . . for mixing with the natron to make a sort of soap».

[16] Il dizionario citato si è probabilmente basato sulla notizia di Spiegelberg (P. dem. Zen. p. 9) che non conosceva però la parte demotica del documento **12**.

[17] B. P. Grenfell, *Revenue Laws of Ptolemy Philadelphus* (1896); J. Bingen, *Papyrus Revenue Laws*, Nouvelle édition du texte (Sammelbuch, Beiheft 1, 1952); cf. A. S. Hunt - C. C. Edgar, *Select Papyri* II n. 203.

j ἐκ τοῦ Ἀρσινοίτου (*l.* 6), più preciso ἐκ Φιλαδελφείας (*l.* 19-20): i chicchi consegnati provengono dal latifondo di Apollonios a Philadelphia e sono una parte soltanto di quei chicchi di ricino che l'intero Arsinoites deve dare al Memphites (v. l'introduzione del nostro documento).

k σήκωμα «a weight in the balance, standard weight». Penso che la quantità messa a parte come campione avesse il peso normale dei campioni. Il testo demotico rende forse la stessa idea con l'uso dell'articolo: «il loro campione». Il peso normale di un campione di grano è una mezza artaba (P. Lond. 7 1940, 62, nota).

Il nostro testo è l'unico documento papiraceo in cui figura, prima dell'epoca bizantina, la parola σήκωμα, che prenderà allora il significato specifico di una misura di capacità di vino.[18]

l φορω (*l.* 7 e 21; P. Cairo Zen. 1 59.012, 104 e 114) = *pwr3(.t)*  (*l.* 13).[19]
Non si sa quale sia l'origine della parola, che ritorna più tardi in Copto: ⲡⲟⲣⲟ. Il determinativo della grafia demotica fa suppore che si tratti di un sacco di cuoio.[20]

In questo sacco si metteva il campione (*mn.t*) di ricino ed il kheiristes lo sigillava. Vedere ASA 33 (1933) 62-64 (con una tavola) per un sacco di cuoio che conteneva un campione di orzo e Crum (*Coptic Dictionary*, 268*a*) per un ⲡⲟⲣⲟ sigillato contenente dell'olio d'olivia.

Il testo demotico precisa che il campione si trova in un solo sacco.

m μέτρον (*l.* 8 e 22) = *ḳws* (*l.* 12). Si ignora l'etimologia della parola demotica; è una «misura» (di legno, v. il determinativo).

n Siccome la capacità di una artaba è variabile (come pure la capacità di un keramion, v. P. Cairo Zen. 2 59.271, intr.), il nostro documento precisa che si tratta di artabe misurate con la misura di 29 khoinikes: μέτρον ἐννεακαιεικοσαχοίνικον (**12** 8-9, 22-23), nel mentre si usano delle artabe di 30 khoinikes nel documento **13** (6, 19): μέτρον τριακονταχοίνικον.

In demotico le espressioni corrispondenti sono:

12 12: *rtb n p3 ḳws* «*n* ꜣ 29» 

13 12, 26: *rtb* . . . «*n* ꜣ 30.*t*» 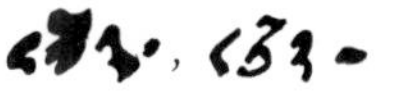

Qui la lettura e l'interpretazione del segno ꜣ (che rassomiglia all'articolo femminile *t3*) sono problematiche. Premettiamo che, per via del greco, ci deve essere questione, in un qualche modo, di khoinikes e che la parola demotica per khoinix deve essere femminile per via della desinenza femminile della cifra nel documento **13**: 30.*t*. Però, l'unica denominazione egizia della misura khoinix che si conosca è la parola *hn*, «hin» e questa parola è maschile.[21] Penso che gli egiziani abbiano semplicemente

[18] Cf. M. Hombert - Claire Préaux, CdÉ 14 (1939) 167 (12).

[19] La parola greca non è, quindi, una «abbreviation» (Liddell-Scott, *Greek-English Lexicon*, s.v.).

[20] Non so se si possa collegare φορω con πήρα «leathern pouch». Liddell-Scott (*Greek-English Lexicon*, 1952) e Crum (*Coptic Dictionary*, 268 *a*) suppongono, a torto quanto pare, che φορω/πορο sia un «vessel».

[21] Molto più tardi, soltanto in copto, si riscontrerà una parola femminile: ϭⲁⲡⲓϫⲉ «a dry measure», χοῖνιξ (Crum *Coptic Dict.*, 827 *b*).

adottato la parola greca femminile χοῖνιξ per designare la loro misura «hin», nella stessa maniera quindi che, nell'epoca persa, avevano addottato la parola «artaba» per designare la loro misura «oipe» (ČERNÝ-PARKER, JEA 57 [1971] 128-131).

Ora vedo due possibilità per interpretare il segno in ogetto:

(1) il segno sta per «khoinix»: *rtb n* ⁊ 30.*t* «artaba di 30 khoinikes»; v. l'espressione simile nei testi dell'epoca persa: *rtb hn* 40 «artaba di 40 hin» (MALININE, Kemi 11 [1950] 16-17); in questo caso la trascrizione di ⁊ sarebbe [hieroglyph], da leggere — almeno nell'epoca tolemaica — come «khoinix»; [nella stessa maniera *rtb n p3 ḳws n* ⁊ 29, sarebbe «artaba (misurata) con la misura di 29 khoinikes»];

(2) il segno è una parola per «capacità», essendo la parola «khoinix» sottintesa: *rtb n* ⁊ 30.*t* «artaba della capacità di 30 (khoinikes)»; in questo caso si potrebbe trascrivere ⁊ come [hieroglyph] e leggere *mḥ*, v. il copto ⲙⲟⲩϩ «contents» (CRUM, *Coptic Dict.* 209*b*); [nella stessa maniera *rtb n p3 ḳws n* ⁊ 29, sarebbe «artaba (misurata) con la misura della capacità di 29 (khoinikes)»].

A causa della paleografia, la seconda possibilità mi sembra preferibile: ⁊ = *mḥ* «capacità» e questa interpretazione mi pare tanto più probabile per il fatto che vi è un gruppo di testi dell'epoca persa dove si legge *rtb hn* 40 *mḥ* «artaba di 40 hin di capacità» (MALININE, Kemi 11 [1950] 16, esempi 4-7).[22]

o *brbrj*(.*t*)

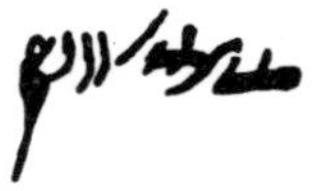

12 11

13 12

13 26

V. *blbjl3.t* (ERICHSEN, *Glossar*, 120) e ⲃⲗⲃⲓⲗⲉ «a single grain», «a single fruit» (CRUM, *Coptic Dict.*, 37*b*); la parola indica, nei nostri documenti, che si tratta di «chicchi» (e non di olio) di ricino; nel testo citato da Erichsen designa una bolla di scottatura. Poiché la lettura *ḳrtns* di SPIEGELBERG (P. dem. Zen. 3 e p. 8 n. 4) è erronea, bisogna cancellare la parola *ḳrtns* dal dizionario di Erichsen (545 e 662).

p La lettura *irm* sembra essere sicura in base a P. L. Bat. 19 doc. 2, 5.

q *mn.t* «campione» (v. doc. **13**, nota *j*); solo il testo demotico precisa che la quantità sigillata nel sacco è un campione. Questo campione è stato sigillato da un dipendente di Zenon; ciò che prova che il campione non doveva rimanere nelle mani di Zenon, ma che era mandato via, insieme al resto del ricino (nel caso contrario il campione sarebbe stato sigillato da Korragos e Khaiophis).

r *ḏbʿ*: restituito dal doc. **13**, 12 e 27.

[22] Si riscontra questo segno *mḥ* assai sovente nei documenti tolemaici; v. ad esempio SETHE - PARTSCH, *Bürgsch.*, Urk. 10, 17: una misura *ntj nmṯ.w r-ḫ p3 ḳws n mḥ* 29 «che va secondo la misura del contenuto di 29 (khoinikes)»; MALININE, RdÉ 19 [1967] pl. 3 (P. Mosc. 123, 4): *r p3 kws* (scritto col gruppo *k3*) *n mḥ* 29.*t* «secondo la misura del contenuto di 29 (khoinikes)»; KAPLONY-HECKEL, *Gebeḷen-Urk. Heidelberg*, Urk. 15: *n p3 ḳws n mḥ* 50 «con la misura del contenuto di 50 (khoinikes)».

13

RICEVUTA DI CHICCHI DI RICINO

Consegna alle autorità del Memphites

Archivio di Zenon | A. × L. = 27,8 × 16,8 cm. | 14 Aprile 252

PSI 4 358 [Firenze, Biblioteca Medicea Laurenziana]. Il testo principale è stato scritto sul recto di una striscia verticale di papiro, tagliata dall'intera altezza di un rotolo [v. l'introduzione § 5]. La scrittura è parallela alle fibre del recto. Vi è, dall'alto in basso, una incollatura; il bordo del foglio sinistro è incollato sopra quello del foglio destro, nella direzione della scrittura greca. Il bordo sinistro del papiro è leggermente danneggiato; la forma dei posti danneggiati e la regolarità con cui essi rivengono e diventano, dall'alto in basso, sempre più grandi, dimostrano che il danno è stato causato quando il documento era ancora arrotolato.

Documento doppio [v. l'introduzione § 4]. La scriptura interior è stata originariamente arrotolata e sigillata con un sigillo che è andato perduto. La scriptura interior e quella exterior contengono tutte e due un testo greco ed un testo demotico; nel verso si trova una breve annotazione archivistica in greco, scritta in calce del foglio.

Bibliografia

Testo greco: PSI 4 358 (G. Vitelli ed altri, 1917); cf. P. dem. Zen. 3; *testo demotico*: P. dem. Zen. 3 (W. Spiegelberg, 1929); cf. PSI 1010 D [traduzione] e U. Wilcken, Archiv für Papyrusforschung 9 (1930) 75 e 238-239; *fotografia*: P. dem. Zen., tav. 3 n. 3 (*l.* 9-28).

Contenuto: ricino per il Memphites [doc. **12**, introduzione].

Si tratta di una ricevuta che appartiene al gruppo dei documenti che riguardano l'amministrazione degli *affari esterni* del latifondo.

Come due anni prima (doc. **12**), il latifondo di Apollonios consegna ai rappresentanti del Memphites la sua parte di quel ricino che l'intero Arsinoites deve fornire al Memphites: 100 artabe di 30 khoinikes = 3000 khoinikes (contro 2919⅓ nel 254). Anche questa volta, il ricino viene consegnato sotto forma di chicchi che si trovano ancora nelle loro capsule; una quantità di 300 khoinikes viene messa da parte per il controllo, che sarà probabilmente effettuato nel magazzino stesso del «luogo (cioè recinto) degli Dei Adelphoi» a Philadelphia dove queste 300 khoinikes sono state depositate sotto sigillo. Il resto è stato subito trasportato nel Memphites sulle bestie da soma che Zenon ha dovuto affittare a questo scopo (P. Lond. 7 1982, v. doc. **12**, introduzione).

Gli uomini interessati sono in gran parte gli stessi di due anni prima: l'oikonomos Hermolaos manda lo stesso suo impiegato Korragos; questi arriva a Philadelphia, accompagnato dal medesimo Khaiophis, il controllore da parte di Har(tephnakhthis) il basilikos grammateus. A Philadelphia ricevono i chicchi di ricino e rilasciano una ricevuta greca che porta il contrassegno in demotico del controllore, contrassegno che è scritto, questa volta, non da Khaiophis stesso (come era il caso nel 254), ma da un suo impiegato, Peteharmais figlio di Pratis, che non ritroviamo in altri documenti Zenoniani, probabilmente per il fatto che viene, anche lui, dal Memphites.

Chi consegna il ricino da parte di Zenon, non è più il Phanesis menzionato nel doc. **12**, ma Kleitarkhos, lo stesso che nel 257 lavorava per il nomarkhos Damis (v. p. 18-19).

Trascrizione

recto [tavola XIII]: scriptura interior

1 [Β]ασιλεύοντος Πτολεμαίου τοῦ Πτολεμαί[ο]υ Σωτῆρος
2 ἔτους λδ [a] μηνὸς Μεχὶρ κ̅β̅. Ἔχει Κόρραγος [b] ὁ παρὰ
3 Ἑρμολάου [c] καὶ Χαιῶφις [d] ὁ παρὰ Ὥρου [e] βασιλικοῦ γραμ-
4 [μ]ατέως [f] παρὰ Κλειτάρχου [g] τοῦ παρὰ Ζήνωνος [h]
5 ἐκ Φιλαδελφείας κροτῶνος [i] ἀδειγματίστου [j]
6 μέτρωι τριακονταχοινίκωι μετρήσει δικαί-
7 αι ἀρτάβας ἑκατόν. Τούτων ὑπολελείμμε-
8 [θ]α εἰς δειγματισμόν,[j] ὃ κατεσφράγισται ἐν κυ-
9 ψάλῃι [k] ἣ κεῖται ἐν τῶι σιτοβολῶνι [l]· ἀρτάβαι
10 δέκα.

11 *ḥ3.t-sp* 33 [a] *ntj ir ḥ3.t-sp* 3⸢4⸣ [a] *ibd-2 pr.t* (*sw*) 22 *iw* (*n*) *dr.t Gljt3rk3ws* [g] *p3 rd n Snn* [h]
12 *rtb tgm brbrj* [i] *r p3j=w stḥ* [m] *ẖn=w n mḥ* [n] 30.*t* 100 *t3j=w pš* 50 *r* 100 *ʿn* ⟨ [o] *ntj ḏbʿ n p3*
r3 [l] *n p3 ʿ.wj n3 ntr.w* [*sn.w*] [p]
13 *ẖn* 1.*t šʿ.t* [k] *n ʿm wb3 mn.t*[j] *rtb tgm* 10 *sẖ P3-dj-Ḥr-m-ḥb* [q] *s3 P3-rtj* [r]

○

scriptura exterior

14 Βασιλεύοντος Πτολ[εμ]αίου τοῦ Πτολεμαίου Σω-
15 τῆρος (ἔτους) λδ μην[ὸ]ς Μεχὶρ κ̅β̅. Ἔχει Κόρραγος ὁ πα-
16 ρὰ Ἑρμολάου καὶ Χαιῶφις ὁ παρὰ Ὥρου βασιλι-
17 κοῦ γραμματέως παρὰ Κλειτάρχου τοῦ παρὰ
18 [Ζήνω]νος ἐκ Φιλαδελφείας κροτῶνος ἀδει-
19 [γ]ματίστου μέτρωι τριακονταχοινίκωι
20 μετρήσει δικαίαι ἀρτάβας ἑκατόν. Τούτων
21 ὑπολελείμμεθα εἰς δειγματισμόν, ὃ κατε-
22 σφράγισται ἐν κυψάλῃι ἣ κεῖται ἐν τῶι σιτο-
23 βολῶνι· ἀρτάβαι δέκα.

24 *ḥ3.t-sp* 33 *ntj ir ḥ3.t-sp* 34 *ibd-2 pr.t* (*sw*) 22 *n Pr-ʿ3* ʿ.w.s. *Ptwlmjs*⸢ ʿ.w.s. *s3 P*⸣*twlmjs* ʿ.w.s
p3⸢*ntj nḥ*⸣[*m ḏd Ḫʿj=f*]
25 *p3 rd n Ḥr-t3j=f-nḫṱ* [e] *p3 sẖ* [f] *Pr-ʿ3* ʿ.w.s. *n p3 tš Mn-nfr irm Ḳwhr3ḳws* [b] *p3 rd n*
Hrmwl3w⸢*s*⸣ [c] [--- *n*]
26 *Gljt3rk3ws p3 rd n Snn dj=k n=n rtb tgm brbrj r p3j=w stḥ ẖn=w n mḥ* 30.*t* ⸢100⸣
27 *t3j=w pš* 50 *r* 100 *ʿn* ⟨ *ntj ḏbʿ ẖn* 1.*t šʿ.t n ʿm n p3 r3 n p3 ʿ.wj n3 ntr.w sn.w wb3 mn.t*
28 ⸢*rtb*⸣ *tgm* 10 *sẖ P3-dj-Ḥr-m-ḥb* (*s3*) *P3-rtj p3 rd n Ḫʿj=f* [d]

verso [tavola XII]: annotazione archivistica

29 (Ἔτους) λδ Μεχεὶρ κ̅β̅.
30 Κόρραγος καὶ
31 Χαιῶφις. Κροτῶν(ος) ἀρ(τάβαι) [ρ].

2, 15 ἔχει: *l.* ἔχουσι 19 -ματίστου: ισ corr.; μέτρωι: ε corr. da σ 21 δειγμα-: Pap. ι  23 -βολῶνι: Pap. ι  31 κροτῶν(ος) ἀρ(τάβαι): Pap. 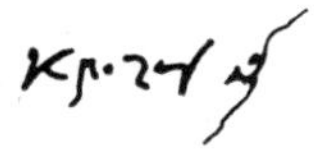

scriptura interior

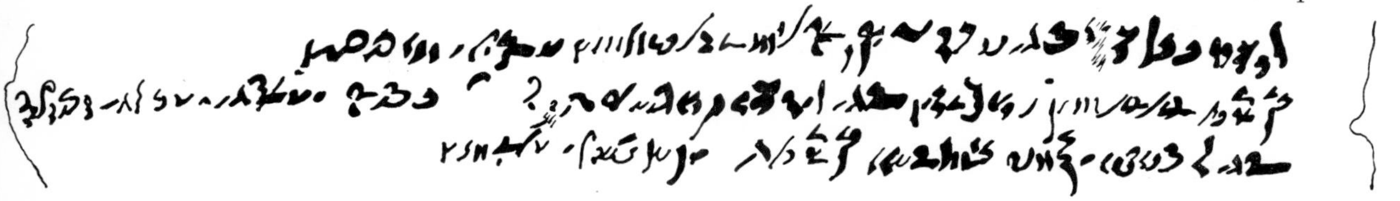

scriptura exterior

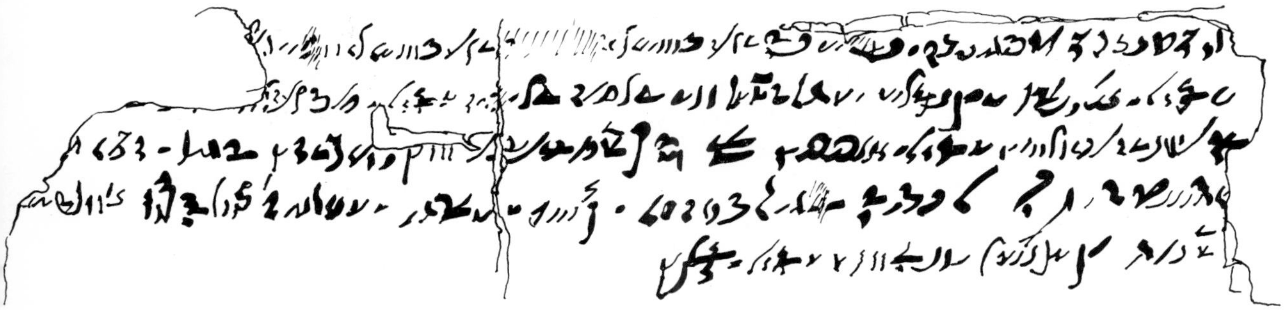

Traduzione

Testo Greco (*l.* 14-23):

Regnante Ptolemaios, figlio di Ptolemaios Soter, anno 34º, il 22 del mese Mekheir.

Korragos — che (agisce) da parte di Hermolaos — e Khaiophis — che (agisce) da parte di Horos, il basilikos grammateus — hanno avuto da Kleitarkhos, che (agisce) da parte di Zenon:

da Philadelphia 100 artabe di chicchi di ricino non controllati, (misurati) con la misura di trenta khoinikes e con misuratura giusta.

Di quei chicchi abbiamo tolto per il controllo (ciò) che è sigillato in un recipiente che si trova nel granaio: dieci artabe.

Testo Demotico (*l.* 24-28):

Anno 33 — che corrisponde all'anno 34 — secondo mese della stagione *pr.t*, giorno 22, sotto Faraone Ptolemaios, figlio di Ptolemaios, colui che salva.

Khaiophis — il rappresentante di Hartephnakhthis, lo scriba di Faraone del distretto di Memphis — e Korragos — il rappresentante di Hermolaos, il ... — hanno detto a Kleitarkhos, il rappresentante di Zenon:

«Tu hai dato a noi chicchi di ricino — mentre le loro capsule si trovano (ancora) tra loro — (misurati con la misura) della capacità di 30 (khoinikes): 100 artabe —

la loro metà è 50, fa 100 di nuovo — fra le quali [1] (ci sono quelle) che si trovano sigillate in un recipiente d'argilla nel granaio del recinto degli Dei Adelphoi (di Philadelphia), per il controllo: 10 artabe di ricino».

Peteharmais, figlio di Pratis, il rappresentante di Khaiophis, ha scritto.

Testo Greco (*l.* 29-31):

Anno 34°, Mekheir 22. Korragos e Khaiophis. 100 artabe di chicchi di ricino.

Note

a L'anno 34 del testo greco (*l.* 2, 15 e 29) e demotico (*l.* 11 e 24) è finanziario e l'anno 33 del testo demotico (*l.* 11 e 24) egizio.

b Κόρραγος (*l.* 2, 15 e 30) = *Ḳwhr3ḳws* (*l.* 25): si noti che il demotico rende l'aspirazione del ρ.

c Ἑρμόλαος (*l.* 3 e 16) = *Hrmwl3ws* (*l.* 25).

d Χαιῶφις (*l.* 3, 16 e 31) = *Ḫʿj=f* (*l.* 28): v. doc. **12** nota *c*.

e ⸢Ὧρος (*l.* 3 e 16) = *Ḥr-t3j=f-nḫt* «Hartephnakhthis» (*l.* 25): v. doc. **12** nota *d*.

f βασιλικὸς γραμματεύς scil. del Memphites (*l.* 3-4 e 16-17) = *sẖ Pr-ʿ3* ʿ.w.s. *n p3 tš Mn-nfr* (*l.* 25): v. doc. **12** nota *e*.

g Κλείταρχος (*l.* 4 e 17) = *Gljt3rk3ws* (*l.* 11 e 26): si noti che il χ è reso mediante il gruppo *k3*  i.e. 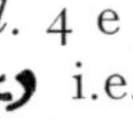, cf. doc. **1**, 27: ⸢*Glwtrk3s*⸣.

h Ζήνων (*l.* 4 e 18) = *Snn* (*l.* 11 e 26); il demotico rende lo ζ con *s* e omette η e ω:

Snn  doc. **13** 26

 doc. **12** 11

 P. dem. Zen. 4, 3

 P. dem. Zen. 2 *a*, 3

Cf. inoltre P. dem. Zen. 5, 1; 6*a*, 4 e 17, 1. Il nome Ἀγρεοφῶν del padre è menzionato una sola volta in demotico:

3ḳrpn  P. dem. Zen. 4, 3

i κροτών (*l.* 5, 18 e 31) = *tgm brbrj(.t)* «chicchi di ricino» (*l.* 12 e 26): v. doc. **12**, le note *h* e *o*.

j ἀδειγμάτιστος «non controllato, non verificato» (*l.* 5 e 18-19); manca nel testo demotico. L'espressione non ci informa sulla questione se il ricino sia καθαρός o ῥυπαρός (doc. **12** nota *i*).

Dieci artabe di ricino sono messe a parte per essere controllate: εἰς δειγματισμόν (*l.* 8 e 21) = *wb3 mn.t* «per il controllo» (*l.* 13 e 27). Il vocabolo *mn.t* è raro in demotico;

[1] Piuttosto «di cui», «fra le quali» che «meno» (v. nota *o*, 3 e 4) perché Korragos e Khaiophis dichiarano di aver ricevuto tutte le 100 artabe.

figura col significato «controllo» = δειγματισμός nel nostro documento, col significato «campione» (cioè δεῖγμα) nel doc. **12** e col significato «qualità, maniera» nella locuzione *n t3 mn.t n.*[2] In tutti questi casi si tratta della stessa parola [3] che si ritrova pure nel verbo *mn* «accertare»: [4] P. Louvre 7845, 9 [5] parla di un danno eventuale *p3 ntj mn* «che sarà accertato», e la versione demotica della Rosettana (*l.* 17) di *p3 st3 ntj mn* «la mancanza che sarà accertata»; che si tratta sempre ancora della stessa nozione viene provato dalla parola δειγματισμός che ritroviamo nella versione greca τὰ πρὸς τὸν δειγματισμὸν διάφορα (*l.* 30 = SB 5 8299).

k κυψάλη (*l.* 8-9 e 22) = κυψέλη «any hollow vessel» (LIDDELL-SCOTT, *Greek-English Lexicon*) = *š*ʿ.*t n* ʿ*m*:

l. 13

l. 27

La parola *š*ʿ.*t* 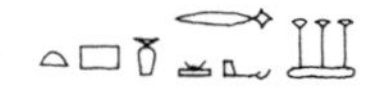 indica, a giudicare dai determinativi, un recipiente rettangolare. In questo caso il recipiente è d'argilla (*n* ʿ*m*) e deve essere assai grande per poter contenere almeno 300 khoinikes (10 artabe di 30 khoinikes), cioè circa 300 litri. Non era quindi trasportabile; difatti si trovava collocato (κεῖται) nel granaio.

l σιτοβολών (*l.* 9 e 22-23) è un vocabolo raro che si incontra solo più in due altri documenti dell'archivio di Zenon. Indica un tipo di magazzino dove si possono conservare sesamo (P. Col. Zen. 1 53, 2), ricino (il nostro documento) e foraggio per i tori (P. Lond. 7 1974, 19). I primi due documenti parlano di «il» σιτοβολών come se si trattasse di uno solo, ma il terzo fa vedere che ve ne era anche uno speciale per i tori: σιτοβολὼν τῶν ταύρων. Di tali magazzini ce n'erano quindi almeno due, l'uno per l'olio (situato nel Temenos degli Dei Adelphoi; nota *p*) e l'altro per il foraggio dei tori, ambedue a quanto pare a Philadelphia. Penso che siano diversi da quei magazzini che sono chiamati θησαυροί.[6]

Nel testo demotico si riscontra la parola *r3* (*l.* 12 e 27) che significa, molto in generale, «magazzino», perché può indicare un θησαυρός (sovente) o un σιτοβολών (nel nostro documento e forse nel P. Lond. inv. 2756 A recto, 19 [P. Lond. 7 1974] e verso II, 4-5 [P. dem. Zen. 22]). Per rimediare all'indefinitezza del termine, il testo demotico precisa il luogo dove il magazzino in oggetto si trova: il Temenos degli Dei Adelphoi (nota *p*).

---

[2] Setne I 5, 17 e probabilmente P. dem. Zen. 1, 6.

[3] Cf. Wb 2 65 *mn.t*: «die Art und Weise» (belegt seit MR); CRUM, *Coptic Dict.* 172 **ⲘⲒⲚⲈ**: «sort, quality, manner».

[4] Forse è il verbo *mn* «rimanere».

[5] G. R. HUGHES, *Saite Demotic Land Leases*, doc. III = M. MALININE, *Trois documents de l'époque d'Amasis relatifs au louage de terre*, Revue d'égyptologie 8 (1951) 135-141. Penso che la frase in oggetto sia da interpretare così: *p3 nbj --- iw=k dj.t n=j p3j=f šmw --- r ḫ.t n p3 ntj mn* «in quanto riguarda il danno, tu mi darai il suo (equivalente della) raccolta, conformemente alla (grandezza del danno) che sarà accertata».

[6] Uno solo θησαυρός statale si trovava a Philadelphia, ed alcuni privati (di Apollonios o Zenon) in questo villaggio e nei dintorni (CPJ 1 p. 139-140).

m *sṯḥ* 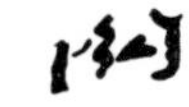 *l.* 12

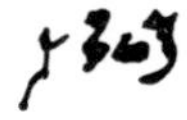 *l.* 26

La parola *sṯḥ* (accompagnata dal determinativo «pianta»; in altri testi qualche volta dal determinativo «male») viene spesso usata in relazione a grano e prende allora il significato di «pula»; nel nostro documento, avendo a che fare con semi di ricino, deve significare «capsula»: i semi consegnati si trovano ancora nelle loro capsule (v. doc. **12** nota *i*); è strano che il testo greco non ne parli.

n *mḥ* «capacità»: doc. **12** nota *n*. Il passo completo sarebbe *rtb* (*n p3 ḳws*) *n mḥ* (χοῖνιξ) 30.*t* «artaba (misurata) con la misura della capacità di 30 khoinikes».

o Il segno ⁄ è uno di quei segni che si riscontrano nei papiri greci, ma che sono stati presi a prestito dall'egizio; altri sono / *r* (Erichsen, *Glossar*, 238: «macht») interpretato come γίνεται, γίνονται e ⌒ o ⌒ *sp* (Erichsen, *Glossar*, 426-427: «Rest») interpretato come λοιπόν.[7] È assai interessante di constatare come questi segni egizi già venissero usati in testi greci nei tempi di Zenon. Penso che Zenon avesse impiegato molti Egiziani indigeni per fare compilare i suoi conti, giornali ed altri documenti simili in cui si trovano questi segni [8] [cf. Horos e la sua lettera citata alla fine di questa nota].

Per quanto riguarda il nostro segno ⁄ (*l.* 12 e 27), lo ritroviamo in egizio sotto diverse forme, come ad esempio:

 P. Wilbour (vol. II p. 92); [9] ieratico

 idem

 Leiden I 431, verso 15; ieratico anormale [J. Černý, *Studies Griffith*, 55 n. 56]

 P. Strasb. 2, 3; demotico antico [M. Malinine, JEA 54, 1968, 190]

 P. Sorb. inv. 2301, 10; demotico tolemaico [Fr. de Cenival, Recherches de Pap. 4, 1967, 100]

 O. Leid. Nur el-Din 192, 2; demotico romano

---

[7] V. in generale A. Blanchard, *Sigles et abréviations dans les papyrus grecs* (1974) 30-31 e 42-43. Per quanto riguarda il segno greco L per ἔτος, non credo che sia d'origine egizia (come pensa J. Dietrich, *Die Herkunft des graeco-ägyptischen Jahreszeichens* L, Schweizer Münzblätter 76 [1969] 69-77); questo segno deve essere d'origine greca, v. ciò che Skeat scrive a proposito di P. Lond. 7 1986, 1 (p. 85): «The ε is written in unusual fashion, with a shallow bow rising high above the line, and

ed in greco, ad esempio come:

 P. Cairo Zen. 3 59.317, 4 (tav. III); terzo sec. a.C.

 P. Sorb. inv. 2301 (tav. IV) = SB 10 10.452, 2; terzo sec. a.C. [B. BOYAVAL, Recherches de Pap. 4, 1967, 104]

 BGU 3 994 col. 1, 3; secondo sec. a.C.

Nei testi egizi [10] bisogna, penso, trascriverlo come *wp st*, poiché queste parole si riscontrano in testi geroglifici cogli stessi significati del segno ⁄ in demotico.[11] Il verbo *wp* «dividere», «separare» prende nell'espressione *wp st* il senso di «elencare pezzo per pezzo», «specificare» ecc.: *wp st* = «specificalo»; [12] a secondo del contesto bisogna tradurre in diversi modi:

1) quando il segno introduce *un elenco o una citazione*, si può renderlo semplicemente con due punti:
   — *n3j=f mtr.w* 16 *wp st* ... «i suoi (i.e. quelli del documento) 16 testimoni: ...» (segue l'elenco dei nomi) [P. Ryl. III 12 H: p. 261 e tav. LX]
   — dopo l'esposizione di un problema matematico da risolvere, si trovano le parole *p3 gj ir=f wp st* «la maniera di risolverlo: ...» (segue la descrizione della maniera in cui si deve risolvere il problema) [R. A. PARKER, *Dem. Mathematical Papyri*, n. 7, 18: p. 19 e tav. 2]
   — *ẖ.t n t3j wtj n inr Jb ntj n ẖft-ḥr n Imn wp st* «testo di quella stele di pietra d'Elefantine, che si trova davanti a Amun: ...» (segue l'intero contenuto del testo) [P. Ryl. III 9 col. 21, 11; tav. XLIII]

---

a short cross-bar. This form lends some support to the theory that the abbreviation for ἔτος originated in a large ε of this type, cf. P. Cair. Zen. 59842, 4-5, n.» La supposizione di Dietrich, che il segno L sia un segno egizio inversato, pare poco probabile, per il semplice fatto che negli altri casi il segno egizio veniva adottato dai greci, esattemente come era, e senza inversione. (Il gruppo menzionato doc. **1** nota *l* mi pare sia troppo raro per poter aver dato origine al segno greco).

[8] Anche Anosis, il famoso κωμογραμματεύς di Philadelphia (v. doc. **1**, intr.) era d'origine egizia. È interessante la lettera scritta da Zenon il 23 *Mesore* dell'anno 28 (C. C. EDGAR, JEA 14 [1928] 288-289) = Suppl. doc. **B**, quando cioè Zenon abitava ad Alessandria e non si serviva ancora di mesi egizi per datare i suoi documenti. Edgar suppone che Zenon non abbia scritto la lettera di persona, ma l'abbia dettata «to a local scribe» (Zenon si trova attualmente vicino a Philadelphia), ciò che spiegherebbe l'uso del mese egizio; cf. pure P. Cairo Zen. 1 59.129 (*Tybi* dell'anno 29).

[9] Il vero significato di questo segno nel P. Wilbour è difficile da stabilire. Suppongo che si tratti del significato (3) citato più avanti; nel caso citato da B. MENU (*Le régime juridique des terres et du personnel attaché à la terre dans le Papyrus Wilbour*, p. 106) si tratta di un terreno di Praʿhiwenmaf: 20 (arure) ⁄ 5 (ar.) $\frac{1}{2}$ (ar.) $1\frac{2}{4}$ (misure di grano) [i numeri $\frac{1}{2}$ e $1\frac{2}{4}$ sono scritti in rosso sul papiro per farli risaltare di più], ciò che significa, penso, che Praʿhiwenmaf possiede un terreno di 20 arure, ma che deve pagare, soltanto per una parte (5 arure), $\frac{1}{2} \times 1\frac{2}{4} = \frac{3}{4}$ misure di grano [secondo questa interpretazione il significato del segno ⁄ è uno di quelli che sono conosciuti; inoltre il calcolo è semplice da fare: basta moltiplicare i due numeri rossi]. Nella interpretazione della signora Menu però (loc. cit. p. 106) Praʿhiwenmaf dovrebbe pagare $(20 : 5) \times \frac{1}{2} \times 1\frac{2}{4} = 4 \times \frac{3}{4} = 3$ misure di grano.

[10] Nelle pubblicazioni di testi greci si suole risolverlo con (ὧν) o (ἀφ' ὧν).

[11] D. MEEKS, *Le grand texte des donations au temple d'Edfou*, ad esempio p. 9[x], 7, 8, 11 e 17 (v. p. 22) e soprattutto l'importante nota 68 (p. 73). [*Addendum*: FR. DE CENIVAL, Enchoria 7, 20].

[12] R. A. CAMINOS, *Late-Egyptian Miscellanies*, p. 110 (vs. 6, 2): «*wp st*, literally 'specify it'.»

2) quando il segno introduce *un elenco di cose che sono totalizzate* si può renderlo nella stessa maniera, ossia con due punti:
— *rmt s 3 p3j=w rn wp st ... r rmt s 3 ntj ḥrj ʿn* «tre persone; il loro nome: ... (seguono i nomi) ..., fanno le tre persone menzionate qui sopra, di nuovo» [P. dem. Zen. 2 *b*, 2-3; tav. 2]
— πήχεις στερε(οί) ε̄ ⟨ Ταελολοῦς γ Πετεαρσεμθεὺς β / (i.e. γίνονται) ε «(un terreno di) 5 cubiti quadrati: Taelolous 3 e Peteharsemtheus 2, fanno 5 (cubiti quadrati)» [BGU 3 994 col. 1]
— P. Cairo Zen. 3 59.476 («a list of the donkeys that have been struck off the roll from Mesore to Phaophi»); dopo l'enumerazione si legge (*l.* 16-18): ⟨ ἄρσενα η θηλυκὰ δ / (i.e. γίνονται) ιβ

3) quando il segno introduce *la specificazione di una parte di quello che precede,* si può renderlo con «di cui», «fra i quali» (greco τούτου, τούτων, ὧν):
— *ipd 21 wp st hmj ipd* 1, «21 oche, di cui una oca (è) per spese di trasporto» [P. Strasb. 2, 3; M. Malinine, JEA 54, 1968, 190; tav. XXX]
— *n3 isw.w 27 wp st ḥwṯ 7* «27 pecore, di cui 7 (sono) maschi» = πρόβατα κζ ⟨ ἄρ(σενα) ζ [P. Sorb. inv. 2301, Recherches de Pap. 4, 1967, tav. IV; testo demotico (p. 100), *l.* 10; testo greco (p. 104 = SB 10 10.452), *l.* 2]

4) quando il segno introduce *qualche cosa che è da sottrarre da quello che precede,* si può renderlo con «meno» (greco ἀπὸ τούτου, ἀπὸ τούτων, ἀφ' ὧν; cf. doc. **13**: τούτων ὑπολελείμμεθα):
— *ḥḏ* 4 *ḳt* $7\frac{1}{2}$ *wp st ... ḥḏ ḳt* $2\frac{1}{2}$ ... *ḥḏ ḳt* $2\frac{1}{2}$ ⌜*r ḳt* 5⌝ *sp ḥḏ* 4 *ḳt* $2\frac{1}{2}$ «4 deben e $7\frac{1}{2}$ kite meno ... $2\frac{1}{2}$ kite d'argento (e) ... $2\frac{1}{2}$ kite d'argento, fa 5 kite: il resto (è) 4 deben e $2\frac{1}{2}$ kite» [O. Leid. Nur el-Din 218, 7-9]
— (ἄρουραι) υ ⟨ 'Οννώφρει τὸ τρίτον ρλγ γ' λοι(πὸν) (ἄρουραι) σξς β' «400 arure, meno la terza parte (che è) per Onnophris (cioè) $133\frac{1}{3}$: il resto (è) $266\frac{2}{3}$ arure» [P. Cairo Zen. 2 59.252].

Citiamo infine una parte di una lettera che Horos (senz'altro uno scriba egizio) scrive a Zenon e che ci offre un bell'esempio dell'uso dei segni d'origine egizia (P. Cairo Zen. 3 59.317; tav. III):

l. 3-6: ἀνηλώσω δὲ εἰς ταῦτα χάρτας δ̄ ⟨ (i.e. ὧν o due punti) εἰς τὸν οἰκοδομικὸν λόγον γ̄ καὶ εἰς τὰ ἔργα ἀμπελουργῶν ᾱ.

l. 9-12: καὶ περὶ τοῦ ὀψώνιον (*l.*-ίου) ἀπὸ μηνὸς Παχῶνος [13] ἕως Μεσορὴ μηνῶν δ̄ / (i.e. γίνονται) (δραχμαὶ) μ. Εἰς τοῦτο ἔχω παρὰ Κάλλωνος (δραχμὰς) ι, ◠ (i.e. λοιπὸν) (δραχμαὶ) λ ⟨ (i.e. ὧν) ὑπολόγησύν (*l.*-σόν) με (*l.* μοι) εἰς ὃ προσοφείλω (δραχμὰς) ιε, ◠ (i.e. λοιπὸν) (δραχμαὶ) ιε.

p *p3 ʿ.wj (n) n3 ntr.w sn.w* «il luogo degli Dei Adelphoi»

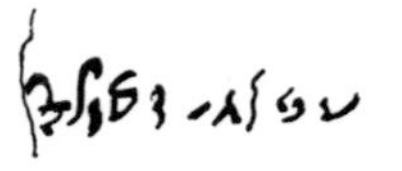
l. 12

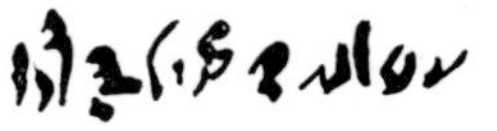
l. 27

[13] Penso che Παχῶνος sia il genitivo di Παχών (come nel P. Cairo Zen. 2 59.175, 7); cf. Παώπιος (P. Lond. 7 2061, 1) e Φαώφιος (P. Cairo Zen. 3 59.346, 2) che considero pure come genitivi.

È difficile identificare questo «luogo».[14] Non può essere Philadelphia ché si chiama *P3-ʿ.wj-t3-mr-sn*[15] «il luogo della (Dea) Philadelphos» = κώμη τῆς Φιλαδέλφου[16] = Φιλαδέλφεια; è dedicato alla regina Arsinoe Philadelphos e possiede un suo tempio, τὸ Ἀρσινοεῖον o τὸ ἱερὸν Ἀρσινόης.[17]

Spiegelberg ha dapprima pensato che il nostro «luogo degli Dei Adelphoi» fosse Theadelphia,[18] poi che fosse Philadelphia e che si trattasse di un secondo nome di quel villaggio,[19] ed infine che dovesse essere il nome non del villaggio intero, ma di una parte soltanto:[20] il nostro «luogo» potrebbe essere il τέμενος, che si incontra in alcuni documenti di Zenon per il fatto che veniva costruito nei suoi tempi.[21] Il nome ufficiale di questo recinto è, a quanto pare, θεῶν Ἀδελφῶν τέμενος[22] e questo nome corrisponde davvero esattamente a *p3 ʿ.wj* (*n*) *n3 ntr.w sn.w* «il luogo (= τέμενος, recinto) degli Dei Adelphoi». Penso che fosse in questo recinto che Apollonios intendeva costruire [τὸ ἱερὸν?] τοῦ βασιλέως καὶ τῆς Φιλα[δέλφου θεῶν Ἀδελφῶν].[23]

q *P3-dj-Ḥr-m-ḥb* (*l.* 13 e 28) deve corrispondere a Peteharmais, cf. *Ḥr-m-ḥb* = Ἁρμάις (doc. **2**).

r Benché il nome *P3-rtj* (*l.* 13 e 28), scritto con l'articolo *p3*, sia nuovo, si conosce il nome *Pa-rṯ* (scritto con *pa*) che corrisponde probabilmente a Φαράτης, Παράτης (cf. ERICHSEN, *Dem. Lesestücke* II. 2 p. 218). Penso quindi che *P3-rtj* possa corrispondere a Πρᾶτις (SB 6 8967; 239 a.C.). I nomi sono da considerarsi, tutti e due, come vezzeggiativi di nomi formati con Harpokhrates, essendo *Ḥr-p3-ẖrd* «Horos, il figlio» il vicario (*rd*) di suo padre.[24]

---

[14] La parola *ʿ.wj* indica uno spazio delimitato e significa «luogo» (v. WB I 157 in calce: ʿ «Gegend», «Stelle»), cioè, a secondo del contesto: casa, tempio (FR. DE CENIVAL, *Ass. Religieuses*, p. 21-22), villaggio (P. Lond. 7 1954, 1 nota), regione (D. MEEKS, *Donations au temple d'Edfou*, p. 59-60, *c*); il significato originale «luogo» si trova inoltre nelle locuzioni *ʿ.wj n* + infinitivo o sostantivo «luogo di ...» (v. gli esempi citati da SPIEGELBERG, *Dem. Grammatik* § 34; *m3ʿ n* è una variante più recente).

[15] Ad esempio P. dem. Zen. 12, 8.

[16] P. Lond. 7 1954, 1 nota.

[17] V. ad esempio resp. P. Lond. 7 1974, 14-15 e 2046, 2.

[18] PSI 9 1010 D, nota 3 (cf. U. WILCKEN, Archiv für Papyrusforschung 9 [1930] 75).

[19] P. dem. Zen. p. 10 n. 9; Wilcken non ci credeva e pensava che lo scriba si fosse sbagliato scrivendo Theadelphia invece di Philadelphia (Archiv für Papyrusforschung 9 [1930] 238-239).

[20] W. SPIEGELBERG, *Zu dem vermeintlichen Doppelnamen von* Φιλαδέλφεια, Archiv für Papyrusforschung 10 [1932] 17.

[21] V. ad esempio P. Cairo Zen. 3 59.499.

[22] C. C. EDGAR, P. Cairo Zen. 4 59.745, 34-37, nota.

[23] P. Cairo Zen. 2 59.169 = doc. **28**.

[24] Vedere E. BRESCIANI, *Testi demotici nella collezione Michaelidis*, p. 26 n. *c* e la letteratura citata da H.-J. THISSEN, Enchoria 1 (1971) 25; però egli è scettico sulla significazione del nome *Pa-rṯ*.

INDICI

I. SOVRANI

Ptolemaios I Soter

Πτολεμαῖος **5** 2
Πτολεμαῖος Σωτήρ **1** 2, 11-12; **2** 2, 9; **3** 2, 9; **4** 2, 8-9; **5** 10; **6** 2, 8-9; **7** 2, 9; **8** 2, 9; **9** 2, 9; **10** 2, 10; **13** 1, 14-15
*Ptlwmjs*ᶜ.ʷ.ˢ. *pꜣ ntj nḥm* «Ptolemaios, colui che salva» **1** 24; **13** 24 (*Ptwlmjs*ᶜ.ʷ.ˢ.)

Ptolemaios II Philadelphos

Βασιλεύοντος Πτολεμαίου τοῦ Πτολεμαίου **5** 1
Βασιλεύοντος Πτολεμαίου τοῦ Πτολεμαίου Σωτῆρος **1** 1, 10-11; **2** 1, 8; **3** 1, 8; **4** 1, 8; **5** 9; **6** 1, 8; **7** 1, 8; **8** 1, 8; **9** 1, 8; **10** 1, 9; **13** 1, 14
*Pr-ᶜꜣ*ᶜ.ʷ.ˢ. *Ptlwmjs*ᶜ.ʷ.ˢ. *sꜣ Ptlwmjs*ᶜ.ʷ.ˢ. *pꜣ ntj nḥm* **1** 23; **13** 24 (*Ptwlmjs*ᶜ.ʷ.ˢ.)

Ptolemaios II Philadelphos e Arsinoe

nꜣ ntr.w sn.w «gli Dei Fratelli»: *pꜣ ᶜ.wj* (*n*) *nꜣ ntr.w sn.w* (θεῶν Ἀδελφῶν τέμενος?) **13** 12, 27 (nota *p*)

II. DATAZIONE

1. *Anni* (introduzione § 3)

Regno di Ptolemaios II Philadelphos:

anno 29 = 28	L κθ Παῦνι κθ	= *ḥꜣ.t-sp* 28	**1**
	L κθ Μεσορὴ ια	= *ḥꜣ.t-sp* 28	**2**
	L κθ Μεσορὴ ιβ	= *ḥꜣ.t-sp* 28	**3**
	L κθ Μεσορὴ κγ	= *ḥꜣ.t-sp* 28	**4-8**
	L κθ Μεσορὴ κθ		**9**
anno 29 = 29	L κθ Θῶυθ β		**10**
	L κθ Θῶυτ κε	= *ḥꜣ.t-sp* 29	**11**
anno 32 = 31	L λβ Ἐπεὶφ κβ	= *ḥꜣ.t-sp* 31.*t*	**12**
anno 34 = 33	L λδ Μεχὶρ κβ	= *ḥꜣ.t-sp* 33 *ntj ir* 34	**13**

2. *Stagioni*

ꜣḫ.t: la prima stagione dell'anno; contiene i mesi Θῶυθ, Φαῶφι, Ἁθύρ e Χοιάκ
ibd-1 *ꜣḫ.t* (= Θῶυθ) **11** 13
pr.t: la seconda stagione dell'anno; contiene i mesi Τῦβι, Μεχείρ, Φαμενώθ e Φαρμοῦθι
ibd-2 *pr.t* (Μεχείρ) **13** 11, 24
šmw: la terza stagione dell'anno; contiene i mesi Παχώνς, Παῦνι, Ἐπείφ e Μεσορή
ibd-2 *šmw* (Παῦνι) **1** 23
ibd-3 *šmw* (Ἐπείφ) **12** 11
ibd-4 *šmw* (Μεσορή) **2** 14; **3** 16, 21; **4** 14; **5** 17; **6** 15; **7** 15; **8** 15

3. *Mesi*

Ἐπείφ	(*ibd*-3 *šmw*)	**12** 1, 14
Θῶυθ	(*ibd*-1 *ꜣḫ.t*)	**10** 3, 11; **11** 18; Θῶυτ: **11** 1, 7, 20
Μεσορή	(*ibd*-4 *šmw*)	**2** 3, 10; **3** 3, 7, 10, 14; **4** 3, 9; **5** 2, 11; **6** 2, 9; **7** 2-3, 10; **8** 2, 9; **9** 3, 10
Μεχείρ	(*ibd*-2 *pr.t*)	**13** 2, 29; Μεχίρ: **13** 15
Παῦνι	(*ibd*-2 *šmw*)	**1** 3 (Πυνι o Πυινι, nota *b*), 12, 31

4. *Giorni*

	β	**10**
(*sw*) 11	= ια	**2-3**
(*sw*) 12	= ιβ	**3**
(*sw*) 22	= κβ	**12-13**
(*sw*) 22	= κγ	**4** (nota *a*)
(*sw*) 23	= κγ	**5-8**
(*sw*) 25	= κε	**11**
sw 29	= κθ	**1**
	κθ	**9**
sw ʿrḳj		**3**

III. NOMI DI PERSONA

1. *Nomi Greci*

a. *Greco*

Ἀπολλώνιος, *3pwrns, 3pwrnis, 3pwrnjs* (**1** nota *v*)
— γῆ Ἀπολλωνίου **1** 5-6, 15; *3ḥ.w* di Apollonios **1** 29; **2** 17; **3** 22; **4** 16; **5** 20; **6** 17; **7** 18; **8** 18; **11** 17
— Πανακέστωρ ὁ παρὰ Ἀπολλωνίου **4** 6, 12; **5** 6, 14; **6** 6, 13; **7** 6, 13; **8** 6, 13; **9** 6, 13; **10** 6, 14
Δᾶμις **1** 4, 14; *T3ms* **1** 28; v. Κλείταρχος
Διόδωρος **1** 5, 14
Ἑρμόλαος **12** 2, 15; **13** 3, 16; *Hrmwl3ws* **13** 25; v. Κόρραγος
Ζήνων, *Snn* f. di *3ḳrpn* (**13** nota *h*) **12** 5, 18; **13** 4, 18; *Snn* **12** 11; **13** 11, 26; v. Κλείταρχος e Φανῆσις
Ἡγησίας **6** 4, 11; **9** 4, 11
Θεόφιλος, f. di *Tim3ḳrts*, giardiniere e viticoltore **3** 5, 13; *Ṯwprs* **3** 18
Κλείταρχος, *Gljt3rk3ws*, ⌜*Glwtrk3s*⌝
— ὁ παρὰ Δάμιδος **1** 4, 13; *p3 rd* di Damis **1** 27
— ὁ παρὰ Ζήνωνος **13** 4, 17; *p3 rd* di Zenon **13** 11, 26
Κλεῖτος, f. di Νικάδας **9** 4, 11
Κόρραγος, *Ḳwhr3ḳws* **13** 30; ὁ παρὰ Ἑρμολάου **12** 1, 14; **13** 2, 15; *p3 rd* di Hermolaos **13** 25
Νικάδας, p. di Κλεῖτος **9** 4, 11
Νικίας **11** 2, 8; *Nigis* **11** 13
Πανακέστωρ, *Pngsṭr* (**2** nota *f*) **2** 5, 12; ὁ παρὰ Ἀπολλωνίου **4** 5, 11; **5** 5, 13; **6** 5, 12; **7** 5, 12; **8** 5, 12; **9** 5, 12; **10** 5, 13; *Pngsṭr* **2** 15; **3** 19; **4** 14; **5** 18; **6** 15-16; **7** 16; **8** 16; **11** 14
Πτολεμαῖος, *Ptlwmjs, Ptwlmjs*: indice I

b. *Demotico*

2. *Nomi Egizi*

a. *Greco*

Ἀμεννεῦς, p. di Σαμῶυς **4** 4, 10; **10** 4, 12; *Imn-iw* **4** 14
Ἁρμάις, f. di Παχῆς **2** 4, 11, 18; *Ḥr-m-ḥb* **2** 14
Ἑθφεῦς, p. di Ὀννῶφρις **3** 5 (Ἑφθ-), 12; *Ḥtp.w* **3** 17
Ἰναρῶς, f. di Πάις, uomo proveniente da Meidum **1** 7, 17 (gen. -ῶδος), 32 (gen. -ῶτος); *Ir.t-Ḥr-r.r=w* **1** 25

Κολλούθης, p. di Πετεῦρις **3** 4, 11; *Kꜣrḏ* **3** 17
Νεχθῶυς, p. di ῟Ωρος (= Harpaesis) **8** 3, 10; *Nḫṱ=w* **8** 15
᾿Οννῶφρις, f. di ῾Εθφεῦς, giardiniere, viticoltore **3** 4-5, 12; *Wn-nfr* **3** 17
Πάις, p. di ᾿Ιναρῶς **1** 8 (gen. -ιδος), 18 (gen. -ιδος, corretto da -ιτος); *Pa-ḥi* **1** 25
Πᾶσις, f. di Σαμῶυς **6** 3, 10; *Pa-sj* **6** 15
Παχῆς, p. di ῾Αρμάις **2** 4, 11, 19; *Pa-⸢ꜣḫ.t⸣* **2** 14
Παῶς, p. di Φερνοῦθις **5** 3, 12; **7** 3-4, 11; *Pa-ḥr* **5** 17; **7** 15
Πετεῦρις, f. di Κολλούθης, giardiniere, viticoltore **3** 4, 11; *Pꜣ-dj-Ḥr* **3** 17
Πογᾶς **8** 4, 11
Ποκᾶς, Ποκῶς, p. di ῟Ωρος **5** 4, 12 (-κᾶς); **7** 4, 11 (-κῶς)
Σαμῶυς, f. di ᾿Αμεννεῦς **4** 4, 10; **10** 3, 12; *Ṯꜣj-n.im=w* **4** 14
Σαμῶυς, p. di Πᾶσις **6** 3, 10; *Ṯꜣj-n.im=w* **6** 15
Φανῆσις, *Pa-n-Is.t* (**12** nota *f*), χειριστής, ὁ παρὰ Ζήνωνος **12** 4, 17; *pꜣ rd* di Zenon **12** 11
Φερνοῦθις, f. di Παῶς **5** 3, 11; **7** 3, 10; *Pꜣ-(i.)ir-nṯr* **5** 17; **7** 15
Χαιῶφις, *Ḫꜥj=f* (**12** nota *c*), scriba **13** 28, 31; v. *Pꜣ-dj-Ḥr-m-ḥb*
ὁ παρὰ ῞Ωρου βασιλικοῦ γραμματέως **12** 2, 15; **13** 3, 16; *pꜣ rd n Ḥr* (o *Ḥr-tꜣj=f-nḫṱ*) *pꜣ sḫ Pr-ꜥꜣ* ꜥ.w.s. **12** 13; **13** 24
῟Ωρος, f. di Ποκᾶς **5** 4, 12; di Ποκῶς **7** 4, 11
῟Ωρος = Harpaesis, f. di Νεχθῶυς, δεκάταρχος
῟Ωρος **8** 3, 10; *Ḥr-pa-Is.t* **8** 15
῟Ωρος = Hartephnakhthis, βασιλικὸς γραμματεύς; v. Χαιῶφις
῟Ωρος **12** 3, 16; **13** 3, 16; *Ḥr* **12** 13; *Ḥr-tꜣj=f-nḫṱ* **13** 25

b. *Demotico*

Imn-iw v. ᾿Αμεννεῦς
Ir.t(-n)-Ḥr-r.r=w v. ᾿Ιναρῶς
ꜥn=w=ṯꜣj (῎Ανοσις, ῎Ανοθις; **1** nota *n*), f. di *Ḏḥwṱ-i.ir-rḫ*, scriba **1** 25, 30
Wn-nfr v. ᾿Οννῶφρις
Pꜣ-(i.)ir-nṯr v. Φερνοῦθις
Pꜣ-rtj, p. di *Pꜣ-dj-Ḥr-m-ḥb* **13** 13, 28
Pꜣ-dj-Ḥr v. Πετεῦρις
Pꜣ-dj-Ḥr-m-ḥb, f. di *Pꜣ-rtj*, scriba, *pꜣ rd* di Χαιῶφις **13** 13, 28
Pa-⸢ꜣḫ.t⸣ v. Παχῆς
Pa-n-Is.t v. Φανῆσις
Pa-ḥi v. Πάις
Pa-ḥr v. Παῶς
Pa- sj v. Πᾶσις
Nḫṱ=w v. Νεχθῶυς
Ḥr v. ῟Ωρος, *Ḥr-pa-Is.t* e *Ḥr-tꜣj=f-nḫṱ* (**12** nota *d*)
Ḥr-pa-Is.t v. ῟Ωρος
Ḥr-m-ḥb v. ῾Αρμάις
Ḥr-tꜣj=f-nḫṱ v. ῟Ωρος
Ḥtp.w v. ῾Εθφεῦς
Ḫꜥj=f v. Χαιῶφις
Kꜣrḏ v. Κολλούθης
Ṯꜣj-n.im=w v. Σαμῶυς
Ḏḥwṱ-i.ir-rḫ (Τοτορχόις, var. Θοτορχῆς; = *Ḏḥwṱ-i.ir-rḫ-s*? **1** nota *o*), p. di *ꜥn=w-ṯꜣj* **1** 25, 30

IV. NOMI GEOGRAFICI E TOPOGRAFICI

a. *Greco*

᾿Αρσινοίτης (νομός) **12** 6
Μοιθυμίτης **1** 8, 18; *pꜣ rmt (n) Mr-Itm* «l'uomo proveniente da Meidum» **1** 25
Σύριος, πυρὸς Σύριος **1** 8, 19; *sw n Ḫr* «frumento di Siria» **1** 26
Φιλαδέλφεια **12** 19-20; **13** 5, 18

b. *Demotico*

Mn-nfr «Memphis»: *p3 tš* (*n*) *Mn-nfr* «il nomos di Memphis» **13** 25
Mr-Itm «Meidum»: *p3 rmt* (*n*) *Mr-Itm* v. Μοιθυμίτης
Ḫr «Siria»: *sw n Ḫr* «frumento di Siria», πυρὸς Σύριος v. Σύριος
Kmj «Egitto»: *sw n Kmj* «frumento d'Egitto» **1** 26; πυρὸς ἐπιχώριος **1** 9, 20

V. TITOLI E PROFESSIONI

a. *Greco*

ἀμπελουργός **3** 23; v. κηπουρός
βασιλικὸς γραμματεύς (del nomos di Memphis): ῏Ωρος o Hartephnakhthis
12 3, 16-17; **13** 3-4, 16-17; *sḫ Pr-ʿ3*$^{c.w.s.}$ «scriba di Faraone» **12** 13; **13** 25
δεκάταρχος: ῏Ωρος Νεχθώυτος **8** 4, 11
ἐργάτης **11** 5, 11
κηπουρός (var. di ἀμπελουργός): Πετεῦρις Κολλούθου, Ὀννῶφρις Ἑθφεῦτος e Θεόφιλος
3 6, 13; *k3m* «giardiniere» **3** 16
χειριστής: Φανῆσις **12** 4, 7, 17-18, 21

b. *Demotico*

Pr-ʿ3$^{c.w.s.}$ «Faraone» **1** 23; **13** 24; cf. βασιλικὸς γραμματεύς
sḫ Pr-ʿ3$^{c.w.s.}$ «scriba di Faraone» v. βασιλικὸς γραμματεύς
k3m «giardiniere» v. κηπουρός

VI. MONETE

a. *Greco*

δραχμή (= 6 oboli)
⊦ (δραχμή) **3-11**; δραχμή **3** 15
ὀβολός
— (ὀβολός) **11** 5, 12
ϟ (τριώβολον) **4** 7; **5** 8; τριώβολον **4** 13; **5** 16
ϟ- (τετρώβολον) **11** 6
δεκόβολο[ν] **11** 12

b. *Demotico*

ḳt «kite»
— l'equivalenza
1 kite = 2 dracme
$\frac{1}{2}$ kite = 1 dracma
$\frac{1}{3}$ kite = ($\frac{2}{3}$ dracma =) 4 oboli
$\frac{1}{4}$ kite = ($\frac{1}{2}$ dracma =) 3 oboli
— la metà (si nota la metà di $\frac{1}{4}$ kite = $\frac{1}{10}\ \frac{1}{60}\ \frac{1}{120} = \frac{15}{120} = \frac{1}{8}$ kite)
ḳt $1\frac{1}{4}$ (la metà è *ḳt* $\frac{1}{2}\ \frac{1}{10}\ \frac{1}{60}\ \frac{1}{120}$) **4** 15 (= 2 dr. + 3 ob.)
ḳt 2 (la metà è *ḳt* 1) **8** 16-17 (= 4 dr.)
ḳt $2\frac{1}{2}$ (la metà è *ḳt* $1\frac{1}{4}$) **3** 20; **6** 16 (= 5 dr.)
ḳt $6\frac{1}{4}$ (la metà è *ḳt* $3\frac{1}{10}\ \frac{1}{60}\ \frac{1}{120}$) **5** 18-19 (= 12 dr. + 3 ob.)
ḳt 7 (la metà è *ḳt* $3\frac{1}{2}$) **7** 16-17 (= 14 dr.)
ḳt $\frac{2}{3}\ \frac{1}{6}$ (la metà è *ḳt*$^{1}\ \overline{3}\ \overline{12}$) **11** 15 (oppure: kite $\frac{1}{2} + \frac{1}{3}$ = 1 dr. + 4 ob.)

VII. PESI E MISURE

ἄρου(ρα) **4** 7, 13; **5** 8, 15; **6** 7, 14; **9** 7; **10** 8
ἀρτάβη, *rtb*
— ἀρτάβη **1** 19; **12** 9, 23; **13** 7, 9, 20, 23
— ἀρ(τάβη) **1** 9; **13** 31
— *rtb* «artaba» **1** 26; **12** 11; **13** 12, 13, 26, 28

μέτρον, *ḳws*
— μέτρον ἐννεακαιεικοσαχοίνικον **12** 8-9, 22-23; *pꜣ ḳws n mḥ* 29 «la misura della capacità di 29 (khoinikes)» **12** 12
— μέτρον τριακονταχοίνικον **13** 6, 19; *n mḥ* 30.*t* «(la misura) della capacità di 30 (khoinikes)» **13** 12, 26
σήκωμα **12** 6, 20
χοῖνιξ v. μέτρον

VIII. INDICE GENERALE

a. *Greco*

ἀδειγμάτιστος **13** 5, 18-19
ἄλως **1** 7, 17
ἀμπελουργός v. indice V
ἀν(ά) **11** 5, 12
ἀπό **1** 6, 16
ἀργυρικός **11** 19
ἄρουρα v. indice VII
ἀρτάβη v. indice VII

βασιλεύω v. indice I
βασιλικὸς γραμματεύς v. indice V

γῆ **1** 6, 15; **11** 3, 9
γραμματεύς v. indice V, βασιλικὸς γραμματεύς

δειγματισμός **13** 8, 21
δέκα **2** 7, 13; **13** 10, 23
δεκαδύο **5** 16
δεκάταρχος v. indice V
δεκατέσσαρες **7** 14
δεκόβολο[ν] v. indice VI
διά **6** 4, 10; **8** 4, 11; **9** 4, 11
διάχωμα **7** 6-7, 13-14; **8** 6-7, 13; **11** 4, 10-11
δίκαιος **13** 6-7, 20
δίμοιρος **12** 9-10, 24
δραχμή v. indice VI
δύο **4** 13

εἰκοσημερία κ̅ ημ̅ **3** 6, 14
εἰκοσιεπτά **1** 20
εἰμί **3** 6, 13
εἷς **1** 19
εἰς **2**; **4-11**; **13**
ἐκ **1** 5, 15; **12** 6, 19; **13** 5, 18
ἑκατόν **12** 9, 23; **13** 7, 20
ἐμπυρισμός **4** 6, 13; **5** 7, 15; **6** 7, 14; **9** 7; **10** 7-8
ἐν **12** 7, 21; **13** 8, 9, 22
ἐννεακαιεικοσαχοίνικος v. indice VII: μέτρον ἐ.
ἐπιχώριος, πυρὸς ἐπιχώριος **1** 9, 20
ἐργάτης v. indice V
ἔτος **13** 2; L (ἔτος), passim
ἔχω
1) «avere», «avere ricevuto da qualcuno»
ἔχω παρά
— **2** 5, 11; **4** 5, 11; **5** 5, 13; **6** 5, 12; **7** 5, 12; **8** 5, 12; **10** 5, 13; **11** 2, 8
— ἔχει invece di ἔχουσι **12** 1, 14; **13** 2, 15
— omesso **3** 6, 13; **9** 4, 11
2) «tenere», «possedere» **11** 3, 9

ἥμισυς **1** 21

κατασφραγίζω **12** 6-7, 20-21; **13** 8, 21-22
κεῖμαι **13** 9, 22
κηπουρός v. indice V
κριθή **1** 21; κρ(ιθή) **1** 9
κροτών **12** 5, 18-19; **13** 5, 18, 31
κυψάλη **13** 8-9, 22

μετρέω **1** 6, 16
μέτρησις **13** 6, 20
μέτρον v. indice VII
μήν **1** 3, 12; **2** 3, 10; **3** 3, 10; **13** 2, 15

ξυλοκοπία **2** 6, 13; **4** 6, 12; **5** 7, 14-15; **6** 6, 13; **9** 6-7; **10** 7

ὀβολός v. indice VI
ὁμολογέω **1-10**; ὁμολογεῖ invece di ὁμολογοῦσι **1**; **3**; **5**; **7**
ὀψώνιον **3** 14; omesso **3** 6

παρά (1) ἔχω παρά; (2) X ὁ παρὰ Y: passim
πέλεκυς **2** 7, 13
πέντε **3** 15; **6** 14
πυρός
1) πυρὸς Σύριος **1** 8, 18-19
2) πυρὸς ἐπιχώριος **1** 9, 20

ῥυπαρός **12** 5-6, 19

σήκωμα v. indice VII
σιτοβολών **13** 9, 22-23
Σωτήρ, *pꜣ ntj nḥm* v. indice I

τέσσαρες **8** 14
τεσσαρακονταπέντε **1** 21-22
τετρώβολον v. indice VI
τριακονταχοίνικος v. indice VII: μέτρον τ.
τρίτος **1** 22
τριώβολον v. indice VI

ὑπολείπω **13** 7-8, 21

φορω **12** 7, 21

χειριστής v. indice V

ὥστε **2** 6, 12

b. *Demotico*

ꜣḥ «terra», *ꜣḥ.w* **1** 29; **2** 17; **4** 16; **5** 20; **6** 17; **7** 17; **8** 17; **11** 16 (= γῆ), 17; *nꜣ ꜣḥ.w ḳꜣj* «le terre alte» **3** 21
ꜣḫ.t, la prima stagione dell'anno, v. indice II.

iꜣbṯ «Est», *pr iꜣbṯ* Suppl. **A** § b
iw «venire», *iw (n) dr.t (n)* «venuto, ricevuto dalla mano di» **12** 11; **13** 11
iw «essere», v. *r*
ibd «mese», v. indice II
imnṯ «Ovest», *pr imnṯ* Suppl. **A** § b
ir «fare», *ḥꜣ.t-sp* 33 *ntj ir ḥꜣ.t-sp* 34 «l'anno 33, che corrisponde all'anno 34» **13** 11, 24; v. *r*
irm «e», «con» **1** 27 (= καί); **13** 25 (= καί); nella cifra «100 *irm* ⅔» **12** 12
it «orzo» **1** 26 (= κριθή)

ꜥ.wj «casa», «tempio» *pꜣ ꜥ.wj (n) nꜣ ntr.w sn.w* «il tempio, recinto degli Dei Fratelli» **13** 12, 27
ꜥm «argilla» **13** 13, 27
ꜥn «di nuovo» **2** 16; **3** 20; **4** 15; **5** 19; **6** 16; **7** 17; **8** 17; **11** 15; **12** 12; **13** 12, 27
ꜥrḳj l'ultimo giorno del mese **3** 21

wꜣḥ ausiliare del Perfetto I: *wꜣḥ . . . ḫꜣj* «(Inaros) ha misurato» **1** 25
wbꜣ «per» *wbꜣ mn.t* «per il controllo» **13** 13, 27 (εἰς δειγματισμόν)
wp st ⟨ **13** 12, 27
wn «diga» **11** 15
wḥm «ripetere», *wn wḥm* «diga che ripete» (διάχωμα) **11** 16

bꜣk «lavoro» **4** 16; **5** 19; **6** 17; **7** 17; **8** 17; v. i verbi *mḥ*, *sf* e *ṯꜣj*
brbrj(.t) «chicco», *tgm (n) brbrj(.t)* «ricino sotto forma di chicchi», «chicchi di ricino» (κροτών) **12** 11; **13** 12, 26

pꜣ **1**, **3**, **12** e **13**
pꜣj=w **13** 12, 26
pwrꜣ(.t) un sacco di cuoio **12** 13 (= φορω)
pr.t la seconda stagione dell'anno, v. indice II
pš(.t) «metà» **2** 16; **3** 20; **4** 15; **5** 19; **6** 16; **7** 16; **8** 16; **11** 15; **12** 12; **13** 12, 27

m-ẖn v. *ẖn*
mj-nn «idem»; ripete la parola *kꜣm* «giardiniere»: *kꜣm* X *ḥnꜥ mj-nn* Y *ḥnꜥ mj-nn* Z **3** 17-18
mn.t (1) «campione» **12** 12; (2) «controllo» *wbꜣ mn.t* (εἰς δειγματισμόν) **13** 13, 27
mḥ «capacità», «capienza» **12** 12; **13** 12, 26
mḥ (< *mḥ*) «bruciare» *bꜣk . . . mḥ sṯ* «il lavoro di bruciare (il legno) con fuoco» (ἐμπυρισμός) **5** 20; **6** 17
mḥṯ «Nord», *pr mḥṯ* Suppl. **A** § b

n genitivo «di» **1** 26; **12** e **13**; scritto sopra il segno che segue **1** 26 (*n Kmj*) e **12** 11 (*Pa-n-Is.t*)
n dativo «a», *ḏd n* «dire a» (v. *ḏd*); *dj n* «dare a»: *n=j* **2** 15; **4** 15; **5** 18; **6** 16; **7** 16; **8** 16; **11** 14; *n=n* **3** 19; **13** 26
n (< *m*)
1) compl. di luogo «in» *n pꜣ rꜣ* «nel granaio» (ἐν τῶι σιτοβολῶνι) **13** 12, 27
2) compl. di tempo «sotto» *n Pr-ꜥꜣ ꜥ.w.s.* «sotto Faraone N.N.» **13** 24
3) compl. di strumento «con» *n.im=w* **2** 16; *n pꜣ ḳws* **12** 12
4) compl. d'identità «come» *n pꜣ ḥbs* **3** 20; *n dnj* **1** 28
nꜣ **3** 21; **13** 12, 27
nꜣ.w **1** 28
nꜣj=n **11** 16
nb (ναύβιον) terra per le dighe *ṯꜣj nb* **7** 17; **8** 17
nḥm «salvare» *pꜣ ntj nḥm* (Σωτήρ) v. indice I
ntj **1** 24; **13** 11, 12, 24, 27; *ntj iw* **12** 12
ntr «dio» *nꜣ ntr.w sn.w* v. *ꜥ.wj*

r preposizione (1) di tempo *r sw ꜥrḳj* «fino all'ultimo giorno del mese» **3** 21; (2) di scopo *r wn* «per la diga» **11** 15 (= εἰς), *r sf* «per tagliare» **2** 16
r (= *iw* «essere») *r pꜣj=w stḥ ẖn=w* «mentre le loro capsule si trovano tra loro» **13** 12, 26
r (= *irj.n* «fare»?) *r s* 3 «fanno 3 persone» **3** 18 (= ὄντες γ); *r hrw* 20 «fanno 20 giorni» **3** 21; «x, la sua metà è ½x, fa (*r*) x di nuovo» **2** 16; **11** 15; **12** 12; **13** 12, 27
rꜣ «granaio» **13** 12, 27 (= σιτοβολών)
rmt «uomo» *pꜣ rmt (n) Mr-Itm* «l'uomo proveniente da Meidum» **1** 25 (= Μοιθυμίτης)
rsj «Sud», *pr rsj* Suppl. **A** § b
rtb, ἀρτάβη v. indice VII
rd «rappresentante» *pꜣ rd n* (ὁ παρά) **1** 27; **12** 11, 13; **13** 11, 25-26, 28
rd «crescere» **1** 28

hrw «giorno» **3** 21

ḥꜣ.t-sp v. indice II
ḥbs «vestimento», «stipendio» *pꜣ ḥbs* **3** 20 (= ὀψώνιον)
ḥnꜥ **3** 17, 18 (= καί)
ḥḏ «argento» *ḥḏ ḳt* «kite d'argento» **4** 15

ḫꜣj «misurare» **1** 26 (= μετρέω)
ḫt «legno» **2** 16; **4** 16; **5** 20; **6** 17; v. *sf*

ẖn «dentro» **1-8** e **11-13**; *m-ẖn* (**3** 12); *ẖn=w* (**13** 12, 26); *ẖn* (= ἐν): **12** 13; **13** 13, 27

s «persona» **3** 18
sꜣ «figlio» passim (omesso: **1** 30; **7** 15; **13** 28); scritto sotto il determinativo del nome precedente **3** 17; **4** 14; **5** 17; **8** 15

sw giorno del mese **1** 23; **3** 21 (sovente omesso, v. indice II)
sw «frumento» *sw n Ḫr* «frumento di Siria» **1** 26 (= πυρὸς Σύριος); *sw n Kmj* «frumento d'Egitto» **1** 26 (= πυρὸς ἐπιχώριος)
swṯ «consegnare» **1** 30
sf «tagliare» *sf ḫt* «tagliare il legno» **2** 16; *b3k sf ḫt* «il lavoro di tagliare il legno» (ξυλοκοπία) **4** 16; **5** 20; **6** 17
sẖ, γραμματεύς v. indice V
sẖ «scrivere», *sẖ* X, «(lo scriba) X ha scritto (questo documento)» **1** 30; **12** 13; **13** 13, 28; il nome dello scriba è omesso: **2** 17; **3** 22; **4** 16; **5** 21; **6** 17; **7** 18; **8** 18; **11** 17
sṯ(.t) «fuoco» **5** 20; **6** 17, v. *mḥ* «bruciare»
stḥ «capsula» *r p3j=w stḥ ḫn=w* «mentre le loro capsule si trovano tra loro» **13** 12, 26 (cf. ῥυπαρός)

*š*ʿ*.t* un recipiente *š*ʿ*.t n* ʿ*m* «recipiente d'argilla» **13** 13, 27
šmw la terza stagione dell'anno, v. indice II

ḳ3j «alto» *p3 k3m ḳ3j* «il giardino alto» **3** 17; *n3 3ḥ.w ḳ3j* «le terre alte» **3** 22
ḳws «misura» (μέτρον) *p3 ḳws n mḥ* 29 «la misura della capacità di 29 (khoinikes)» **12** 12, v. indice VII
ḳrbn «scure» **2** 15 (= πέλεκυς)
ḳt «kite» v. indice VI

k3m «giardino», «vigna» *p3 k3m ḳ3j* **3** 16
k3m «giardiniere» (κηπουρός), «viticoltore» (ἀμπελουργός), v. indice V

t3j=f **2** 16; **3** 20; **4** 15; **5** 19; **6** 16; **7** 16; **8** 16; **11** 5; *t3j=w* **12** 12; **13** 12, 27
tš «distretto», «nomos» **13** 25
tgm «ricino» **13** 13, 28; *tgm (n) brbrj* «ricino sotto forma di chicchi», «semi di ricino» **12** 11; **13** 12, 26 (= κροτών)

ṯ3j «prendere» *b3k ṯ3j nb* «il lavoro di prendere (o portare) naubia (cioè terra per le dighe)» **7** 17; **8** 17

dj «dare» (1) *dj=k n=j* (o *n=n*) «tu hai dato a me (o a noi)» v. *n* (dativo); (2) *dj rd* «far crescere» **1** 28
dnj «imposte» **1** 28
dnj(.t) «parte» *dnj(.t) 3ḥ.w* **1** 29; **2** 17; **3** 21; **4** 16; **5** 20; **6** 17; **7** 17; **8** 17; **11** 17
dr.t «mano», plurale *dr.w(t)* **1** 27
1) *(n) dr.t* «dalla mano di», «da» **12** 11; **13** 11
2) *(r) dr.t* «nella mano di», «a» **1** 27

*ḏb*ʿ «sigillare» **12** 13; **13** 12, 27 (= κατασφραγίζω)
ḏd «dire» **1** 24; *ḏd n* **2** 14; **3** 16; **4** 14; **5** 17; **6** 15; **7** 15; **8** 15; **11** 13; **13** 24

IX. SIMBOLI E ABBREVIAZIONI

a. *Greco*

	ἀν(ά)		**11** 5
	ἄρου(ρα)		**6** 14
			**4** 7
	ἀρ(τάβη)		**1** 9
⊢	(δραχμή)		**6** 14
			**8** 7
κ̄ ημ̄	(εἰκοσ)ημ(ερία)	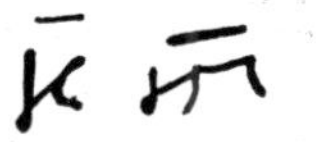	**3** 14
L	(ἔτος)		**3** 3
			**3** 10
		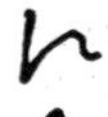	**11** 7
			**13** 15
c	(ἥμισυς)		**1** 9
	κρ(ιθή)		**1** 9
—	(ὀβολός)		**11** 5
ꟸ	(τριώβολον)		**4** 7
ꟸ-	(τετρώβολον)		**11** 6

b. *Demotico*: segni egizi adottati in Greco (v. doc. **13** nota *o*)

⟨ *wp st* → (ὧν), (ἀφ' ὧν)
/ *r* → (γίνεται)
∩ ∩ *sp* → (λοιπόν)

II

GREEK TEXTS FROM THE ARCHIVE OF ZENON

EDITED BY

W. CLARYSSE, M. MUSZYNSKI, A. SCHUTGENS,
W. J. TAIT, J. K. WINNICKI

14

ARCHILOCHUS (?), TETRAMETERS

H. × W. = 5.5 × 10 cm. Mid third cent. B.C.

Brit. Mus. (now Brit. Library) inv. 2652 A V°: **P. Lond. lit. 54**, with plate IV A. See also DIEHL, *Anthologia Lyrica Graeca* 3^{3}, pp. 25-26, no. 56 A; TREU, *Archilochos*, pp. 66-68; ROBERTS, *Greek Lit. Hands*, pl. 4 *b*. See further PACK, *Greek and Latin Literary Texts*, 2nd ed. (1965) no. 130, and add G. TARDITI, *Arciloco* (1968), no. 92 (text p. 114, translation p. 270) and M. L. WEST, *Iambi et elegi graeci ante Alexandrum cantati* I (1971), fragm. 106.

The text was acquired in 1925 together with a large number of Zenon-papyri and probably belongs to that archive. It is written along the fibres in an uncial hand of earlier type, without lectional signs. On the recto are the remains of an account (unpublished), written in a hand common in the Zenon archive.

Contents The text consists of eight partially preserved lines, assigned to the tetrameters of Archilochus by Crönert, who compares it with fr. 56 (Diehl). It belongs therefore to the small group of texts of a literary character which probably come from the Zenon archive; the others are no. **15** (and perhaps no. **16**), P. Cairo Zen. 4 59.532, 59.533, 59.535; P. Col. Zen. 2 60; compare P. Cairo Zen. 4 59.534 and 59.561, 21. See further C. PRÉAUX, *Les Grecs en Égypte d'après les archives de Zénon*, p. 12.

- -
[ ]γ̣ται νῆες <ἐ>μ πόντωι θοαί
[π]ο̣λλὸν δ' ἱστίων ὑφώμεθα
[λύσαν]τ̣ες ὅπλα νηὸς ⟦ιστι⟧ οὐρίην δ' ἔχε
[ἑταί]ρ̣ους ὄφρα σέο μεμνεώμεθα
[ ] ἄπισχε μηδὲ τοῦτον ἐμβάλῃς
[ ]ν ἵσταται κυκώμενον
[ ]χ̣η̣ς ἀλλὰ σ̣ὺ προμήθεσαι
[ ]υμος
- -

3 ⟦ιστι⟧: from the line above

S.

15

EURIPIDES, HIPPOLYTUS

H. × W. = 9.3 × 11.5 cm. Mid third cent. B.C.

Brit. Mus. (now Brit. Library) inv. 2652 B: **P. Lond. lit. 73**, with plate IV B. See also ROBERTS, *Greek Lit. Hands*, pl. 3 *a*; PACK, *Greek and Latin Literary Texts*, 2nd ed. (1965) no. 397.

This fragment was acquired in 1925 together with a large number of Zenon papyri and may reasonably be considered as being a part of this archive. The text is written along the fibres in an uncial hand of early type, without lectional signs.

Contents The text, which preserves portions of two columns, contains Euripides, Hippolytus, lines 1165-1179 and 1194-1204. The text has been collated with the editions of Barrett and Murray.

The papyrus offers two readings that differ from the testimony, in each case unanimous, of the other MSS.: ὑπῆγε (1194) against ἐπῆγε (which gives a better sense), and ἁμαρτῆι (1195) against ὁμαρτῆι.

In cases where the later MSS. disagree, the papyrus is not consistantly allied with any group of MSS.: αἰσχύναντά με (1172) and χῶρον (1198) seem to be preferable readings, while ἀναστρέφοι (1176), πώλους (1195), and perhaps δέ (1203) are to be rejected.

The ῥ]οπτον of 1172 is plainly a mistake for ῥ]όπτρον, which the papyrus shares with two MSS., perhaps by coincidence.

Col. I

- -
[ὅτου κατήισχυν’ ἄλοχο]ν̣ ὡς πατρὸς βίᾳ̣[ι]; Θη.
[οἰκεῖος αὐτὸν ὤλεσ’ ἁ]ρμάτων ὄχος Αγ.
[ἀραί τε τοῦ σοῦ στόμ]α̣τος, ἃς σὺ σῶι πατρὶ
[πόντου κρέοντι π]αιδὸς ἠράσω πέρι.
[ὦ θεοί, Πόσειδόν θ’]· ὡ̣ς ἄρ’ ἦσθα ἐμὸς πατὴρ Θη.
[ὀρθῶς, ἀκούσας τῶ]ν ἐμῶν κατευγμάτων.
[πῶς καὶ διώλετ’; ε]ἰπέ, τῶι τρόπωι̣ δ̣[ίκη]ς̣
[ἔπαισεν αὐτὸν ῥ]όπτ<ρ>ον αἰσχύναντά [με];
[ἡμεῖς μὲν ἀκτῆ]ς̣ κυμοδέγμονος πέλας̣ Αγ.
[ψήκτραισιν ἵππ]ων ἐκτενίζομεν τρίχας
[κλαίοντες· ἦλθε γ]άρ τις ἄγγελος λέγων̣
[ὡς οὐκέτ’ ἐν γῆι] τῆιδ’ ἀνασ̣τρέφοι πόδ̣α̣
[Ἱππόλυτος, ἐκ σο]ῦ τλήμονας φυγὰς ἔχ[ων].
[ὁ δ’ ἦλθε ταὐτὸν] δακρύων ἔχων μέ[λος]
[ἡμῖν ἐπ’ ἀκτάς, μυ]ρία [δ’ ὀπισθόπους]
- -

1169 ἦσθα ἐμός Pap., ἦσθ’ ἐμός B(arrett) and M(urray). 1172 ῥ]όπτον Pap., the same error in Parisinus Gr. 2713 and Laurentianus 31.10; αἰσχύναντά [με] Pap., -αντά με B, -αντ’ ἐμέ M. 1176 ἀνασ̣τρέφοι Pap., -στρέψοι B and M

Col. II

κἀν τῶιδ' ὑπῆγ[ε κέντρον ἐς χεῖρας λαβὼν]
πώλους ἁμαρτῆι· π[ρόσπολοι δ' ὑφ' ἅρματος]
πέλας χαλινῶν εἱπ[όμεσθα δεσπότηι]
τὴν εὐθὺς Ἄργους κἀ[πιδαυρίας ὁδόν].
ἐπεὶ δ' ἔρημον χῶρο[ν εἰσεβάλλομεν],
ἀκτή τις ἔστι τοὐπ[έκεινα τῆσδε γῆς]
πρὸς πόντον [ἤδη κειμένη Σαρωνικόν].
ἔνθ[ε]ν τις ἠχὼ [χθόνιος, ὡς βροντὴ Διός],
[β]ạρὺν βρόμ[ον μεθῆκε, φρικώδη κλύειν]·
[ὀρθὸ]ν̣ δὲ κρᾶ[τ' ἔστησαν οὖς τ' ἐς οὐρανὸν]
[ἵπποι, π]ạρ' ἡ[μῖν δ' ἦν φόβος νεανικὸς]

1194 ὑπῆγ[ε Pap., ἐπῆγε B and M. 1195 πώλους Pap., πώλοις B and M; ἁμαρτῆι Pap. and B, ὁμαρτῇ M. 1198 χῶρο[ν Pap., χῶρον B and M, var. χῶραν and χώραν 1203 δέ Pap. and M, τε B

S.

16

MYTH CONCERNING A GOD (?)

H. × W. = 11.2 × 9.1 cm. Mid third cent. B.C.

Heid. inv. 1891 recto: the text was published by GERHARD as **P. Baden 6 176** recto (with plate I) in 1938 and, thoroughly revised, by SIEGMANN as P. Heid. 2 10 in 1956. See further PACK, *Greek and Latin Literary Texts*, 2nd ed. (1965) no. 2460, and R. SEIDER, *Paläographie der Griechischen Papyri* II, 2 (1970), plate IV, no. 8. The text contains two incomplete columns: the beginnings of the lines are missing in Col. I and the ends of those in Col. II. Above there is a margin of about 1.2 cm. On the verso are a few lines of a legal document (see no. **73**).

The papyrus is apparently recorded at Heidelberg as belonging among the papyri acquired from the Zenon archive, but neither the text on the recto nor the text on the verso (see no. **73**, intr.), contains any indication to confirm this provenance. As a matter of fact it is not even possible to be certain that the other Heidelberg documents published in this volume really belong to the Zenon archive: nos. **17** (inv. 1832), **18** (inv. 1834), **19** (inv. 1880) and **33** (inv. 1881). Prof. Seider has kindly sent us photographs of the other documents from this group which are still unpublished but they leave the question undecided: inv. nos. 423 (probably later than Zenon), 1758 (uncertain), 1786 (letter to Apollonios) and 1796 (letter from Euklês to Hêragoras).

The provenance of the papyrus edited here is of course of importance for establishing the date when the literary text was written. Siegmann (P. Heid. 2 10) suggested *c.* 280 B.C.—which is a surprisingly early date for a Greek text from Egypt—probably on account of the fact that the verso of the papyrus was used later for a legal document by someone who was supposed to be Zenon. Although there is no proof that the date 280 B.C. is too early, we prefer a date in the mid third century.

Contents The text begins with a number of epic hexameters, in which evidently metamorphoses of a god are described. Towards the end of Col. I a transition to prose seems to be made, which probably is continued in Col. II. Siegmann's reconstruction of line 11 of Col. I, which seems quite satisfactory, shows that the lines of the first, and probably also of the second, column originally contained about 23-24 letters. We print here Siegmann's version of the text, although we are not convinced by his reading of some letters, especially the dotted ones, but since these readings raise problems beyond the scope of the present reedition, and since Prof. Seider has sent us an excellent photograph of the text, we prefer to reproduce it here (see plate XIV) so that the reader may judge for himself. At any rate, in Col. I line 12 Gerhard's reading εἰς is certainly correct and not the reading ὄ̣ις, and the former is printed here.

[plate **XIV**]:

Col. I

[ ] τοῖς ἔπεσιν:
[ ]ονα καλὰ δι
[ ]α̣ τέρ⟦α⟧`ε΄μνα: ε̣ἶδος
[ ]ς τοτὲ̣ μὲν κυα̣-
[ ]ος: φωνὴν καὶ μορ-
[φὴν]ς τοτὲ δ' οἰοπόκοιο:
[ ]ερω τοτὲ̣ δ' εἴκελο̣ς
[:δ]ε̣σπο̣ίνη` λευκοι-
[ ] ἄλλοτε ταύρωι <:>
[μ]εγάλω̣ι τε κορυσ-
[σομένωι κερ]ά̣εσσιν : ἄλλοτε
[ ] ἐφαίνετο εἰς
[ ]: ἀλλοι.υ̣θ' ἱε̣ρῶν
[ ] θ̣ε Ζεὺς κ̣α̣ὶ 'Α.[ ]
[ ] τομμ[.].[ ]
[ ]σ̣ασ̣[ ]
- -

Col. II

σὺν [α]ὐτῶι κ[ ]
Ζ̣εὺ̣[ς] τὸν [ ]
τὴμ Φερσεφ[όνην]
σ̣θαι καὶ τω̣ι̣[ ]
σαιτο ἐξ ἀλλ̣[ ]
θεῶν ἡ δεσ̣[ ]
.ην γιγνω[σκ]
παρὰ τὸν ω[ ]
δι..[..]λε̣[ρά]-
⟦α⟧`β΄δο̣ν[ ]
κατα[ ]
ῥάβδ[ ]
θ̣εισα.[ ]
ῥάβδ̣[ ]
- -

S.

17

PETITION TO THE KING

H. × W. = 7.1 × 10.4 cm. Date unknown

Heid. inv. 1832: R. SEIDER, *Beiträge zur Ptolemäischen Verwaltungsgeschichte. Der Nomarches. Der Dioiketes Apollonios* (Quellen und Studien zur Geschichte und Kultur des Altertums und des Mittelalters, Reihe D, Heft 8, 1938), pp. 74-5; **SB 8 9796**; R. SEIDER, *Paläographie der Griechischen Papyri* I, no. 6, p. 39, with plate 4 (only *ll.* 1-8).

The text is written across the fibres. There is a margin at the top (0.8 cm.) and at the bottom (0.3 cm.), but we possess only the central portion of the text, which is broken on the left and on the right. The last two lines are written in a different hand, no doubt by one of the clerks in the office of the strategos.

Contents As can easily be seen from *ll.* 6-8, the text is a petition addressed to the king by an unknown person, and directed against two Egyptians, Horos and Harmiusis. A previous petition made by Zenon seems to be mentioned. The object of both petitions is largely unknown, because of the damaged state of the papyrus. It is impossible to decide whether or not this document comes from the Zenon archive (see no. **16** above, intr.); the mention of "Zenon" in lines 1 and 5 is quite inconclusive.

[plate XIV]:

[Βασιλεῖ Πτολεμαίωι χαίρειν X. Ἐπιδε]δωκότος ἔντευξιν Ζήνων[ος ---]
[κ]ατὰ Ὥρου καὶ Ἁρμιύσιος τῶν α[---]
[ ]ατο αὐτοὺς καὶ καταστάν[των αὐτῶν ἐπὶ ---]
[ ]ṭας ἡμῖν δοῦναι Ἁρθωύτην μ̣[---]
[ ]ῳσιν ἐπιδοῦναι Ζήνωνι καθ' οὗ [---]
[Δέομ]α̣ι οὖν σου, βασι[λ]εῦ, εἴ σοι δοκεῖ π̣[ροστάξαι]
[τῶι ἐπιστά]τηι καπαρ̣υχι δ̣ιακοῦσαι ἡμῶ[ν. Τούτου δὲ]
[γενομένου, τύχωμεν διὰ σέ, βασιλεῦ, τ]ὸμ πάντων σωτ̣ῆρα τοῦ δικα[ίου.]
[Εὐτύχει.]

Second hand:

[ ]ς πρὸς ⟦του⟧ Παχοῖριν καὶ ἑλόμενοι κ.[---]
[ ]μας ⟦ọτε Ὧρος καὶ Ἁρμιῦσις⟧ *vacat*

1 [Βασιλεῖ Πτολεμαίωι χαίρειν supplevimus; Ζήνων[ι Seider, Ζήνων[ος supplevimus 2 τῶν ἀ[ρχιφυλακιτῶν Seider 3 καταστασ.[Seider, καταστάν[των legimus 4 Ἁρθωίτην κ̣[αὶ Παάγχιν Seider (cf. 7), Ἁρθωύτην μ[legimus 5]ẹσιν Seider,]ῳσιν legimus 7 Ἁρθωί]τηι καὶ Παάγκι Seider, τῶι ἐπιστά]τηι καπαρ̣υχι legimus et rest. 7-8 ἡμῷ[ν ἵνα τύχωμεν διά] | [σε, βασιλεῦ, τ]όμ Seider, ἡμῶ[ν. Τούτου δὲ] | [γενομένου, τύχωμεν διὰ σέ, βασιλεῦ, τ]όμ supplevimus 10]πρὸς τὸν Πεχοῖριν Seider,]ς πρὸς ⟦τον⟧ Παχοῖριν legimus; κο[Seider, κ.[legimus 11]μαν ἄλεστρον (?) καὶ ... αγομεν. Seider,]μας ⟦ọτε Ὧρος καὶ Ἁρμιῦσις⟧ legimus

Notes

1 The text is no doubt a petition to the king, and therefore the introductory formula Βασιλεῖ Πτολεμαίωι χαίρειν ὁ δεῖνα can confidently be restored: cf. ANNA DI BITONTO, *Le Petizioni al re, Aegyptus* 47 (1967), p. 11. For the first sentence of the petition proper one has a choice between [Ἐμοῦ ἐπιδε]δωκότος ἔντευξιν Ζήνων[ι] and [Ἐπιδε]δωκότος ἔντευξιν Ζήνων[ος], and the latter seems preferable in view of *l.* 4: cf. *ibidem*, pp. 50-5.

The greeting formula, which is never lacking from petitions to the king, proves that Seider's supplement in *ll.* 7-8 was too short. As a matter of fact the length of the lacuna can be established by a different method. In his introduction to the Enteuxis papyri, P. Ent. pp. xix-xxii, O. GUÉRAUD has shown that the enteuxeis to the king were always written across the fibres on the recto of a first quality papyrus roll measuring from 31 to 33 cm. in height. This is no doubt also the case with the present petition, and it can safely be assumed that about two thirds of the text are lost. It is not difficult to find a suitable restoration for *ll.* 7-8 on this basis, since there is considerable variety in the final formulae of enteuxeis.

2 Ὥρου καὶ Ἁρμιύσιος τῶν α[---]: I do not think the supplement ἀ[ρχιφυλακιτῶν] is correct. Ἁρμιῦσις is not a rare name, and Ὧρος is extremely common, therefore the identifications proposed by SEIDER, *Beiträge*, pp. 74-5 are far from compelling. Moreover, Horos is attested as φυλακίτης as late as 241/40 (year 7 of Euergetes—one of the latest dated documents in the archive) and so the supplement ἀ[ρχιφυλακιτῶν] would necessitate us to assume that our text was written after 241/40, *and* that Horus had in the meantime been promoted to archiphulakites, *and* that at that moment there were two archiphulakitai in Philadelphia. If anything, I would suggest restoring τῶν ἀ[πό + place name]. For τῶν ἀπό as a synonym for τῶν ἐκ (which is more common in the Ptolemaic period) see E. MAYSER, *Grammatik* II, 2, p. 377. However, it is perhaps preferable to offer no supplement at all.

3 καταστάν[των αὐτῶν ἐπὶ ---]: both καθιστάναι and καταστῆναι often mean "to bring to court" and "to appear in court" (*Wörterbuch* I 717). This would well suit the context here: Zenon has brought a petition against Horos and Harmiusis. Consequently they have appeared in court, and now, for some reason, an unknown person brings a new petition against them.

5 A possible restoration is [ὅπως ἀναγκασθ]ῶ̣σιν ἐπιδοῦναι Ζήνωνι. If this is right, the subject matter of the petition is some arrears in payments made to Zenon. The petition would thus fall within the group which ANNA DI BITONTO, *op. cit.*, discusses on pp. 32-9, "Inadempienza ad obbligazioni".

6-7 The supplement [Ἁρθωί]τηι (better [Ἁρθωύ]τηι) at the beginning of *l.* 7 is surely wrong. Scores of parallel passages in the Enteuxeis papyri prove abundantly that we can expect [Δέομ]αι οὖν σου --- π̣[ροστάξαι τῶι δεῖνι τῶι στρατηγῶι γράψαι τῶι δεῖνι τῶι ἐπιστά]τηι, but this is too long for the lacuna. This and the unexplained letters καπαο̣υχι have prevented us from giving a supplement for this passage.

10-11 These lines, written in a second hand, are clearly the subscription made in the office of the strategos, although they do not conform to any of the "apostilles" studied by O. GUÉRAUD, P. Ent., introd., pp. I-LIII. In *l.* 12 we can recognize *in rasura* the names of the accused.

C.

18

FRAGMENT OF A PETITION (?)

H. × W. = 5.4 × 8.5 cm. Date unknown

Heid. inv. 1834: R. Seider, *Beiträge zur Ptolemäischen Verwaltungsgeschichte. Der Nomarches. Der Dioiketes Apollonios* (Quellen und Studien zur Geschichte und Kultur des Altertums und des Mittelalters, Reihe D, Heft 8, 1938), p. 75; **SB 8 9797**.

The text on the front is written along the fibres, and, as a join between two *kollemata* can be identified towards the right-hand edge of the fragment, the text is evidently upon the recto surface. The papyrus is damaged on all sides, but the lines of text are complete at the right. The poor condition of the fragment is reminiscent of that of many papyri extracted from cartonnage, and it is not possible to be certain that it really belongs in the Zenon archive (see above no. **16**, intr.).

Contents Seider's hypothesis that the text was concerned with a maternal inheritance (based on the words τὴν μητρικὴν in *l.* 5) was rejected both by C. Préaux, *Chronique d'Égypte* 15 (1940), p. 174, and by U. Wilcken, *Archiv für Papyrusforschung* 14 (1941), p. 157. Too much is lost for us to recover even the general sense of the text, and although the two other Heidelberg texts published here (nos. **17** and **19**) are portions of petitions, it is far from certain that the present text is also a petition. The main point of interest is the new reading in *l.* 3 (see n. *ll.* 3-4).

[plate XIV]:

[ ]. . τ̣οῦ 'Απολλο̣δό̣τ̣ο̣υ̣ . . . .
[ ]. βασιλεικοὶ γρα̣μ̣μ̣α̣τ̣ε̣ῖ̣ς̣ ρα
[ ] 'Απολλοδότου Εἰδουμαῖο̣ς τῆς
[ἐπιγονῆς --- ἐν Κρο]κοδείλων πόλει το. . . . .
[τ]ὴν ὑπάρχουσάν μοι μητρικὴν
[ ]. . α τῆς Ἡρακλείδου μερείδος
[ἀπ]ο̣δημησ̣[αμ]ε̣νου μετὰ κυρίου

3 εισ. . ασαι. . Seider, Εἰδουμαῖος legimus 4 [ἐπιγονῆς] supplevimus; τοῦ̣ 'Α̣ρ̣σ̣ι̣ν̣ο̣ίτου Seider, το. . . . . legimus 5 μητρικόν Seider, μητρικήν legimus 7 [ἀπ]οδημησ̣ά̣[μ]ε̣νον Seider, [ἀπ]ο̣δημησ̣[αμ]ε̣νου legimus

Notes

3-4 Our reading Εἰδουμαῖο̣ς, which fits the surviving traces perfectly, may be regarded as certain. The patronymic Apollodotos is therefore of interest here: as Qōs, the chief god of the Idumaean Pantheon, was identified with Apollo, theophoric names beginning with 'Απολλο- are very common among Idumaeans (see the remarks of F. Zucker, *Abhandl. der preuss. Akad. Wissensch. Philol. - histor. Klasse*, 6 (1937), pp. 15 and 20). The supplement [ἐπιγονῆς] is assured by the "Nomenklaturregel" (see F. Uebel, *Die Kleruchen Ägyptens*, 1968, pp. 11-13), whereby soldiers do not mention their patronymic, whereas the members of the epigone always do. The son of

Apollodotos is one of the earliest Idumaeans known in Egypt, and the qualification τῆς [ἐπιγονῆς] identifies him as the son of a soldier. For Idumaeans in Egypt, see the recent account of U. Rapaport, *Les Iduméens en Égypte, Rev. de Philol.* 43 (1969), pp. 73-82.

Between *ll.* 3 and 4, there is rather a large space, but this is not sufficiently wide for another line of text.

4 It is very tempting to adopt Seider's reading τοῦ̣ 'Ạρσ̣ι̣ν̣ο̣ίτου which might plausibly follow [ἐν Κρο]κοδείλων πόλει, but this does not seem to fit the surviving traces.

6 A place-name is to be expected before τῆς Ἡρακλείδου μερίδος: [εἰς Φαρβ]α̣ῖ̣θ̣α̣ is a possible but very doubtful supplement.

C.

19

PETITION TO THE KING

H. × W. = 22.5 × 26.5 cm. Date unknown

Heid. inv. 1880: R. SEIDER, *Beiträge zur Ptolemäischen Verwaltungsgeschichte. Der Nomarches. Der Dioiketes Apollonios* (Quellen und Studien zur Geschichte und Kultur des Altertums und des Mittelalters, Reihe D, Heft 8, 1938), pp. 76-7; **SB 8 9798**.

Professor R. Seider has kindly informed us, in a letter of 14 May 1976, that this papyrus is now lost. We are therefore dependant upon his edition (see bibliography) for the text and for the physical description. The papyrus survived in a very fragmentary state, being badly damaged at its numerous folds. These are explained in detail in Seider's introduction. The top margin measures 2.5 cm., the left-hand margin 2.8 cm., and the bottom margin about 3.5 cm. Up to 0.9 cm. of the right-hand margin survives on the small fragment that preserves part of *ll.* 3 and 4. According to Seider, *l.* 16 is written upon a piece of papyrus glued on, which is about 4 cm. high. Εὐτύχει stands half on the upper and half on the added sheet.[1] It is not clear whether, as seems likely, this represents a normal join between two *kollemata* of a manufactured roll, or there is some reason to suppose that the sheet had been enlarged *ad hoc*. Seider does not state the direction of the fibres, but the writing may be expected to be across the fibres.

Contents This document is certainly a petition addressed to the king. The regular and characteristic formula of an ἔντευξις, "Δέομαι οὖν σου, βασιλεῦ", is preserved in *l.* 12. The name of the sender—certainly a single sender—is lost, but from Seider's reading in *l.* 15 (possibly supported by βουλομένη[in *l.* 10) this must be a woman. From what is preserved, little of the substance of the petition can be made out. Seider suggested that the woman might have been conceded a piece of rented land by a certain Teos, and that a certain Menes had given security for the sum to be paid to the woman. Herakleides had not carried out his obligations, and so should be summoned to court. The only point that is certain here, is that some kind of security is involved. A number of Seider's useful and constructive supplements have here been relegated to the apparatus as less than certain. The papyrus is apparently recorded at Heidelberg as belonging among the papyri acquired from the Zenon archive, and Seider published it with three other texts that he thought belonged to the archive, including another document (SB 8 9800), apparently quite unrelated. There is little in the present document itself to connect it with the archive (see above no. **16**, intr.), although the mention of Philadelphia (*l.* 10) tends to confirm the provenance. The two names that can fairly certainly be read, Teos and Herakleides, are common enough both within and outside the Zenon archive, and there are no precise grounds for proposing any particular identification of them. The text has been duly noted without further discussion by C. PRÉAUX, *Chronique d'Égypte* 15 (1940), p. 174; U. WILCKEN, *Archiv für Papyrusforschung* 14 (1941), p. 157; and listed by M. T. CARASSINI, *Aegyptus* 35 (1955), p. 305, no. 160.

[1] "Außerdem ist Zeile 16 auf ein angeklebtes Papyrusstück geschrieben, das ca. 4 cm. hoch ist. Εὐτύχει steht zur Hälfte auf dem oberen und zur Hälfte auf dem angesetzten Papyrusblatt".

Βασιλεῖ Π[τολεμαίωι χαίρειν c. 50]
μοι Τεῶ[c. 70]
σε τὸν σω[c. 65]λον
μαχίμῳ[ι c. 65]δης
ἀπολαβεῖ[ν c. 65]
῾Ηρακλειδη[c. 40]αληθη προ[c. 15]
-νος προστο[c. 40]. . σθαι με[.]εο̣[c. 15]
ὁ απ̣[c. 55]κ[c. 16]
ἐνοχλησ[c. 70]
ὁ ἐμ Φιλαδελ[φείαι c. 25] βουλομένη [c. 25 α]
-ναγκασθεισ[c. 30]έδωκεν τε. [c. 25]
-γύημαί τε μ[c. 30]. Δέομαι οὖν σου, β[ασιλεῦ, c. 15]
-λέσασθαι ἐπὶ [c. 25]ιδην κἂν ηιδ̣[c. 30]
της διεγγ[υ c. 30]. . . γω[c. 30]
ἀνωμολογειτ[c. 25 ἐπὶ] σ̣έ, βα[σιλ]εῦ, κ̣α̣τ̣α̣φυ̣γ[ο]ῦ̣[σα, c. 15]
τύχω τοῦ δικ[αίου.] Εὐτύχει. [*vac.*]

Textum et rest., quantum supra proferuntur, omnes e S(eideri) op. cit. deprompsimus 1-2 [ἐπιχωρήσαντός] | μοι Τεῶ[τος] Bilabel apud S. 2-3 [ἐπὶ] | σὲ τὸν σω[τῆρα καταφεύγω] S. 6 ῾Ηρακλείδη[ι] S.; [ἐὰν ἦι ἃ γράφω] ἀληθῆ, προ[στάξαι] S. 7 Με[ν]έο̣[υς] S. 8 ὁ ᾿Απ̣[ολλωνίου] S.; [῾Ηρα]κ[λείδην] S. 9 ἐνοχλῆσ[αι] S. 10-11 [ἐπα]-|ναγκασθείς S. 11-12 [διηγ]-|γύημαί τε Μ[ενεῖ] S.: δι- e *l.* 14 haud improbabile est 12-13 Δέομαι οὖν σου β[ασιλεῦ, εἴ σοι δοκεῖ, ἀνακα]-|λέσασθαι ἐπὶ [τὸ καθῆκον δικαστήριον ῾Ηρακλε]ίδην κἂν ἦι δ̣[ύνατον] S. 14 τῆς διεγγ[υήσεως] S.;], . . . γω[S., fort. ob spatium quidquam? 15 ἀνωμολογεῖτ[αι] sic S. (ἀνωμολόγειτ[αι], *l.* -ηται; vel ἀνωμολογεῖτ[ο]?); [ἵνα ἐπὶ] σ̣έ, βα[σιλ]εῦ, κ̣α̣τ̣α̣φυ̣γ[ο]ῦ̣[σα, τὸν πάντων σωτῆρα]| S. 16 quantum papyri supersit incertum est

Notes

The mere existence of plausible restorations other than those offered by Seider is not spelled out in these notes, nor are all his suggestions discussed.

1 Despite Seider's n. *l.* 1, there seems to us adequate room to restore the common, but not obligatory, formula ἀδικοῦμαι ὑπό in *l.* 1. For examples of ἐντεύξεις in which both the sender and the party complained against are given only a single name in the opening formulae, see P. Ent. 35 and 64. The tendency, which does not constitute a rule, for ἐντεύξεις complaining of officials' (rather than private individuals') conduct to avoid the ἀδικοῦμαι formula, is mentioned at P. Ent., pp. xxiii-xxiv.

2-3 If something like Seider's restoration is correct, it is surprising for this kind of phrase to occur so early in the petition.

6 ἐάν, etc. (Seider): it would be especially surprising for this phrase in quite this form to occur so early in the petition.

7 Seider here read the proper name Μενῆς (also in *l.* 12 below), which occurs occasionally in the archive (see *Prosopography*, P. L. Bat. 21. IX, Μενῆς: cf. also the name Μενῆις), in the strictly incorrect but possible genitive form Μενέους (the form does not happen to be attested in the archive). This restoration is possible, but not compelling. Even without questioning Seider's readings, it is not in fact necessary to restore *any* proper name here (for example, read μέν, μεθ' ἑορτ.).

8 Presumably Seider's restorations here, as in several other places, are to be taken merely as hints as to the possible trend of the text.

11-12 Apart from trivial doubts as to whether or not this is a compound, and as to the precise orthography, the question remains whether it is to be understood in a Middle or Passive sense: either "I have accepted as surety", or "security has been put up for me".

12 Μ[ενεῖ]: see n. *l.* 7.

12-13 Seider's ἀνακαλέσασθαι + a phrase meaning "into court" is very probable. T.

20

ADVANCE OF RENT IN THE FORM OF A LOAN OF MONEY

H. × W. = 12.5 × 9 cm.[a]; 14.2 × 4.6 cm.[b] 1 May, 252 B.C.

Cairo JdE 48707[a+b]: **P. Cairo Zen. 2 59.257**[a]; P. Cairo Zen. 3, p. 290, republication of only the front, with the addition of fragment (b) at the right-hand side; H.-A. RUPPRECHT, *Untersuchungen zum Darlehen*, 1967, p. 25, n. 7.

The text on the front is written along the fibres, presumably on the recto surface. The docket on the back is written across the fibres. Edgar (P. Cairo Zen. 2 59.257, n. *l.* 1) plausibly suggested that the document may have been written in duplicate: compare the duplicate form of P. Col. Zen. 1 49.

Contents This text is related to a number of Zenon and other papyri of various kinds, but has no precise parallel (the closest is P. Col. Zen. 1 49). The document is explicitly a loan, in the form ὁμολόγει N. ἔχειν δάνειον, "N. acknowledges that he has received a loan". No interest charge is mentioned. Instead of any stipulations as to the return of the money, it is stated that the lender is to deduct the amount of the loan from the rent in grain for the following year that is due from him to the borrower. The document is thus in effect a receipt for an advance of rent:—Zenon has advanced four drachmas to Asklepiades, a cleruch from whom he is renting land. No penalty or praxis clause is included, and plainly in the circumstances none is necessary. Neither the type of grain, nor the rate of exchange between grain and money is stated; instead it is laid down that the price is to be the current price (presumably after the next harvest) at the threshing-floor of Moithumis, which clearly is specified because it is the local threshing-floor serving the plot of land in question.

front [plate XVII]:

L δλ Φαμενῶφι θ. [Ὁμολο]γεῖ Ἀσκληπιάδης
Λύκιος τῶν Νικάνορος κλ[ηροῦχος] ἀρου(ρῶν) ο ἔχειν
δάνειον παρὰ Ζήνωνος τ[οῦ Ἀγρε]οφῶντος Καυ-
νίου τῶν περὶ Ἀπολλώνι[ον τὸν δι]οικητὴν ἀργυρίου δραχμὰς τέσσαρας. Ε[ἰς δὲ τοῦ]το ὑπολογη-
σάτω αὐτῶι Ζήνων εἰς τὰ γ[ινόμεν]α ἐχφόρια
τοῦ λε L σῖτον ὡς ἄ[ν ἐπὶ τ]ῆς ἅλω πωλῆ-
ται ἐμ Μοιθύμει τοῦ Με[μφίτου.] vacat
Ἔγραψεν τὸ σύμβολον Αρ[......]ης διδάσκαλος
Ἀσκληπιάδου συντά[ξαν]τος.

back [plate XVI]:

11 Ἀσκληπιάδης ὧν ἔχει εἰς τὸ ἐκ[φό]-
ριον τοῦ λε L ⊢δ, ἀνθ' ὧν ὑπολο[γη]-
θήσεται σῖτος.

1 L δλ τοῦ Φαῶφι θ ed. princ., L δλ Φαμενῶφι θ Muszynski

Translation

Year 34, Phamenophi (i.e. Phamenoth) 9.

Asklepiades the Lycian, one of Nikanor's men, a cleruch of 70 arouras, acknowledges the receipt of a loan of four silver drachmas from Zenon son of Agreophon, the Caunian, on the staff of Apollonios the dioiketes. In respect of this, Zenon is to deduct for him in respect of the rent due for the 35th year corn at whatever price it may be being sold at the threshing-floor in Moithumis in the Memphite nome.

Ar.......es the teacher wrote this document on Asklepiades' instructions.

Docket:

Asklepiades, concerning his receiving 4 drachmas towards the rent of year 35, for which corn will be deducted.

Notes

1 L δλ: for the other examples in the archive of inverted digits in ordinal year numbers, see the *Chronological Survey*, P. L. Bat. 21. VII *a*, under the years 28, 31, 33-6, and 38.

— Φαμενῶφι (cf. P. Cairo Zen. 2 59.265 with Wilcken's note, *Archiv für Papyrusforschung* 8, 1927, p. 283) is plainly to be understood as Φαμενώθ.

— Asklepiades: see *Pros. Ptol.* 2 3846; 4 8837; F. Uebel, *Die Kleruchen Ägyptens*, 1968, p. 35, no. 8; cf. *Prosopography*, P. L. Bat. 21. IX, Ἀσκληπιάδης (no. 5). This cleruch may be the same man as the Asklepiades who is the author of the letter P. Cairo Zen. 3 59.407, but there is little there to connect them beyond the mention of Moithumis (*l.* 4).

3-5 The document is expressed as a loan, δάνειον, without any mention of interest. This one document cannot decide the question whether the loan was made without interest, or the sum stated already included the interest to be paid (see H. Kühnert, *Zum Kreditgeschaft*, 1965, p. 42; H.-A. Rupprecht, *Untersuchungen zum Darlehen*, 1967, pp. 81-4; and P. W. Pestman, *Loans bearing no interest?*, *The Journal of Juristic Papyrology*, 16-17 (1971), pp. 14-15). The three accounts in the Zenon archive that illustrate the regular practice of making advances of rent to cleruchs, P. Cairo Zen. 3 59.325-6 and P. Cairo Zen. 4 59.724, give no hint of the calculation of interest, but this is in no way conclusive. The sum of 4 drachmas is low for a loan (see Kühnert, *op. cit.*, pp. 183-4), but is not exceptional in the light of the accounts just cited, and is comparable to the value of the 4½ artabas of wheat advanced as rent in P. Col. Zen. 1 49.

6-7 We should expect rent for agricultural land to be payable each year out of the produce of the same year once it had been harvested (see for example the supplementary agreement to share crops after the harvest in P. Col. Zen. 2 85) and that any question of an advance of rent would naturally arise in the preceding 12 months, and not sooner. In the present text, "year 34, Phamenophi (i.e. Phamenoth) 9" by the Financial year would be 1st May 252, and by the Egyptian and Macedonian year would be 1st May 251 B.C. For us, "the rent due for the 35th year" is ambiguous. By the Egyptian regnal year, the rent would be due in, roughly speaking, the summer of 250 B.C.; by the Financial year, in the summer of 251 B.C.

P. Col. Zen. 1 54, a document of 250 B.C., quotes in Col. I a contract, dated year 30, Epeiph 10, for the cultivation of land, which specifies that the rent is to be paid in the month Daisios of year 31. Daisios of year 31 can only be July-August 255 B.C. Epeiph 10 of year 30 could be (by the Egyptian regnal year) 31st August 255 B.C., or (by the Financial year) 31st August 256 B.C. The former date is impossible in the context, and therefore the Financial year must be being used. P. Cairo Zen. 2 59.258 is a receipt dated to year 34, Phaophi 18, for all the rent of cleruchic land "for the 34th year". Phaophi 18 of year 34 can only be 11th December 252 B.C. As the document is plainly not an advance of rent, "the 34th year" can only be the Financial year, ending in March 251 B.C., and including the harvest of the summer of 252 B.C.

Thus it is safe to assume that the phrase "the rent due for the 35th year" in the present papyrus must refer to the Financial year, and that the rent was due within a twelve-month, as we should expect. The same conclusion will apply to P. Col. Zen. 1 49, a receipt for an advance of rent in kind for cleruchic land, dated to 11th December 252 (year 34, Phaophi 18), which similarly refers to "the rent due for the 35th year".

9 Ἀρ[......]ης: *Pros. Ptol.* 6 17163; *Prosopography*, P. L. Bat. 21. IX. We cannot be sure whether a Greek or Egyptian name should be restored here, nor precisely what is meant by the term διδάσκαλος: it is presumably used here as a professional "title", but this is not certain. The other occurrences of διδάσκαλος in the archive all clearly belong in the context of Greek education. In P. Cairo Zen. 1 59.098, 4, and P. Lond. 7 2017, 3 and 11, the word is not used as a title, but rather to express a relationship. In P. Mich. Zen. 77, 5-6 the context is Greek. The letter is written with heavy-handed humour, and is, perhaps, a patchwork of quotations: it is a serious possibility that Philon is not in fact to be understood literally as a professional διδάσκαλος. Cf. *Pros. Ptol.* 6 pp. 286 ff.

9-10 Compare PSI 4 394, 7-10 (year 6): Ἔγραψεν Ἀπολλόδωρος Ἀνδραγάθου Μακεδὼν συντάξαντος Ἰάσονος.

T.

21

DEPOSITION OF A WITNESS

H. × W. = 7 × 35.5 cm. 20 November, 246 B.C.

Brit. Mus. (now Brit. Library) inv. 3083: This papyrus was part of the Michaelides private collection, previously in Cairo. First published by EDGAR in *Annales du Service des Antiquités* 20 (1920) pp. 183-184 (P. Edgar 56) from where it was reproduced in **SB 3 6762** (cf. BL 6 p. 134); republished by A. S. HUNT and C. C. EDGAR in *Select Papyri* II, pp. 185-187 (no. 253).[1]

The fact that the width of the papyrus corresponds rather well to the usual height of a papyrus roll and that, moreover, there is no κόλλημα visible on the photograph induces us to see in the front side a small strip of papyrus cut from the recto of the papyrus roll. After being cut away, the papyrus strip was then turned over 90° and inscribed across the fibres. Once inscribed, the papyrus was folded first inwards along an axis running between the fourth and the fifth line of writing, then further on as indicated in the sketch below. The back, whose top corresponds to the bottom of the front side, is inscribed to the left along the fibres. The front side has numerous ink smudgings, especially in the upper and lower margins.

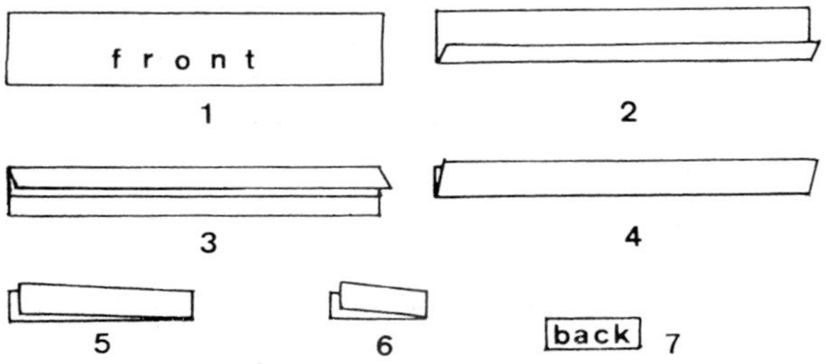

Contents The present papyrus contains the deposition of a witness called Euphronios, witnessing in favour of a certain Antipatros. This document has a companion piece in P. Cairo Zen. 3 59.347, relating to the same affair and dated one month later.[2] Although the latter text is fragmentary, the wording in both cases seems to be more or less the same. This is a clear indication that the persons who drew up such legal instruments had a fair knowledge of the requirements imposed by law on witness depositions.

The act of summoning witnesses to give evidence to be duly submitted to the legal authorities is a procedure to which people had normally recourse in their litigations. These depositions, called μαρτυρία, had to comply with certain requirements mainly

[1] The present edition is based on a collation made on photographs in my possession and reproduced here.

[2] We know of four witness depositions dating from the third century B.C.: P. Cairo Zen. 3 59.347, P. Hamb. 1 105, P. Gurob ined. (cf. W. CLARYSSE in *Ancient Society* 4, 1973, p. 134 bottom) and the present papyrus.

stipulated, as far as Alexandrian law is concerned, in the *Dikaiomata* [3] under the heading εἰς μαρτυρίαν κλῆσις. The summoning, made in the presence of two witnesses, was performed by the party. The witness was called upon to give detailed information or evidence of what he had seen or heard in person that might be of interest to the party summoning him. The latter then had to write down the evidence, to the truth of which the witness later made an oath—ἐπὶ τῆι ἀρχῆι καὶ ἐπὶ τῶι δικαστηρίωι (*l.* 226). The party who had taken the proof could then introduce the deposition in court.[4] It appears thus that the Alexandrian law was very explicit in pointing out the role of the witness and the way in which the evidence thus obtained could be presented to the court.

Outside Alexandria however, witnesses were called upon in a different way: "Quite different rules prevailed in the χώρα. The summons was official. The examination of the witness took place before the *strategos* or the *epistates* and not before the court, to which only the record of the testimony was presented. Such records, commencing with the word μαρτυρεῖ, name in the dative the person in whose favour the deposition had been made, then in the nominative the name of the witness, his patronymicon, age, description; then follows an account of the facts which the witness has seen. In contrast with the Alexandrian rules, such a μαρτυρία was never confirmed by oath." [5]

front [plate XV]:

Μαρτυρεῖ Ἀντιπάτρωι Εὐφρόνιος Ἀπολλωνίδου Ἀμμωνιεὺς `ὡς (ἐτῶν) λε εὐμεγέθης εὔρωστος κλαστὸς μελί̣χ̣ρους τετανὸς οὐλὴ ὀφρύων δ̣ε̣ξ̣ιᾶι΄. Οἰκῶ ἐμ Φιλαδελφείαι τοῦ Ἀρσινοΐτου.

Τοῦ δὲ β (ἔτους) μηνὸς Πανήμου, ὄντος μου καὶ Νίκωνος καὶ ἄλλων τινῶν ἐν τῶι Εὐδόξου κουρείωι, παραγενόμενος

Ἀντίπατρος καὶ Σῖμον, οἷς μαρτυρῶ, εἰς τὸ κουρεῖον τοῦτο ἠξίουν Νίκωνα ἀποδοῦναι αὐτοῖς τὸν υἱὸν αὐτῶν Θεο-

δόσιον. Νίκων δὲ ὁ κρινόμενος πρὸς Ἀντίπατρον οὐκ ἔφατο εἰληφέναι τὸ παιδάριον παρ' αὐτῶν οὐδὲ ἔχειν αὐτὸ

παρευρέσει οὐδεμιᾶι.

back [plate XV]:

6 Εὐφρονίου.

(Ἔτους) β Γορπιείου κϛ. Φέρει

Ἀντιπάτρωι πρὸς ἀντίδ̣ικον

Νίκωνα.

1 τετανὸς --- δ̣ε̣ξ̣ιᾶι legi, ὀρ̣θ̣όγωνος --- δ̣ε̣ξ̣ιᾶι Edgar, ASAE ("I have marked the reading as doubtful but have not had an opportunity of revising it on the original"), om. SB (vide BL 6 p. 134), ὀρθογώνιος (?) --- δεξιᾶι Hunt-Edgar, Sel. Papyri 7 φέρει, sc. μαρτυρίαν

---

[3] P. Hal. I, *ll.* 223-233.

[4] Cf. R. TAUBENSCHLAG, *The Law of Greco-Roman Egypt*, p. 515.

[5] R. TAUBENSCHLAG, *o.c.*, pp. 515-516.

Translation

Gives evidence, in favour of Antipatros, Euphronios, son of Apollonides, from the Ammonieian deme, whose age is about 35 years, of good size, stout, curly haired, honey coloured, upright, having a scar on the right eyebrow.

"I live in Philadelphia of the Arsinoite nome. In the second year, month of Panemos, whilst I and Nikon and some other men were in Eudoxos' barber's shop, Antipatros and Simon, in whose favour I am giving this testimony, dropped by to this barber's shop and requested Nikon to give back to them their son Theodosios. Nikon however, who has been brought to trial by Antipatros, denied having taken the boy from them and holding him under any pretence."

Back, to the right:

(Evidence given) by Euphronios.

Back, to the left (*docket*):

Year 2, 26th of Gorpiaios. Bears (witness) in favour of Antipatros against the defendant Nikon.

Notes

1 Ἀμμωνιεύς: Alexandrian demotic.

— τετανός "upright": the epithet τετανός occurs often in connection with the hair,[6] which it then depicts as being straightened, smooth as opposed to κλαστός "curly".[7] In the present case however, τετανός cannot possibly describe Euphronios' hair since the latter has already been said to be κλαστός. The adjective τετανός must therefore pertain to the witness' general appearance, which was "straight", "upright".

Edgar had first read ὀρθόγωνος, later changed it into ὀρθογώνιος without being able to check his transcription with the original again and obviously full of doubt himself as to the correctness of his text. It must be noted that, even if one can pretty well understand how the confusion was possible,[8] the word ὀρθογώνιος,[9] with the probable meaning of "square shouldered", would at least have been redundant, since Euphronios has already been described as hefty and stout.

For the physical description of witnesses, see G. Hübsch, *Die Personalangaben als Identifizierungsvermerke im Recht der gräko-ägyptischen Papyri*, Berlin 1968 (Berliner Juristische Abhdl. 20), p. 73.

2 Πανήμου: in 246 B.C., the month of Πάνημος fell in August-September.

3 Ἀντίπατρος: see p. 108.

— ἀποδοῦναι αὐτοῖς τὸν υἱόν: for the story behind this demand, see pp. 108-109.

— Θεοδόσιον: see p. 108.

5 παρευρέσει οὐδεμιᾶι: see p. 108.

Zaki Aly
Prof. Emeritus Cairo Univ.

[6] C. Gini, *La pigmentazione degli abitanti*, Roma 1932, pp. 28-50.

[7] The full words are respectively τετανόθριξ and κλαστόθριξ, meaning persons "with long straight hair" or "with curly hair".

[8] What is interpreted by me as an ink smudge before τετανός was read as ο, in ligature with ρ - the actual first τ of τετανός. The ε was misread as θ, the second τ as ογ and the α as ω, the latter being in reality less deeper when written in ligature with ν.

[9] *LSJ* registers only ὀρθογώνιον "rectangle" and ὀρθογώνιος "rectangular". For square-faced animals, the Greek has a word τετραγωνοπρόσωπος.

Notes complémentaires [10]

A. *Notes à la traduction*

3 Ἀντίπατρος: le nom d' Ἀντίπατρος, de sa femme Σῖμον et de leur fils Θεοδόσιος sont grecs, mais il convient de noter que:
a) Ἀντίπατρος est un nom dynastique fréquemment porté par les Juifs;
b) Σῖμον (très rare) est proche du nom masculin Σίμων, presque typiquement juif;
c) Θεοδόσιος est un nom théophore relativement rare à cette époque et, ne renvoyant pas à une divinité précise, souvent adopté par des Juifs.
Prises isolément, ces trois remarques n'auraient que peu de poids; mises côte à côte, elles rendent toutefois vraisemblable qu'il s'agissait là d'une famille juive. Cpr. CPJ 1 p. 132 n. 1 in fine.

— Θεοδόσιον: un παιδάριον de ce nom est mentionné dans le P. Cairo Zen. 4 59.569, aux lignes 13 (9 Phaophi = 1er décembre 246) et 117 (1er Choiak = 22 janvier 245). Reekmans, *Sitométrie*, p. 43 n. 19, pense qu'il s'agit du fils d'Antipatros et de Simone, maintenu en détention par Nikôn en garantie de la dette contractée par sa mère (voir ci-dessous). «La *dôrea*», poursuit Reekmans, «semble avoir liquidé cette dette et reçut en échange le droit de disposer des services du garçon». Cette supposition me paraît toutefois erronée, puisque le παιδάριον en question relève de la δωρεᾷ au moins dès le 1er décembre 246 (P. Cairo Zen. 4 59.569 *l.* 13) alors que la déposition du témoin Eudêmos ne fut faite que le 19 décembre suivant (P. Cairo Zen. 3 59.347, voir ci-dessous). Il y a donc deux personnes du nom de Théodosios.

5 παρευρέσει οὐδεμιᾶι: ces deux mots sont probablement empruntés tels quels au vocabulaire des ordonnances royales: cpr. C. Ord. Ptol. p. 355 s.v. παρεύρεσις. Dans notre texte, οὐδὲ ἔχειν αὐτό eût suffi à exprimer la pensée de Nikôn.

B. *L'affaire Théodosios*

Les archives de Zénon nous ont conservé quatre documents relatifs à l'affaire qui opposa Nikôn à Antipatros et à Simone:

1. *P. Col. Zen. 2 83*: une pétition adressée au roi par Antipatros (sans date). Il s'agit probablement d'une copie plutôt que de l'original (cf. les remarques des éditeurs aux pp. 78-79);
2. *P. L. Bat. 20 21*: déposition d'Euphronios en faveur d'Antipatros (26 Gorpiaios = 20 novembre 246, le présent texte);
3. *P. Cairo Zen. 3 59.347*: déposition d'Eudêmos en faveur d'Antipatros (25 Hyperberetaios = 19 décembre 246);
4. *P. Cairo Zen. 4 59.617*: fragment d'une lettre, vraisemblablement adressée à Zénon ou à Euklês (sans date). La première ligne mentionne Ν̣ίκωνος τὴν ἔντευξιν (cpr. P. Col. Zen. 2 p. 79).

Il est possible de résumer comme suit la succession des événements. Simone, la femme d'Antipatros, avait emprunté à Nikôn 70 drachmes à un intérêt de 6% par mois,[11] s'il faut en croire la pétition d'Antipatros, qui avait garanti le remboursement de la dette. Peu après, Artemidôros, l'agent d'Apollônios, aurait porté contre Antipatros des accusations — fausses selon ce dernier, — et Antipatros préféra emmener sa femme et son fils Théodosios à Hermopolis Magna où il ouvrit boutique. Comme Simone ne remboursait pas sa dette, Nikôn profita d'un déplacement d'Antipatros à Philadelphie pour se rendre lui-même à Hermopolis et y menacer Simone de la faire saisir par le πράκτωρ si elle ne le suivait pas de sa propre volonté, ce qu'elle fit accompagnée de son fils Théodosios. Nikôn les mena à Hérakléopolis, où il les tint en détention, chacun séparément. Simone réussit à s'échapper, mais Théodosios se trouverait toujours entre les mains de Nikôn au moment où Antipatros adresse au roi sa pétition, du moins l'affirme-t-il.

Nous ne savons pas ce qu'il advint de la pétition d'Antipatros: celui-ci demande au souverain de confier son cas au tribunal des χρηματισταί, mais ce n'est qu'un souhait de sa part.

---

[10] Le texte no. **21** avait déjà été traduit et commenté par moi, lorsque j'appris que le professeur Zaki Aly en possédait des photos et qu'il était disposé à en assurer lui-même la réédition. Une partie de mon commentaire ne faisant toutefois pas double emploi, il a semblé bon de l'imprimer à la suite de la contribution de Z. Aly.

[11] Pour les problèmes soulevés par ce prêt, voir la discussion détaillée dans P. Col. Zen. 2 pp. 76 sqq., ainsi que H. Kühnert, *Zum Kreditgeschäft in den hellenistischen Papyri* et H.-A. Rupprecht, *Untersuchungen zum Darlehen*.

Toujours est-il qu'à un certain moment on fit appel à Zénon (ou à Euklês, son successeur à Philadelphie),[12] soit comme membre du tribunal amené à juger de cette affaire, soit plus probablement en tant que personne chargée par le tribunal de réunir les informations nécessaires.[13] C'est vraisemblablement à cette occasion que fut envoyée la lettre P. Cairo Zen. 4 59.617, à laquelle était sans doute jointe la copie de la pétition.

Les accusations portées par Antipatros contre Nikôn sont doubles: d'une part, le taux du prêt dépasse le maximum légal (cpr. P. Col. Zen. 2 pp. 78-81), de l'autre Nikôn aurait saisi la débitrice et son fils illégalement, c'est-à-dire personnellement et non par l'entremise du πράκτωρ (cpr. P. Col. Zen. 2 pp. 81-82).

Il est naturellement important de savoir si Théodosios, le fils d'Antipatros et de Simone, garantissait ou non avec son père la dette contractée par sa mère. Les éditeurs du P. Col. Zen. 2 83 font remarquer à juste titre que, si tel fut le cas, Antipatros l'a probablement passé sous silence dans sa pétition pour mieux pouvoir noircir Nikôn. La documentation dont nous disposons ne nous permet pas de trancher ce point, mais il semble certain que Nikôn se soit, à un moment donné, emparé de l'enfant.

Les deux déclarations de témoins que nous avons conservées concernent précisément le fait de savoir si Nikôn détenait, oui ou non, Théodosios. Euphronios et Eudêmos rapportent que, à deux occasions diverses, Nikôn repondit aux accusations d'Antipatros en affirmant ne pas avoir pris l'enfant et ne pas l'avoir chez lui.

Il est heureux que les deux témoins affirment qu'ils témoignent en faveur d'Antipatros, car leurs témoignages respectifs ne suffiraient pas à l'établir: ils peuvent en effet se comprendre tant dans un sens favorable à Nikôn — et serviraient alors à prouver que ce dernier a toujours nié s'être saisi de Théodosios, — que dans un sens favorable à Antipatros — Nikôn ne pourrait alors pas dire qu'Antipatros ne l'a jamais interpelé au sujet de l'enfant, à moins qu'Antipatros n'ait tenté d'établir que Nikôn avait affirmé à certaines reprises avoir pris Théodosios, à d'autres ne s'en être jamais emparé.

M.

---

[12] Nous savons qu'Euklês était ἐπιστάτης τῆς δωρεᾶς (P. Cairo Zen. 3 59.366, 5) et il aurait donc pu agir ici, tout comme l'ἐπιστάτης τῆς κώμης, en tant qu'assistant en matière judiciaire du stratège (cpr. ce qui est dit ci-dessus, p. 106, à propos des témoignages dans la χώρα); on ne saurait toutefois exclure la possibilité que c'est à Zénon que l'on fit appel.

[13] Dans le premier cas, la présence des quatre documents dans les archives de Zénon (ou dans celles d'Euklês, d'où elles passèrent dans les archives de Zénon avec les autres textes qui lui seraient venus d'Euklês, cpr. p. 5 et E. Seidl, *Ptolemäische Rechtsgeschichte*, pp. 41-42) s'explique aisément; dans le second cas, il aurait conservé la copie de la pétition et la lettre par laquelle on lui demandait sa collaboration, ainsi que les déclarations de deux témoins, si rien ne s'est perdu. S'il en est ainsi, est-ce parce que ces deux déclarations sont trop ambivalentes que Zénon ne les aurait pas envoyées au tribunal?

22

BRIEF DES AMMONIOS AN ZENON

H. × Br. = 11,5 × 24 cm.[a]

Geschrieben 1. März 257 v. Chr., empfangen 3. März 257 v. Chr.

Biblioteca Medicea Laurenziana[a+b]: **PSI 5 489**[a]; PSI 6 S. XVI[b].

Inhalt Ammonios macht Zenon bekannt, dass er die für den König bestimmten Kränze aus Granatblüten an Apollonios gesandt hat. Zenon soll aber die Sendung übernehmen und wohl den weiteren Transport besorgen. Ferner schreibt Ammonios über einem roten Farbstoff (ἐρυθρύδανον): ein Agent des Zenon hatte 3 Talente davon gekauft zu 25 Drachmen das Talent; tatsächlich war damals (wenn wir den Text richtig verstehen) der Marktpreis 30 Drachmen pro Talent. Er verspricht Zenon noch einen Sklaven zu senden, der ihm Auskünfte geben kann und er bittet seine Briefe rechtzeitig dem Apollonios zu übergeben und ihre Beantwortung zu beaufsichtigen.

Vorderseite:

Ἀμμώνιος Ζήνωνι χαίρειν. Ἀπεστάλκαμεν Ἀπολλωνίωι
τοὺς υ στεφάνους τῶν βαλωστ̣ί̣[ω]ν περὶ ὧν ἔγραψεν ἡμῖν
κατασκευάσαι ὥστε τῶι βασιλεῖ. Καλῶς ἂν οὖν ποιήσαις ἐπιμεληθεὶς
ὅπως τὸ τάχος παραληφθῶσι παρ[ὰ] τ̣[*c* 22]ην
τὸν Ἀπολλωνίου ὅτι ἀπέχει. Τὸ δὲ ἐρυθρύδα[ν]ο̣[ν] γίνωσκε συν-
ηγορασμένου ⟦τ̣ο̣ῦ παρὰ σοῦ ἐκ ⊢ κε⟧ \`ὅσου ἔφη χρείαν ἔχειν τ̣ο̣ῦ̣ παρὰ σοῦ ⊼ γ ἐκ [⊢] κε'
τὸ τάλαντον, ἐπωλεῖτο δὲ ἀνὰ ⊢ λ.
Ἵνα οὖν εἰδῆις γέγραφά σοι. Καὶ Χάρμον δὲ τὸν παῖδα ἀποστελῶ πρὸς σὲ
τὸ τάχος διωικημένον περὶ πάντων. Χαρίζοιο δ' ἂν μοι φροντίσας ὅπως
αἱ λοιπαὶ ἐπιστολαὶ αἱ παρ' ἡμῶν ἀποδοθῶσι Ἀπολλ̣[ω]νίωι εὐκαίρως καὶ ἵνα
ἀντιγραφῆι ἡμῖν πρὸς ἕκαστα ἐπιμεληθείς.
Ἔρρωσο. ∟ κη Τῦβι ζ.

Rückseite:

Ζήνωνι.
Ἀμμωνίου. Στεφάνων.
∟ κη Αὐδναίου κη,
ἐν τῶι Βερενίκης ὅρμωι.

2 τῶν in der ed. princ. ausgelassen; nachträglich (PSI 8, S. XVI) angegeben 4 τ̣[ῶν ed. princ., aber τ̣[οῦ ist auch moglich

Übersetzung

Ammonios grüsst Zenon.

Ich habe an Apollonios die 400 Kränze aus Granatblüten gesandt, worüber er mir geschrieben hat sie für den König herzurichten. Du wirst also gut tun zu besorgen, dass sie unverzüglich von . . . übernommen werden . . .

Und über den roten Farbstoff musst Du wissen, dass Dein Agent so viel gekauft hat als er sagte nötig zu haben, 3 Talente zu 25 Drachmen pro Talent; er wurde aber (damals) zu 30 Drachmen verkauft.

Damit Du es erfährst, habe ich Dir geschrieben. Und ich werde auch unverzüglich den Sklaven Charmos, der über alles instruiert ist, zu Dir senden.

Du würdest mir einen Gefallen erweisen, wenn Du Dich darum kümmerst, dass meine übrigen Briefe rechtzeitig an Apollonios übergeben werden, und wenn Du besorgst, dass er auf alles pünktlich antwortet.

Lebe wohl.
Im 28. Jahr, am 7. Tybi.

Anschrift:

An Zenon.

Empfangsvermerk:

Von Ammonios. Über Kränzen. Im 28. Jahr, am 28. Audnaios, in Berenikes Hormos.

Anmerkungen

1 Das Amt des Ammonios ist nicht sicher. Edgar (P. Cairo Zen. 1 59.062 a, Anm. zur Z. 3) hat die Vermutung geäussert, dass Ammonios Bankier wäre. Einen Bankier dieses Namen in Athribis kennen wir jetzt wirklich aus P. Lond. 7 1938, 1, 9 (2. April 257 v. Chr.); 1943 a, 3 (5. Mai 257) 1944, 2 (5. Mai 257), welche Texte zeitlich nicht viel von einander entfernt sind. Der Text liefert uns aber zu wenig Angaben, um diese beide Männer gleichstellen zu können.

2 στεφάνους τῶν βαλωστ̣ί̣[ω]ν: derartige Kränze (στέφανοι βαλαύστινοι) kommen sonst nur in PSI 4 333, 8 vom 20. Februar 256 v. Chr. vor. Aus jenem Text wissen wir, dass die Herstellung 300 solcher Kränze ungefähr einen Monat in Anspruch genommen hat. Dazu kommen noch einige Tage für den Transport. Auch hier ist es klar, dass fertige Kränze gesandt wurden (περὶ ὧν ἔγραψεν ἡμῖν κατασκευάσαι). Das alles stimmt aber nicht zu unseren Vorstellungen über die beschränkte Haltbarkeit der Blumen.

Ein anderes Problem ist die Bestimmung dieser Kränze. Das erste, was uns einfällt, ist, dass sie ein Geschenk sein mussten für eins der Feste, welche der König im Monat Dystros feiern würde: die Feier seiner Thronbesteigung am 25. Dystros (= 28. April 257), und am 12. Dystros (= 15. April 257) sein Geburtstag (für das Datum vgl. F. Uebel, *Proceedings of the XIV International Congress of Papyrologists*, London 1975, S. 320 Anm. 2).

4 In der Lücke wurde wohl jemand genannt, dem die Sendung anvertraut war. Es konnten aber ein oder mehrere Leute gewesen sein. Die Zeilen 5 und 8-9 lassen hier auch die Erwähnung eines Briefes vermuten, der diese Sendung ankündigte. Der grammatische Bau des nach der Lücke gelesenen Textes ist nicht klar, und demgemäss kann die grammatische Rolle des Apollonios hier nicht festgestellt werden.

5 Für die Benutzung von ἐρυθρύδανον siehe P. Cairo Zen. 3 59.326 bis, 23, 24 (ἐρεθρύδανον), wo es zusammen mit anderen für einen βαφεύς bestimmten Farbstoffen erwähnt wird, und den fragmentarischen P. Cairo Zen. 4 59.781, 13 (ἐρυ]θ̣ρόδανον). Die rote Farbe war sehr populär in Ägypten. Siehe darüber Th. Reil, *Beiträge zur Kenntnis des Gewerbes im hellenistischen Ägypten*, Borna-Leipzig 1913, S. 99-101.

6 Sowohl in dem getilgten Teil der Zeile als auch in den hinzugeschriebenen Worten hat man in der editio princeps vor παρὰ σοῦ 2 bezw. 3 Buchstaben nicht gelesen. M.E. muss man an beiden Stellen τοῦ παρὰ σοῦ ergänzen. Damit erhalten wir das Subjekt zu συνηγορασμένου und zu ἔφη. Weniger wahrscheinlich scheint es mir, dass man in Apollonios (Z. 1) das Subjekt zu ἔφη sehen kann. Für seine Kränzebestellung steht in Z. 2 schon das Verbum ἔγραψεν.

Es ist schwer diesen Satz, worin Ammonios selbst schon Änderungen vorgenommen hat, zu verstehen. Wir nehmen an dass er nach dem genitivus absolutus συνηγορασμένου ὅσου ἔφη χρείαν ἔχειν τοῦ παρὰ σοῦ keinen Hauptsatz mehr geschrieben hat, sondern dass er einen zweiten Satz ἐπωλεῖτο ἀνὰ ⊢ λ durch δέ mit diesem genitivus absolutus verbunden hat.

— $\overline{\Lambda}$ γ: bemerkenswert ist hier die grosse Menge des eingekauften Farbstoffs. Der oben angeführte βαφεύς brauchte einmal ein Talent (± 21½ kg), einmal ein halbes Talent ἐρυθρύδανον. In P. Cairo Zen. 4 59.781, 13 kauft man nur eine Mine ἐρυθρύδανον.

— ἐπωλεῖτο: wir nehmen an, dass der Agent trotz des laufenden Preises (vgl. πωλεῖται in P. Cairo Zen. 5 59.823, 3) von 30 Drachmen per Talent die nötige Menge billiger gekauft hat.

7 Die Formel ἵνα οὖν εἰδῆις κ.τ.λ. o.ä. kommt sehr oft als Schlussformel eines Briefes oder zum Schluss einer Nachricht vor. Hier bleibt es aber unsicher, ob Charmos den knappen Brief erklären sollte oder dass er andere Geschäfte mit Zenon besprechen sollte. Der Sklave Charmos war längere Zeit als selbstständiger Agent des Apollonios tätig.

15 Berenikes Hormos ist uns nur aus dem Zenonarchiv bekannt. Die Belege lassen uns die Ortschaft entweder in der Nähe von Memphis oder von Heliopolis lokalisieren. Siehe Calderini, *Dizionario dei nomi geografici e topografici*, Bd. 2, S. 41 und Nr. **29**, 14, Anm.

W.

23

BRIEF DES AMYNTAS AN ZENON

H. × Br. = 11 × 27,3 cm. Empfangen 16. März 257 v. Chr.

Societas Archaeologica Atheniensis: **P. S. A. Athen. 1**. Von der Rekto-Seite und der Verso-Seite des Papyrus sind Photographien vorhanden in „The International Papyrological Photographic Archive" in Brüssel. Der Text wurde mehrmals ergänzt und berichtigt: Kougeas (vergl. Kunkel, *Zeitschr. Savigny-Stiftung* RA 61, 1941, 419-420); Wilcken, *Archiv für Papyrusforsch.* 14 (1941) 158; Heichelheim, *JEA* 27 (1941) 177; Bingen (vergl. BL 6, S. 171).

Der rechte Rand des Textes ist nicht erhalten, es sind aber wohl nur einige Buchstaben verloren gegangen. Die Zeilen laufen senkrecht zu den Fasern. Mitten unter dem Text auf der Rekto-Seite befinden sich Abdrücke in Spiegelschrift einiger Buchstaben von Z. 5.

Inhalt Amyntas bittet seinen Freund Zenon dem κοιλουργός Chares dessen Verfehlung zu vergeben. Von Interesse ist hier der Beruf des Chares: κοιλουργός ist sonst unbekannt und dies legt die Vermutung nahe, dass wir mit einem selten ausgeübten Beruf zu tun haben.

Vorderseite:

Ἀμύντας Ζήνωνι χαίρειν. Παρεγενήθη πρὸς ἡμᾶς ὁ κοιλουργὸς ἀξ[ιῶν με γράψαι]
πρὸς σὲ ἵνα μὴ ἀδικηθῆι. Καλῶς ἂν οὖν ποιήσαις ἀφεὶς αὐτὸν εἴ τι μὴ μέγα ἡμ[άρτηκεν],
εἰς δὲ τὸ λοιπὸν φησὶν εὐτακτήσειν· ἐπετιμῶμεγ γὰρ αὐτῶι καὶ ἡμεῖ[ς ἐπειδὴ]
περιτρέχει καὶ οὐκ ἐργάζεται. [2. H.] Ἀξιοῖ δὲ ἐν Μέμφει ἀπολειφθεὶς ἐργάζεσθαι. Εἰ
οὖν μ[ηδέν τι ?]
ἄλλο Ἀπολλώνιος συντάσσει καλῶς ἂν ποιήσαις ἐπιχωρήσας αὐτῶι.
Ἔρρωσο. [L ---]

Rückseite:

Ζήνωνι.
[3. H.] Ἀμύντας περὶ Χάρητος
κοιλουργοῦ. L κη
Περιτίου ιβ,
[ἐ]μ Βουβάστωι. [4. H.] αν( )

1 ἀξ[ιῶν ἀπολογεῖσθαι (?)] ed. princ., ἀξ[ιῶν γράψαι] Kougeas, Heichelheim, ἀξ[ιῶν με γράψαι] Wilcken 2 ἠ[δίκησεν (?) ed. princ., ἡμ[άρτηκεν] Bingen 8 περὶ Χάρητος ed. princ., Wilcken, περὶ χάρητος, *l.* χάριτος Kougeas 11 . . Βουβάστου Α˙ scil. ἀν(αγέγραπται)? ed. princ., [ἐ]μ Βουβάστωι. ạṿ Bingen

Übersetzung

Amyntas grüsst Zenon.

Zu mir ist der κοιλουργός angekommen mit der Bitte an Dich zu schreiben, damit er nicht ungerecht behandelt würde. Du wirst also gut tun ihn freizulassen, wenn er eine nicht zu grosse Verfehlung begangen hat. Und für die Zukunft verspricht er, seine Pflicht pünktlich zu erfüllen; denn auch ich habe ihm öfters Vorwürfe gemacht, da er herumbummelt und nicht arbeitet. Und er wünscht in Memphis zurückgelassen zu werden, um zu arbeiten. Wenn also Apollonios nicht etwas anderes anordnet, wirst Du gut tun, es ihm zu gestatten.

Lebe wohl.

Anschrift:

An Zenon.

Empfangsvermerk:

Amyntas über Chares, den κοιλουργός.
Im 28. Jahr, am 12. Peritios, in Bubastos.

Anmerkungen

1 Zu Amyntas siehe P. L. Bat. 21. IX, s.v., Nr. 6, sowie Rostovtzeff, *Large Estate*, S. 29-31 und Świderek, *Eos* 50 (1959/1960) 82-85.

— κοιλουργός: das Wort ist sonst unbekannt und der Text bietet keine Anweisung wie man es deuten muss; κοιλουργός ist eine Zusammensetzung von κοιλός und ἔργον, also ein Mann der sich mit κοιλά beschäftigt, ,,hohle Sachen''. Der Herausgeber hat κοιλουργός als ,,Töpfer'' erklärt (so auch unter Vorbehalt Liddell-Scott-Jones, *Suppl.* S. 85), Kougeas, *loc. cit.* als ,,Zimmermann''; vgl. κοιλόσταθμος in Bezug auf Häuser, Fenster, Schiffe gebraucht.

3 εὐτακτήσειν: das Verbum εὐτακτέω bedeutet in den Papyri fast immer ,,voll und pünktlich zahlen''. Der Brief gibt aber keine Indizien dass Zenon den Chares wegen finanziellen Verfehlungen strafen wollte. Nach unserer Meinung hatte Zenon ähnliche Vorwürfe gegen Chares als Amyntas: περιτρέχει καὶ οὐκ ἐργάζεται. Deshalb meinen wir dass hier εὐτακτεῖν mit ,,seinen Pflicht pünktlich erfüllen'' zu übersetzen ist. Diese Bedeutung von εὐτακτεῖν ist schon bekannt aus P. Lond. 7 2045, 5 (vgl. die Anm. zu dieser Z.).

11 Bubastos = Tell Basta. Der Text stammt von der kurzen Periode (16-26. März 257 v. Chr.), als Zenon im Ostdelta weilte. Zu den anderen Urkunden dieser Zeit siehe P. L. Bat. 21. VIII, *c* (Chronology).

— αν( ). Die Lesung dieser Abbreviatur scheint mir sicher. Dieser Vermerk wurde in einer andren Hand geschrieben und wir können wohl annehmen dass der Vermerk im Büro des Zenon zu dem Empfangsvermerk hinzugefügt worden ist. Auf Grund des Archivs gibt es zwei Möglichkeiten die Abbreviatur zu deuten. Die Rückseite von PSI 4 359 enthält die Notiz ἀ[ντ]έγραψα Διογένους ἐπ(ιστολῆι) und P. Cairo Zen. 4 59.562 enthält Abschriften von verschiedenen Briefen. Wir können uns also leicht einen Schreiber vorstellen, der bei seiner Arbeit die erledigten Briefe gekennzeichnet hat. Demgemäss ist der Vermerk etwa ἀν(έγραψα) ,,ich habe (in das Verzeichnis) aufgenommen'' oder ἀν(τέγραψα) ,,ich habe (den Brief) beantwortet'' zu ergänzen. In Ermangelung weiterer Belege muss doch diese Erklärung nur eine blosse Vermutung bleiben. Siehe auch Wilcken, *Archiv für Papyrusf.* 6 (1920) 390.

W.

24

BRIEF DES AMYNTAS AN ZENON

H. × Br. = 14 × 28 cm. Empfangen 11. April 257 v. Chr.

Biblioteca Laurenziana Medicea: **PSI 4 329**; der gesamte Text mit den Ergänzungen WILCKENS (*Archiv für Papyrusforschung* 6 [1920] 386) und denen des ROSTOVTZEFF, wurde in dessen *Large Estate*, S. 30, Anm. 39 gedruckt (vgl. BL 1, S. 396).

Der Text ist unvollständig erhalten. Eine unregelmässige Lücke läuft senkrecht durch seine ganze Höhe. Auch der rechte Rand fehlt (etwa 4-9 Buchstaben).

Inhalt Ein von Zenon gekaufter Sklave ist entflohen und bleibt unter den Kappadoken in der Gegend von Athribis. Amyntas macht dies dem Zenon, der zu dieser Zeit auf Reisen ist, bekannt, damit er die entsprechenden Massnahmen treffen kann um den Flüchtling festzunehmen.

Vorderseite:

Ἀμύντας Ζήνωνι χαίρει[ν. Γίνωσκε ὅτι ὁ μά]γειρος, ὃν ὑμεῖς ἐπρίασ[θε, ...]
λαβὼν χαλκοῦ (δραχμὰς) π, ὥστ[ε εἰς χόρτασμ]α τοῖς ἵπποις, ἀποδέδρακ[εν, συνήν]-
τηκε δέ τισιν περὶ Ἀθλῖβιν, ὅς καί ἐστιν [παρὰ] τοῖς Καππάδοξιν τοῖς ἐκε[ῖ σταθμὸν ἔ]-
χουσιν. Καλῶς ἂν οὖν ποιήσαις τοῖς τ[ε] παισὶ πᾶσι διαγγείλας καὶ γρά[ψας πρὸς]
οὓς ἂν ὑπολαμβάνηις χρήσιμον εἶν[αι, ἵ]να, ὡς ἂν οἱ παρ' ἡμῶν ἐπιλαμβ[άνων]-
ται αὐτοῦ, συναντιλάβωνταί τ[ε τοῦ κ]ατασταθῆναι αὐτὸν πρὸ[ς ὑμᾶς].
Ἔρρωσο. L κη [--]

Rückseite:

Ζήνωνι.
L κη Δύστρου η̄, ἐν Μένδητι.
Ἀμύντας περὶ τοῦ μαγείρου
τοῦ ἀποδράντος.

1 Γίνωσκε ὅτι ὁ Rostovtzeff; ἐπρίασ[θε] Rostovtzeff, ἐπρίασ[θε . . . . . .] Preisigke (BL 1, S. 396) 2 ὥσ[τε εἰς χόρτασμ]α Wilcken; ἀποδεδρακ[έναι ed. princ., ἀποδέδρακ[εν Wilcken 3-4 τοῖς ἐκε[ῖ τεί]-|νουσιν Rostovtzeff, τοῖς ἐκε[ῖ σταθμὸν ἔ]-|χουσιν Vitelli (PSI 5, S. IX) 5 εἶν[αι .]. . .σαν ed. princ., εἶν[αι ὅ]πως ἄν Rostovtzeff, εἶν[αι ἵ]να ὡς ἄν Vitelli (PSI 6, S. X); ἐπιλαμβ[άνων]ται Rostovtzeff 6 συναντιλαμβάνωνται PSI 6, S. X; τ[ε τοῦ κ]ατασταθῆναι Wilcken; πρὸ[ς ὑμᾶς] Rostovtzeff

Übersetzung

Amyntas grüsst Zenon.

Wisse, dass der Koch, den Ihr gekauft habt [--] entflohen ist mit 80 Kupferdrachmen, die für Pferdefutter bestimmt waren und dass er sich einigen Leuten um Athribis angeschlossen hat. Er ist jetzt unter den Kappadoken, die ihren Sitz dort haben. Du wirst also gut tun, es allen Sklaven (?) bekannt zu machen und an diejenigen, die nach Deiner Meinung nützlich sein können, zu schreiben, damit sie, wenn meine (Diener) ihn packen, mithelfen, ihn zu Dir zu bringen.

Lebe wohl. Im 28. Jahr . . .

Anschrift:

An Zenon.

Empfangsvermerk:

Im 28. Jahr, am 8. Dystros, in Mendes.
Amyntas über dem entflohenen Koch.

Anmerkungen

1 Über entflohene Sklaven lesen wir öfter im Zenonarchiv. Siehe dazu I. BIEŻUŃSKA-MAŁOWIST, *Les Esclaves fugitives dans l'Égypte gréco-romaine, Studi in onore di Edoardo Volterra,* Bd. VI, S. 75-90; vergl. Nr. **36** und Nr. **43**.

2 Zu χόρτασμα siehe M. SCHNEBEL, *Die Landwirtschaft im hellenistischen Ägypten,* München 1925, S. 213.

3 Die Anwesenheit von Kappadoken und Nachbarvölker in Ägypten wird auch durch andere Quellen bestätigt. Siehe F. HEICHELHEIM, *Die auswertige Bevölkerung im Ptolemäerreich,* Leipzig 1925, S. 75-76 und 91, und M. LAUNEY, *Recherches sur les armées hellénistiques,* I, Paris 1949, S. 483-485.

9 In Mendes war Zenon vom 11. bis zum 20. April 257 v. Chr. Für die anderen Urkunden dieser Zeit siehe P. L. Bat. 21. VIII, *c* (Chronology).

W.

25

LETTER FROM APOLLONIOS TO ZENON

H. × W. = 17.5 × 24 cm.[a]; 16 × 7 cm.[b]

Sent 8 July, 257 B.C.,
received 10 July, 257 B.C.

Col. inv. 232[a] + Cairo JdE 48919[b]: **P. Col. Zen. 1 14** and **P. Cairo Zen. 4 59.583**; C. C. EDGAR, *A new letter of Apollonios the dioiketes, Archiv für Papyrusforschung* 11 (1935), pp. 218-19, first publication of the combined text; P. M. FRASER, *Ptolemaic Alexandria*, vol. 2, p. 72, n. 165; p. 75, n. 174; and p. 260, n. 129.

The two fragments of this letter were first combined by Edgar (see bibliography). The text on the front is written across the fibres (evidently on the recto surface) in a "chancellery" hand, which the editors of P. Col. Zen. 1 14 compared to that of P. Cairo Zen. 3 59.388 (see loc. cit. Plate 15), although they believed it to be the work of a different scribe, partly because of its "many ligatures". From the evidence of the folds, they suggested that the original width of the letter would have been about 34 cm., and this estimate is presumably still valid. They also gave a description of the traces of the letter's seal on the verso.

Contents Apollonios the dioiketes writes to Zenon, instructing him to attend to the unloading and safe storage of a consignment of (olive-?) oil at the docks of Alexandria. The text has received a little discussion in connection with Alexandrian trade. The outstanding problem concerns the source of the oil—whether it was imported from abroad, or shipped from Apollonios' Egyptian estates—and its ultimate destination. The text is securely dated to a well-documented period of Zenon's career, and belongs to his two months' stay in Alexandria in the summer of 257 B.C. (see the chronological tables in P. L. Bat. 21. VIII, *c*).

front:

Ἀπολλώνιος Ζήνωνι χαίρειν. Τ[ὸ] ἔλαιον τὸ
παραγεγενημένον ἡμῖν ἐξ [οἴ]κου κατ̣[---]
εἰς Ἐμπόριον ἐξελοῦ καὶ λαβὼν [π]αρ' Ἡγήμον[ος]
ἀπόστασιν ὅ τι ἀσφαλεστάτην κατάστησ[ον]
τῶν παίδων τοὺς τηρήσοντας ἕως ἃ̣[ν]
παραγενόμενοι προσαγ̣άγωμ̣ε̣ν οἰκονομία[ν.]
Ἔρρωσο. L κθ [Δ]αισίου η, Παχ[ὼν ---]

back:

8 Ζήνωνι.
Ἀπολλώνιος περὶ τοῦ παραγεγο-
νότος ἐλαίου ἐξ οἴκου.
L κθ Δαισίου ι, ἐν Ἀλεξ(ανδρείαι).

Textum, minimis mutatis, et rest. ex E(dgar, *Archiv* 11 [v. bibl.]) deprompsimus 2 κατ̣[αβάς?] E.: at P. Cairo Zen. 4 59.583]κου κα̣. . . .[relicta ut plura designat? alias quoque rest. in nota l. 2 dedimus 6 προσαγάγωμεν E., προσαπάγωμεν Westermann (?) apud E.: cf. P. Col. Zen. 1 14, προς απαγωγη̣[ν 7 Παχ[ὼν ις] E.: aut Παχ[ὼν η]

Translation

Apollonios to Zenon, greetings.

Go down to (?) the Emporion and unload the (olive-?)oil that has arrived for us from home. When you have got as safe as possible a warehouse from Hegemon, post some of the servants to guard it until we arrive and can settle the matter.

Fare well.

Year 29, Daisios 8, Pach[on 16?].

Address:

To Zenon.

Docket:

Apollonios about the (olive-?)oil that has arrived from home.

Year 29, Daisios 10, in Alexandria.

Notes

1 ἔλαιον, as is generally recognized, can either signify "olive-oil" or "oil" in general, and the mere form of words here cannot determine which interpretation is correct in this papyrus. The importance of this point lies in the fact that olive-oil was exempt from the oil-monopoly.

As far as can be judged from the editions, the line-lengths on the front may vary, and there perhaps remains a little latitude in the length of restorations that can be made at the line ends. However, there is no particular reason to suggest restoring anything after ἔλαιον τό (e.g. ἤδη might be a possibility), and the sense is not in doubt.

2 παραγεγενημένον: cf. παραγεγονότος, *ll.* 9-10. There is every reason to accept Edgar's interpretation "that has arrived", rather than the view put forward in P. Col. Zen. 1 14, "that has accumulated" (in excess of household requirements). On the latter view, there is also considerable awkwardness in the expression ἐξ οἴκου that follows both in *l.* 2 and in *l.* 10.

— ἐξ οἴκου, "from home": cf. *l.* 10. It is highly improbable that this phrase can mean or imply, as suggested by Edgar, "from our own property (overseas)". Edgar was perhaps only led to this interpretation because he felt that the possibility that the oil might have come from one of Apollonios' estates in Egypt was ruled out by "the regulations of the oil monopoly". This is not an inescapable conclusion. Further, if the oil concerned was olive-oil, it would be exempt from the monopoly (thus Fraser, *op. cit.*, vol. 2, p. 260, n. 129). Although Edgar plausibly explains that the phrase might have been included to distinguish oil produced on an estate belonging to Apollonios himself from oil *purchased* abroad, he does nothing to show that it can bear the weight of the sense he puts upon it. Οἶκος occurs in the Zenon archive seven times without the article in vague common phrases, "at home", "homewards", "from home", and twice with the article where parts "of houses", etc., are mentioned, P. Cairo Zen. 4 59.847, 40 and PSI 5 546, 4 (in a further occurrence at P. Hamb. 1 105, 9 the context is unclear, and a compound could be in question). Here the vague sense "from home" is certain, and can only well refer to Apollonios' Egyptian estates.

— At the end of the line, the restoration of καταβάς is plausible, although the word is perhaps a little redundant in the context: Zenon may or may not need to be told where the oil now is, but he hardly requires instructions in so many words "to go down", and the text would hardly emphasise "go *in person*" (cf. παραγενοῦ in **27**, 4). It is perhaps not impossible to restore a transitive verb here (e.g. κατάξας, καταγαγών, καταλαβών, κατέχων: cf. the phrase κατάγει ... εἰς Ἐμπόριον in **76** A and B, 4-5). For example, the translation might be "Fetch the oil that has arrived for us from home down to the Emporion, and, when you have ...". The chief effect of these alternatives would be to make it much less certain that the situation we are to visualise is that the oil has arrived by boat, and is at the quays of the Emporion. Other possibilities should be kept in mind.

3 The editors of P. Col. Zen. 1 14 asserted that ἐμπόριον here ought on philological grounds to signify merely *a* marketplace (n. *l.* 3; cf. P. Col. Zen. 2 73, n. *l.* 5), but the evidence of other

occurrences of the word is insufficient and inconclusive (instances in the archive other than the two just cited are P. Cairo Zen. 1 59.025, 9 and PSI 4 413, 5). Edgar, n. *ll.* 2-3, believed that the great Emporion at Alexandria must be meant, and in this he is followed by FRASER, *op. cit.*, vol. 2, p. 72, n. 165. There is a striking resemblance between the wording of this papyrus and the phrase in Strabo's description of Alexandria καὶ τὸ Ἐμπόριον καὶ <αἱ> ἀποστάσεις (17.1.9). See also for the Emporion text **76** and A. CALDERINI, *Dizionario dei nomi geografici*, I. 1, pp. 110-11.

It is a separate question whether or not the oil was imported (or was intended for export).

— Hegemon here is presumably the member of Apollonios' Alexandrian household: see p. 250, n. 5 and *Prosopography*, P. L. Bat. 21. IX, Ἡγήμων (no. 2). Thus FRASER, *op. cit.*, vol. 2, p. 75, n. 174, following a slightly less positive suggestion by Edgar, suggests that Apollonios had his own warehouses at the Emporion.

6 Edgar cites P. Cairo Zen. 2 59.240, 10 for this phrase, although his translation of that passage, "tell me what arrangements you have made (τίνα οἰκονομίαν προσαγήγοχας) with the toll-collectors", is unjustifiably precise: merely, as in *LSJ*[9], "what steps you have taken"? As he believed the oil was imported, Edgar suggested that it was "stored in bond" until the dues to be paid could be arranged with the customs officials. C. PRÉAUX plausibly suggested that there may have been some dispute about the consignment (*L'Économie Royale des Lagides*, p. 86, n. 3). Certainly the central point of the letter is the need for security (cf. P. Cairo Zen. 2 59.179, 12 and 18). We can only speculate as to what precisely Apollonios had to "settle": it need not have been anything to do with either import or export dues.

Presumably Westermann had actually expressed a preference to read προσαπάγωμεν, knowing of the Cairo fragment, and Edgar in n. *l.* 6 is not merely drawing an inference from the reading of the edition of P. Col. Zen. 1 14. However, it is not clear what the sense of this could be: "until we bring off a deal in addition"?

7 On our present knowledge, the equivalent Egyptian date should be Pachon 16, as Edgar restored. It is not quite impossible that Apollonios might have merely used the fictional Egyptian equivalent date, Pachon 9 (see the chronological information in P. L. Bat. 21. VIII, introduction).

T.

26

LETTER FROM APOLLONIOS TO ZENON

H. × W. = 13.2 × 10.5 cm.[a]; 13.2 × 9.5 cm.[b]

Sent 2 February, 255 B.C., received 26 February, 255 B.C.

Cairo JdE 48609[a+b]: **P. Cairo Zen. 2 59.162**; P. Cairo Zen. 3, p. 290, republication of only the front, with the addition of fragment (b) at the right-hand side. (The contents of this text were briefly mentioned by EDGAR in *Annales du Service des Antiquités* 24 in his introduction to the closely related letter P. Edg. 96 = SB 3 6811 = P. Cairo Zen. 2 59.159).

The text on the front is written along the fibres, presumably on the original recto surface. The central portion of the papyrus has still to be located, although the essential information it contained can safely be restored from the docket on the back.

Contents Apollonios the dioiketes writes to Zenon from Alexandria, informing him that he has sent various cuttings and plants of vines and pomegranate trees to Philadelphia, and instructing him diligently to organize their planting. As Edgar originally pointed out, this letter presumably refers to the same batch of plants—"further vine plants, and other types, [as many as] may prove useful"—that Apollonios had promised to send to Zenon in a letter dated 7 January, 255 B.C. (P. Cairo Zen. 2 59.159, mentioned above, *ll.* 5-6).

A calender of vineyard work copied by Zenon is republished in this volume as text no. **64**, and see also text no. **52** below.

front:

Ἀπολλώνι̣[ος Ζήνωνι χαίρειν. Ἀπεστάλκα]μεν εἰς Φιλαδέλφειαν
φυτὰ ἀμπέλ̣[ινα μύρια, μοσχεύματα χί]λια πεντακόσια,
ῥόϊνα πεντ̣[ακόσια ----------------]ος τῶν παίδων.
Ἐπιμελῶς οὐ̣[ν -------------- φύτε]υ̣σον.
[Ἔρρωσο. L λ, Ἀπελ]λ̣αίου κ̣α̣, Χ̣ο̣ιὰχ̣ ι.

back:

Ζ̣[ήνωνι.]
Φυτῶν.
L λ, Αὐδναίου δ, Τῦβι δ.
Ἀπολλώνιος φυτῶν ἀμπελίν(ων) $\overset{\alpha}{M}$
μοσχευμάτων Ἀφ
ῥ̣όϊνα φ

Textum et rest. e P. Cairo Zen. 3 (*ll.* 1-5) et P. Cairo Zen. 2 (*ll.* 6, 8-11) deprompsimus 7 scriptum in fragm. *b*, om. Edgar, legit Muszynski 10 Ἀψ P. Cairo Zen 2

Translation

Apollon[ios to Zenon, greetings.

We have sent] to Philadelphia [ten thousand] vine cuttings, one thousand five hundred [young plants,] and five [hundred] pomegranate. [. . .] . . . of the servants. Therefore diligently [. . .]plant [. . .].

[Fare well. Year 30, Apel]laios 21, Khoiak 10.

Address:

To Zenon. Concerning cuttings.

Docket:

Year 30, Audnaios 4, Tubi 4.

Apollonios: vine cuttings, 10,000; young plants, 1,500; pomegranate, 500.

Notes

2 The term μόσχευμα has been exhaustively discussed by H. CADELL, *Le substantif* μόσχευμα *et les techniques de reproduction fruitière dans l'Égypte grecque, Revue de Philologie* 46 (1972), pp. 256-65, who brings a wealth of philological argument and horticultural information to bear on the problem (cf. *eadem, La viticulture scientifique dans les archives de Zénon*: PSI 624, *Aegyptus* 49 (1969), pp. 105-20). She proposes that μόσχευμα in the Zenon archive signifies a plant produced by grafting. The evidence of the present letter is specifically discussed on pp. 260 and 264. By contrast, φυτόν signifies a plant (in general) suitable for planting, and, in the context of the present letter, will signify ordinary plants, as opposed to the special grafted plants, of which only a relatively small number could be dispatched (see, in addition to pp. 260 and 264, the specific comment on φυτά, p. 259, last paragraph.)

The present letter is here translated in accordance with the view that μόσχευμα is used in the archive as a general term for young plants, and that φυτόν in the present case signifies "cutting", as it demonstrably does in P. Cairo Zen. 4 59.736, and probably does in some other texts (e.g. P. Cairo Zen. 1 59.072; 2 59.156-7, 59.222). The μοσχεύματα here may well in fact be "rooted cuttings". Compare the remarks on text no. **3**, pp. 31-32.

It should be pointed out that on any interpretation the list given in the present letter cannot be made to tally exactly with what is said in P. Cairo Zen. 2 59.159, 5-6, where apparently only μοσχεύματα are mentioned. However, several plausible explanations might be offered for this difference, and it does not throw any light on the terminology used. The natural interpretation of the wording of the present letter is that the μοσχεύματα are of vines, and P. Cairo Zen. 2 59.159 supports this view: however, it is not beyond all doubt.

3 Probably μοσχεύματα is to be understood with ῥόϊνα.

— In the second half of the line, could Apollonios have used a phrase such as ὅτι πλεῖστα κατὰ τὸ πλῆθος τῶν παίδων?

4 Apollonios seems fond of placing a participle and object before a bare imperative with the same object understood (for example restore "so diligently [unpack them and] plant (them)"), or the imperative may simply have no object expressed, and the sentence may have run something like "so diligently [organize the men and] plant (them)"? Probably καταφύτε]υσον is to be restored (cf. P. Cairo Zen. 2 59.156, 4; 59.157, 3; 59.159, 4).

8 Apollonios' letter took 24 days to reach Zenon (cf. at roughly the same time of year in the same year P. Col. Zen. 1 31 (22 days), P. Cairo Zen. 2 59.154 (24 days), and P. Cairo Zen. 2 59.156-7 (both 20 days). We may assume that the cuttings and plants had to survive a journey of about the same duration: we cannot tell whether or not the present letter travelled with them.

T.

27

LETTRE D'APOLLÔNIOS À ZÉNON

Dimensions non connues — 17 décembre 254

Académie d'Athènes: S. B. Kougeas, dans Ἑλληνικά 9 (1936) pp. 7-10 et planche face à la p. 5; reproduit dans **SB 5 8242**.

Le texte est inscrit perpendiculairement aux fibres sur le recto. Un *kollêma* court horizontalement à peu de centimètres du bord supérieur, un rien au-dessus de la première ligne d'écriture.

Contenu Apollônios a acheté, par l'entremise de Phanêsis, du bois (τὰ ξύλα) qui doit être amené à Philadelphie. Acheté sans doute quelque part en Haute Égypte, le bois sera transporté d'abord par bateau jusqu'à Ptolemaïs Hormou (voir note à la *l.* 3), pour être ensuite chargé sur des péniches de plus faible tonnage qui l'achemineront à Philadelphie en empruntant le canal.

Une première lettre a été envoyée par Apollônios à Nikêratos, qui doit veiller au déchargement des madriers et les faire garder jusqu'à l'arrivée des péniches qu'affrêtera Zénon. Apollônios envoie également une lettre à Zénon pour lui donner ordre d'affrêter les embarcations nécessaires (cpr. P. Cairo Zen. 3 59.449) et d'assurer le transport des madriers jusqu'à Philadelphie, aussitôt que Nikêratos lui aura signalé leur arrivée. Apollônios joint à la lettre à Zénon la copie de celle qu'il a envoyée à Nikêratos.

Ἀπολλώνιος Ζήνωνι χ[αί]ρειν. Ἀπέσταλκά σοι τῆς πρὸς Νικήρατον ἐ[π]ι̣στολῆς τἀντίγραφα. Ὡς ἂν οὖν καταχθῆι τ[ὰ] ξύλα εἰς τὴν̣ [*c.* 6], παραγενοῦ καὶ σύνταξον παρακ̣[ομί]σ̣αι δ̣ι̣[ὰ τ]ῆς διώρυγος εἰς Φιλαδέλφ[ε]ιαν, καὶ τοῦτο ἐπιμελῶς γενέσθω.

Ἔρρωσο. L λβ Ὑπερβερ(εταίου) $\overline{\kappa\epsilon}$, Φαῶφι $\overline{\kappa\epsilon}$.

Νικηράτωι. Τὰ ξύλα τὰ ἠγορασμένα ἡμῖν διὰ Φανήσιος συντετάχαμεν ἐμβαλομένους εἰς πλοῖα ἀποστεῖλαι πρὸς σέ. Ὡς ἂν παραγένηται σύνταξον ἐξελέσθαι καὶ ἐπιμελές σοι γενέσθω ἵνα διατηρηθῆι· συντετάχαμεγ γὰρ Ζήνωνι διὰ τῆς διώρυγος παρακομίσαι εἰς Φιλαδέλφειαν. Ἔρρωσο.

Au dos:

14 Ζήνωνι.

1 χαίρειν ed. 2 ἐπιστολῆς ed. 3 τὰ ξύλα ed.; εἰς τὰ π̣ε̣[. . . . .] ed. 4 π[αρακομίσαι] ταῦτα δ[ιὰ τῆς] ed. 5 Φιλαδέλφειαν ed. 7 Ὑπερβερεταίου ed.

Traduction

Apollônios salue Zénon.

Je t'envoie la copie de ma lettre à Nikêratos. Dès que les madriers auront été amenés à ...., sois présent et ordonne leur transport à Philadelphie par le canal, et que cela se fasse avec soin.

Porte-toi bien. An 32, 25 Hyperberetaios 25 Phaôphi.

À Nikêratos.

Nous avons donné ordre de charger sur des navires les madriers achetés pour nous par l'entremise de Phanêsis et de te les envoyer. Dès qu'ils arriveront, donne ordre de les décharger et prends soin qu'ils soient gardés; car nous avons donné ordre à Zénon de les transporter à Philadelphie par le canal.

Porte-toi bien.

Adresse:

À Zénon.

Notes

3 τὰ ξύλα: vraisemblablement des madriers destinés à des travaux de construction. Nous savons par d'autres textes que les travaux de construction n'avaient pas encore cessés en l'an 32: voir p. ex. le P. Cairo Zen. 2 59.233. Pour le bois en Égypte au temps de Zénon, cfr. la note aux *ll.* 191-211 du P. Tebt. 3.1 703 (pp. 98-99).

— εἰς τὴν [......]: le papyrus est cassé à cet endroit et légèrement replié, de manière à nous cacher le dernier mot de la ligne. Serait-ce peut-être Λίμνην? Quel qu'ait été le mot manquant, il semble qu'il doive s'agir de Ptolemaïs Hormou: le bois vient en effet du Sud (καταχθῆι) et doit être amené à Philadelphie, si bien qu'en empruntant l'actuel Bahr Yussuf, les gros navires de transport arrivaient tout naturellement à Ptolemaïs Hormou. De là, les péniches pouvaient rejoindre Philadelphie en empruntant successivement le Bahr Yussuf, le Bahr Selâ et le Bahr Wardân (cpr. la carte du nome arsinoïte à pl. III du second volume des P. Tebtunis).

7 L λβ Ὑπερβερ(εταίου) κ̅ε̅, Φαῶφι κ̅ε̅: il s'agit d'une double date fictive. Si Apollônios écrivait d'Alexandrie, c'est probablement le 25 Hyperberetaios = le 17 décembre 254 qui est la date réelle, donnée selon le calendrier macédonien. Le 25 Phaôphi de l'année égyptienne correspondrait au 19 décembre, soit une différence de deux jours seulement.

8 Νικήρατος: vraisemblablement à identifier au Νικήρατος qui nous est connu par les archives de Kleôn (voir à son sujet la note à la *l.* 1 du texte **42**). Nikêratos y apparait deux fois (P. Petrie II 13, textes 3 et 4), toujours en rapport avec des travaux de construction.

— Φανῆσις: voir la note à la *l.* 1 du texte **57**.

11 διατηρηθῆι: le prix élevé du bois en question est confirmé par le fait qu'Apollônios recommande à Nikêratos de le faire garder durant l'entreposage (διατηρηθῆι).

M.

28

LETTER FROM APOLLONIOS TO ZENON

H. × W. = 16 × 21 cm. Date unknown

Cairo JdE 48616: C. C. Edgar, *Selected papyri from the archives of Zenon*, XI, *Annales du Service des Antiquités* 24 (1924), pp. 23-4 [P. Edg. 92]; SB 3 6807; **P. Cairo Zen. 2 59.169**.

The text on the front is written across the fibres, presumably on the original recto surface. The address on the back is written parallel to the fibres. The letter, when written, was folded twice horizontally. In consequence, an inverted ink offset of 'Αντίκ- in *l.* 2 is visible above 'Απολλώ- *l.* 1. The various restorations mentioned *exempli gratia* by Edgar in his notes all assume the fairly short line-length of the transcription printed here. Apollonios' other letters to Zenon of about this date (the date of the present letter can, of course, only be inferred) show a similar line-length.

Edgar, in his final edition in P. Cairo Zen. 2, confined nearly all restorations to the notes, perhaps wishing to emphasize that several interpretations of the text were possible. U. Wilcken, who had discussed the P. Edg. 92 edition in *Archiv für Papyrusforschung* 8 (1927), pp. 66-7, suggested several restorations ibid., p. 280, when reviewing P. Cairo Zen. 2. Finally, one alternative restoration has been mentioned by T. C. Skeat in P. Lond. 7 2164, n. *l.* 8. The transcription given here contains a series of supplements based on this work, and it is perhaps easier to appreciate the problems of restoring the text when it is presented in this form: however, it should be stressed that there are many other possibilities, not only involving trivial differences in the wording, but also affecting the interpretation of the text.

Contents This letter from Apollonios the dioiketes instructs Zenon to show an important visitor by the name of Antikritos around the village of Philadelphia, including the site of the as yet unbuilt temple of the Gods Adelphoi, and around Apollonios' estate.

The letter must presumably date from after Zenon's arrival at Philadelphia, or, at any rate, from after the moment early in 256 B.C. when he became involved with the Philadelphia estate. It probably relates to an early stage in Apollonios' schemes for the development of Philadelphia, and the tone of enthusiasm perhaps apparent in the letter would suit a date near the beginning of Apollonios' correspondence with Zenon there. Edgar's restoration of κώμην in *l.* 7, which met with Wilcken's approval, makes the letter expressly indicate this, but it is possible that *ll.* 7-8 should be restored to refer rather to some particular part of the village or estate. A considerable amount of evidence survives for the various building projects carried out at Philadelphia, much of it unfortunately undated (see the general account in P. Mich. Zen., pp. 27-30). The work appears to have been at its height in 254 B.C. The present letter might plausibly be dated to 256 or 255 B.C. However, nothing is known about the actual building of the shrine of the Gods Adelphoi. Our only evidence that such a temple was completed consists of the phrase *p3 ʿ.wj n n3 ntr.w sn.w*, "The House of the Gods Adelphoi", in text no. **13**, 27 (cf. *l.* 12) of 14 April 252 B.C., which clearly from the context refers to a fully-built and operative shrine (see n. *p* on this text above). Thus a date for its building of about 254 B.C. would be quite plausible.

The reference in the present letter to a temple of the Gods Adelphoi (Ptolemy II Philadelphos and Arsinoë Philadelphos) in fact depends upon a restoration made by

Wilcken (*Archiv* 8, 280), and is supported chiefly by the possibility of restoring a rather differently worded reference to the same projected temple in P. Cairo Zen. 2 59.168, 3-4, where Wilcken suggested reading τὸν ὥ[στε τοῖς βασιλεῦσιν] ἀπολ[ελειμμένον τόπον, "the site left free for the sovereigns". He admitted that the full listing of the cult-names in the present text, τοῦ βασιλέως καὶ τῆς Φιλα[δέλφου θεῶν Ἀδελφῶν] might be thought a little redundant, but suggested it was quite understandable. In his P. Cairo Zen. 2 editions of 59.168 and of 59.169, Edgar was evidently considering the possibility that both texts might contain a reference to a temple of the sovereigns, but was unwilling to make an appropriate restoration in either text. Edgar abandoned here his earlier suggestion (*ASAE* 24, 23) to restore in P. Cairo Zen. 2 59.168, 3-4 τὸν ὥ[στε τοῖς Ἀδελφοῖς] ἀπολ[ελειμμένον τόπον], perhaps only because of Wilcken's strictures in *Archiv* 8, 66. However, this restoration later received support from the phrase Ἐνεύχομαι οὖν σου κατὰ τῶν Ἀδελφῶν καὶ τοῦ βασιλέως at P. Cairo Zen. 3 59.462, 7. Edgar in his note on this line merely remarked "Note τῶν Ἀδελφῶν without θεῶν, contrary to what Wilcken says in *Archiv* VIII, p. 66", but the possibility of reinstating his original restoration should perhaps be born in mind. For evidence as to the arrangement of the shrines at Philadelphia, see, apart from these Cairo texts, P. Mich. Zen. 84, and the texts relating to the Arsinoeion mentioned in n. *l.* 5 below.

Edgar's suggestion in P. Cairo Zen. 4 59.745 n. *ll.* 34-7 (cf. P. Cairo Zen. 3 59.499 n. *l.* 3), that the shrine of the Gods Adelphoi might in some sense be identified with the Arsinoeion, deserves serious consideration.

Antikritos, who is not otherwise attested in the archive, was evidently an important visitor. He is not given any title, nor is his identity clarified in any way. Edgar plausibly suggested that he came from the Alexandrian court. (C. Préaux in *L'Économie royale des Lagides* (1939), p. 561, compared P. Cairo Zen. 2 59.247, 2-3, where Philiskos mentions that he had been ordered to go to meet "Ariston, who had sailed up from the king to see the nome", Ἀρίστωνι \`τῶι' παρὰ τοῦ βασιλέως ἀναπεπλευκότι ἐπὶ θέαν τοῦ νομοῦ). In *ASAE* 24, 23, Edgar suggested (to expand here a very brief comment) that the point of the special mention of [---] τοῦ βασιλέως καὶ τῆς Φιλα[δέλφου] (at that time, Edgar had "statues" or "altars" in mind) was that Antikritos should be impressed by Apollonios' loyalty. It is of course also possible that Antikritos was merely a friend, who had to see all the sights at Philadelphia; or he may have had some particular interest in, or even involvement with, the building project of the temple.

front [plate XVIII]:

Ἀπολλώνιος Ζήνωνι χαίρε[ιν. Ὡς ἂν παραγένηται]
Ἀντίκριτος, τήν τε κώμην [πᾶσαν δεῖξον αὐτῶι]
καὶ τὸν τόπον οὗ μέλλομε[ν οἰκοδομεῖν τὸ ἱερὸν]
τοῦ βασιλέως καὶ τῆς Φιλα[δέλφου θεῶν Ἀδελφῶν]
καὶ τὸν δρόμον καὶ τὸ ἄ[λσος. Δεῖξον δὲ αὐτῶι]
καὶ τὰ περιχώματα καὶ τ[*c.* 5 τῆς δωρεᾶς μου,]
καὶ ἐμφάνισον ὅτι νεωστὶ ἤ[ργμεθα τὴν κώμην]
κτίζειν.
Ἔρρωσ[ο.]

back [plate XVIII]:

Ζήνωνι.

1 et 2 rest. Edgar, *ASAE* 24 3 et 4 Edgar, *ASAE* 24: — e.g. ἀναθεῖναι τοὺς ... ἀνδριάντας, et in P. Cairo Zen. 2 sugg. quoque βωμούς; οἰκοδομεῖν τὸ ἱερὸν ... θεῶν Ἀδελφῶν Wilcken *Archiv* 8, 280 5 καὶ τὸ Ἀ[ρσινοεῖον. Δεῖξον δέ]| Wilcken *Archiv* 8, 280, καὶ τὸ ἄ[λσος sugg. Skeat, P. Lond. 7 2164, n.*l.* 8 6 καὶ τ[....... τῆς δωρεᾶς μου] Wilcken, *Archiv* 8, 280

Translation

Apollonios to Zenon, greetings.

[Whenever] Antikritos [arrives, show him] both the [whole] village, and the site where we propose [to construct the temple] of the king and of (Queen) Phila[delphos, the Gods Adelphoi,] and the sacred-way, and the [sacred-grove. And show him] both the irrigation-basins and the [--- of my estate;] and make it clear that we have only recently [begun] to establish [the village.]

Fare well. [*Date.*]

Address:

To Zenon.

Notes

2 Apollonios, perhaps self-consciously, refers to Philadelphia simply as "the village", its correct title: M. Rostovtzeff, *A Large Estate in Egypt* (1922), p. 69, mentions letters where the term πόλις is used, referring to PSI 4 341, 3 and (the text later published as) P. Lond. 7 1954, 6: there Skeat refers also to PSI 4 402, 5.

2-3 The text as restored here might perhaps reasonably be translated "... the whole village, and, in particular, the site ...".

3-4 The restorations here have been discussed in the *contents* above. It does not seem possible to suggest any restoration of a kind widely different from those put forward by Edgar and Wilcken.

5 The Arsinoeion at Philadelphia, a reference to which Wilcken suggested should be restored here, is well-attested. P. Cairo Zen. 4 59.745, 29-33 and P. Lond. 7 1974, 14-15 seem to relate to its construction: both have been dated to 254 B.C. on grounds of general probability—the editions should be consulted for possible links with other texts. P. Lond. 7 2046 is a request to be considered for employment in connection with "the projected (?) temple of Arsinoe". Possibly the writer, and his kinsmen, wished to be hired for some aspect of the building-work. The letter is undated, and Skeat therefore assigned it to "about 254 B.C." (n. *l.* 2).

Wilcken (*Archiv* 8, 280) suggested that the train of thought in the text as he restored it was a natural one, as the sacred-way perhaps linked the temple of the Gods Adelphoi to the Arsinoeion, and for this he compared P. Cairo Zen. 2 59.168 (see also his comments in *Archiv* 8, 66), where, if the restoration is correct, there is a reference to a δρόμος shared by the Isieion and the Serapeum. It is not quite clear precisely what arrangement Wilcken had in mind. We might perhaps imagine that the δρόμος was a substantial processional-way, along which the various shrines were situated; or δρόμος in P. Cairo Zen. 2 59.168, 5 might refer just to the entrance-way to the individual shrines.

However, the train of thought is as natural, or perhaps more natural, if we adopt Skeat's suggestion to read καὶ τὸ ἄ[λσος]. The word ἄλσος, "sacred grove", is otherwise attested in the archive only at P. Lond. 7 2164, 8. It would then be plausible to understand δρόμος as referring to the entrance-way to the shrine. The text would thus mention the temple, and then two features belonging to it.

Edgar's suggestion that the shrine of the Gods Adelphoi and the Arsinoeion were not separate entities has already been mentioned in the *contents* above. If the Arsinoeion is interpreted as a part of the shrine, it might yet be a plausible restoration in *l.* 5 of the present letter. If it is interpreted as merely another way of referring to the shrine (perhaps its Greek name was changed at some point?), then it plainly cannot be restored here.

— It is perhaps not essential to restore the beginning of a new sentence and a second imperative verb here.

6 For the famous system of περιχώματα, "irrigation-basins", on Apollonios' estate, see below P. Lille 1 (text **A** in the supplement), Edgar's brief account in P. Mich. Zen. p. 31 and the recent comment of Skeat, P. Lond. 7 2164, n. *l.* 3.

— Many restorations might be possible here.

7 A slightly longer restoration might be expected here. It is possible and perhaps even likely that a particular feature of the estate (or the village) is mentioned, rather than the village as a whole. There is no other instance of κτίζειν in the archive: conceivably a compound is in question. Perhaps νεωστὶ ἤδη would be a possible phrase here.

T.

29

LETTER FROM ATHENODOTOS TO ZENON

H. × W. = 25.5 × 14.5 cm.[a] Received 5 March, 257 B.C.

Biblioteca Medicea Laurenziana[a+b]: **PSI 5 484**[a]; PSI 6 p. XV[b].

Few physical details of these two fragments are available. It may perhaps be assumed that the text on the front stands on the recto surface. The end portions of *ll.* 3-10 proved to be preserved on a Cairo fragment (*b*), which was presented to the Biblioteca Medicea Laurenziana; the resulting readings were reported in PSI 6 p. XV, with one small correction in PSI 8 p. XVI. From the transcription alone, it is quite obvious that the positioning of this new fragment is correct. However, it is puzzling that, although *ll.* 7-8, for example, each contain 64 letters, *l.* 3 contains only 52. There may be a very straightforward explanation for this, but it cannot at present be checked. The consequence is that it is not possible to judge whether a supplement of about 3-4 letters is necessary in *ll.* 1-2, to match *l.* 3, or a longer restoration is possible.

Contents What is certain in this letter, is that Athenodotos, a person not otherwise known in the archive, who is in some sense being detained, writes to Zenon asking him to intervene with Zoilos to secure his release. Zoilos may very plausibly be identified with the *oeconome* of the Arsinoite nome (see *Prosopography*, P. L. Bat. 21. IX, Ζώιλος (nos. 1-2) for this official). The nature of Athenodotos' detention is not at all clear (see the notes below), but it no doubt concerned the *oeconome's* official duties; and in fact it seems almost certain that it was Zoilos who was failing or refusing to grant Athenodotos his release (see n. *l.* 1).

front:

Ἀθηνόδοτος Ζήνωνι χαίρειν. Μὴ θαυμάσηις ὅτι οὐκ ἐνετύχο̣[μεν. Ζωίλωι] γὰρ ταξάμενοι ὥς ποτε αὐτῶι ἐδόκει καὶ συνθέμενος ἡμῖν ἐντ[υχεῖν] περὶ τῆς ἀφέσεως παρῆλκεν ⟦η⟧ ἕως ἀνεζεύξατε. Ἠνάγκασεν οὖν ἡμᾶς ἀναπλεῦσαι εἰς τὴν Λίμνην. Διὸ οὐκ ἠδυνάμεθα συνκαταπ̣λ[ε]ῦ̣σαι ὑμῖν. Δέομαι οὖν σου, ἀξιῶν καὶ Διονυσοδώρου ἕνεκεν τοῦ οἰκείου τοῦ συστήσα[ντος,] καὶ ἡμῶν δὲ αὐτῶν — ἴσως γάρ που καὶ ἡμεῖς πού σοι χρήσιμοι ἐ̣σ̣όμεσθα σωθέν[τες —] γράψαι φιλότιμον ἐπιστολὴν πρὸς Ζωίλον, ἵνα ἡμᾶς ἀφῆι· ἐσμὲν γὰρ πρεσβύτεροι καὶ ἀδύνατοι. Τὰ δὲ καθ' ἡμᾶς ἀναγγελεῖ σοι Φιλίσκος ἕως ἂν οὖν σοι φαίνηται τὴν ταχίστην ἀποφῆναι αὐτῶι.

Ἔρρωσο. ∟ κη Τῦβι . . .

back:

Ζήνωνι. Ἀθηνοδότου. ∟ κη Αὐδναίου̣ λ, ἐν τῶι Βερενίκης ὅρμωι.

1 ἐνέτυχο̣[ν PSI 4 484 2 ἐν τ[PSI 4 484, et in nota e.g. Τ[άσκρυ —], Τ[άνει —]: aut ἐν τ[άχει], aut e.g. ἐντ[είλασθαι] 6 εσομεσθα PSI 8 p. xvi, corrigens PSI 6 p. xv ἐ̣σ̣όμεσθα 10 ∟ κη Τῦβι . . . PSI 6 p. xv: fortasse ∟ κη Τῦβι η?

Translation

Athenodotos to Zenon, greetings.

Do not be surprised that we did not put in an appearance. For when we had settled with [Zoilos], just on the terms he wished, and when he had agreed with us [to meet] about our release, he kept putting it off, until you had moved on. So he forced us to sail up to the Lake (The Faiyûm). Because of this, we could not sail down together with you. Therefore, I beg you, and I ask both for Dionusodoros' sake, your friend, who introduced (us), and indeed for our own sake—for perhaps somehow even we shall in some way be of service to you, if we are rescued—write a polite letter to Zoilos, so that he may release us. For we are aged and powerless. Philiskos will relate our plight to you, until you decide to give him his instructions as quickly as possible.

Fare well. Year 28, Tubi . . .

Address:

To Zenon.

Docket:

From Athenodotos. Year 28, Audnaios 30, in Berenikes Hormos.

Notes

1 The length of the restoration here poses a problem (see in the description of the fragments above). The structure of more than one of the sentences of this letter is evidently somewhat rambling; but, unless we suppose that the writer (or dictator) completely lost the thread of his sentence, it is essential to restore a personal-name at the end of *l.* 1.

The person concerned here had failed to give Athenodotos his release. As, in *l.* 7, Zenon is to write to Zoilos, "so that he may release us", the obvious restoration in *l.* 1 is of Zoilos' name. It is of course conceivable that a lesser official had been involved, and that Zenon is asked to approach his superior, Zoilos the *oeconome*. But the Greek of *l.* 7 does not naturally suggest that Zoilos is to intervene as a superior, and the letter as a whole perhaps reads better if no further person is involved (see also n. *l.* 8-9).

It might therefore be plausible to restore ὅτι οὐκ ἐνετύχο̣[μέν σοι. Ζωίλωι]| γάρ etc. Although it is impossible to be sure, this does seem to be too long a supplement. The restoration ἐνέτυχό̣[ν σοι. Ζωίλωι]| γάρ is shorter, but it seems very questionable if the use of a singular verb here in *l.* 1 would make the antecedent of ταξάμενοι in *l.* 2 clear; and also Athenodotos uses the plural throughout the letter, except for Δέομαι οὖν σου ἀξιῶν in *l.* 5, which is perhaps used as being partly a set phrase, common, for example, in enteuxeis (although it should be pointed out that Athenodotos' use of the plural in this letter could be explained, not as a point of style, but as referring to himself and his party). Therefore ἐνετύχο̣[μεν. Ζωίλωι]| γάρ is suggested here, ἐνετύχομεν being used absolutely, in the sense, "to put in an appearance".

2 The only possible way of making sense of ταξάμενοι here is as a nominativum pendens, referring to the writer of the letter. As such it seems quite plausible, provided ἐνετύχο̣[μεν] is restored in *l.* 1: there certainly cannot be enough room to restore ἡμεῖς with ταξάμενοι.

Professor M. Manfredi has kindly confirmed, in a letter of 20 August, 1976, that ταξάμενοι is a certain reading here, and thus the possibilities of reading ταξαμένοις or [Ζώιλος]| γὰρ ταξάμενος etc. ("when Zoilos had arranged things to suit himself") are not pursued here.

The participle ταξάμενοι might have a wide range of meanings, but the sense "when we had settled" seems correct here, and probably a payment is involved.

2-3 In PSI 5 484, n. *l.* 2, the interpretation of καὶ συνθέμενος ἡμῖν --- περὶ τῆς ἀφέσεως intended is perhaps "and having reached an agreement with us (*or* given us a promise) . . . about our release", with an indication of where the agreement was reached to be restored at the end of *l.* 2 ("in Taskru", which is in the Memphite nome, or "in Tanis" are suggested). This might be correct. The same construction after συνθέμενος would be retained if, for example, ἐν τάχει were restored.

The alternative is to restore an infinitive after συνθέμενος. The obvious possibilities are an infinitive of ἐντέλλειν, or ἐντυχεῖν. The former would give the sense "having promised us to give orders for our release" (for the use of ἐντέλλειν, see for example P. Cairo Zen. I 59.048, 5; 3 59.408, 6; 59.416, 6; 59.488, 1). The latter might mean "having promised us to discuss our release", almost "having promised us an interview". Of all these possibilities, ἐντυχεῖν has been put in the text here, because it best explains the mention of Zoilos' delaying in *l.* 3 and of Athenodotos' being "forced" to sail up to the Faiyûm in *ll.* 3-4.

Thus the interpretation favoured here is that, although Athenodotus says that he had "settled *or* payed ... just on the terms he wished", there was in fact some dispute about this, or, at any rate, the matter had to be discussed. Zoilos kept putting off the interview, and finally Athenodotos had to follow him up to the Faiyûm, where, at the time of writing, he had still not obtained his release.

The nature of the "release" requested by Athenodotos is not certain. It is perfectly possible that Athenodotos was under some form of arrest, perhaps for debt. However, Ἠνάγκασεν οὖν ἡμᾶς | ἀναπλεῦσαι εἰς τὴν Λίμνην suggests more that Athenodotos was seeking an interview with Zoilos, than that he was transferred as a prisoner, and the general tone of the letter does not demand such an interpretation. Compare P. Petrie II 13.19 *l.* 8 (= Sel. Pap. I 94), where ἀφεθῆναι suggests a retirement from office.

6 The punctuation here is not, of course, present in the original.

7 φιλότιμον, "polite", or possibly "effusive"?

8-9 The last sentence of the letter is perhaps just a little humorous. Conceivably Philiskos was notably garrulous or had instructions to be persistent, and the sense may be that he will keep on telling the story, until Zenon decides to give him his instructions or to give him a decision. It is natural to suppose that Philiskos was the bearer of Athenodotos' letter to Zenon, and perhaps Philiskos was also meant to bring back Zenon's letter to Zoilos. This interpretation has been followed in the translation above.

It would be very hazardous to suggest that the Philiskos of this letter should be identified with the later *oeconome* of the Arsinoite nome (see further in the *Prosopography*, P. L. Bat. 21. IX).

Two possible alternative interpretations are rejected here. First that αὐτῶι in *l.* 9 could refer to the obstructive official detaining Athenodotos, who (it is suggested in n. *l.* 1) is probably to be identified with Zoilos in *l.* 7:—"until you decide to explain to him"? Secondly, that Philiskos himself is in fact the obstructive official:—"Philiskos will give you an (unfair?) account of our position", etc.?

10 Because the month Audnaios in year 28 should contain only 29 days, the date Audnaios 30 in *l.* 13 presumably is to be understood as equivalent to 1 Peritios, and the corresponding day by the Egyptian calendar would be 11 Tubi. In PSI 6 p. XV it was indicated that the date of dispatch consisted of both tens and units (Τῦβι ..): the only such reading possible would be Τῦβι ια, Tubi 11. This would mean that the letter was written and received on the same day, which is unlikely to be correct. If the traces suggested the presence of two letters here, the obvious reading that springs to mind is η, which is often deceptively broad. In this case the date of sending would be 2nd March, 257 B.C.

14 For the problem of the location of Berenikes Hormos, probably not far to the north of Memphis, see text no. **22**, n. *l.* 15 above. The geographical indications in the present letter are quite clear. By the time the letter was written, Zenon had sailed north to Berenikes Hormos (*l.* 3 and *l.* 4), and Athenodotos had been forced to sail south to the Faiyûm (*l.* 4). The conclusion seems virtually certain that they had both been in Memphis, where in fact the evidence from the archive places Zenon in January 257 B.C.: he probably arrived at Berenikes Hormos on 3rd February 257 B.C. (see the chronological information in P. L. Bat. 21. VIII, *c*).

T.

30

LETTER FROM DEMETRIOS TO ZENON

H. × W. = 12.3 × 8.6 cm. — Sent 5 April, 242 B.C. (Financial Year) or 4 April, 241 B.C. (Egyptian Year)

Berl. inv. 17487: **BGU 10 1994**, with plate 22.

The papyrus is well-preserved with margins on all sides. The text on the front is written along the fibres, and continues upside down on the back. The writing is a small, fluent cursive. The letter was folded nine times from the top downward; the folds are clearly visible on the verso.

Contents Zenon had ordered Demetrios to give Antipatros 100 drachmae from the proceeds of the remaining wine. Demetrios replies in this letter that this is impossible because part of the wine has gone bad. He asks Zenon to send him some jars of fragrant wine, as he hopes to clear his stock of the old wine at the same time. He finally informs Zenon that the latter's debt to Antipatros totals 190 drachmae. We do not know if the wine was stemming from Zenon's involvement with the *apomoira* (see no. **34**, introduction) or if it was the produce of his own vineyards.

front:

Δημήτριος Ζήνωνι χα̣ί̣ρειν.
Γράφεις μοι δοῦναι Ἀντιπ̣ά̣τρωι
ἐκ τῶν περιόντων οἰναρί̣ω̣ν ⊦̣ ρ·
ἔστιν δὲ τὰ περιόντα κερ(άμια) η, ἐν οἷς
ἔνεστιν γ τὰ διαφωνοῦντα,
ἃ καὶ ἔγευσαν Ἀντίπατρο̣ν καὶ
Νίκανδρον, ὥστε μηδὲ δραχμῆς
τὸν χόα ἄξιον εἶναι. Καὶ εἰ μὴ τὴν
ἐπιγραφὴν ἑώρων, τοὺς παρα-
κομίζοντας ἂν ᾐτιώμην. Καλῶς
οὖν ποιήσεις εὐώδους ἀποστεί-
λας κεράμια πλέονα. Ἱκανὸς γάρ
⟦και⟧ `τις´ ὄχλος ἐνδημεῖ διὰ τὸ καὶ τὰς
ὠνὰς πωλεῖσθαι καὶ ζητοῦσι
εὐώδη καὶ ἅμα τὸν περιόντα
ἐξώσει. Ἀπέστειλα δέ σοι καὶ
πρότερον τὸν παρ' αὐτοῦ λόγον

back:

καὶ νῦν ἐπὶ κεφαλαίου ὧν
τὸ καθ' ἓν ὑπάρχει ἵνα εἰδῇς
ἕως Μεχεὶρ ι̅α̅ ⊢ ρϙ κα[ὶ]
μετὰ λόγον ⟦ἐπισκεψάμενος⟧
γραφήσεταί σοι.
"Ερρωσο L ϛ̣ Μεχεὶρ ι̅ε̣̅.

Ζ̣ήνωνι.

14 ζητήσει ed. princ. 23 L ζ ed. princ.

Translation

Demetrios to Zenon, greetings.

You write to me to give 100 drachmae to Antipatros from (the proceeds of) the remaining wine. What remains is 8 keramia, three of which have gone bad—and they have let Antipatros and Nikandros taste it—so that it is not even worth one drachma per chous. And if I had not seen the label, I would have blamed those who brought it. Please, therefore, send several jars of fragrant wine. For there is a considerable crowd here, because they are selling the "farms"; they are looking for fragrant wine, and at the same time you will be rid of the remainder. I have already sent you his account. The grand total, of which a detailed account exists, for your information, is now, up to the 11th of Mecheir, 190 drachmae. And we shall write to you after settling the account.

Fare well. Year 6, 15 Mecheir.

Address:

To Zenon.

Notes

2-3 γράφεις μοι δοῦναι 'Αντιπάτρωι ἐκ τῶν περιόντων οἰναρίων ⊢ ρ: Müller translates this "du schreibst mir, du hast Antipatros für den übriggebliebenen Wein 100 Drachmen gegeben", but the Greek rendering of "für den Wein" would be εἰς τὰ οἰνάρια, not ἐκ τῶν οἰναρίων. Moreover the aorist infinitive after γράφω, instead of the usual ὅτι, more often than not indicates a command: cf. the well-known formula of the enteuxeis: δέομαι --- προστάξαι τῶι στρατηγῶι γράψαι + infinitive aorist.

Our interpretation of this passage brings with it a new view of the rest of the letter as well: it continues with a rejection of Zenon's proposal, with a counterproposal for finding buyers for the remaining wine, and a rough account of what Zenon owes to Antipatros.

6 ἔγευσαν: the *nu* appears to have been inserted afterwards, the writer changing from the first person sing. to the third person plural. For the active γεύω "to let have a taste", cf. also P. Lond. 7 1948, 6: ἔγευσεν δέ με καὶ τοῦ οἴνου.

7-8 ὥστε μηδὲ δραχμῆς τὸν χόα ἄξιον εἶναι: Müller's translation "so dass die Lieferung nicht eine Drachme wert ist" does not seem justified. As far as I know, χοῦς is never used in the sense of "Lieferung", "supply". I therefore prefer the following translation: "so that it (the wine) is not even worth one drachma per chous". The article in τὸν χόα has a distributive sense (E. MAYSER, *Grammatik* II, 2, pp. 43 and 336; see also P. Cairo Zen. 3 59.516, 20-21: ἐξ ἐννέα ὀβολῶν τὸν χόα and P. Cairo Zen. 3 59.591, 8-9: ἀγοράζειν ἐξ χαλκῶν τὴν δέσμην.) The subject of εἶναι can easily be understood from οἰναρίων in *l.* 3. The same word has also to be supplied in *ll.* 11 and 15.

When dealing with a normal wine-keramion of six chous, one drachma per chous is indeed the usual price (T. REEKMANS, *Monetary History, Studia Hellenistica* 5, 1948, p. 34). This level has not been reached in this case, because three keramia have gone bad.

13-14 διὰ τὸ καὶ τὰς ὠνὰς πωλεῖσθαι: the reference is to the practice of putting up for sale the contracts for the farming of taxes, and other sources of revenue. For the expression, see for example P. Rev. Laws 60, 13-14 and Sylloge I^3 284, 9-10. Here, as in P. Cairo Zen. 3 59.371 (cf. Edgar's note ad loc.), the auction takes place in Mecheir, at the beginning of the financial year.

14 ζητοῦσι: Müller reads ζητήσει, but, having checked the original in Berlin, I think ζητοῦσι is a more likely reading. The *constructio ad sensum* ὄχλος ἐνδημεῖ --- καὶ ζητοῦσι raises no difficulty.

16 In my opinion ἐξώσει is a second person middle ("you will shake off to your advantage") and not a third person active (Müller: "man wird .... abstossen"). This is the only attestation of ἐξωθέω in the papyri. The middle form of the verb is not recorded in Liddell-Scott-Jones, but see G. W. M. LAMPE, *A Patristic Greek Lexicon*, s.v.

C.

31

BRIEF DES DORION AN ZENON

H. × Br. = 12 × 33 cm.

Geschrieben 25. März 249 v. Chr.,
empfangen 4. April 249 v. Chr.

Bibliotheca Medicea Laurenziana: **PSI 4 369**; nachträglich berichtigt von Grenfell (PSI 5, S. X), Edgar (PSI 6, S. XII) und Wilcken (*Archiv für Papyrusforsch.* 6, 1920, 390).

Der rechte Rand des Textes ist nicht völlig erhalten; es sind aber wohl höchstens vier Buchstaben verlorengegangen. Auf der Rückseite befinden sich Anschrift und Empfangsvermerk.

Inhalt Dorion berichtet Zenon über verpfändete Gegenstände und ihren Wert, sowie Zins und Dauer der Verpfändung. In der zweiten Hälfte des Briefes bittet er Zenon ihm zu helfen Geld von Sostratos zu erhalten; danach berichtet er über eine grosse Summe Geldes, welche in Auftrag des Sostratos in Memphis zur Verfügung gestellt werden muss.

Der Brief war dem Zenon wahrscheinlich aus Memphis gesandt worden, denn sowohl Dorions Nachrichten als seine Aufgaben hängen mit dieser Stadt zusammen. Der hier erwähnte Thrason (Z. 9) ist gut bekannt als Zenons Agent im Memphitischen Gau.

Vorderseite:

Δωρίων Ζήνωνι χαίρειν. Ἐπυθόμεθα ἀφ᾽ οὗ χρόνου κεῖται τὰ διὰ Χάρμου ἐνέχυρα [ποτη]-
ρίδια καὶ κοσμάρια· ἔστιν τὸ κεφάλαιον ἀργυρίου ⊦ χ καὶ τόκος ἑκάστης μνᾶς ἀργυ̣(ρίου) [⊦ . ὁ δὲ]
χρόνος ἔτη β̅ καὶ μῆ(νες) ια. Ὁμοίως δὲ καὶ τὰ ἕ<τε>ρα· τὸ κεφάλαιον ἀργυ(ρίου) ⊦ ⸓, ἀφ᾽ ὧν
παρὰ Πετάλιος ἐμ πόλει ἀργυ(ρίου) <⊦>χ καὶ ἐμ Μέμφει Κάλλωνι ἀργυ(ρίου) ⊦ τ (γίνονται) ἀργυ(ρίου) [⊦ ⸓]·
ὁ δὲ χρόνος ἐνιαυτὸς καὶ μῆ(νες) ε̅. Περὶ δὲ τῶν ⸓ ⊦ τοῦ τόκου μὴ φρόντιζε, ἀλ<λ᾽> ὡς ἄ[ν σοι]
φα̣ίνηται, οὕτως ποίει. Καλῶς δὲ ποιήσεις καὶ παρὰ Σωστράτου ἀργυ(ρίου) ⊦ λβ ἃ̣ς̣ [ἔχω]
διὰ τραπέζης ὑπὲρ Διονυσίου φροντίσας ὅπως ἀποσταλῇ μοι. Συνέθηκε δὲ ⊼ α
ἀποδόσθαι ἐμ Μέμφει, ὃ συνέταξεν δοῦναι εἰς τὰ ὀψώνια Πάιτι καὶ Φαλοῦτι καὶ
ἄλλα ⊼ β (γίνεται) ⊼ γ. Ἔγραψε δέ μοι πρὸς Θράσωνα ἐπιστόλιον ὑπολογῆσαι ὧν
τὴν τιμὴν οὐθεὶς δέδωκεν.

Ἔρρωσο. L λς Μεχεὶρ β̅.

Rückseite:

Ζήνωνι.
L λς Μεχεὶρ ιβ. Δωρίων
ποτηριδίων, Σωστράτ(ου)
ἀ(ργυρίου) ⊦ λβ.

1-2]|ριδια ed. princ., [ποτη]|ρίδια Edgar 2 ἀρ̣γ̣υ̣[ρίου ⊦. ὁ δέ] ed. princ.: nur in Z. 2 (Mitte) steht ἀργυρίου vollständig geschrieben; in Z. 3, 4 und 6 steht die Abkürzung ἀργυ(ρίου) welche ich auch hier annehme, aber trotzdem bleibt diese Zeile ein wenig länger als die anderen 3 τὰ ερα (?) ed. princ., τὰ ἕ<τε> ρα Wilcken 4 [⊦.] ed. princ., [⊦ 𐅵] Wilcken 5 ἀλωσα[ἔαν σοι] ed. princ., ἀλ<λ'> ὡς ἄ[ν σοι] Grenfell 6 ⊦ λβ ἅ̣ς̣ [ed. princ., ⊦ λβ ἃς [ἔχει] Edgar 7 Die editio princeps nimmt an, dass nach ⊼ α in der Lücke noch etwas geschrieben war; m.E. braucht man hier (und in Z. 8 und 9) nichts mehr zu ergänzen; die Zeilenlängen variieren stark in diesem Text 8 Φαλοῦτι κατ̣[ed. princ., Φαλοῦτι καὶ [Grenfell; vgl. auch Anm. zu Z. 7 9 ὑπολογῆσαι ...[ed. princ., ὑπολογῆσαι ὧν [Grenfell; vgl. auch Anm. zu Z. 7 14 π̣οτηρίου(?) ων ed. princ., ποτηριδίων Wilcken.

Übersetzung

Dorion grüsst Zenon.

Wir haben erfahren, seit welcher Zeit die durch Charmos verpfändeten Becherchen und Schmucksachen verpfändet sind: die Hauptsumme beträgt 600 Silberdrachmen und der Zins ist für jede Mine .. Silberdrachmen und die Zeitdauer ist 2 Jahre und 11 Monate. Und ähnlich auch die anderen Gegenstände: die Hauptsumme beträgt 900 Silberdrachmen, von denen von Petalis in der Stadt 600 Silberdrachmen und in Memphis für Kallon 300 Silberdrachmen; das ist zusammen 900 Silberdrachmen und die Zeitdauer ist ein Jahr und 5 Monate. Und für den Zins der 900 Drachmen musst Du Dir keine Sorgen machen, aber tue so, wie es Dir gut scheint.

Und Du wirst auch gut tun, wenn Du Dich darum kümmerst, dass von Sostratos 32 Silberdrachmen, welche ich durch die Bank für Dionysios (empfangen) habe, zu mir gesandt werden. Und er hat Massnahmen ergriffen, dass 1 Talent in Memphis gegeben würde — welches Talent er befahl dem Païs und dem Phalus als Löhne zu geben — und weitere 2 Talente, das macht 3 Talente. Und da hat er doch einen Brief an Thrason geschrieben, die Posten in Abzug zu bringen, wofür keiner den Preis bezahlt hat.

Lebe wohl.
Im 36. Jahr, am 2. Mecheir.

Anschrift:

An Zenon.

Empfangsvermerk:

Im 36. Jahr, am 12. Mecheir.
Dorion über Becherchen, (und) 32 Silberdrachmen von Sostratos.

Anmerkungen

1 Dorion scheint sonst unbekannt zu sein. Vgl. aber P. Col. Zen. 2 100, 11-12, Anm.; PSI 6 608, Einl. und Wipszycka, Klio 39 (1961) 166.

— Charmos hat Sachen verpfändet betreffs eines Darlehens von 600 Drachmen; ebenso Petalis betreffs eines Darlehens von ebenfalls 600 Drachmen. An Kallon wurden 300 Drachmen (gegen Unterpfand) ausgeliehen. In dem Brief wird nicht expressis verbis erwähnt ob Zenon der Gläubiger ist, der diesen 3 Leuten das Geld ausgeliefert hat, oder ob er der Schuldner ist, für den diese drei Männer gehandelt haben. Da Dorion aber in Z. 5-6 sagt, dass Zenon hinsichtlich des Zinses der 900 Drachmen nach Belieben handeln kann, kann man vielleicht folgern dass Zenon der Gläubiger war.

Für Verpfändung siehe TAUBENSCHLAG, *Law of Greco-Roman Egypt*, S. 285-286 und SEIDL, *Ptolemäische Rechtsgeschichte*, S. 141-142, wo auch die anderen Urkunden des Archivs, worin Verpfändung erwähnt wird, zusammengestellt sind.

1-2 ἐνέχυρα [ποτη]ρίδια: vgl. P. Cairo Zen. 3 59.327, 1-2 und PSI 6 608, 3, wo verpfändete ποτήρια vorkommen.

4 ἐμ πόλει: es ist hier wahrscheinlich Alexandria gemeint.

6 παρὰ Σωστράτου ist mit dem folgenden Teil des Satzes schwer zu verbinden. Kann man annehmen, dass dieser Satz ursprunglich anders, etwa ,,Und Du wirst gut tun, 32 Silberdrachmen von Sostratos zu nehmen (o.ä)'' formuliert werden sollte und während des Schreibens eine Änderung eingetreten ist? Vgl. auch den Empfangsvermerk.

Sostratos scheint hier einen höheren Posten zu bekleiden. Obwohl der Name im Archiv öfter vorkommt, kann unser Sostratos mit einem der anderen gleichnamigen Männer schwer gleichgestellt werden. Vgl. aber den fragmentarischen Brief des κυβερνήτης Pais (P. Lond. 7 2063), wo ein Sostratos wahrscheinlich auch in Verbindung mit Opsonia genannt ist.

8-9 Pais und Phalus kommen in mehreren Urkunden des Archivs vor, aber niemals zusammen in einem Text. Immer behandeln sie verschiedene mit Schiffen verbundenen Angelegenheiten. Pais ist in P. Mich. Zen. 60, 15 als κυ(βερνήτης) bezeichnet und den Beruf des Phalus lesen wir nur in P. dem. Zen. 5, 3:*p3 nf*; diese demotische Bezeichnung wird in der griechischen Übersetzung von P. dem. Berl. 3116, Kol. 5, Z. 13-15 (113 v. Chr.) mit κυ(βερνήτης) wiedergegeben (UPZ 2 180a, Kol. 10, Z. 10-11, Kol. 11, Z. 1). Bemerkenswert ist hier die grosse Summe, die für Opsonia ausgezahlt werden sollte. In anderen Urkunden (P. Cairo Zen. 4 59.649, 6; 59.754, 13; PSI 4 357, 18) variiert sie von 8 bis 10 Drachmen. Es ist aber möglich, dass dieses Talent für das ganze Gesinde bestimmt war, und Löhne für eine längere Periode bildeten.

W.

32

LETTER FROM HELIODOROS TO ZENON

H. × W. = 5.5 × 7.5 cm.[a]; 13.5 × 7.5 cm.[b]; 19 × 11.8 cm.[c]; 11 × 7 cm.[d]

Sent 9 February, 258 B.C., received 5 March, 258 B.C.

Col. inv. 306e3[a] + Col. inv. 305c[b] + Brit. Mus. (now Brit. Library) inv. 2326[c] + Cairo JdE 48466[d]: **P. Col. Zen. 2 61**[a] and **P. Lond. 7 1931**[c] (which incorporated P. Col. Zen. 2 115g[b] and P. Cairo Zen. 1 59.017[d]).

The original dimensions of the whole letter may be estimated to have been 19 cm. (height) by (very roughly) 25-28 cm. (width). The text of the letter on the front is written across the fibres. The arrangement of the various fragments may most easily be appreciated from the following schematic figure, in which the papyrus is naturally viewed from the front:

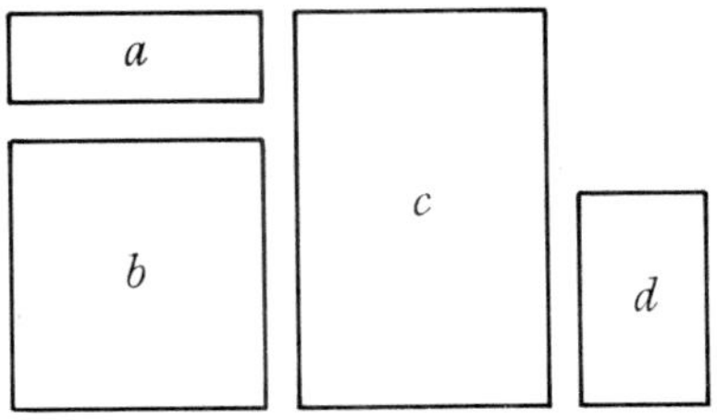

A fragment is still missing at the top right-hand corner. The address, "To Zenon", on the back, stands almost entirely upon the B.M. fragment (*c*), with just part of the first letter being preserved upon P. Col. Zen. 2 61 (*a*), which also bears on its back surface the docket. Skeat describes the hand as of a chancery type, and gives the colour of the B.M. fragment as medium-brown. We are most grateful to Dr. R. Bagnall for examining and collating the two Columbia portions and informing us that all the indications favour Pestman's suggestion that they belong to the same papyrus.

Contents This letter asks Zenon to take delivery of a large quantity of wheat and barley at Ptolemais/Acre. The nature of the grain transaction involved remains uncertain, chiefly because of the lacunae at the ends of *ll.* 1-4 of the text, due to the small portion of the papyrus still missing. The possibilities are discussed in the notes below, especially n. *ll.* 2-3. The letter as now combined provides us with our latest date for Zenon's stay in Syria-Palestine.

front:

Ἡλιόδωρος Ζήνωνι χαίρειν. Ἔγραψεν ἡμ̣[ῖν Ἀπολλώνιος]
τὸν προσοφειλό̣μενον σῖτον Μηδείωι εκτ̣[*c.* 8-12]
τα μετρῆσαί σοι ἵνα διαθῆι̣. Καλῶς οὖν [ποιήσεις κατα-?]
μετρησάμενος αὐ̣τ̣ὸν ἐμ Πτολεμαίδι [*c.* 8-12]
του παρ' ἡμῶν. Καὶ τοῦτο ποιήσα[ς] ἐ̣ν τάχει χαριεῖ ἡ[μῖν.]
Ἔστι δὲ τὸ πλῆθος πυ(ρῶν) ἀρ(τάβαι) 'Γσπδ, κριθ̣ῶν̣ ἀρ(τάβαι) 'Βχνγ.
Ἀπέσταλκα δέ σοι καὶ τὴν παρ' Ἀπολλωνίου ἐπιστολὴ[ν]
περὶ τούτων. Ἔρρωσο. L κζ Αὐδναίου κε.

back:

9 Ζήνωνι.
10 [. . . . .] . . . . ου
[᾽Απολ]λ̣ω̣ν̣ίου. L κζ
[Περιτ]ί̣ο̣υ̣ ιθ̄, ἐν Κυδί̣σωι.

Textus cum P. Col. Zen. 2 61 et P. Lond. 7 1931 hic collatus est, differentias minores non notavimus

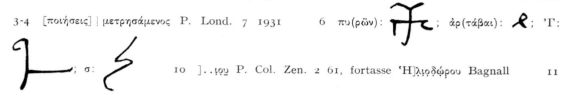

3-4 [ποιήσεις] | μετρησάμενος P. Lond. 7 1931   6 πυ(ρῶν): ; ἀρ(τάβαι): 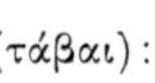; ᾽Γ: ; σ:    10]. .ι̣ο̣υ̣ P. Col. Zen. 2 61, fortasse ῾Η]λ̣ι̣ο̣δ̣ώ̣ρου Bagnall   11 ᾽Απολ]λ̣ω̣ν̣ίου Pestman, β]αλα̣ν̣ίου P. Col. Zen. 2 61   12 Περιτ]ί̣ο̣υ̣ rest. Pestman,]ί̣ο̣υ̣ legit Bagnall,]ο̣υ̣ P. Col. Zen. 2 61.

Translation

Heliodoros to Zenon, greetings.

[Apollonios] wrote to us that the corn still owing [---] to Medeios [---] should be measured for you so that you could settle (the matter). So please have it measured in Ptolemais [---] from us. And you will oblige us if you do this speedily. The amount is 3284 artabas of wheat, and 2653 artabas of barley. I have also sent you the letter from Apollonios about these matters.

Fare well. Year 27, Audnaios 25.

Address:

To Zenon.

Docket:

[---]. . . . . . . of Apollonios. Year 27, [Perit]ios 19, in Kudisos (Qadesh).

Notes

1 There seems no sufficient reason to identify the Heliodoros who wrote this letter with any other Heliodoros known, and in the *Prosopography*, P. L. Bat. 21. IX, he has been included as an unidentified person (no. 5). We do not know from where he wrote, whether from Egypt or from elsewhere. His (Greek) name does not give any indication whether or not he was from Egypt. The form of the date in *l.* 8 (employing the symbol L, and a regnal year) is, of course, Egyptian, but might be found throughout the Ptolemaic sphere of influence. The general manner of the letter, in particular the way in which Apollonios is mentioned, suggests that Heliodoros was an employee or associate of Apollonios; but it is conceivable that the letter should be differently interpreted (see n. *ll.* 2-3 below).

— In P. Col. Zen. 2 61, 1, the [after Ηλιοδωρος Ζη was omitted by a misprint.

— The restoration of Apollonios' name here is virtually certain, in view of the mention of his letter in *ll.* 7-8 below.

2-3 It remains impossible to be sure of the structure of the sentence here. We might restore Μηδείωι ἐκτ̣[εῖσαι καὶ κα]|ταμετρῆσαι, "Apollonios has written to us that the corn still owing should be paid out to Medeios, and (*i.e.* 'more precisely') should be measured for you, so that you can settle (the matter)", *or* "deal (with it—*i.e.* the corn)"; but there are many other possibilities. The verb ἐκτίνειν, "to pay in full" is not common in the archive (P. Cairo Zen. 4

59.640, 18 and PSI 4 349, 4) but its usage presents no problem. Skeat's edition does not suggest a restoration for ἐκτ̣[(so printed), but his index gives, with an interrogation mark, a reference to this passage under ἐκτίθημι: apart from other meanings ("publish", "narrate") ἐκτιθέναι occurs in the archive in the sense of "paying out a (small) allowance" (P. Cairo Zen. 1 59.002, 4; 59.049, 6), and Skeat may have speculated that ἐκτιθέναι could here mean simply "to pay", or "to deliver". The natural interpretation of the wording of the letter is that Heliodoros is simply following Apollonios' instructions, and is not suggesting an alteration in the arrangements, and any restoration should take account of this.

A Medeios occurs also in P. Cairo Zen. 1 59.036, 3 and 13; cf. EDGAR, *Annales du Service des Antiquités* 22 (1922), esp. pp. 214-15; U. WILCKEN, *Zur Trierarchie im Lagidenreich, Raccolta Lumbroso*, esp. p. 96; and R. S. BAGNALL, *The Ptolemaic Trierarchs, Chronique d'Égypte* 46 (1971), esp. p. 358: see *Prosopography*, P. L. Bat. 21. IX Μήδειος—for the eponymous priest proposed as an identification by Edgar, see Pros. Ptol. 3 5199.

In his introduction to P. Lond. 7 1931, Skeat saw Medeios as an "agent" at Ptolemais from whom Zenon was to collect the corn, although in his n. *l.* 2 he appears to accept the identification with the Medeios of P. Cairo Zen. 1 59.036, who, according to the generally accepted opinion, was to be paid (in some more or less official capacity, and probably at Alexandria) a large sum of money that had been collected at Halikarnassos for a royal tax. The reading προσοφειλόμενον (which was not in Skeat's text) by itself makes it very difficult to find any restoration here whereby Medeios can be understood only to have been an intermediary, and whereby the purpose of Apollonios' letter to Heliodoros can be understood merely to have been to have the corn placed at Zenon's disposal, without specifying its ultimate destination. If the situation in the present letter even remotely resembles that in P. Cairo Zen. 1 59.036, and the corn here is to be paid to the same Medeios, several questions arise: Medeios' position, and the nature of the debt or payment pose obvious problems; and, further, it is no longer so clear that the grain was being imported for profit by Apollonios from Egypt. Skeat plausibly argued that grain may be expected to be carried from Egypt to Syria, and his suggestion of a connection between the present text and P. Lond. 7 2022 (mentioning Ptolemais and corn from Alexandria) is also plausible. If this point is accepted, we might speculate that Apollonios had contracted to deliver grain to Medeios or his agents in Syria.

A quite different interpretation would be to understand προσοφειλόμενον as indicating that the corn was owed *to* Apollonios. (In this case, it would be natural, judging from the way the letter is expressed, to suppose that it was owed directly or indirectly *by* Heliodoros). However, if so, it is a great problem to know what kind of restoration is to be made at the end of *l.* 2. Conceivably διαθῆι might be understood as indicating that Zenon was to take delivery of the grain and "dispose" of it, i.e. "sell" it—but this also would make *l.* 2 difficult to restore or to understand: it might be suggested that the grain was to be "offered for sale" (ἐκτιθέναι) to Medeios, but this is a dubious interpretation.

3-4 The supplement [ποιήσεις] at the end of *l.* 3, which could easily be expanded, might seem rather short, although Skeat perhaps observed some special reason for accepting it. One possibility is to read κατα-]|μετρησάμενος.

4 Skeat's translation, "so please have it (i.e. the corn) measured out in Ptolemais", is followed here. To judge from the parallels he cites (P. Cairo Zen. 4 59.577 passim; 59.649, 26), Skeat understood this in the sense of "receiving the measured corn", rather than of "organizing its measurement" and such a nuance, difficult to express in a literal translation, would best suit the context.

— Skeat had already argued that "in view of the date of the letter, the only Ptolemais which comes into consideration is the Palestinian port of Acre". The letter is now known to have been received by Zenon at Qadesh (*l.* 12), less than 50 km from Ptolemais/Acre.

4-5 Several kinds of restoration are possible here. One possibility might be διά (or another preposition) N. τοῦ παρ' ἡμῶν; or [ἐκ τοῦ σίτου]|τοῦ παρ' ἡμῶν might mean "from the corn we have sent", and might conceivably support the idea that the grain was owed to Apollonios by Heliodoros (see n. *ll.* 2-3 above), although the inference might only be that Heliodoros was responsible for its shipment.

6 Skeat n. *l.* 6 suggests that "πυ(ροῦ) might perhaps be better expanded as πυρ(ῶν), seeing that κριθῶν follows", and the expansion has been made in the plural here.

7 The sense of ἀπέσταλκα (in the singular, as Skeat n. *l.* 1 points out) is clearly "I am now sending herewith" and this sense is supported by the apparent use of ἀπεστάλ[καμεν] in P. Lond. 7 1934, 1 to refer to a letter of which a copy is written out below, although ὑπογέγραφα is the

common expression for this. Cf. n. *l.* 10. It is possible that Apollonios' letter was actually enclosed here, rather than copied, not just for information, but because it was required or would be helpful to secure the issue of the corn. However, such an explanation cannot apply to all the letters addressed to other people that found their way into Zenon's hands.

10-11 Dr. Bagnall has kindly confirmed on the original that Pestman's suggestion to read]λ̣ω̣ν̣ιου in *l.* 11 is plausible. The amount to be restored to the left is not certain, although probably little is lost (cf. *l.* 12). We might simply restore [Ἡλιο]δ̣ω̣ρου | [Ἀπολ]λ̣ω̣ν̣ιου, assuming that the docket referred to Apollonios' letter enclosed within. The traces in *l.* 10, read by the Columbia editors]. .ι̣ο̣υ̣ are too badly damaged to confirm or deny the restoration of Heliodoros' name here. The docket could have been more extensive and more explicit.

12 The ι̣ of]ι̣ο̣υ̣ has been read by Dr. Bagnall, who also confirms the readings ιθ̄ ἐν Κυδ̣ίσωι.

The restoration Περιτ]ί̣ο̣υ̣ ιθ̄ (5th March, 258 B.C.) is the earliest date that can be restored for the receipt of the letter, and is plainly correct. Accepting the reading]ι̣ο̣υ̣, the next month name in -ιος that could be restored would be Artemisios, and this would mean the letter was received on Artemisios 19th = 1st July, 258; but this date should belong to Year 28, and also would imply an improbably long delay before the letter reached Zenon.

If the reading]ι̣ο̣υ̣, rather than the Columbia editors']ο̣υ̣, is not thought sufficiently secure to be the basis of a chronological argument, then Peritios Embolimos, Dystros, and Xandikos might come into consideration, yielding dates of 3rd April, 3rd May, and 2nd June 258. The first of these three involves a more extensive restoration than it was suggested in n. *ll.* 10-11 was probable in the docket, and implies a surprising delay in the delivery of the letter: the other two possibilities imply increasingly improbable delays, and Xandikos 19 should belong to Year 28.

What emerges for certain is that this letter, which duly found its way into Zenon's archive, was endorsed as received in Qadesh on a date that at the earliest must be **5th March, 258**, and this provides us with a reliable new *terminus post quem* for Zenon's departure from Syria-Palestine.

The question of when Zenon returned to Egypt has received some discussion. It is generally assumed that Zenon's stay in Syria-Palestine was a continuous one—that he did not return to Egypt at all in the meantime. This is perhaps plausible, and there is no evidence to contradict it, but our evidence for the latter part of Zenon's stay is scanty, and it cannot be regarded as proven.

In **April/May 259** (Xandikos, Year 27), we know from P. Cairo Zen. I 59.003 that Zenon was in Palestine; and it is reasonable to infer from P. Cairo Zen. I 59.016 that near the beginning of 258 he was somewhere in this area, as on the **30th December 259** it was appropriate for a visitor to the coast of Phoenicia/The Lebanon to write to him for a supplement to his travel allowance, and the letter evidently arrived. Thereafter, we have no proof of his presence back in Egypt until the **Autumn of 258**, nor is there any firm evidence as to his activities in the Spring and Summer of that year. V. A. Tcherikover, in *Palestine under the Ptolemies, Mizraim* 4-5 (1937), pp. 11-12, argued that it was possible to deduce from P. Cairo Zen. I 59.015 verso and 59.018 a fairly precise indication of when Zenon returned to Egypt—that he arrived "probably in February, at the latest at the beginning of March, 258".

Tcherikover reasoned as follows: While Zenon was travelling back to Egypt (Ἡμῶν 'δ'' εἰς Αἴγυπτον εἰσπορευομέ̣[νων], P. Cairo Zen. I 59.015 verso, 18), some slaves recently purchased in Idumaea escaped. After he had received information that they had returned to their former owners, Zenon sent a certain Straton from Egypt to Idumaea to recover them, and gave him various letters to assist him in this task—letters of which we possess the undated drafts in P. Cairo Zen. I 59.015 verso. However, from I 59.018, we learn that a Straton, obviously the same man, had been attempting to carry out another mission (the recovery of a debt) for Zenon, on or shortly before **4th April, 258**. Edgar assumed that this incident took place in Palestine, and, although nothing in the text proves this, the events would suit a Palestinian context, and were discussed in this light by Tcherikover in CPJ, on text no. 6 (the same papyrus). Thus, if Straton had been sent from Egypt, Zenon must have been in Egypt to send him, and in good time before 4th April 258.

There are a number of minor uncertainties in this argument, but there is also one major difficulty—that it is neither certain nor especially likely that Straton was sent by Zenon from Egypt to Palestine. More probably he was in Palestine all the time, and, in the case of the escaped slaves, Zenon sent letters and instructions to him there. The phrases Στράτωνι | τῶι κομίζοντί σοι τὸ ἐπιστόλιον, "Straton, who brings you this letter" (P. Cairo Zen. 1 59.015 verso, 8-9), and Στράτωνι τῶι τὰς ἐπιστολὰς ὑμῖν | κομίζοντι, "Straton, who brings you these letters" (*ibid.*, *ll.* 33-4: "letters" has been corrected from "letter"), do nothing to establish that Straton travelled from Egypt. Thus P. Cairo Zen. 1 59.015 verso need not be dated well before 59.018, and in fact the order of the texts could just as easily be the reverse. There is nothing in P. Cairo Zen. 1 59.018 that shows whether or not Zenon was in Palestine at the time. Edgar mentioned the possibility "far from certain" that P. Cairo Zen. 5 59.804, dated 7 September 258, might refer to the same slaves as P. Cairo Zen. 1 59.015 verso (n. *l.* 2).

As a pendant to his discussion of the dates of Zenon's stay in Palestine, Tcherikover suggested (*Mizraim* 4-5, p. 13) the possibility that Zenon was recalled hastily and unexpectedly back to Egypt by Apollonios, but none of the evidence for this seems at all satisfactory. Edgar in his introduction to P. Mich. Zen. (pp. 19-20) discussed the possibility that the political situation within and outside Egypt led to Zenon's return, but, surely rightly, concluded this was unlikely.

Edgar, in his introduction to P. Cairo Zen. 5 59.803 (see text no. **76 A** below), pointed out that if this damaged letter was addressed to Zenon, it might indicate that he was already in Egypt in January 258; but it is in fact plausible to suppose Zenon was not the addressee.

The present text shows that Zenon was still in Palestine on **5th March, 258**. It would just conceivably be possible to reconcile this with the essence of Tcherikover's view that Zenon must have been back in Egypt on a date suitably in advance of 4th April, 258. However, it has been suggested above that Tcherikover's argument probably rests on no foundation at all. The present papyrus might suggest that Zenon was still travelling, and still had business to attend to on 5th March; but really we do not know why or when Zenon returned to Egypt, except that it was between 5th March, 258 B.C. and a date in the Summer of 258 B.C. that would permit us to find him already travelling with Apollonius probably by **1st September, 258**, certainly by **5th October, 258**. For this whole question, see further the chronological material in P. L. Bat. 21 VIII, *b*.

T.

33

MEMORANDUM FROM HERIEUS

H. × W. = 33.2 × 5.7 cm. Date unknown

Heid. inv. 1881: R. SEIDER, *Beiträge zur Ptolemäischen Verwaltungsgeschichte. Der Nomarches. Der Dioiketes Apollonios* (Quellen und Studien zur Geschichte und Kultur des Altertums und des Mittelalters, Reihe D, Heft 8, 1938), pp. 78-9; **SB 8 9799**.

The text on the front is written along the fibres with a brush. If it is on the recto surface, which is probable but cannot at present be proved, the roll from which the piece for this memorandum was cut was a fairly tall one, with a height of over 33 cm. The original left-hand edge of the piece is preserved, and there is here a margin of about 1 cm. (less towards the bottom). The bottom edge is also preserved with a margin of about 2 cm. The top edge is damaged, and here up to 1.5 cm. of the top margin survive. The papyrus is broken at the right-hand edge, and a portion of the text is lost (see n. *l.* 24). No information concerning the back surface is available.

Contents This memorandum from Herieus, probably addressed to Zenon (but see no. **16**, intr.), deals with the breeding of calves. It is very difficult to comprehend the details of the text, although the portion lost on the right need not necessarily be very extensive (see *l.* 24 with note for a probable restoration). Herieus seems to be putting forward a proposal to undertake calf-breeding on Zenon's behalf, and he states the terms on which he wishes to do so. The text has briefly been discussed by C. PRÉAUX, *Chronique d'Égypte* 15 (1940), p. 174; and U. WILCKEN, *Archiv für Papyrusforschung* 14 (1941), p. 157. An important new text on the breeding of calves has recently been published by J. SCHERER, *Note de frais concernant l'élevage de cinq veaux*, in *Le monde grec, Hommages à Claire Préaux*, 1975, pp. 578-84.

[plate XVII]:

Ὑπόμνημ[α Ζήνωνι
παρὰ Ἑριέω[ς
τοὺς ἀπ[μόσ-]
χους οὓ`ς´ ἔχ[ω καὶ]
οὓς ἂν ἀποσ[τέλλῃις (?)
χορηγήσω [
μοσχοτροφ̣[
λαμβάνω̣ [
δέκα μὲ̣[ν
ἐφ' ὧ̣ι τελ̣ε̣[ίους
παρέξω [
εἰς αὐτοὺ̣[ς
καὶ παρα̣[
ἵνα μηθ̣[

ὃς βλάβηι .[
..λωσ..[
βάλλειν .[
χορηγήσω [
τ' εἰς ἐγγύ[ην ἀνθρώπους
ἀξιοχρέου[ς
"Ερρω[σο

Δεῖ οὖν δοθ[ῆναι
μόσχωι τῶι [
χωι χόρτου ἑ̣[κάστης ἡμέρας δέσ-]
μας δύο .[
ετε̣ι̣ καὶ ..[
δέσμας δύ[ο

2 γράφω σοι περὶ] supplevit Seider 3 ἀπ[ὸ σοῦ supplevit Seider 5 ἀποσ[τέλλειν supplevit Seider, ἀποσ[τέλλῃς supplevimus 8 λαμβάνῳ Seider, aut ἃ λαμβάνω? 10 δὲ καὶ τελε[ίους Seider, ἐφ' ὧ̣ι τελ̣ε̣[ίους legimus 13 παρα[δώσω Seider 16 ἥ̣γησον (?) Seider, ..λωσ.. legimus 23 μοσχοτρόφ[οις Seider, μόσχωι τῶι [legimus 24 ἕ̣[ως τῆς ἡμέρας Seider, ἑ̣[κάστης ἡμέρας supplevimus 26 ἔτου(ς) κγ ἱε[Seider, ετε̣ι̣ καὶ ..[legimus

Notes

2 Herieus: Seider identifies Herieus with the βούκολος of P. Cairo Zen. 4 59.719, 7 see n. *l.* 24 below, and *Prosopography*, P. L. Bat. 21. IX, 'Εριεύς (no. 13).

10-11 Seider's reading δὲ καί is clearly wrong. Our reading ἐφ' ὧι, apart from being more probable palaeographically, receives some support from the occurrence of the future indicative παρέξω in *l.* 11. The sense might be "providing that I deliver them fully grown".

22-27 The last 6 lines of the text are plainly in the same hand as the rest of the memorandum, and presumably form a postscript, specifying further details.

24 Seider rightly compared this passage with P. Cairo Zen. 4 59.719, 7-9, καὶ 'Εριεῖ 'βουκ̣ό̣λ̣ω̣ι̣ ε̣ἰ̣ς̣ μόσχον α̣' ἀπὸ Φαρμοῦθι ιδ ἕως λ ἡμερῶν ιζ ὡς τῆς ἡμέρας δέσμαι β / λδ ("and to Herieus the cow herd, for one calf, from Pharmouthi 14 until 30, that is for 17 days, each day 2 bundles, total 34 bundles"). Seider's supplement ἕ̣[ως τῆς ἡμέρας], clearly suggested by ὡς τῆς ἡμέρας in the Cairo papyrus, cannot stand: ὡς there is used in a distributative sense, and should not be confused with ἕως (see MAYSER, *Grammatik* II. 2, pp. 43-4). The supplement suggested here, ἑ̣[κάστης ἡμέρας δέσ]|μας may establish the length of the lacuna, but unfortunately the *epsilon* is not a certain reading, and a similar expression with the same meaning might have been used.

C.

34

LETTER FROM HERMAPHILOS (?) TO ZENON CONSTITUTING AN ORDER FOR PAYMENT OF SALARY IN WINE

H. × W. = 9.2 × 18.7 cm. Date unknown

Cairo JdE 53757: **P. Cairo Zen. 4 59.615**; T. Reekmans, *Notes sur quelques papyrus du 3ᵉ siècle av. J.-C., Antidorum Peremans*, Studia Hellenistica 16 (1968), pp. 227-8.

The text on the front is written across the fibres, presumably on the original recto surface. The address and docket on the back are written parallel to the fibres. The papyrus was folded horizontally just below *l.* 6, and some inverted ink offsets below the fold come from *l.* 6, and are to be disregarded.

The present papyrus is closely similar to P. Cairo Zen. 5 59.834. Both are very fragmentary, and thus the nature of the texts was not recognizable until it became possible to compare the two papyri. Some improvements in the reading and restoration of the present letter were made in the edition of P. Cairo Zen. 5 59.834, and then the text was fully revised by T. Reekmans (see above), who treated it together with other parallel material; and the text printed here is not very different from his. Few physical details are available of either of the Cairo papyri. Jouguet/Guéraud (P. Cairo Zen. 5, p. 32, n. 1) reported that a comparison of the two papyri showed that they were by the same hand. Apparently, before his sudden death, Edgar worked on the material for vol. 5 only from photographs, and this may be the reason why his manuscript did not include such a suggestion (rather than that he had thought otherwise). Edgar described P. Cairo Zen. 5 59.834 as "in a good official hand", and noted that the ἔρρωσο and the date were added by "the author himself", comparing P. Mich. Zen. 65 (a letter from the same Hermaphilos, where the final portion was in a second, more cursive hand), although he did not specifically state if any similarities in the hands were apparent. In the edition of P. Cairo Zen. 4 59.615 (the present letter), Edgar identified the hand of *l.* 6 as Zenon's own, and the note "The subscription is of course the work of the recipient" in the introduction to P. Cairo Zen. 5 59.834 presumably means that the same is true of the docket there.

Contents This letter addressed to Zenon instructs him to pay the salary of an individual (whose name is badly damaged in the text, and cannot be recognized), who had undertaken the collection of the oil tax. Zenon is not known to have held any official position, and his responsibility for these salary payments was explained by Edgar (P. Cairo Zen. 5 59.834, introduction) as stemming from his known involvement with the *apomoira*. A general discussion of Zenon's position was given by Edgar in his introduction to P. Mich. Zen., pp. 38-40 and 46-7 and see also P. L. Bat. 21, VI, note 9. The date of the letter is not known, except that it bears on the back a docket from which only the month-name and day-date "... Mesore 20" survive: however, it is quite likely that it belongs to a date close to that of the very similar letter P. Cairo Zen. 5 59.834, which is dated either to 244 or to 241.

front:

[Ἑρμάφιλος (?) Ζή]νωνι χαίρειν. Δ̣ὸ̣ς̣ [ἀπὸ τῆς ἕκτης τῆς γινομένης τῆι]
[Φιλαδέλφωι ἐ]κ τῶν πε̣ρ̣ὶ̣ Φ̣ι̣λ̣α[δέλφειαν ἀμπ]ελών[ων . . .]ται̣[c. 6 τῶι]
[ἐξειληφότι] τ̣[ὴ]ν ἐλαικὴν ἀ̣[ντὶ τοῦ γι]ν[ο]μ̣ένου αὐτῶι ὀψω[νίου c. 5]
[οἴνου με(τρητὰς) τέσσαρας δ]ω̣δ̣ε̣κ̣α̣[τον καὶ σύμβολον ποίησαι c. 5].τ̣ην.
Ἔρρ[ωσο. L].
[χρημά]τισον οἴνου με(τρητὰς) δ ι̣'[β'].

back:

Ζήνωνι.

[L . Μ]εσορὴ κ.

Text. et rest. Edgari sunt, nisi aliis ascriptae 1 [Ἑρμάφιλος (?) Reekmans; Δọ́ς̣ Jouguet/Guéraud, P. Cairo Zen. 5 59.834 n. *l.* 1 1-2 rest. Reekmans e P. Cairo Zen. 5 59.834 2-3 [...]ταί̣[ωι τῶι | ἐξειληφότι] Reekmans, cf. Edgar introd. P. Cairo Zen. 5 59.834 τῶι δεῖνα τῶι e.g. ἐξειληφότι 4 [με(τρ.)] Reekmans, at [οἴνου με(τρ.)] imprimi voluit?; [τέσσαρας δ]ω̣δε̣κ̣α̣[τον, Reekmans,].δο̣σ̣κ̣.[Edgar; καὶ σύμβολον ποίησαι περὶ αὐ]τ̣ῶν Reekmans,]τ̣ην Edgar 6 δ ι̣'[β'] Reekmans, δ.[Edgar, qui δ̣έ[κα] legeret, si e n. *l.* 6 indicaremur

Translation

[Hermaphilos(?) to Ze]non, greetings.

[From (the proceeds of) the one-sixth tax due to the (goddess) Philadelphos] from the vineyards around Philadelphia, deliver to ..., who has [undertaken] the (collection of the) oil (tax), in lieu of the salary due to him [for the ...th year, four] and one twelfth [metretai of wine, and make out a receipt for] them.

Fare well. [*Date.*]

(2nd hand)

[(?)] provide $4\frac{1}{12}$ metretai of wine.

Address:

To Zenon.

Docket:

[Year ..., M]esore 20.

Notes

1 The name Ἑρμάφιλος was restored in P. Cairo Zen. 5 59.834, 1, apparently by Edgar, simply on the grounds that an order of this kind might be expected to come from the *oeconome* (cf. P. Col. Zen. 1 55, 6). Hermaphilos is attested in the archive from Year 38, Epeiph 30 (18 September, 248) to Year 6, Khoiak 1 (20 January, 240), and thus he would be the appropriate holder of the office to restore in 59.834, whether the text is ascribed to 241 B.C., as Edgar read the year number, or to 244 B.C., the possibility mentioned by Jouguet/Guéraud in their n. *l.* 5. Reekmans, who apparently accepted that 59.834 and the present text were of the same date, made the corresponding restoration Ἑρμάφιλος (?) here, and cited the footnote by Jouguet/Guéraud to the introduction of 59.834, where it was stated that the two letters were in the same hand. It is plainly unlikely that the same scribe would have written letters for two different officials. The only serious doubt, therefore, is if both letters might not have been written by an official other than the *oeconome*.

2 ...]ται̣[: the name of the individual who was to receive his salary has plainly to be restored here, followed by τῶι ἐξειληφότι, or something very similar. Reekmans printed ...]ταί̣[ωι τῶι | ἐξειληφότι, and mentioned *exempli gratia* the names Aretaios, Pantaios, Diktaios, and Euktaios. These names do not occur elsewhere in the archive, but there is no particular or strong reason to expect that the recipient of this payment would have had other dealings with Zenon. However, it seems possible that a slightly more extensive restoration is required at the end of the line here. A longer name might be supplied, or less probably, an adverbial phrase added to τῶι ἐξειληφότι.

3 A phrase such as "for the ...th year" might be expected at the end of this line, for example, simply τοῦ x (ἔτους). Compare the small amount of room available at the corresponding point in P. Cairo Zen. 5 59.834, 3.

4 Reekmans quoted with approval Edgar's restoration of P. Cairo Zen. 5 59.834, 4 (partly made in the note *ad loc.*) [οἴνου μετρητὰ]ς δέκα ἥμυσυ τρ[ί]τ̣[ο]ν δ̣ω̣δέ̣κ̣α̣τον καὶ [σύμβολον ποίησαι], to which

he would add [περὶ αὐτῶν] in *l.* 5, on the basis of P. Petrie II 15 (2), 8-9 [= III 43 (7)], where presumably he would read καὶ σύμβολον ποίησα[ι περὶ] | αὐτ[ῶ]ν. He would therefore also restore [καὶ σύμβολον ποίησαι περὶ αὐ]τ̣ῶν in the present letter. He himself pointed out that this involves correcting Edgar's reading]τ̣ην in *l.* 4, and in fact the ω is not a possible reading.

5 The date of this letter cannot be deduced with certainty. The note on the outside (the back) of the letter preserves the date "... Mesore 20". During Zenon's time at Philadelphia, this date will have fallen in early October, and thus might be a plausible date for the (early) delivery of the new vintage's wine. It may be noted that the dates preserved in P. Grenf. 1 9 of 239-8 B.C., which is printed with the incorporation of various improvements in REEKMANS *op. cit.*, p. 229, would not be very far from the date in the present papyrus (esp. *l.* 8,] L η Μεσορεὶ ιδ [: note the mention of the *apomoira* (in *l.* 6). In P. Col. Zen. 1 55 n. *l.* 1, the editors put forward a plausible case for dating this receipt for wine to the month of Παῦνι, but the fact that the wine concerned is called "sweet wine" might be relevant to this difference.

Jouguet/Guéraud were apparently struck by the occurrence of the day-date 20 both in *l.* 8 of the present text, and in *l.* 7 of P. Cairo Zen. 5 59.834, and in their footnote to the introduction of 59.834, they suggested that the two texts were of the same date. It is conceivable that both texts belonged to the same year, and that a note was made on the back when the wine was paid out from the new vintage. As far as the present text is concerned, this would present no problem. However, in the case of 59.834, a difficulty arises from the date when the letter was sent. The month-name was read by Edgar as Τῦ[βι], without any indication that it was doubtful; and, if Mesore is restored on the back, this would imply a delay of about seven months between the writing of the letter and the placing of the note on the back. Of course it is conceivable that this is precisely what occurred: that such letters were written in the last month of the Financial year, and the payments were made in Mesore, either because it was the last month of the Egyptian year, or, more probably, because it was when the new vintage became available.

However, it should be stressed that only one month-name is preserved in each text, and the evidence in no way demands an interpretation of this kind. Nor, on present evidence, does it seem desirable to restore the month-name Τῦβι in *l.* 5 of the present text, rather than a date closer to that on the back. There remains, however, a probability of a vaguer kind, that the only two letters of this type that survive in the archive, which, furthermore, are written in the same hand, were in fact dealt with by Zenon at roughly the same time.

Unfortunately, Jouguet/Guéraud's n. *l.* 5 on P. Cairo Zen. 5 59.834 is so expressed as to make it necessary to regard the date of that text as uncertain:—either 244 B.C. or 241 B.C. Reekmans, in dating the present text to 241 B.C., evidently preferred Edgar's original reading of Year 6 in 59.834, and dated the present text to the same year.

6 χρημά]τισον: or possibly ἔκ]τισον?

T.

35

ACCOUNT SUBMITTED BY HERMIAS TO ZENON

Dimensions unknown | Date unknown

Jand. inv. 364; H. G. Gundel, *Verlorene Papyri Jandanae, Aegyptus* 41 (1961), pp. 13-15; F. Uebel, *Zu P. Iand. Inv. 364, Archiv für Papyrusforschung* 17 (1962), p. 188, only *ll.* 1-16; **SB 8 9682.**

This papyrus, together with a number of others, was lost at the end of the Second World War. In 1961, Gundel (see above) gave an account of all this material, and was able to publish a "rough copy" that had been made of Jand. inv. 364 by T. C. Skeat in 1932. Similar copies of Jand. inv. 361-3 were also printed: see texts nos. **45**, **60** and **72** below. Subsequently Uebel (see above) was able to point out that the text could in part be restored from P. Cairo Zen. 3 59.429. No physical details are available, except that in *Aegyptus* 41 (1961) p. 15 Gundel put forward a reason for supposing that the backs of all the Giessen Zenon papyri had been blank.

Contents This papyrus probably preserves just the opening of a long and varied account of goats, rendered to Zenon by Hermias the goat-herd. The first sixteen lines are concerned with an account of kids delivered to various persons out of a total of 160 kids that Hermias had received from Amortaios in the month of Mecheir. Hermias the goat-herd is well-known in the archive. See *Prosopography*, P. L. Bat. 21. IX, Ἑρμίας (no. 2). As parallels to the present account (apart from the closely related text P. Cairo Zen. 3 59.429 discussed below) see especially P. Wisc. 2 78, an account rendered by Hermias in 248 B.C., and P. Mich. Zen. 67, an account in the form of a *hypomnema* rendered by Menodoros in 242 B.C. (for Hermias, see *ll.* 15 and 26). It is not possible to deduce the date of the present papyrus.

P. Cairo Zen. 3 59.429 is an account rendered by Hermias of the same kids as those mentioned at the beginning of the present account, recording those disposed of, specifically described as kids, down to Mecheir 27, obviously the same month as that in which they were acquired. The disposal of various goats (not described as kids) and some "unweaned kids" is then noted without dates (*ll.* 12-17:—see n. *l.* 22 below). Edgar pointed out that (at least in one case?) these goats were not "perpetual" (ἀθάνατοι), that is, they were not goats that would have to be replaced if they died. The final "remainder" given in the last line of the Cairo text takes into account only the kids listed in *ll.* 3-9, and ignores the entries of *ll.* 12-17. The text perhaps was written roughly at the end of Mecheir (but see n. *l.* 22 below): the year-date cannot be deduced.

The present account is perhaps of a slightly later date. Lines 1-14 reproduce almost exactly the account of kids in P. Cairo Zen. 3 59.429, 1-11, including the total given there of kids disposed of up to Mecheir 27. The text then proceeds to record various further transactions. Dates in Phamenoth and in Pharmouthi can be read. As no physical details are available, it is unfortunately impossible to be entirely sure that the text does not come to an end in *l.* 40, the last line preserved; but there is no clear sign of a total or remainder at this point, and it is here assumed that the papyrus is not complete. What survives of the text perhaps runs down to the end of Pharmouthi, or into the next month, Pachons.

The nature of the continuation of this account in *ll.* 17-40 poses something of a problem. UEBEL (*op. cit.*, pp. 188-9) suggested that all mention of the goats dealt with in P. Cairo Zen. 3 59.429, 12-17 had naturally been postponed until the end of the present account, and that it was in fact lost in the lacuna after *l.* 40. He suggested that what survives of the continuation of the present account dealt with ἔριφοι and also with ἔριφοι θανάσιμοι, "kids that do not have to be replaced".

However, there are several difficulties here. First, the phrase ἔριφοι θανάσιμοι nowhere occurs in the text: instead there is a puzzling neuter expression, which is discussed below (n. *l.* 18), and which may refer to goats of some kind rather than kids. Secondly, after *l.* 16, the word ἔριφοι can first be read again only in *ll.* 36-9, although the masc. forms in *ll.* 28-9 might suggest that kids were in question there.

Clearly the portion of the text after *l.* 16 does not necessarily have to be a strict continuation of the account of 160 kids. In fact the parallel accounts mentioned above contain entries of varied kinds, each transaction perhaps being entered as it occurred, or in convenient groups, rather than being arranged on any strict accounting principle. It is therefore necessary to ask if the deliveries of goats mentioned in *ll.* 12-17 of the Cairo text cannot in fact be identified in the present account, and it seems at least a possible suggestion that the entries relating to Doxaios in *ll.* 21-30 (cf. Doxaios in *l.* 35) might be interpreted in this way. The relevant portion of the Cairo text is reproduced in n. *l.* 22 below.

Λόγος Ζήνω[νι παρ' Ἑρμίου τοῦ αἰπόλου.]
Ἔχω παρ' Ἀμ̣ορ̣[ταίου ἐρίφους ρξ]
μηνὸς Μεχεί[ρ, ἀφ' ὧν ἔχει Κρότος]
Κρότου ἔριφ[ον α καὶ Ἀπολλώνι-]
ος ἔριφον α [καὶ οὓς εἰς Μέμφιν]
ἀπέστειλα ἐρί[φους λε οὓς κα-]
τ̣άγει Ἀ̣μο̣ρτα̣[ῖος *vacat*?]
καὶ ἄλλους {ι}β [οὓς Νικίας ἀπέ-]
δοτο ὧν τὴν τ[ιμὴν ἔχει Δοξαῖ-]
ος, καὶ ἄλλου̣[ς ἐρίφους κ τοὺς]
εἰς Μέμφ[ιν ἀποσταλέντας]
διὰ Σίμων̣[ος καὶ ἄλλους ἐρί-]
φους ιγ ἐν τῆ̣[ι δευτέραι κατα-]
γωγῆι οὓς παραλαμ̣[βάνει Σίμων (?) .]
Ἕως Μεχεὶρ κζ {τ} οὓ̣[ς ἐκτεταμί-]
ευται ἐρίφους δι' ἐμοῦ̣ [οβ. Νουμη-]
νίαι Παμενὼ Λυκο.[ ]
καὶ πέμπτηι θ̣α̣ν̣[ασιμ-]
ἐνάτηι ἔχει Ν̣[ὁ-]
μολογεῖ κ[ ]

πέντε κα[ὶ δεκάτηι]
δ ἔχει Δοξ[αῖος]
ἄλλο θανά̣σιμ̣[ον]
πέμπτη̣ καὶ εἰ̣κ̣ά[δι θανά-]
σιμον α ἔχει Δοξαῖος [ ]
τρίτηι ἄλλο θανάσιμ̣[ον Δο-]
ξαῖος Παρμούτει τρίτ[ηι]
τοὺς παραλαμβα̣[-]
-νους Δοξαῖος ῥ̣.[ ]
ἔχει Δοξαῖος .δ̣[ ]
ἑβδόμηι ...[ἀρνα-]
κίδα τοι ...[ ]
..........[ ]
πέντε καὶ δεκάτ̣[ηι]
δ ἔχει Δοξαῖος θ[ανάσιμ-]
καὶ οὓς αὐτὸς π['Ιου-]
δαίοις ἐρίφους λ[ ]
τὰ πάντα θ̣α̣ν̣[άσιμα]
ται τῶν ἐρίφ[ων]
τρία κ̣αὶ τα .[ ]
- -

1-16 cf. Uebel, *op. cit.* 2 Skeat: 'Αχοά̣[πιος 7 Skeat: παγειχομαρτα̣[16-17 νουμη]-|νίαι Skeat 17 *l.* Φαμενώθ 21 πέντε κα[ὶ δεκάτηι Skeat 22 δ' ἔχει SB 25 ἃ ἔχει SB 27 *l.* Φαρμοῦθι 31-32 [ἀρνα]|κίδα Skeat 35 δ' ἔχει SB 36-37 ['Ιου]|δαίοις Skeat

Translation (*ll.* 1-17)

Account (rendered) to Zenon, [from Hermias the goat-herd.]
I have received from Amor[taios 160 kids] in the month of Mecheir:
[from which Krotos,] son of Krotos has received 1 kid
[and Apollonios] 1 kid
[and those] I sent [to Memphis] [35] kids
[which] Amortaios brings down(-river)
and another {1}2
[which Nikias] sold, and the [price] of which
[Doxaios has]
and another [20 kids]
[that were sent away] to Memphis in the
charge of Simon
[and another] 13 kids
in the [second] transportation, of which
[Simon (?)] took delivery.
Up to Mecheir 27, the kids [accounted out] (to Zenon) through me:—[72]
On the first day of Phamenoth, ...

Notes

1-16 The small differences of wording between the present text and P. Cairo Zen. 3 59.429, 1-11 are not all noted here. Generally, as is to be expected, corrections and additions made to the Cairo text appear duly incorporated into the present account. One figure, ιβ in *l.* 8, seems to be wrong, as the Cairo text has β, and, if β is accepted, then the Cairo text's total in *l.* 11 is correct. However, the corresponding total in the present text is not preserved (see *l.* 16), so that we cannot check the figures, and it is conceivable that it is the Cairo text that is in error here.

2 Skeat's "rough copy", for which we are very grateful, as being our only record of this text, reads at this point εχω παρ Αχοα̣[πιος, where in the Cairo papyrus Edgar confidently read Ἀμορταίου. Similarly, where Edgar read the same name inserted between *ll.* 5 and 6 of the Cairo text, here at the corresponding point in *l.* 7 Skeat read παγειχομαρτα̣[, which appears in the transcription printed here as [κα]-|τ̣άγει Ἀμορτα̣[ῖος]. Skeat was not, of course, at that time aware that the text had a parallel in Cairo. Concerning *l.* 7 of the Jand. text, Gundel reports Skeat's comment "These letters are only pencilled in in my copy; I obviously had failed to find a satisfactory reading". In fact Amortaios is well-attested in the archive as a goat-herd and shepherd (see *Prosopography*, P. L. Bat. 21. IX, Ἀμορταῖος [nos. 1 and 2] for references), and plainly his name should be read in the present text.

8 {ι}β: P. Cairo Zen. 3 59.429, 5 reads β. See n. *l.* 1-16 above.

14 οὓς παραλαμ[βάνει N.]: P. Cairo Zen. 3 59.429 has instead οὓς κατάγει Σίκων, inserted as an afterthought *before* ἐν τῆι δευτέραι καταγωγῆι (as Edgar notes, presumably read Σίμων here). Probably, therefore, Σίμων is to be restored in *l.* 14 of the present text; but it is possible that the name of the man who took delivery of the kids from Simon was given here instead.

15 {τ} οὓ̣[ς: P. Cairo Zen. 3 59.429, 10 reads οὕς, the relative pronoun that we should expect to find here. The τούς in the present text is presumably merely a copying error.

15-16 ἐκτεταμί]|ευται: in P. Cairo Zen. 3 59.429, 10-11, ἐκτετα|μίευσαι was read by Edgar. This abrupt use of the 2nd pers. in accounts is not uncommon. Edgar, in his introduction to the Cairo account, deduced from it that the goats belonged to Zenon, to whom the account is addressed, or to the estate. The 3rd pers. form ἐκτεταμίευται would presumably refer to Zenon also. In fact ἐκτεταμίευται here may be a copying mistake, or perhaps ἐκτεταμίευσαι actually should be read. In any case, this use of the verb is surprising: for other occurrences of ἐκταμιεύειν, see P. Cairo Zen. 1 59.008, 21 and 29, and PSI 7 855, 3 and 8; cf. ἀποταμιεύειν, P. Cairo Zen. 2 59.176, 47 and PSI 4 428, 28; in P. Cairo Zen. 4 59.539, 2, the ἀπο- is restored.

18 θ̣α̣ν̣[: this, if correctly read, is the first instance of the word θανάσιμον, which occurs several times later in the text: cf. *ll.* 23, 24-5, 26, 35, and 38. The word is nowhere completely preserved, but a comparison of all these instances can leave no doubt that this is the word in question and that it must be restored at least in most cases; and there is sufficient reason to restore it in every case. The word appears to be used in the same way each time, and to stand alone, unaccompanied by a noun. In *ll.* 23 and 26, ἄλλο suggests that θανάσιμον is neuter, and this seems to be confirmed by τὰ πάντα in *l.* 38. (The SB reading ἃ ἔχει in *l.* 25, which would also support this, is not accepted here: see n. *ll.* 24-5). It would perhaps be perverse to suggest reading ἄλλο θανασίμ[ου] in *l.* 23, and again exactly the same in *l.* 26, and τὰ πάντα θ̣α̣ν̣[ασίμων] in *l.* 38, which would permit us to understand θανάσιμον there and elsewhere as masculine.

Uebel suggested that θανάσιμος was used in this text as the opposite of the well-attested adjective ἀθάνατος, "perpetual", which signifies that an animal is to be replaced when it dies. This sense of ἀθάνατος is common in Greek in quite different contexts also. Uebel's suggestion may be correct, but there are serious difficulties raised by it. The word θανάσιμος is not found anywhere else in this sense, and indeed its only other occurrence in documentary papyri seems to be in SB 6 9239, 12 (A.D. 548) πληγὰς θανασίμους, "deadly blows". The commonest meanings of θανάσιμος in Greek, "deadly" etc., do not suggest it would very naturally be used as the opposite of ἀθάνατος in the context of herds of animals, and it never seems to be used quite in the sense of "mortal".

The use of a neuter form is also strange. It is not very satisfying to regard it as a common gender form, coined to match ἀθάνατος. One possible explanation is to restore or supply as appropriate δέρμα, "skin" (cf. P. Cairo Zen. 3 59.429, 13; P. Wisc. 2 78, 6-14). However, the expression would be an odd one; it might be surprising if nearly all the entries in *ll.* 17-40 mentioned skins; the necessary restorations are difficult to effect; and *l.* 38 becomes very hard to explain. The problems raised by reading ἄλλο θανασίμ[ου] in *l.* 23, and interpreting other passages similarly (this possibility has been mentioned above), and by understanding this as "another (skin) of a non-perpetual (goat)" appear insuperable. There seems no other neuter noun that can plausibly be supplied (certainly not δεῖγμα, P. Wisc. 2 78, 27, nor γάλα, P. Wisc. 2 78, 43 etc.); and it is surely impossible that something other than goats are in question (e.g. πρόβατον).

A completely different approach is to regard the apparent connection of θανάσιμος with the well-attested ἀθάνατος as misleading, and to understand θανάσιμον as signifying either "dying" or "condemned" or "dead". The last of these three senses might most naturally be expected in such an account, and we might compare P. Mich. Zen. 67, 25-6, καὶ ἐτελεύτη|σαν...; but it is also the sense which the evidence least suggests we might find in a document. Each of these three senses at any rate raises fewer difficulties than the sense of "non-perpetual". The problem of the neuter form remains: it might or might not be judged less acute if the animals are to be thought of as dead. It may be noted that, although instances of θανάσιμα predominate in the latter part of the account, they are, in the case of *ll.* 23, 24-5 and 26, certainly (and, in the case of *l.* 35, possibly) single animals that are so designated: the plural is certain only in *l.* 38. This might support the idea that the animals were dying or had died, perhaps of disease or lack of food. On this interpretation, whichever of the three senses is accepted, the θανάσιμα might or might not be goats as distinct from the kids: the passage in *ll.* 35-7, which may report that Doxaios had one θανάσιμον, and some kids that he handed over to the Jews, "all of them θανάσιμα", naturally suggests that a θανάσιμον mentioned without any qualification was not a kid; but this is not a certain conclusion from the wording. The same considerations would apply if θανάσιμον were understood, as Uebel suggests, to mean "non-perpetual".

22 δ ἔχει: The *Sammelbuch* here and in *l.* 35 printed δ' ἔχει, whereas Skeat's copy as reproduced by Gundel has no accents, etc., throughout. In both cases δ might better be taken as a numeral. Compare n. *ll.* 24-25.

— Δοξ[αῖος]: In the *contents* above it is tentatively suggested that this passage concerning deliveries to Doxaios might roughly relate to P. Cairo Zen. 3 59.429, 12 ff. The uncertainties are too many to settle the question, or for precise restorations to be suggested. The Cairo passage runs

12 καὶ ἣν ἔλ{εβ}αβεν αἶγα Δοξαῖος τῆι δορκάδι
`ἀπέχει αὐτήν´ καὶ δέρμα αἰγὸς τελείας δ ἔλαβεν
Δοξαῖος καὶ ἄλλας αἶγας δ τὰς εἰς
15 Μέμφιν καὶ ἄλλην αἶγα στεῖραν
καὶ χιμαίρας β / αἶγες θ
καὶ ἐρίφους γαλαθηνοὺς ζ

If this suggestion is correct, it is perhaps not too surprising that just the transactions with Doxaios were entered in P. Cairo Zen. 3 59.429: in fact it may even be that the Cairo text is not later in date than the present account, but is in some sense a draft for it.

For Doxaios see *Prosopography*, P. L. Bat. 21. IX, Δοξαῖος.

24-25 [θανά]|σιμον α ἔχει: the *Sammelbuch* printed ἃ ἔχει, whereas Skeat's copy as reproduced by Gundel has no accents, etc., throughout. The α might better be taken as a numeral. Compare n. *l.* 22, on δ ἔχει.

26 Presumably the sequence of the dates is slightly disturbed here?

31-32 Skeat suggested restoring [ἀρνα]|κίδα, "a sheepskin coat": cf. P. Cairo Zen. 4 59.633, 7 and 800, n. *l.* 4.

35 δ ἔχει: cf. n. *l.* 22.

38 τὰ πάντα θ̣α̣ν̣[άσιμα]: the obvious interpretation of this phrase is "all of the above being θανάσιμα".

T.

36

LETTER FROM MENES TO ZENON

H. × W. = 10 × 16.5 cm.[a] Received 21 July, 257 B.C.

Mich. inv. 3217[a] + one Cairo fragment[b]: **P. Mich. Zen. 18**; the readings of the Cairo fragment are given in the introduction to the Michigan papyrus.

Few physical details are available. The text on the front is presumably written on the recto surface. Like the closely related text P. Lond. 7 1951, the letter is written in a fairly broad format, and no doubt, as in the case of the London papyrus, the writing is across the fibres.

Contents This letter is one of a group of three that were written to Zenon by Menes, evidently from Alexandria, either all on the same day, or else on two consecutive days. Of these, P. Cairo Zen. 5 59.812, received by Zenon on 21 July, seems only to deal with news concerning some honey that is being purchased. P. Lond. 7 1951, sent and received on 20 July, begins by announcing the arrival of the men who are bringing to the house of Amuntas two recaptured slaves, named as Donax, and "the slave of Zenodoros". The recapture of one further slave, whose name probably was not given in the letter, is reported, and then the subject changes to various provisions that are being sent to Zenon. Donax (cf. P. Col. Zen. 1 5, 63), who is simply referred to by his name, was presumably a slave belonging to Apollonios; and one plausible restoration of the London papyrus put forward by Skeat (n. *l.* 3) would suggest that the third slave also belonged to him, although this is not certain.

The present letter, received by Zenon the day after the London papyrus, expressly forms a postscript to it: Menes announces the recapture of Stakhus. In his introduction to P. Mich. Zen. 18, Edgar suggested that Stakhus should be identified with "the slave of Zenodoros" mentioned in P. Lond. 7 1951, 2 and 8. He also suggested that this Stakhus might be the author of P. Cairo Zen. 1 59.035 (where the reading of the writer's name is uncertain) perhaps only because "Zenodoros is again mentioned" there (in *l.* 1), and compared P. Cairo Zen. 2 59.266, 11 and PSI 6 616, 24. Although Edgar, at the time of the Michigan volume, was aware of the existence of the London portion of the text now known as P. Lond. 7 1951, he had perhaps been able to study only the Società Italiana portion, PSI 5 505. From the latter, it was very plausible to identify Stakhus and the slave of Zenodoros. However, the letter as printed in P. Lond. 7 shows that the slave of Zenodoros had *already* been recaptured, and apparently had not just recently been recaptured by Menes, but was being "brought in" by others. It is very difficult to understand the present letter as announcing anything but a fresh capture, and the identification with "the slave of Zenodoros" has plainly to be abandoned. It is of course plausible to suppose that the slave in the present letter belonged to Apollonios, as this would explain why Menes hastened to inform Zenon, to save him "anxiety". The "ultimate" owner of "the slave of

Zenodoros" might also be Apollonios, as Skeat seems to suggest: certainly it is clear that all the slaves are eventually to be brought to the house of Amuntas.

Skeat therefore plausibly concluded that altogether four fugitives were involved.

It is not possible to be entirely sure where these slaves were being held at the time of writing of each letter. The third slave of P. Lond. 7 1951 is expressly said to be ἔσω, "within", and this probably means that he was in Menes' own house. However, it is uncertain whether the two slaves (Donax and "the slave of Zenodoros") who were being brought into the house of Amuntas had arrived at Menes' house when P. Lond. 7 1951 was written, or had arrived at the house of Amuntas. The former view seems the more probable, and *l.* 3 of the present text has been restored accordingly. See nos. **24** and **43** for some other fugitive slaves.

front:

Μένης Ζήνωνι χ̣[α]ί̣ρε̣ι̣ν̣. [Μετὰ τὸ ἀποστεῖλαι τὴν πρότερον γ]ραφεῖσαν ἐπιστολήν,
μικρῶι ὕστερον συνέλαβον Στάχ[υν] ἀπαγαγὼν εἰς τὰ
᾽Αμύντου παρέδωκα μετὰ τῶ̣[ν ἄλλων παιδαρίων. Καὶ τήνδε νῦν] γεγράφαμέν σοι
ἵνα εἰδὼς μὴ ἀγωνιαῖς.
[῎Ερρωσο. L κθ Δαισίου]

back:

Ζήνωνι.
Μένης περὶ Στάχυος.
L κθ Δαισίου κα,
ἐν ᾽Αρσινόηι.

2 Στάχ[υν τὸν παρὰ Ζηνοδώρου παῖδα καί] Edgar 3 μετὰ τω̣[Edgar, P. Mich. Zen. 18, at idem in introd. huius text.: μετὰ το[ῦ ἄλλου παιδαρίου. καὶ τήνδε νῦν]

Translation

Menes to Zenon, greetings.

[After sending off my previously] written letter, a little later I captured Stakhus [--- and], taking him to the house of Amuntas, I handed him over with the [other slaves. So we have now] written this (letter) to you to let you know and to save you anxiety.

[Fare well. *Date*]

Address:

To Zenon.

Docket:

Menes concerning Stakhus. Year 29, Daisios 21, in Arsinoe.

Notes

2 The reasons why Edgar's restoration for this line has to be abandoned are set out in the *contents* above. Of course, it is not now established that Stakhus *could not* by chance also be a slave of Zenodoros. Several different kinds of restoration might be made after Στάχ[υν here, and it is perhaps not even certain that we can restore καί immediately before ἀπαγαγών.

3 Edgar in his transcription printed μετὰ τῳ̣[, and it may perhaps be assumed that this was the reading that the traces most suggested. It should be noted that he probably only printed the reading μετὰ το[ῦ ἄλλου παιδαρίου] in his introduction because the portion of the text preserved in PSI 5 505 suggested to him, reasonably enough, that only *two* slaves were involved in the whole affair. In all, it seems highly probable that the plural can be restored here. Presumably the three other slaves of P. Lond. 7 1951 are meant (see further in the *contents* above), although conceivably *l.* 2 might be restored in such a way that only two of them were involved here.

4 ἀγωνιαῖς: "lest you should worry", or "lest you should go to further trouble"?

9 ἐν 'Αρσινόηι: the Arsinoe close to Alexandria. The fact that P. Lond. 7 1951 was written and received on the same day shows how near to Alexandria Arsinoe must have been. See Edgar's introduction to P. Mich. Zen. 18, and P. Lond. 7 1951 n. *l.* 10. It is impossible to judge if the present letter was written on the 20th or 21st Daisios.

T.

37

LETTRE DE NIKÔN À ZÉNON

H. × L. = 8,7 × 23,3 cm. Envoyée le 1er avril 257 a.C., reçue le 14 avril 257 a.C.

Biblioteca Medicea Laurenziana: **PSI 9 1013** (comprenant PSI 6 638) et **PSI 7 863 p.** Voir aussi T. Reekmans dans *Chronique d'Égypte* 43 (1968), p. 167 (corrections reprises dans BL 6 p. 183) et T. C. Skeat dans l'introduction à P. Lond. 7 1937 (identifie le fragment 863*p* comme faisant partie de la lettre). Grâce à l'obligeance de M. le Professeur M. Manfredi, il m'a été possible de collationner sur photo les deux fragments PSI 1013.

Ce papyrus se compose actuellement de trois fragments, qui préservent la presque totalité d'une lettre, écrite contre le sens des fibres. Le premier fragment (PSI 6 638), qui contient le début des lignes, est monté sous verre ensemble avec le troisième fragment (PSI 9 1013), l'appartenance du fragment médian (PSI 7 863*p*) à ce même texte n'ayant été reconnue que récemment. L'adresse se trouve au dos du fragment médian, le docket au dos du premier fragment, dans le sens des fibres, à 3,5 cm. du bord supérieur (qui est le bord inférieur de la lettre), à hauteur des *ll.* 2 et 3 du texte de la lettre. Le fragment médian (PSI 7 863*p*) est actuellement introuvable.

Contenu Comme tant d'autres textes des archives de Zénon, celui-ci aussi concerne le payement de salaires, arriérés ou non. Les jardiniers ont reçu, en accord avec les instructions envoyées par Zénon, le salaire du mois de Tybi, qui précède immédiatement le mois de Mecheir. Mais les jardiniers prétendent aussi obtenir quelque chose de plus, et menacent même de s'en aller à défaut de payement. Or écrit Nikôn, c'est précisément en ce moment — et il a ajouté le νῦν après coup, — qu'on a un besoin urgent d'eux pour certains travaux, vraisemblablement d'irrigation, à effectuer dans la δωρεά memphite — où Nikôn était un agent d'Apollônios.

Νίκων Ζήνωṿ[ι χ]αίρειν. Καθάπερ ἡμῖν ἔγραψας, δεδώκαμεṿ [τοῖς κηπουροῖς]
τὸ ὀψώνιον τοῦ [μηνὸ]ς Τῦβι. Γράψον οὖν εἰ δεῖ δί`δο´σθαι αὐτοῖς κατα[*c.* 13].
Εἰ δὲ μὴ `ἔ´φασαν ἀπ[οδρ]αμεῖσθαι. Ἡ δὲ χ[ρ]εία ἐστὶν ἀναγκαία `νῦν´ διὰ τὸ [τὸν ἀμπελῶνα]
περισκάπτ[εσθαι]. Ἔρρωσο. L [κη Μεχεὶρ .].

au dos:

Ζήνωνι.
[L κη Δύσ]τρου ια.
[ ] ⟦. . ẹκ. . . . ωι⟧
[ ]. .θ. κηπουρῶν.

2 κατὰ [συγγραφήν] Hellebrand (Festschrift Koschaker III, p. 266, n. 81), κατα[φυτείαν e.g. τῆς γῆς] Reekmans 3 ἀπ[οχωρεῖν. Ἡ δὲ καταφυτ]εία suppl. Reekmans 3-4 διὰ τὸ [τὸν ἀμπελῶνα] | περισκάπτ[εσθαι] suppl. edd. e.g. 4 L [κη Μεχεὶρ .] suppl. Skeat 6 [L κη suppl. Skeat; Δ]ύστρου edd., Δύσ]τρου legimus 8]μẹθα edd.,]. .θα̣ vel]. .θẹ legimus

Traduction

Nikôn salue Zénon.

Ainsi que tu nous l'avais écrit, nous avons donné aux jardiniers le salaire du mois de Tybi. Écris-nous par ailleurs s'il faut leur donner [---]. Sinon, ils ont dit qu'ils s'en iront. Or, le besoin est impérieux, pour le moment, parce qu'on doit creuser autour du vignoble.

Porte-toi bien. An 28, 8 (?) Mecheir.

Adresse:

À Zénon.

Docket:

An 28, 11 Dystros, [---] des jardiniers.

Notes

1 Νίκων: voir au sujet de cet administrateur de la δωρεά memphite d'Apollônios, E. Wipszycka, *The* Δωρεά *of Apollonios the Dioeketes in the Memphite Nome*, *Klio* 39 (1961), pp. 154-156.

3 ἀποδραμεῖσθαι: cpr. PSI 4 421, 7-9: ὥστε εἰ μὲν διδοῖς ἡμεῖν· εἰ δὲ μή, ἀποδραμούμεθα.

6 [L κη Δύσ]τρου ια: 14 avril 257 a.C. Zénon, qui se trouvait à Mendès depuis la veille, reçut le même jour trois autres lettres de Nikôn (cpr. l'introd. à P. Lond. 7 1937), envoyées toutes trois le 8 Mecheir (1er avril). Il n'est dès lors pas impossible que la présente lettre également ait été redigée ce même jour (auquel cas il faudrait restituer à la *l.* 4 [Μεχεὶρ η]), mais elle peut tout aussi bien leur être antérieure ou postérieure de quelques jours.

M.

38

LETTER FROM ONNOPHRIS TO ZENON

H. × W. = 15 × 26.5 cm. Received 7 November, 253 B.C.

One Biblioteca Medicea Laurenziana fragment[a] + Col. inv. 357[b] + Col. inv. 333[c]: the first two fragments (**PSI 6 639**[a] and **P. Col. Zen. 2 114 j**[b]) were joined by E. Van 't Dack, *Une lettre d'Onnophris à Zénon, Chronique d'Égypte* 36 (1961), pp. 179-181, with plates (fig. 47); his text was reproduced in SB 6 9565. The third fragment (**P. Col. Zen. 2 78**[c]) is here added for the first time.

Fragment *a* preserves the left-hand half of the first column and measures 12 × 8 cm.; fragment *b* preserves the right-hand half and measures 12.5 × 6 cm.; fragment *c* contains the upper half of the second column and measures 15 × 12 cm. The text continues on the back of fragment *c* (col. III); various figures and letters have been jotted on the back of fragments *a* and *b* and both the address (*l.* 44) and the docket (*ll.* 45-46) stand on the back of fragment *a*.

The upper margin is preserved along all the top edge (about 1 cm. above col. II), but at the bottom about half of the original text is lost. There are margins to the left of col. I (about 1.5 cm.), between col. I and II (about 2 cm.), and to the right of col. II, where it is rather small (see the end of *l.* 26, where the line was too long for the available space). All the fragments join with virtually nothing lost between them. The main text is written parallel with the fibres on the recto surface. There is a join between two sheets in the middle of the second column.

Both on the front and the back of the text there are numerous ink-traces, caused by the folding of the letter before the ink was dry. They are clearly visible on our photographs in the left-hand margin (especially by *ll.* 2, 3 and 4), in the right-hand margin (where the figures δʹηʹ at the end of *l.* 18 are reproduced in mirror-writing in the margin) and on the back, where under *l.* 34 and above *l.* 39 respectively, we see traces of the Π from Ποινείτας (*l.* 20) and of ϶Ξ from Ξένων (*l.* 13). The traces to the left of *l.* 13 were read by the editors as τῶν and thus contributed to their misunderstanding of this passage; in fact they are caused by the wet ink of *l.* 27.

The folds in the papyrus can also be seen on the photograph: there are nine of them and the fissures between fragments *a*, *b* and *c* run exactly along two of these folds.

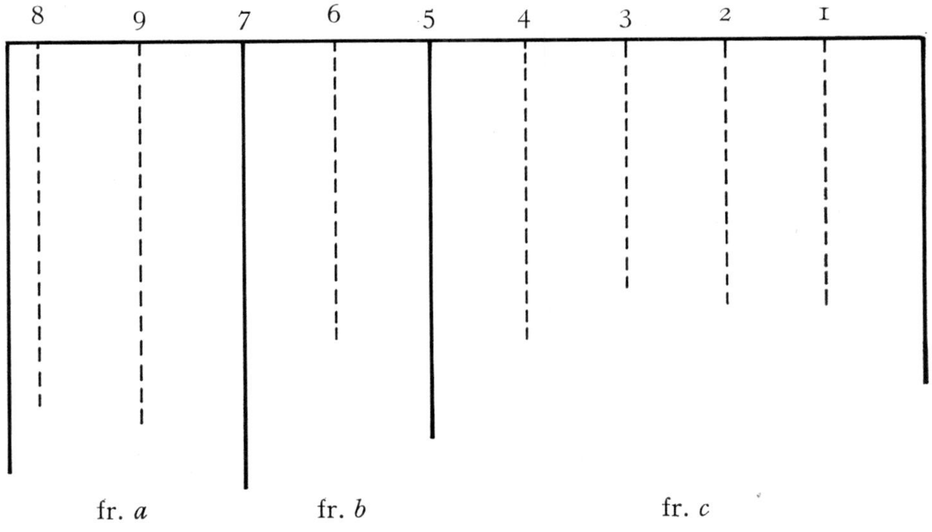

The offsets in mirror-writing and the location of the address on the back of fragment *a* make it possible to reconstruct the original letter as shown in the diagram on p. 157 (the surviving folds are represented by dotted lines).
Onnophris began by folding his letter up from right to left (folds 1-7), as is clear from the offsets on fr. *c* (front and back). To protect the left-hand edge of the letter he then folded-in a narrow strip (fold 8): see the traces in the left-hand margin of col. I. Finally (fold 9), he folded this strengthened flap over the bundle created by folds 1-7. He then wrote the address on the back of fr. *a*, on the strip between folds 9 and 7, which now formed one of the outside surfaces of the letter. No doubt the whole letter was doubled over and fr. *c* (measuring 51 cm. in height) preserves exactly the upper half of the original letter.

The first column was studied thoroughly by Van 't Dack in his *Chronique d'Égypte* article (see above), which contained special discussions of the πρεσβύτεροι στρατιῶται and of the reference to Andromachos in *ll.* 6-7.

Contents In this letter Onnophris reports to Zenon the results of his measurement and assessment of land allotments held by veteran soldiers in two 10,000-arourae estates. The total amount of land in each is stated and special mention is made of the over-all proportion of the first estate rendered uncultivable by rising salt. Then follows a list of individual holdings, in which the total holding of land, the uncultivable portion, and the remaining portion of cultivated land are given for each cleruch. In the first column this specification (διαστολή) is lost except for the first line, but in col. II more than half of it is preserved ($123\frac{1}{4}\ \frac{1}{8}\ \frac{1}{16}$ arourae out of a total of $200\frac{1}{2}\ \frac{1}{16}$). The verso recapitulates in col. III the totals of uncultivable and cultivable land for both estates together and specifies the crops of the cultivated area.

Onnophris' survey had been ordered by Zenon (see *l.* 2) and plainly concerns Zenon's leasing and cultivation of cleruchic land (see the general account by Edgar in P. Mich. Zen., *introduction* pp. 40-43).

The information provided by the newly reconstructed text is still fragmentary, but some interesting facts can be deduced from it (compare the table on p. 159). It is highly significant that the amount of γῆ ἁλμυρίς "salt land" in the estate of Andromachos is about 15% of the total area, but in the estate of Panouphis only about 3.6%, and also that in Andromachos' estate no more land, as far as we can judge, is lost over and above this salt land, whereas in Panouphis' estate a further $10\frac{1}{2}$ arourae (i.e. about 5% of the total area) are taken up by dykes and canals. The two estates are therefore quite different in character: Panouphis held an old estate, which had been well-managed for years, whereas the estate of Andromachos was more recent, and the land had yet to be made fertile (compare Supplement text **A**).

Onnophris writes in a fluent and individual hand, although it could not be described as regular. The most typical features are the *epsilon* with a small tail underneath  and the two different forms of the *tau*  and 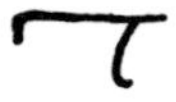 (they even occur together in *l.* 12, for example); the *lambda* appears throughout as a semi-circular curve , whereas *mu* and *pi* are written as capitals  and . The special form he uses for a half aroura (**c**, see n. *l.* 8, but also the normal sigle ∠ opposite *l.* 32) is noteworthy; and so is the writing = for the figure 6 in *l.* 35 (elsewhere he uses the normal form ). His spelling is far from faultless: cf. πρεζβυτων (for πρεσβυτέρων) in *l.* 3, διωρυγον (for διωρύγων) in *l.* 18, the faulty repetition of τῶν in *l.* 27, and λο<ι>παί in *l.* 33.

The writer's unfamiliarity with Greek is apparent from these various details, and it therefore becomes very tempting to ascribe the expression γῆς ἄρουραι in *l.* 13 to the influence of his native language: it could be a literal translation of the common demotic expression *st3* x *n 3ḥ*, "x arourae *of land*".

Table

	the two holdings together (col. III of the text)	Andromachos' holding (col. I of the text)	Panouphis' holding (col. II of the text)
ἡ πᾶσα γῆ	498 $\frac{1}{2}$ $\frac{1}{8}$ $\frac{1}{32}$ ar.	298 $\frac{1}{32}$ ar.	200 $\frac{1}{2}$ $\frac{1}{16}$ ar.
uncultivable land:			
ἁλμυρὶς γῆ	51 $\frac{1}{4}$ $\frac{1}{8}$ $\frac{1}{16}$ $\frac{1}{32}$	44 $\frac{1}{8}$ $\frac{1}{16}$ $\frac{1}{32}$ (about 15%)	[3$\frac{1}{4}$] + 4 (about 3.6%)
διώρυγες	4 $\frac{1}{2}$ $\frac{1}{4}$ $\frac{1}{16}$		[2$\frac{1}{8}$] + 2 $\frac{1}{2}$ $\frac{1}{8}$ $\frac{1}{16}$
σκάμματα and χώματα	6 $\frac{1}{8}$		[2$\frac{1}{4}$] + 3 $\frac{1}{2}$ $\frac{1}{4}$ $\frac{1}{8}$
total	62 $\frac{1}{4}$ $\frac{1}{8}$ $\frac{1}{32}$	[44 $\frac{1}{8}$ $\frac{1}{16}$ $\frac{1}{32}$]	[7 $\frac{1}{2}$ $\frac{1}{8}$] + 10 $\frac{1}{2}$ $\frac{1}{16}$
cultivable land:			
κριθοφόρος γῆ	80		
σησαμοφόρος γῆ	356 $\frac{1}{4}$		
total	436 $\frac{1}{4}$	[253 $\frac{1}{2}$ $\frac{1}{4}$ $\frac{1}{16}$]	[69$\frac{1}{2}$] + 112 $\frac{1}{2}$ $\frac{1}{4}$ $\frac{1}{8}$

front [plate XX]:

I

Ὀννῶφρις Ζήνωνι χαί[ρ]ειν.
Εἶπάς μοι γεωμετρῆσαι
τὴν τῶν πρεζβυτων
γῆν. Ἐγεωμέτρησα οὖν αὐ-
τὴν καὶ εὗρον ἐν αὐτῆι ἁλμυρίδος ἀφόρου. Ἐ̣ν τῆι Ἀνδρο-
μάχου (μυρι)αρού(ρου) εἰ[σ]ὶν ἄρου(ραι) σϙῆ λʹβ (ὧν)
ἁλμυρίδος ἀφόρου μδ 𐅵 ηʹ ιςʹ λʹβ.
Τούτων ἡ διαστολὴ ἐν ἑ[κάστωι]
κλήρωι·
[Διο]νύσ[ιο]ς [ ]δ̣ʹ ηʹ ιςʹ (ὧν) ἁλ̣[μυρίδος]δʹ
- -

2 [μ]ετρήσηι P. Col. Zen. 2 114*j*, γεωμετρῆσα̣ι Van 't Dack 3 *l.* πρεσβυτέρων 4-5 αὐτ̣|[ῶι] P. Col. Zen. 2 114*j*, αὐ|τὴν Van 't Dack 7 (μυρι)αρού(ρου): , sic legit Van 't Dack, PSI 6 639 habet: ν. ἀρου( ); ἄρουραι: ; σ: ; ϙῆ: 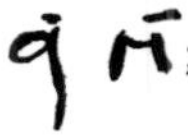; (ὧν):  cf. p.76 supra 11 (ὧν): 

II

Καὶ ἐν τῆι τοῦ Πανούφιος
(μυρι)αρού(ρου) γῆς ἄρου(ραι) σ c ι'ς' (ὧν) διαστολή·
× Εὔνομος ιη (ὧν) διώρυγος δ' η'
σκαμμάτων c η' / α ⌒ ιζ
—
ἄβ(ροχος) ἔν-εστιν — Μενοίτιος κα δ' η' ι'ς' (ὧν) διωρύγων δ' η'
σκαμμάτων c η' ι'ς' / α ι'ς' ⌒ κ δ' η'
—
× Σωτάλας ιη (ὧν) διωρύγον δ' η'
σκαμμάτων c η' / α ⌒ ιζ
—
ἔστιν δὲ Λυσάνδρου — Ποινείτας κβ δ' ι'ς' (ὧν) διωρύγων δ' η' ι'ς'
σκαμμάτων c η' ι'ς' ἁλμυρίδος α
/ β η' ⌒ κ η' ι'ς'
—
× Ξένων ιη (ὧν) διώρυγος δ' η' σκαμμ-
ά[των c] η' [ἁ]λμυρίδος α / β ⌒ ις
—
/ Πρω[ ] κε c η' ι'ς' (ὧν) διώρυγος c δ'
[σκαμμάτων] c η' ἁ[λμυ]ρί(δος) β / γ δ' η' ⌒ κβ 'δ' ι'ς''

- -

13 τῶν $\overset{α}{Μ}$ ἀ(ρουρῶν) P. Col. Zen. 2 78, 2; διὰ τὸ σῆ(μα) P. Col. Zen. 2 78, 2 18 *l.* διωρύγων
20 διωρύγον P. Col. Zen. 2 78, 9

back [plate XXI]:

III

ἡ πᾶσα γῆ τῶν {τῶν} δύο
μισθώσεων ἄρου(ραι) υϙη 'c' η' λ'β [ι']ς'
ἁλμυρίδος να δ' η' ι'ς' λ'β
διωρύγων δ c δ' ι'ς'
σκαμμάτων καὶ χωμά[τ]ων ς η'
σ∠ ι'ς' ρκβ∠δ' — / ἄρου(ραι) ξβ δ' η' λ'β
/ ἄρου(ραι) τκγ δ' ι'ς' — λο<ι>παὶ ἄρου(ραι) υλς δ' (ὧν)
κριθοφόρου π
σησαμοφόρου τνς δ' (ὧν)
ἀβρόχου τῆς χορτοφόρου ι
.[.].αφορου εισ[......]..ει[..]σ[--]
⌒ σημα.[ ]...φυτου

28 ς' scriptum in fragm. *b* verso 35 τις δ' P. Col. Zen. 2 78,24, τνς δ' legimus 37 γῆ[ς] ἀφόρου P. Col. Zen. 2 78, 26 38 (γίνονται) δι(ά) P. Col. Zen. 2 78, 28, ⌒ legimus; [ἄρ(ουραι) τῆς] συμφύτου P. Col. Zen. 78, 28

IV

. .
. ι̣
γ β
δʹ ηʹ δ̣ʹ
κ αν( ) ν

V

Ζήνω[νι.]
[L λ]γ Θῶυθ ιδ,
παρὰ Ὀννώφριος.

Translation

Col. I

Onnophris to Zenon, greetings.

You told me to measure the land of the veterans. Therefore I measured it, and I found salt, unproductive (land) in it.

In the (land) of Andromachos, the ten-thousand arourae holder, there are $298\frac{1}{32}$ arourae, of which $44\frac{1}{2}\ \frac{1}{8}\ \frac{1}{16}\ \frac{1}{32}$ are salt and unproductive. The specification of them individually in each holding is:

Dionusios: [---] $\frac{1}{4}\ \frac{1}{8}\ \frac{1}{16}$ (arourae),
of which for salt land [---];

Col. II

And in the (land) of Panouphis, the ten-thousand arourae holder, (there are) $200\frac{1}{2}\ \frac{1}{16}$ arourae of land, of which the specification is:

Eunomos: 18 (arourae),
of which for a canal $\frac{1}{4}\ \frac{1}{8}$, for trenches $\frac{1}{2}\ \frac{1}{8}$, total 1, remainder 17;

Menoitios: 21 $\frac{1}{4}\ \frac{1}{8}\ \frac{1}{16}$ (arourae),
of which for canals $\frac{1}{4}\ \frac{1}{8}$, for trenches $\frac{1}{2}\ \frac{1}{8}\ \frac{1}{16}$, total 1 $\frac{1}{16}$, remainder 20 $\frac{1}{4}\ \frac{1}{8}$;

in margine:
contains unirrigated land

Sotalas: 18 (arourae),
of which for canals $\frac{1}{4}\ \frac{1}{8}$, for trenches $\frac{1}{2}\ \frac{1}{8}$, total 1, remainder 17;

Poineitas: 22 $\frac{1}{4}\ \frac{1}{16}$ (arourae),
of which for canals $\frac{1}{4}\ \frac{1}{8}\ \frac{1}{16}$, for trenches $\frac{1}{2}\ \frac{1}{8}\ \frac{1}{16}$, for salt land 1, total $2\frac{1}{8}$, remainder $20\frac{1}{8}\ \frac{1}{16}$;

in margine:
it belongs to Lusandros

Xenon: 18 (arourae),
of which for a canal $\frac{1}{4}\ \frac{1}{8}$, for trenches [$\frac{1}{2}$] $\frac{1}{8}$, for salt land 1, total 2, remainder 16;

Pro[---]: $25\frac{1}{2}\ \frac{1}{8}\ \frac{1}{16}$ (arourae),
of which for a canal $\frac{1}{2}\ \frac{1}{4}$, [for trenches] $\frac{1}{2}\ \frac{1}{8}$, for salt land 2, total $3\frac{1}{4}\ \frac{1}{8}$, remainder $22\frac{1}{4}\ \frac{1}{16}$;

Col. III

The total land of the two leases: $498\frac{1}{2}\,\frac{1}{8}\,\frac{1}{32}$ arourae, (of which)

- for salt land $51\frac{1}{4}\,\frac{1}{8}\,\frac{1}{16}\,\frac{1}{32}$
- for canals $4\frac{1}{2}\,\frac{1}{4}\,\frac{1}{16}$
- for trenches and dykes $6\frac{1}{8}$
- total: $62\frac{1}{4}\,\frac{1}{8}\,\frac{1}{32}$ arourae;

in margine:
$200\frac{1}{2}\,\frac{1}{16}$, $122\frac{1}{2}\,\frac{1}{4}$, total
$323\frac{1}{4}\,\frac{1}{16}$ arourae

remainder: $436\frac{1}{4}$ arourae, of which

- for barley-bearing land 80
- for sesame-bearing land $356\frac{1}{4}$, of which for unirrigated hay-bearing land 10

Col. V

Address:

To Zenon.

Docket:

[Year 3]3, Thoth 14. From Onnophris.

Notes

1 For Onnophris and his son Horos, frequently employed by Zenon on work connected with the cleruchies, see the *Prosopography*, P. L. Bat. 21. IX, Ὀννῶφρις (no. 8) and Ὧρος (no. 10). Van 't Dack refers to the information collected by F. UEBEL, *Die Kleruchen im Ptolemäischen Ägypten* (1959) p. 53 n. 4 (to no. 184, p. 52). In the subsequent publication *idem*, *Die Kleruchen Ägyptens unter den ersten sechs Ptolemäern* (1968), see especially p. 25 n. 3, p. 43 n. 4 (on no. 32), p. 67 n. 2 (on no. 122), p. 86 n. 3 (on nos. 195-197), p. 101 n. 2 (on no. 266), and p. 117 n. 2 (on no. 332).

6-7 ἐν τῆι Ἀνδρομάχου (μυρι)αρού(ρου): see the *Prosopography*, P. L. Bat. 21. IX, Ἀνδρόμαχος (nos. 1 and 3) and the prosopographical discussion by VAN 'T DACK in his article in *Chronique d'Égypte* 36 (1961) pp. 184-186. In combining the two fragments PSI 6 639 and P. Col. Zen. 2 114*j*, Van 't Dack was able to clarify suggestions made by Uebel: plainly ἡ Ἀνδρομάχου (scil. γῆ?) in the present text is to be identified with τὸ Ἀνδρομάχου ἐποίκιον of P. Cairo Zen. 3 59.325, 12-13 (this text is a list of cleruchs and the remainder of rent due to them from Zenon for Year 36:—250/249 B.C.). See subsequently UEBEL, *op. cit.* (1968), p. 43.

Several cleruchs were settled on Andromachos' estate, holding altogether $298\frac{1}{32}$ arourae. The list of their names and holdings was plainly given in the lower half of col. I, but only the first item survives.

7 The numeral ϙ is quite clear on the photograph, and is here printed without a dot. *Pace* Van 't Dack, the editors of P. Col. Zen. 2 114*j* rightly read the figure here as σϙη̄, but wrongly interpreted this as $290\frac{1}{8}$ instead of 298. For $\eta' = \frac{1}{8}$ see *l.* 8. Thus they were able to suggest in their n. *l.* 10 that "the remaining fractions [those that survive in *l.* 10, now *l.* 11] indicate that the number which appeared here was obtained by subtracting the acreage in *l.* 8 from that in *l.* 7". That is, $290\frac{5}{32} - 44\frac{23}{32} = 245\frac{14}{32}$; and therefore they restored [σμε] δʹ ηʹ ιʹϛʹ. Once Van 't Dack had combined the two fragments PSI 6 639 and P. Col. Zen. 2 114*j*, it became plain that this calculation is irrelevant, and it certainly provides no grounds for reading anything but $298\frac{1}{32}$ in *l.* 7.

— It is noticeable that the signs indicating the fraction $\frac{1}{32}$ have merged here and elsewhere in this text into one group .

8 The scribe of this document uses the symbol c (usually indicating $\frac{1}{2}$ of an obol, but see *Symbols*, P. L. Bat. 21. XIX *a*) to indicate $\frac{1}{8}$ of an aroura. This is unparalleled in the archive.

11 [Διο]νύσ[ιο]ς: see *Prosopography*, P. L. Bat. 21. IX, Διονύσιος (no. 30); Uebel, *op. cit.* (1968), no. 33, p. 43.

—]δ': only a trace, if that, survives of the δ; but the stroke to mark the fraction is quite clear, and thus there can hardly be any doubt as to the reading. The reason for the restoration, now plainly seen to be wrong, printed here in P. Col. Zen. 2 114*j*, 10 (sic), is discussed above in n. *l.* 7.

12-13 ἐν τῆι τοῦ Πανούφιος (μυρι)αρού(ρου) (scil. γῆι?): it is clear now that Panouphis is not a leaseholder as was supposed by the editors of P. Col. Zen. 2 78 and also by Uebel, *op. cit.* (1968), p. 92 n. 3 (who wanted to identify him with a homonymous farmer on Apollonios' dorea), but a rich landholder.

Panouphis is the fifth muriarouros we know by name in Ptolemaic Egypt and the third Egyptian in this position, cf. Clarysse, *Egyptian Estate-holders in the Ptolemaic Period*, in *State and Temple Economy in the Ancient Near East* (Leuven, 1979) II, pp. 737-743.

13 διαστολή: the editors of P. Col. Zen. 2 78 read here διὰ τὸ σῆ(μα), "because of the burial plot". This makes no sense; what is needed is a word meaning "specification" or "detailed account". The word διαστολή fits this sense excellently and it is corroborated by *l.* 9, where it occurs in the same context. The reading as such is less sure: it may be that the papyrus has διατολη, to be corrected into δια<σ> τολή.

14-26 Eunomos, Menoitios, Sotalas, Poineitas, Xenon and Pro[---] all belong to the military class of the πρεσβύτεροι on which see Van 't Dack, *op. cit.*, pp. 182-183. The only one who is perhaps mentioned elsewhere is Eunomos, cf. Uebel, *op. cit.* (1968), no. 217.

The leases range from 18 to 25 arourae, and these six cleruchs held in all $123\frac{7}{16}$ arourae out of the $200\frac{9}{16}$ arourae leased. The remaining $76\frac{2}{16}$ arourae, perhaps divided into 4 holdings, were listed in the lower half of col. II, which is now lost.

As stated in P. Col. Zen. 2 78, "the names of the actual occupants of the farms --- are separated one from the other by *paragraphoi*. Those which are correct as stated were marked in the left margin with an × in three cases, with a slanting stroke in the case of Pro[---] in *l.* 14 [now *l.* 25]. Marginal notations indicate some necessary change in the two cases which are not checked, those of Menoitios and Poineitas".

17 σκάμμα: the term does not occur elsewhere in the papyri. The editors of P. Col. Zen. 2 78 call the σκάμματα "lesser ditches taking off from the διῶρυξ".

28 The total of $498\frac{1}{2}\,\frac{1}{8}\,\frac{1}{32}$ arourae (the fraction $\frac{1}{2}$ was added later) contains an error of $\frac{1}{16}$ aroura:

Andromachos	298			$\frac{1}{32}$
Panouphis	200	$\frac{1}{2}$	$\frac{1}{16}$	
total	498	$\frac{1}{2}$	$\frac{1}{16}$	$\frac{1}{32}$

However, on the back of fragm. *b*, immediately after υϘη 'c' η' λ'β', there is a symbol which at first sight one would read as ε'. It is just possible that this is [ι']ς' and that the writer added $\frac{1}{16}$ afterwards without deleting the fraction $\frac{1}{8}$.

29 By subtracting the amount of salt land in Andromachos' estate (*l.* 8) from the total mentioned here, one obtains $7\frac{1}{4}$ arourae as the amount of salt land in Panouphis' estate. Of these $7\frac{1}{4}$ arourae, 4 are actually mentioned in *ll.* 21-26, and the remaining $3\frac{1}{4}$ plainly figured in the lower part of col. II, which is missing.

30-31 The total amount of land for canals is given as $4\frac{13}{16}$ arourae. A part of it is mentioned in the surviving half of col. II: $2\frac{11}{16}$ arourae, and it is very likely that the remaining $2\frac{2}{16}$ arourae figured in the missing half of this same col. II (in the same way as the arourae of salt land, see above n. *l.* 29). Likewise, out of the $6\frac{1}{8}$ arourae for trenches and dykes, $3\frac{7}{8}$ are mentioned in the first half of col. II and the other $2\frac{2}{8}$ very likely in the missing half (these proportions match the fact that the first half of col. II concerns $\frac{3}{5}$, and the missing half $\frac{2}{5}$, of the land in the estate of Panouphis).

All the canals, trenches and dykes that are mentioned in this document lay, therefore, in Panouphis' estate, and none in the estate of Andromachos.

32-33 The marginal figures seem to include the total of the holdings in Panouphis' estate ($200\,\frac{1}{2}\,\frac{1}{16}$ arourae), to which is added the figure $122\,\frac{1}{2}\,\frac{1}{4}$. There is no hint in the preserved part of the text as to what this figure represents. In PSI 4 432 Onnophris' son Horos is responsible for 120 arourae, but it cannot be affirmed that these are identical with the $122\,\frac{1}{2}\,\frac{1}{4}$ arourae mentioned here (see however below n. *ll.* 34-35). Indeed it is not even impossible that the first figure ($200\frac{1}{2}\frac{1}{16}$) represents a part of Andromachos' estate and the second ($122\frac{1}{2}\frac{1}{4}$) a part of Panouphis' estate.

34-35 Our revised reading of the number in *l.* 35 establishes that the whole of the cultivable area was sown with only two crops: barley (80 arourae) and sesame ($356\frac{1}{4}$ arourae). Among the crops grown on the land sesame is unusually prominent. CL. PRÉAUX, *L'économie royale*, pp. 66-72, lists several instances of this crop (esp. pp. 71-72 n. 5) in Apollonios' dorea and among the cleruchs, but it remains remarkable that out of a total of $436\frac{1}{4}$ arourae of cultivable land $356\frac{1}{4}$ were sown with sesame.

This leads us to PSI 5 522, a letter of Eutuchides docketed by Zenon "περὶ τῆς σησαμί-τιδος". The situation is so similar that the letter almost certainly concerns the same piece of land.[1] The crops, barley and sesame, are the same and they cover more or less the same area. The land is also divided into κλῆροι and Horos, the son of Onnophris (the writer of our text) is responsible for their cultivation. Before the exact relationship between the two texts can be established, however, PSI 5 522 will need close re-examination. The same land is probably also the subject of P. Cairo Zen. 3 59.315.

35 The number 6, usually written  (see *l.* 33) is here written  by means of two parallel horizontal strokes (cf. the symbol for "two obols"). The same form of *sti* is known to us from an unpublished ostracon found by the Belgian excavations at Elkab (3.T.044) and belonging to the same period as Zenon's archive, where we read: L ε Φαρμοῦθι = . Πέπτωκεν etc.

39-42 The numbers on the back of fragm. *b* have no apparent connection with the main text. They were written in two columns; from *ll.* 41-42 it appears that the figures in the first column were half as large again as those in the second.

45 The restoration of [L λ]γ here, "Year 33", is principally based on the known range of dates for Onnophris' activities: see VAN 'T DACK, *op. cit.*, p. 182 and UEBEL, *op. cit.* (1968), n. 4 p. 43. The cleruchic settlements at the end of 253 were the aftermath of the end of the second Syrian War, see CLARYSSE, *A Royal Visit to Memphis and the End of the Second Syrian War*, in *Ptolemaic Memphis, Studia Hellenistica* 24 (1980), pp. 83-89.

C. and T.

[1] PSI 5 522 was, however, written five years later than the present text.

39

BRIEF DES PATAIKION AN ZENON

H. × Br. = 15,5 × 19,5 cm. Geschrieben 23. Januar 250 v. Chr.

Biblioteca Medicea Laurenziana: **PSI 4 363**. Der Text war öfter ergänzt und berichtigt: VITELLI, PSI 6, S. XII; JOUGUET, *Revue Égyptologique*, Nouvelle Série 1 (1919) 124; VIERECK und NORSA, PSI 8, S. XVI.

Der Text wurde in zwei Kolumnen geschrieben. Dazwischen ist eine Lücke, so dass die letzten Buchstaben der ersten Kolumne und die ersten der zweiten verloren gegangen sind. Auf der Rückseite befinden sich Anschrift und Empfangsvermerk.

Inhalt Laut einer Anordnung Zenons sollte sein Angestellter Pataikion dem Isidoros einen Esel im Tausch für einen anderen geben. Das andere Tier ist aber in Herakleopolis und Pataikion schreibt Zenon, dass er es haben will, bevor er sein eigenes Tier weggibt. Deswegen hat er jetzt einen Eseltreiber nach Herakleopolis gesandt.

An Zenon hat Pataikion am selben Tag einen anderen Brief (PSI 6 572) gesandt, der von derselben Hand geschrieben wurde.

Vorderseite:

I

Παταικίων Ζήνωνι
χαίρειν. Ἔγραψάς μ[οι]
δοῦναι τὸν ὄνον Ἰσιδώ-
ρωι, ἐὰν παρ[ῆι], ἢ [καὶ]
τοῖς παρ' αὐτọῦ̣, κ[ομίσα-]
σθαι δέ με παρ' αὐτọῦ̣ τ̣[ὸν]
ὄνον ἀνθ' οὗ δίδωμι α̣ὐ̣τ̣[ῶι.]
Οὐκ ἔφη οὖν Ἀπολλ[ό]δ̣[οτος]
ὁ παρ' Ἰσιδώρου παρεῖναι τ̣ὸ̣ν̣
ὄνον, ἀλλὰ ἐν Ἡρ[ακλήους]
πόλει εἶναι. Οὐκ ἔδοξεν
οὖν μοι χρήσιμον εἶν[αι]
ἀποδοῦναι τὸν ὄνον ἕ̣[ω]ς̣
τοῦ ἐκεῖνον κομίσα[σθαι.]
Ἀπέσταλκα δὲ τὸν ὀνη̣-
λάτην εἰς Ἡρακλήους [πό-]
λιν ⟦εγ̣⟧{δ}δοὺς αὐτῶι ἐφọ́-
διον ⊢ δ· οὐ γὰρ ἠβούλ[ετο]
πορεύ<ε>σθαι, ἂ<μ> μὴ ἐφόδιον [λ]άβηι.

II

[῎Ε]χει δὲ καὶ παρὰ
[᾿Α]πολλοδότου ἐπι-
[σ]τολήν, ὅπως δῶσίν
μο̣ι̣ τὸν ὄνον.
῎Ερρωσο. ⟦L λ.⟧
Ḷ λ̣ε̣ Χο̣ι̣ά̣ιχο ᾱ.

Rückseite:

Ζήνωνι.
L λε Χοιὰχ [--].

4 ἐὰν παρ[..]ι̣[.....] ed. princ., ἐὰν παρ[ῆι] ἢ [καί], Viereck 5-6 αὐτο̣ῦ̣ .[......]| δε ed. princ., αὐτο̣ῦ̣ κ[ομίσα]|σθαι δέ Jouguet 13-14 ὄνον | τοῦ ἐκεῖνον κομί[σαντος] ed. princ., ὄνον <πρὸ> | τοῦ ἐκεῖνον κομί[σασθαι], Jouguet, ὄνον ἕ̣[ω]ς | τοῦ ἐκεῖνον κομίσα[σθαι] Norsa 22-23 ὅπως δωσ..|[.]ν̣ ed. princ., ὅπως δῶσί̣ν | μο̣ι̣ Norsa 25 Ḷ λ̣ε̣ Χο̣ι̣ά̣ιχο ᾱ Vitelli, in ed. princ. nicht gelesen

Übersetzung

Pataikion grüsst Zenon.

Du hast mir geschrieben, dem Isidoros, wenn er da ist, oder auch seinen Leuten, den Esel zu geben und von ihm den (anderen) Esel zu übernehmen im Tausch für denjenigen, welchen ich ihm gebe. Apollodotos, der Mann von Isidoros, sagte aber, dass der Esel nicht da war, sondern dass er in Herakleopolis war. Also schien es mir nicht nützlich zu sein, den Esel zu übergeben, bevor ich jenen empfangen hatte. Und ich habe den Eseltreiber nach Herakleopolis gesandt, nachdem ich ihm 4 Drachmen Reisegeld gegeben hatte; denn er wollte nicht gehen, wenn er kein Reisegeld erhielt. Und er hat auch einen Brief von Apollodotos, damit sie mir den Esel geben.

Lebe wohl.
Im 35. Jahr, am 1. Choiak.

Anschrift:

An Zenon.

Empfangsvermerk:

Im 35. Jahr, am .. Choiak.

Anmerkungen

3 Isidoros und sein Angestellter Apollodotos sind sonst unbekannt.

6 τ̣[όν]: diese Lesung steht in der ed. princ.; man erwartet aber eine andere Lesung, z.B. ἄλλον.

19 ἄ<μ> μή: vergl. S. 169 (1).

25 Χο̣ι̣ά̣ιχο: diese Form für den Monatsnamen Choiak ist nur aus diesem Text und aus PSI 6 572 bekannt; dieser Papyrus enthält einen Brief, den Pataikion, der Schreiber des hier edierten Briefes, am selben Tag geschrieben hat.

27 Χοιὰχ [-]: den oben erwähnten anderen Brief des Pataikion hat Zenon am 30. Choiak empfangen. Es ist auffallend, dass der Brief erst nach so langer Zeit empfangen wurde, denn aus P. Cairo Zen. 2 59.252, 4 und 4 59.787, 19-21 und 69-71 geht hervor, dass Pataikion in Pharbaithos im Faijum ansässig war.

W.

40

LETTER FROM PAUSANIAS TO ZENON

H. × W. = 2 × 8 cm.[a]; 6.9 × 9 cm.[b] Date uncertain (2 August, 228 B.C.?)

Strasbourg inv. gr. 2484[a] + 2486a[b]: **P. Strasb. 7 561**.

Three fragments survive of this papyrus. Two which join bear the number 2486a[b]; and the other, preserving the first two lines of the text, bears the number 2484[a]. It is probable, but not certain, that the two lines on 2484 immediately precede the first line preserved on 2486a. The docket on the back is written the other-way-up relative to the text on the front, and stands close to the left-hand edge (in the case of this papyrus, the "left-hand edge" is the same whether the papyrus is viewed from front or back). The text on the front is written across the fibres. It stands on the recto surface, and the letter may well have been written in a wide format: Schwartz suggests that at least three times as much as survives has been lost. On the back, the address has plainly been lost to the right of the docket. Schwartz indicates that horizontal folds can be seen.

Contents In this fragmentary letter, Pausanias informs Zenon of the circumstances of a dispute between Tboéris and Orses. Evidently violence had been involved, or was alleged to have done so.

For the name Pausanias see P. Cairo Zen. 2 59.176, 114 (255 B.C.) and P. Cairo Zen. 3 59.396, which plainly concerns the exploitation of the cleruchies. For P. Cairo Zen. 1 59.017, cited by Schwartz (n. *l.* 1) as possibly an earlier occurrence of a Pausanias, see now text no. **32** above: the Cairo fragment belongs with others, and the relevant name is now to be read as Apollonios. For the name Orses, see P. Cairo Zen. 3 59.361, 8 (242 B.C.): it suggests the Faiyûm.

front [plate XIX]:

Παυσανίας Ζήνωνι χαίρε[ιν
[ ]. . [
- -
[ ].[.]ν φαιṿ[
[προσενέγκ]ηι τὰς χέρας αλ̣[
[. . . κα]λεσαμενος οὖν τὸν 'Ορσ[ῆν
[. . . τῆ]ς προγεγραμμένης ἡμ[έρας
[. . . 'Ορ]σῆν εἰ ἐγδέδυκεṿ [
Γ̣έ̣γρ̣α̣φα οὖν σοι ἵνα ἰδῆς. *vacat* [
["Ερρωσο *etc.*

back [plate XIX]:

[Ζήνωνι.]
[L κ Δύσ]τ̣ρου κδ Παῦνι ιη.
[Παυσ]ανίας περὶ Τβοήριο̣[ς]
[πρὸ]ς 'Ορσῆν.

4 [προσενέγκ]ηι Clarysse 7 'Ορ]σῆν εἰ Clarysse 11 "Ε]τους κδ ed. princ., Δύσ]τ̣ρου κδ Clarysse

Translation

Pausanias to Zenon, greetings.

--- (*l.* 4) lay hands upon ---. Therefore, summoning Orses, --- on the day mentioned above --- Orses, if he stripped ---. So I have written to you for your information.

[Fare well. *Date*].

Address:

[To Zenon.]

Docket:

[Year 20 Dys]tros 24 Pauni 18: Pausanias about Tboeris against Orses.

Notes

4 Perhaps the sense is "lay violent hands on": cf. P. Cairo Zen. 1 59.018, 8; P. Cairo Zen. 3 59.443, 6 (vol. 4, p. 290); P. Col. Zen. 1 34, 4-5, etc. (presumably as a threat, or as what someone feared might happen:—perhaps [οὐ μόνον] --- ἀλ[λὰ καί might be restored). Alternatively, perhaps [προσενέγκ]ηι τὰς χέρας αὐ̣[τῶι, or αὐ̣[τοῖς, "lay hands on", "catch" (see P. Cairo Zen. 4 59.559, 3: cf. PSI 4 380, 5).

5 Perhaps ['Ανακα]λεσάμενος: we cannot tell whether or not a court was involved here.

7 ἐγδέδυκεν: "to strip [of clothing]"? cf. PSI 4 380, 10-11.

11 Clarysse is certainly right to read -ρου and hence Δύσ]τ̣ρου κδ seems entirely inescapable, and hence Year 20, 228 B.C. seems equally inescapable (see P. L. Bat. 21 VIII). On the other hand the use of an Egyptian month-name together with a Macedonian one in the dockets of letters received by Zenon is not attested after the end of 255 B.C. and perhaps the text does not belong to the archive. See p. 6 n. 10.

T.

41

LETTER FROM PAÜS TO ZENON

H. × W. = 11.4 × 8.9 cm. Not dated

Berlin inv. 18089: W. MÜLLER, *Papyri aus der Sammlung Ibscher*, *JJP* 13 (1961), pp. 76-8; SB 8 9780 (only a version with the orthographic peculiarities normalized is given); **BGU 10 1995**, with plate 23.

Except for the left-hand margin, which is mostly lost, the text is well-preserved. There are only small margins at the top and on both sides, but there is a spacious blank space at the foot. The text is written along the fibres in somewhat clumsy capitals mixed with more cursive forms of α, τ, and υ.

Contents Paüs is trying to secure an appointment as a storekeeper on a ship, and seeks Zenon's recommendation.

We think it likely that Paüs' letter was written in Alexandria. Being an Egyptian, Paüs could more easily make a start there than in the Ptolemaic possessions abroad. It would also be easier for him to get help from Zenon quickly (τὸ τάχος), whether Zenon was already in Philadelphia or still in the travelling party of the dioecetes. This could also explain why Zenon referred him to the logisterion. This office was closely connected with that of the dioecetes. We know, for instance, that the logisterion of Dionusodoros, which according to the Revenue Laws was the central one for the whole of Egypt, accompanied the dioecetes during his tours in the Delta (see *Pros. Ptol.* 1 74 and add.). No wonder that Zenon had personal contacts with clerks or heads of department in this office, the usual seat of which was of course Alexandria.

If this is correct, the opposition in the text between Egypt (*l.* 2) and the place where Paüs is writing (ὧδε, *l.* 3) becomes particularly interesting. At first sight it looks as if he is abroad, but we know that in the Roman period Alexandria was considered to be outside the Imperial province of Egypt, for example in the expressions 'Αλεξάνδρεια ἡ πρὸς Αἰγύπτωι and *Praefectus Alexandreae et Aegypti*. According to P. M. FRASER, *Ptolemaic Alexandria* (1972), I, pp. 108-9, this idea developed during the second century B.C. With the present text, it may be traced back one century earlier. Perhaps it is as old as the foundation of the city.

The plate in BGU 10 shows a good example of an untrained hand. The orthography is hardly any better than the hand-writing. Several irregularities are just plain errors (δύσαι, ἐχθέψαι, δύται, τρίαρχος), but most reflect the actual pronunciation in the middle of the third century B.C.:

1. Simplification of a double consonant within a word (ἄλος) and even between two consecutive words (οὖμοι = οὖμ μοι): cf. E. MAYSER - H. SCHMOLL, *Grammatik* I² 1, pp. 186-91 and for example text no. **39** *l.* 19.
2. Disappearance of the υ in ευ (σκεοφύλακα): cf. *ibid.*, p. 94.
3. Confusion of η and ε (e.g. Ζένωνι, ἐξέθρηψας): cf. *ibid.*, pp. 39-41 and pp. 46-9.
4. Confusion of ει and ι (ἀπόστιλον): cf. *ibid.*, pp. 60-70.
5. Confusion of ωι and οι (ἐν Αἰγύπτοι): cf. *ibid.*, pp. 114-15.

The confusion between ει and ι is common, both in the third and in the second century B.C. However, the case is different with η. In the third century, uneducated writers fail to distinguish properly between η and ε; [1] but from the second century onwards the confusion is generally between η and ι. The confusion between ωι and οι proves that the ι *mutum* was still pronounced in the third century B.C.[2] In the next century, when this ι is dropped from the spoken language, ωι is instead confused with ω.

Thus some of the irregularities in the present letter illustrate the changes in pronunciation that occurred between the third and the second centuries B.C. In general, an instructive comparison can be made between the orthography of certain letters in the Zenon archive,[3] and that of Ptolemaios the katochos and his brother Apollonios in the first volume of UPZ (mid second century B.C.).

front:

Παῦς Ζένωνι χαίρειν. Σύ μ'
ἐξέθρηψας ἐν Αἰγύπτοι, δύσαι
με καὶ ὧδη ἐχθέψαι. Ἔλεγές μοι
δ̣ιελθεῖν εἰς τὸ λογιστήριον καὶ ζη-
τῆσαι Ἡλιόδωρον. Οὗτος δύται
με καταστῆσαι σκεοφύλακα·
Ἀμένανδρός ἐστι τρίαρχος τῆς ἐ-
ννειέρους. Σὺ οὗμοι ἀπόστιλον,
[ἵ]να μοι γένηται τὸ τάχος, ἵνα
μὴ ἄλος παρήλεταί μου.
Ἔ[ρρ]ωσο.

back:

12 Παῦς.

1 *l.* Ζήνωνι 2 *l.* ἐξέθρεψας ἐν Αἰγύπτωι, δύνασαι 3 *l.* ὧδε ἐκθρέψαι 5 *l.* δύναται 6 *l.* σκευοφύλακα 7 *l.* Ἀμύνανδρος, τριήραρχος 8 *l.* ἐννήρους, οὗμ μοι (= οὖν μοι) ἀπόστειλον 10 *l.* ἄλλος παρέληται

Translation

Paüs to Zenon, greetings.

You have brought me up in Egypt, and you can (continue to) bring me up here as well. You told me to go to the accountant's office and to seek out Heliodoros. He can appoint me as a store-keeper, and Amunandros is captain of the *enneres*. Therefore, send me a letter, so that the post may soon be given to me, and no one else may take it away from me.

Fare well.

---

[1] The confusion between ε and αι is not securely attested before the second century B.C. Cf. E. Mayser - H. Schmoll, *Grammatik* I² 1, pp. 85-6. Therefore καλάμε πολλέ in P. Lond. 7 2061, 17 is not written for καλάμαι πολλαί (so Skeat in his critical apparatus), but for καλάμη πολλή (cf. in the same text Ψενταἔς, τὴν γἔν, τρήφω, ἀνέλωκα, σιτωνέσω, οὐκ ἔν ξύλα).

[2] W. Clarysse, *Notes on the use of the iota adscript in the third century B.C.*, *Chronique d'Égypte* 50 (1976) 150-166.

[3] P. Cairo Zen. 3 59.499 (letters of Petosiris), P. Lond. 7 2061 (letter of Psentaes), P. Mich. Zen. 29 (letter of Senchons), P. Mich. Zen. 87 (letter of Kallippos, from prison), and PSI 4 421 (letter from the dyke-guards). See also P. Cairo Zen. 4 59.625 (fragment of a petition).

Notes

2 This passage, in which former protection is invoked in order to obtain further help, is paralleled in two other petitions from Egyptians to Zenon:

P. Ryl. 4 569, 6-8:

'Εσκέπασες[ἡ|μᾶς κ]ạὶ ἀρχῆς, ἔτι δὲ καὶ νῦν οὐδεὶς ἡμᾶς | [μὴ σκε]πάσῃ ἀλλ' ἢ σύ.

PSI 6 596, 2-4:

'Αφ' οὗ τε γε|γόναμεν ἐμ Φιλαδελφέαι | σὺ ἡμᾶς τέτρεφας.

5 Heliodoros: I do not feel so sure he was the head of the logisterion, as is suggested by W. Müller, *JJP* 13 (1961), p. 78, and *Pros. Ptol.* 8. 148a. Paüs is asking for only a minor job, and any head of department within the logisterion probably could procure this.

7 For the trierarchos in the Ptolemaic fleet, see most recently R. S. Bagnall, *The Ptolemaic Trierarchs, CdÉ* 46 (1971), pp. 356-62 and H. Hauben — E. van 't Dack, *L'apport égyptien à l'armée navale Lagide, Das Ptolemäische Ägypten* (Berlin, 1978), p. 82.

7-8 An *enneres* is a very large seagoing warship, having at least two superimposed banks of rowers with e.g. 5 men to each upper roar and 4 to each lower, cf. L. Casson, *Ships and Seamanship in the Ancient World* (Princeton, 1971), pp. 97-140, esp. pp. 106 and 113, where a crew of more than 500 rowers is considered likely for such a ship.

C.

42

LETTRE DE PHILÔNIDÊS À ZÉNON

H. × L. = 9 × 25 cm. | Envoyée le 18 mars 257 a.C.,
reçue le 23 mars 257 a.C.

Col. inv. 290 + un fragment de la Biblioteca Medicea Laurenziana: **P. Col. Zen. 1 7** et **PSI 6 663**; C. C. Edgar dans *JEA* 21 (1935), p. 123 (réunit les deux fragments); cpr. BL 3, p. 43.

La lettre a été écrite dans le sens contraire à celui des fibres. L'adresse et le docket se trouvent au verso du fragment conservé à Columbia. Grâce à l'amabilité de M. le Professeur M. Manfredi, j'ai pu collationner sur photo le fragment conservé à Florence.

Contenu Philônidês écrit à Zénon pour lui demander d'aider Ptolemaios au cas où ce dernier ferait appel à lui. Cette lettre de recommandation (ἐπιστολὴ συστατική) suit le schéma habituel: après avoir indiqué les liens qui le lient à la personne qu'il recommande (parent, ami, concitoyen, connaissance, Grec ...), l'auteur demande d'aider celui-ci dans son entreprise et termine en demandant au destinataire d'indiquer comment il peut, à son tour, lui être utile.

Dans le cas qui nous occupe, nous ne savons pas ce que voulait exactement obtenir Ptolemaios: la lettre de Philônidês est en effet muette à ce sujet et le personnage nous est inconnu par ailleurs. Nous pouvons par contre déduire de la présence-même de cette lettre dans les archives de Zénon que Ptolemaios réussit à le rejoindre à Boubastos — où Zénon se trouvait depuis le 16 mars, — et à lui remettre la lettre dont il était porteur.

Φιλωνίδης ὁ ἱερεὺς τοῦ 'Ασκληπιοῦ Ζήνωνι χ[αίρειν. Καλ]ῶ̣ς ποεῖς εἰ ὑγιαίνεις· ὑ[γιαί-]
νομεν δὲ καὶ ἡμεῖς. Πτολεμαῖος ὁ κομίζων σο̣ι̣ [τὴν ἐπιστολ]ὴ̣ν φίλος ἐστὶν ἡμ[ῖ̣ν καὶ]
ἀναγκαῖος. Καλῶς ἂν οὖν ποήσαις συγ̣[επιλ]αμβ[ανόμενος αὐτοῦ ἐ]άν σε π̣αρα̣[καλῆι].
Τοῦτο δὲ ποιῶν χαρί̣ζοι' ἂν καὶ ἐμοὶ καὶ τῶι θεῶ[ι. Γράφε δὲ ἡμῖν πε]ρὶ ὧν ἂν θέ[λῃις]
ὡς ἐσομένων σοι. ["Ε]ρρωσο. Τῦβι κδ.

au dos:

6 Ζήνωνι.
Φιλωνίδου ἱερέως
τοῦ 'Ασκληπιοῦ περὶ Πτολεμαίου.
L κη Περιτίου ιθ.

2 ἡμ[ῶν καί] ed. 3 συγ̣[....]αμ.[ed., συγ̣[επιλ]αμβ[ανόμενος] Edgar; π̣αρ[ακαλῆι] ed.

Traduction

Philônidês, le prêtre d'Asklêpios, salue Zénon.

Tu fais bien si tu es en bonne santé; nous aussi, nous nous portons bien. Ptolemaios, qui te remettra cette lettre, est un ami à nous et de notre famille. Tu ferais donc bien de l'aider s'il venait à faire appel à toi. Ce faisant, tu obligerais et moi-même et le dieu. Écris-moi au sujet des choses dont tu souhaiterais qu'elles te soient envoyées. Porte-toi bien. 24 Tybi.

Adresse:

À Zénon.

Docket:

De Philônidês, prêtre d'Asklêpios, à propos de Ptolemaios.
An 28, 19 Peritios.

Notes

1 Φιλωνίδης: probablement le fils de Κλέων, l'architecte du nome arsinoite durant la seconde moitié du règne de Ptolémée II Philadelphe.[1] Ainsi que le fait remarquer EDGAR, JEA 21 (1935), p. 123, la présente lettre n'est pas de la main de Philônidês; ce n'est toutefois pas un argument suffisant pour repousser l'identification maintenue ici, car Philônidês a fort bien pu faire appel à (un scribe de) son frère Polykratês: «it is written in ... a ... hand, resembling that of Polycrates» (EDGAR, *l.c.*).

— ἱερεὺς τοῦ 'Ασκληπιοῦ: si le Philônidês de notre texte est bien le fils de Kleôn, ce n'est peut-être pas par hasard que, dans une lettre adressée à son père, il mentionne le temple d'Asklêpios (P. Petr. I 30, 1, 3-5, cpr. EDGAR, P. Cairo Zen. 4 59.556, 9 note): [γίνωσκε δὲ Σάτ]υρον ὄντα ἐν Μέμφει ἀρρωστοῦντα καὶ τ[ὰς δ]ιατρ[ιβὰς ποιούμενον ἐν τ]ῶι 'Ασκληπιείωι. Pour le temple d'Asklêpios ~ Imouthês de Memphis, voir l'introduction d'Edgar au P. Mich. Zen. 31 (p. 95); cpr. D. WILDUNG, Imhotep und Amenhotep (Münch. Äg. Stud. 36, 1977), pp. 58-59.

2-3 φίλος ἐστὶν ἡμῖ[ν καὶ] ἀναγκαῖος: dans P. Lond. 7 2027, 2, l'ordre des mots est inverse: ἀναγκαῖος ὢν καὶ φίλος.

M.

---

[1] La plupart des textes publiés appartenant aux archives de Κλέων sont réunis dans P. Petr. III 42. Cpr. outre les textes **B** et **C** publiés plus bas dans le supplément, *PP* I 534 + Add., A. BOUCHÉ-LECLERCQ, *L'ingénieur Cléon, Revue des Études Grecques* 21 (1908), pp. 121-152, RE Supplem. IV (1924) 909-912, C. C. EDGAR, *Four Petrie Papyri Revised* (Studies Presented to F. Ll. Griffith, 1932), pp. 209-213, T. C. SKEAT, *A Letter from Philonides to Kleon Revised, JEA* 34 (1948), pp. 80-81, E. SEIDL, *Ptolem. Rechtsgesch.* (1962), p. 43 n° 20 «Das Theodoros-Archiv» et T. REEKMANS, *Le salaire de Cléon, Archiv für Papyrusforsch.* 20 (1970), pp. 17-24.

43

MÉMOIRE DE SÔSITIMOS À ZÉNON

H. × L. = 12,5 × 11,3 cm. Non daté

Berlin inv. 18088: W. MÜLLER dans *JJP* 13 (1961), pp. 75-76 (le texte faisait alors partie, sous le numéro 11, de la collection privée de H. Ibscher), reproduit dans SB 8 9779; W. MÜLLER dans **BGU 10 1993** (photo à la pl. XXI).

Les marges gauche, supérieure et droite sont intactes; la cassure au bas du papyrus n'a laissé subsister que le sommet du dernier mot du mémoire (cpr. toutefois la n. à la *l.* 12). Le texte est inscrit, sur le recto de la feuille de papyrus, parallèlement aux fibres; il y a un *kollêma* à gauche, à hauteur du début des lignes.

Contenu Sôsitimos, qui n'est connu que par ce texte, demande à Zénon d'écrire aux policiers des nomes arsinoïte et héracléopolite afin qu'ils aident ses propres hommes dans la recherche de deux de ses esclaves enfuis. (Pour d'autres textes concernant les esclaves fugitifs, voir les n[os] **24** et **36**). Si Sôsitimos s'adresse à Zénon, c'est que ce dernier est vraisemblablement la personne la plus influente qu'il connaisse dans la région où ses esclaves se seraient enfuis. Mais le fait que ceux-ci aient fui dans les nomes arsinoïte et héracléopolite ne constitue pas une raison suffisante pour affirmer «dass Sositimos im Memphites wohnhaft war, wo Apollonios eine δωρεά besass» (MÜLLER, *JJP* 13, 1961, 75).

Ὑπόμνημα Ζήνωνι παρὰ Σωσιτίμου. Παῖδες ἀποκεχωρήκα`σί´ μου δύο, τυγχάνουσι δὲ ἀναστρεφόμενοι ἐν τῶι Ἀρσινοΐτηι νομῶι καὶ ἐν τῶι Ἡρακλεοπολίτηι. Καλῶς ἂν οὖμ ποιήσαις γράψας πρὸς τοὺς ἐκεῖ φυλακίτας, ὅπως ἂν μετὰ τῶν παρ᾽ ἐμοῦ ἀπεσταλμένων συζητήσωσιν α̣ὐ̣[το]ὺ̣ς̣.

Traduction

Mémoire (adressé) à Zénon de la part de Sôsitimos.

Deux de mes esclaves se sont enfuis et se trouvent en ce moment dans les nomes arsinoïte et héracléopolite. Tu ferais bien d'écrire aux policiers de là-bas, afin qu'ils les recherchent ensemble avec ceux qui ont été envoyés par moi.

Notes

11 συζητήσωσιν: suite à une erreur d'impression, le texte BGU 10 1993 a συζητήσουσιν.

12 Les ὑπομνήματα ne contenaient pas nécessairement une formule de salutation finale (v. p. ex. P. Cairo Zen. 2 59.188), mais on ne peut exclure que la présente note ait eu une treizième ligne avec εὐτύχει (ou ἔρρωσο) suivie de la date; dans ce cas, un docket aurait pu se trouver au dos de cette partie manquante.

Dans son état actuel, le texte ne comporte pas de date, et on doit se limiter à dire qu'il est postérieur au retour de Zénon de Palestine en 258 a.C., cpr. MÜLLER dans *JJP* 13 (1961) p. 75.

M.

44

LETTRE DE SÔSTRATOS À ZÉNON

H. × L. = 9,5 × 29,2 cm. 19 mars 253

Société d'archéologie d'Athènes: G. A. Petropoulos, **P. S. A. Athen. 2**. Une photographie du recto de ce texte se trouve à Bruxelles dans «The international photographic archive».

La lettre est écrite dans le sens contraire à celui des fibres.

Contenu Sôstratos écrit à Zénon pour l'informer de la mort d'une de ses chiennes. L'intérêt de Zénon pour la chasse est bien connu (cpr. P. Cairo Zen. 2 59.262 et 4 59.532) et ses chiens l'accompagnaient souvent durant ses déplacements (voir p. ex. P. Cairo Zen. 4 59.710 et 59.712).

Σώστρατος Ζήνωνι χαίρειν. Τῆι κ̅ς̅ ἀναβαίνοντός μου ἐκ τοῦ πεδίου προσήνεγκαν οἱ κυνουλκοὶ τὴν θήλειαν κύνα, τὴν παρ' Ἀπολλωνίου ἀποσταλεῖσαν, τετελευτηκυῖαν. Γέγραφα οὖν σοι ἵνα εἰδῆις.

Ἔρρωσο. ∟ λβ Τῦβι κ̅ς̅.

au dos:

Ζ[ήνωνι].

Traduction

Sôstratos salue Zénon.

Le 26, alors que je revenais de la plaine, les valets de chiens m'ont apporté la chienne — celle qui avait été envoyée de la part d'Apollônios, — morte. Je t'écris afin que tu sois au courant.

Porte-toi bien. An 32, Tybi 26.

Adresse:

À Zénon.

Note

2 πεδίον: c'est là notamment que l'on faisait paître le bétail: P. Cairo Zen. 3 59.362, 23 et 29.

M.

45

DECLARATION TO ZENON FROM STEPHANOS

Dimensions unknown — Date unknown

Jand. inv. 361; H. G. GUNDEL, *Verlorene Papyri Jandanae, Aegyptus* 41 (1961), p. 13; **SB 8 9665**.

This papyrus was lost at the end of the Second World War, and in 1961 Gundel published a "rough copy" made by Skeat in 1932 (see the introduction to text no. **35** above). No physical details are available, except that Gundel (p. 15) put forward a reason for supposing that the backs of all the Giessen Zenon papyri that are lost were blank.

Contents In this declaration, Stephanos makes a statement to Zenon about an improper exaction (perhaps of rent, or in connection with a loan) that he claims Herakleides has made from him. Neither Stephanos nor Herakleides can certainly be identified with other persons known from the archive. However, it is reasonable to speculate that there may be a connection with the kind of dispute referred to in P. Cairo Zen. 3 59.330-1 and PSI 4 384: see therefore *Prosopography*, P. L. Bat. 21. IX, Ἡρακλείδης (no. 4). For other declarations (προσαγγέλματα) in the archive, see P. Col. Zen. 1 53, presumably addressed to Zenon; and PSI 4 396, written by Zenon; and compare P. Cairo Zen. 2 59.167; P. Lond. 7 1980-1; P. Mich. Zen. 34 and 52; PSI 4 393; and PSI 6 677: declarations are mentioned in P. Cairo Zen. 3 59.384, 16; P. Cairo Zen. 3 59.439, 2; and P. Lond. 7 2061, 16.

Προσάγγελμα Ζή̣νων̣ι̣
παρὰ Στεφάνου. Οὗ εἰσ-
πέπρακέμ μου Ἡρακλεί-
δης ἀδίκως [ ]
ε.[ ]
- -

Translation

Declaration to Zenon from Stephanos.
In the matter of the exaction that has improperly been made from me by Herakleides- - -

Notes

2-3 Skeat's copy as printed by Gundel bears no breathings or accents throughout, and the SB left the word ου here without either (although the rest of the text is accented), presumably not wishing to choose between οὐ (*l.* οὐκ) and οὗ. Clarysse has proposed that the reading should be οὗ. Plainly the sense is "Concerning what Herakleides has wrongly exacted from me". The SB notes on *l.* 3 "μου für μοι", but this does not perhaps improve the Greek. Possibly the SB understood the text differently.

T.

46

LETTER ADDRESSED TO ZENON

H. × W. = 8.8 × 30 cm. Sent 7 December, 252 B.C.
(8.8 × 12 cm.[a] and 8.8 × 9.4 cm.[b])

Strassb. Wiss. Gesellsch. 354[a] + Brit. Mus. (now Brit. Library) inv. no. 1994 B[b]: **P. Strasb. 4 228** and **P. Lond. 7 2064**.

The Strassburg and London fragments of this letter were combined as the result of a reexamination of P. Strasb. 228, during a visit made by the present editor to the Bibliothèque Nationale et Universitaire.[1] Both fragments were purchased before the main bulk of the Zenon archive came onto the market. The British Museum portion was acquired in 1911, and the collection of Die Wissenschaftliche Gesellschaft in Strassburg was formed before 1914. The text on the front is written across the fibres in a neat, medium-sized uncial. There are spacious margins at the top (2.5 cm.) and at the bottom (1.5 cm. below the ἔρρωσο and date in *l.* 4). A small portion of the letter is still missing at the left-hand side (see n. *l.* 1 below). At the right-hand side the original edge, although damaged, survives: the right-hand margin is of 1-1.5 cm. The text on the front is written on the recto surface, and a join between two *kollemata* runs between *ll.* 3 and 4. The address, written along the fibres, is on the back of the Strassburg portion, and stands the other way up relative to the text on the front.

Contents The writer has sent five yokes of oxen, probably accompanied by as many drivers. He asks Zenon to provide the men with provisions and [pay, and to send them back (?)] when the work is finished. The work meant here is probably sowing, as the time of year suggests: November-December is the usual season for sowing (see M. Schnebel, *Die Landwirtschaft*, 1925, pp. 138-9).

There is an interesting parallel to the present text in P. Hamb. 1 27, 13-15: Γίνω̣σκε δέ με παρὰ Ὀννώφριος εἰληφότα τὰ ζεύγη ἐχθὲς ὀψέ, ὥστε εἰς τὴν σήμερον ἐργάζεσθαι, ---. Συναφέσταλκεν δὲ καὶ γεωργοὺς γ, οἷς κελεύει ἐμὲ τοὺς [μισθοὺς δοῦναι]. This letter is dated 26 Phaophi (19 December) and deals with the sowing of corn (cf. *l.* 18: οὐ γὰρ ἔχομεν ἀλλ' ἢ ἡμερῶν β σπέρμα).

front [plate XIX]:

[... ... . Ζήνω]νι χαίρειν. Τὰ πέντε ζεύγη ἀπεστάλκαμεν πρὸς σέ.
[Καλῶς οὖν ποιήσεις ἐ]πιμέλειαν π[ο]ιησάμενος ὅπως τά τε ἐπιτήδεια καὶ οἱ
[γενόμενοι μισθοὶ ε]ὐτάκτως διδῶνται καὶ ὡς ἂν ἀπεργάσωνται τὰς εἴκοσι
[ἀρούρας ἄφες αὐτά.] Ἔρρωσο. L λδ Φαῶφι $\overline{\iota\delta}$.

back:

Ζ̣ήνωνι.

1 ζεύγματ[α J. Schwartz, ἀ]πεστάλκαμεν T. C. Skeat; ζεύγη ἀπεστάλκαμεν legimus 3 διδῶνται: littera ν trans dextram partem litterae ω inserta est 4 $\overline{\iota\delta}$ corr. e $\overline{\iota\gamma}$

[1] We should like to thank Professor J. Schwartz and the British Library for providing photographs.

Translation

[N.] to Zenon greetings.

We have sent you the five yokes (of oxen). Please see to it that the provisions and the wages due are given punctually, and release them as soon as they have finished off the twenty arouras.

Fare well. Year 34, Phaophi 14.

Address:

To Zenon.

Notes

1 The very probable supplement καλῶς οὖν ποιήσεις in *l.* 2 suggests that about 15-17 letters are missing at the beginnings of the lines. This would suit the normal roll-height of about 30 cm., and leaves us with 10-12 letters for the name of Zenon's correspondent. The lower number is more likely, since the writer apparently left a space blank after each word in the heading. Spaces can clearly be seen after Ζήνω]νι and χαίρειν, and another can be assumed before Ζήνω]νι, since the custom of dividing up the introductory formula ὁ δεῖνα τῶι δεῖνι χαίρειν in this way is widespread in Zenon's correspondence (see for example the plates of P. Col. Zen. 1 9 and 12). The plural form ἀπεστάλκαμεν does not necessarily imply that the letter was written jointly by two people (cf. E. MAYSER, *Grammatik* II, 1 pp. 40-43).

3 The supplement in this line was suggested by Mr. T. C. Skeat on the basis of P. Lond. 7 2038, 25-7: προστάξας τοὺς μισθοὺς εὐτ[άκτ]ως ἡμῖν ἀποδιδόναι.

4 [ἄφες αὐτά]: Skeat suggested [γράψον ἡμῖν], which is equally possible.

C.

47

COMMUNICATION ADDRESSED TO ZENON

H. × W. = 8.8 × 9.1 cm. Date unknown

A fragment belonging to the Egyptian Papyrological Society (no inventory no.): ZAKI ALY, *New data from the Zenon papyri, Proceedings of the XIV International Congress of Papyrologists 1974*, text no. 1, p. 2 and plates 1-2.

The papyrus is of a dark brown colour. It has suffered damage at what appear to be three vertical folds. The original left- and right-hand margins are preserved. The papyrus is broken at the top edge, although it appears fairly straight (this is apparent from the text, and also a single trace seems to survive from the line preceding the first one fully preserved). The letter was evidently in the narrow format, but it is impossible to judge how much text is lost—possibly only a few lines. The text on the front seems to come to an end in *l.* 5, but it is conceivable that a piece of papyrus is lost at the foot, perhaps bearing a greeting, date, or post-script, as the bottom edge is not straight. The text on the front is written along the fibres in an upright, regular hand, which notably employs two different forms of the letter ν. The two lines of which a little survives on the back are also written along the fibres. The writing here seems to be rapid and sloping, and there is every reason to suppose they are both in the same hand, and a different one from that on the front. Their nature is therefore uncertain (see n. *l.* 6).

Contents The little that is preserved of the end of this note addressed to Zenon seems to announce that some corn due from "the stone-cutters" is ready for collection.

front:

- -

c. 9] . [*c.* 7	*only one trace*
-σόμενον τὸ σιτάριον	. . . . the corn,
τὸ παρὰ τῶν λ[α]τ̣ό-	that (which is due?) from the stone-cutters;
μων· ἕτοιμον γάρ	for it is ready.
ἐστιν.	
vac.?	*blank*?

- -

back:

6	]ει.	] . . .
	] Ζήνωνι.	] To Zenon.

Textum, minimis mutatis, e Zaki Aly, *op. cit.*, deprompsimus.

Notes

1-2 Zaki Aly mentions the possible restorations [συμμετρηθη]σόμενον or [συντασ]σόμενον for the verb here. Probably read [καταμετρη]σόμενον.

Presumably the general thread of the sense is "[Please send someone who may (*for example*) take possession of] the corn due from the stone-cutters; for it is ready".

2-4 Zaki Aly provides a useful discussion of the real difficulty raised by these lines: we do not expect a corn-allowance in any sense to come "from" stone-cutters. He suggests they may themselves have hired labour, and may have paid for it with corn stored on their account by Zenon. It might perhaps fairly be commented that τὸ σιτάριον τὸ παρὰ τῶν λατόμων would be an odd and illogical, although perhaps not impossible way of expressing "the corn-allowance that is to be paid out by the stone-cutters". Although "corn-allowance" is usually the ideal, or, in some cases, a possible translation of σιτάριον, there are a few examples in the archive where it might simply mean "corn", or perhaps "corn that is due", without the connotations of "wages" or "allowance": see P. Cairo Zen. 2 59.150, 29 (it is not clear if the restoration [Θεό]δ̣ωρος, rather than the less probable ['Αρτεμί]δ̣ωρος is certain, but this would perhaps not invalidate the point made here); 59.217, 3; and PSI 4 397, 4. This suggestion does not go far towards explaining the circumstances behind the present text, but may make interpretation easier, if the text simply refers to "corn due from the stone-cutters". On our present evidence, some of the well-known stone-cutters in the archive seem also to have been involved in agricultural work: see *Prosopography*, P. L. Bat. 21. IX, Ἑριεύς (no. 4), Ὧρος (no. 23/24).

6 The reading ει (rather than θι) is fairly secure. These two letters seem to be in the same hand as Ζήνωνι in *l.* 7, although they are not written so large. It would perhaps be perverse to argue that Ζήνωνι is anything but the address of the letter. It is possible only to guess at the nature of *l.* 6.

T.

48

LETTER FROM [DIODORO]S TO APOLLONIOS

H. × W. = 19.5 × 22 cm.   Sent in 258-257 B.C.

Biblioteca Medicea Laurenziana: **PSI 5 496** (cf. 6 p. xvi); BL 1 p. 401.

No physical details of this papyrus other than the dimensions are available. Several restorations suggested by Edgar were given in PSI 6 p. xvi. In incorporating these, the BL reprinted *ll.* 1-5 entire.

Contents   In this letter Diodoros, who was in charge of Apollonios' building-works at Philadelphia, reports to him a difficulty in the supply of wood. Possibly the letter was sent on to Zenon for him to deal with the problem. Edgar in P. Mich. Zen. p. 28 seems to suggest that Zenon eventually took over control of the building-works from Diodoros. This is possible, and Diodoros may well have undertaken other duties after Year 29, but equally he may have been simply in charge of the building operations, with no responsibility for ordering materials. For another letter from the archive concerning wood-supplies, dated to 254 B.C., see text no. **27** above.

front:

         [Διόδωρο]ς Ἀπολλωνίωι χαίρειν. Ἀπέστ[αλκά σοι τὴν]
         [διαγραφὴν τῶ]ν ἔργων ἐν τίσιν ἐστίν, ὅπως εἰδ[ῆις. Τὰ μὲν]
         λίθινα καὶ πλίνθινα οὐθὲν ἐπικωλύσει, τὰ δ[ὲ ξύλινα]
         ἡμᾶς ἐφέξει· ξύλα γαρ οὔτε εἰς ὑπέρθυρα οὔ[τε εἰς]
    5 ἐπιστύλια ὑπάρχει.
                           Ἔρρωσο. Ⳑ κη Μ[   ]

back:

    7   Ἀπολλωνίωι.

2 εἰδ[ῆις. Τὰ μέν]: εἰδ[ῆις. τὰ μὴν οὖν] Edgar; εἰδ[ῆις. Τὰ μὲν οὖν] BL   4 οὔ[τε εἰς]: οὔ[τε — εἰς] PSI 5 496; οὔ[τε τά] Edgar; οὔ[τε εἰς τά] BL

Translation

    [Diodoro]s to Apollonios, greetings. I send you an account of the state that the project for the (building-)works is in, for your information.

    In the case of the stone and brick supplies, there will be no delay; but the wood supplies will hold us back. For there is no stock of wood either for lintels or for architraves.

    Fare well. Year 28, M[...........].

Address:

    To Apollonios.

Notes

1 Diodoros' name was restored here by Edgar, solely on the basis of PSI 5 500, a letter from Maron to Zenon of 6 July, 257, from which it is clear that Diodoros had been and was to continue to be in charge of Apollonios' building works. The precise date of the present letter is uncertain (see n. *l.* 6 below) but it cannot be very far removed in date from PSI 5 500, and may be assumed to concern the same operations.

Apart from the present letter, PSI 5 500 is the only other text in which Diodoros is stated to be connected with building work: see the *Prosopography*, P. L. Bat. 21. IX, Διόδωρος (no. 9; cf. no. 1) for the suggestion that he may be identified with several other instances of the name, and see Edgar's general account of the organization of the building work in P. Mich. Zen. p. 27-9, where Diodoros is discussed.

There might conceivably be a case for seeing P. Cairo Zen. 2 59.193 as a letter from Diodoros, although Edgar and Wilcken argued that it was from an important person for whom a house was being built: see n. *l.* 2 and n. *ll.* 2-4 below.

— 'Απέσταλκα here will have the sense "I am sending herewith" and simply refers to the substance of the letter in the following lines. Compare text no. **32** n. *l.* 7 above.

2 In connection with building works, διαγραφή might be expected to signify an architectural plan or drawing.[1] The only place in the archive where it clearly or very probably does so is in P. Cairo Zen. 2 59.193 (cf. U. Wilcken, *Archiv für Papyrusforschung* 8 (1927), p. 282): all other examples of the word with one exception signify a "notification" to a bank or something similar, or are in broken and obscure contexts (cf. P. Cairo Zen. 1 59.011, n. *ll.* 8-9). The exception is in P. Mich. Zen. 84, 17. In his note *ad loc.* Edgar discusses the use of the word, and argues that it can mean "programme", and evidently he had this sense in mind in suggesting the restoration here in the present text. It is not clear if in his note to P. Mich. Zen. 84 he wished to hint that he preferred a similar interpretation of διαγραφή in P. Cairo Zen. 2 59.193. It is not impossible to restore another word here in the present text, but the general sense is not in doubt.

— The restoration τὰ μέν is here preferred to τὰ μὲν οὖν because of the line-lengths, as far as these can be judged, and because οὖν does not seem very probable in the context. The μήν printed in PSI 6 p. xvi, and tacitly changed to μέν in BL, was no doubt a misprint: such a phrase seems most unlikely, and the use of μήν in the archive is confined to a few well-known expressions.

2-4 Compare the delays mentioned in PSI 5 500, 3-8, and the phrase τὰ δὲ ξύλα οὐκ ἐπικωλύσει in P. Cairo Zen. 2 59.193.

4 Edgar's restoration at the end of this line seems rather short, and perhaps for this reason the BL printed, without comment, οὔ[τε εἰς τά]. The εἰς is a definite improvement to the Greek, but there seems no justification for the τά. Admittedly the restoration printed here is barely longer than Edgar's. It may be noted that the three line-beginnings preserved show no division of words between lines.

6 The month-name here, beginning with M, can only be restored as either Mecheir or Mesore, and no Macedonian month comes into question. It is probable that Diodoros here employed the Macedonian year, in which case the letter might date from September/October 258 B.C. (restoring Mesore), or from March/April 257 B.C. (restoring Mecheir). The various possibilities may best be appreciated from the chronological tables in P. L. Bat. 21. VIII, and the information on the use of the calendars given there should also be consulted. To date the letter by the Financial year to March/April 258 (restoring Mecheir) seems too early (see text no. **32** above for the date of Zenon's return from Palestine).

On any calculation, Zenon cannot yet have taken up his duties in Philadelphia at the time this letter was written. It is perhaps conceivable that he acquired it on his arrival there together with other old papers, but it seems more likely that it was sent to him as Apollonios' secretary to arrange a supply of wood.

T.

1 See P. Petrie II 9.4 *l.* 2: [εἴ]περ οὖν ἔ[στιν ἐν τ]ῆι διαγραφῆι (Clarysse).

49

BRIEF DES EUKLES AN APOLLONIOS

H. × Br. = 21,5 × 11,5 cm. Geschrieben 30. April 244 v. Chr.

Sorb. inv. 282: P. Jouguet, *Petit Supplément aux Archives de Zénon, Cinquantenaire de l'École Pratique des Hautes Études; Bibliothèque de l'École des Hautes Études, Sciences historiques et philologiques*, 230 (1921) 216-228; mit Abbildung der Vorderseite; **SB 3 6800**. Die Umschrift von Jouguet ist von Lesquier und Grenfell durchgesehen und ihre Anmerkungen wurden in der editio princeps angegeben. Vgl. auch Wilcken, *Archiv für Papyrusforsch.* 7 (1926) 296.

Der Text des Briefes ist vollständig erhalten, obgleich darüber noch Schriftspuren von zwei Zeilen sichtbar sind. Die geübte kursive Schrift weist auf einen Berufsschreiber. Sie läuft senkrecht zu den Fasern.

In die Z. 24 und unter die Z. 25 mit Grussformel und Datum sind die Zusätze nachgetragen, die bis auf die Rückseite hinauskommen (Z. 29). Sie sind etwas kursiver geschrieben. Auf der Rückseite befinden sich die Anschrift und der Name des Absenders, der wohl von einer anderen Hand stammt. Über dem Namen des Absenders befindet sich ein brauner Fleck. Der Meinung von Jouguet nach sollte sich dort ursprünglich das Siegel befinden, nach Lesquier aber handelt es sich um Spuren der verlorengegangenen Inhaltsangabe.

Inhalt Eukles schreibt an seinen Grammateus Apollonios. Der Brief enthält eine Reihe ziemlich ausführliche Aufträge, die Apollonios erfüllen muss. Nachher muss er dem Eukles darüber einen Bericht erstatten.

Eukles war Verwalter der Dorea nach Zenon. Wir kennen noch einige Briefe von ihm: P. Col. Zen. 2 88; 91; PSI 5 537 (vgl. auch P. Col. Zen. 2 87, 1). Die Schrift des vorliegenden Textes ist identisch mit der des P. Col. Zen. 2 88 (vgl. ib. Tafel nach S. 100). Sie ist aber verschieden von der des Apollonios, seines Grammateus, und der des P. Col. Zen. 2 91 (vgl. ib., S. 97). Es ist klar, dass Eukles mehrere Schreiber hatte, von denen wir nur einen dem Namen nach kennen.

Eine andere Frage, die hier nur erwähnt werden kann, ist, wie der Brief unter die Zenon-Papyri geraten ist und ob er wirklich dem Zenon-archiv angehört. Bekanntlich war Zenon seit 246 v. Chr. nicht mehr Verwalter der Dorea gewesen und hat in Philadelphia als Privatperson gelebt. Für die Diskussion darüber siehe oben S. 5 und E. Seidl, *Ptolemäische Rechtsgeschichte*, S. 41-42.

Vorderseite:

Εὐκλῆς Ἀπολλωνίωι χαίρειν. Ἀπέσταλκά σοι τὰς ἐπιστολὰς τὰς γραφείσας πρός τε Ὀρσικλείδαν τὸν ἀρχισιτολόγον περὶ τῆς σιτομετρίας ἧς δεῖ χρηματίσαι αὐτὸν κατὰ τὴν παρ' Ἑρμαφίλου ⟦γραφεῖ⟧ `πεμφθεῖ´σαν αὐτῶι ἐπιστολήν. Ἔ̣[πε]ι̣[τα] δὲ καὶ τὰς πρὸς Χρύσιππον, τήν τε περὶ τοῦ ταλάντου ὅπως περιέληι ἐκ τοῦ προστάγματος τοῦ γραφέντος Πύθωνι `καὶ διορθώσηται´, σύμβολον δὲ πόησαι `ἀντὶ τοῦ πρὸς ἐμὲ´ ⟦μὴ πρὸς ἐμὲ ἀλλὰ⟧ πρὸς τοὺς ἀναιρουμένους ἀποχῆς καὶ τὴν περὶ τῆς σιτομετρίας ἵνα μνησθῆι τῶι Ὀρσικλείδαι. Ἐπιμελῶς οὖν ἀποδοὺς αὐτοῖς σπούδασον ἀγαγεῖν εἰς οἰκονομίαν περὶ ὧν γεγράφαμεν καὶ περὶ μὲν Ὀρσικλείδου λαβεῖν ἐπιστολὴν πρὸς Νίκωνα καὶ παρὰ Νίκωνος πρὸς Ἡρακλείδην καὶ πρὸς ἡμᾶς συντόμως πέμψαι, Χρυσίππωι δὲ μνησθῆναι ὅπως συντάξηι Πύθωνι ἐπιστεῖλαι Σκύμνωι χρηματίζειν ἵνα μὴ ἐν ἐπιστάσει ἦι τὰ ἔργα. Πρὸς δὲ ταῦτα παράλαβε καὶ Λυκόφρονα. Ἐντετάλμεθα δὲ καὶ Προίτωι συνλαβεῖν τινα τῶν ὀφειλόντων καὶ τὰ ὑπάρχοντα ἐνεχυράσαι. Παραλαβὼν οὖν Κτησικλῆν καὶ τῶν παρὰ Λυκόφρονος μαχίμων τινὰ συνδίελθε αὐτῶι καὶ ὃν ἄν σοι παραδείξηι, παράδος αὐτοῖς καὶ τὰ ὑπάρχοντα παράθου Λυκόφρονι. Γράψον δὲ καὶ πρὸς ἡμᾶς, ὡς ἂν οἰκονομήσηις.

Ἔρρωσο L δ Φαμενὼθ ῑ.

Rückseite:

30 Ἀπολλωνίωι

31 Εὐκλέους.

Nachtrag

Vorderseite:

24a Καὶ περὶ τῶν $\overline{\iota\theta}$ (τετρωβόλων) δὲ

26 ὧν γράφεις δεῖν με κομίσασθαι ⟦ἐκ παρὰ Παθιώφιος τοῦ ἐξειλη-

27 φότος⟧ ἀπὸ τοῦ γενήματος τοῦ βαλανείου τῆς διὰ Παθιώφιος

28 μισθώσεως, ἐπίστειλόν μοι πόθεν κομίσωμαι· τὸ μὲν γὰρ

Rückseite:

29 διεγγύημα διὰ τῶν λόγων ἀνενήνοχας.

5 ἔ̣[πε]ι̣[τα] Grenfell 8 ποῆσαι ed. princ., πόησαι Wilcken 9 ἀνατ̣ρουμένους ed. princ., ἀνα<με>τ̣ρουμένους Collart (ed. princ., S. 224), ἀναιρουμένους Wilcken (auf Grund der Tafel der ed. princ.) 26 und 27 Παθώφιος ed. princ., Παθιώφιος Bilabel (SB)

Übersetzung

Eukles grüsst Apollonios.

Ich sende Dir die an den Archisitologos Orsikleidas geschriebenen Briefe über die Sitometria, womit er sich zufolge des ihm von Hermaphilos gesandten Briefes beschäftigen muss.

Und ferner auch die (zwei Briefe) an Chrysippos: den (Brief) über das Talent, damit er den Posten auf Grund der an Python geschriebenen Anordnung streicht und ihn berichtigt — und stelle, statt der Bescheinigung an mich, eine an die Empfänger aus, eine Bescheinigung für den Empfang; — und auch den (Brief) über die Sitometria, damit er (Chrysippos) es dem Orsikleidas in Erinnerung bringt.

Nachdem Du die Briefe an sie (Orsikleidas und Chrysippos) gegeben hast, musst Du Dich sorgfältig bemühen die Angelegenheiten, worüber wir geschrieben haben, in Ordnung zu bringen: und zwar, was Orsikleidas angeht, einen Brief an Nikon (von ihm) zu empfangen und von Nikon einen an Herakleides, und diese (Briefe) uns sofort zu schicken; und (ferner) dem Chrysippos in Erinnerung zu bringen, dass er Python beauftrāgt dem Skymnos Auftrag zu geben dass er Massnahmen trifft, dass die Arbeiten nicht eingestellt werden. Und nimm mit Rücksicht darauf auch Lykophron mit.

Und wir haben auch Proitos befohlen, einen der Schuldner zu verhaften und seinen Besitz zu pfänden. Nimm also Ktesikles — und jemanden der Machimoi von Lykophron — und mach Dich mit ihm auf den Weg, und denjenigen, welchen er Dir nur anzeigt, den musst Du ihnen (den Machimoi) überantworten und seinen Besitz musst Du Lykophron zur Verwahrung übergeben. Und schreibe uns auch, wie Du es besorgt hast.

Lebe wohl.
Im 4. Jahr, am 10. Phamenoth.

Anschrift:

An Apollonios.

Empfangsvermerk:

Von Eukles.

Nachtrag:

Und bezüglich der 19 Drachmen 4 Obole, worüber Du mir schreibst, dass ich sie vom Ertrag des von Pathiophis gepachteten Bades erhalten soll, schreibe mir, warum ich sie erhalten soll, denn Du hast schon das Pfand in Deine Rechnungen gebucht.

Anmerkungen

1 Für Eukles siehe oben S. 5, P. L. Bat. 21, IX, *Prosography*, s.v., Nr. 1 und E. Seidl, *Ptolemäische Rechtsgeschichte*, S. 41-42.

2-4 Weil Eukles der Absender des Briefes ist, können wir vermuten, dass die Sitometria für die Leute der Dorea ausgezahlt werden sollte. Aus dem Auftrag an den Archisitologen Orsikleidas auf Grund einer Anordnung des Gauoikonomos Hermaphilos geht hervor, dass die Dorea in dieser Zeit der königlichen Verwaltung unterlag.

6-9 M.E. kann man diesen Passus folgendermassen verstehen: gewisse Leute (τοὺς ἀναιρουμένους, Z. 9) hatten ein Talent geliehen bekommen, aber für diesen Betrag war zu Unrecht ein σύμβολον zu Lasten des Eukles ausgefertigt worden (Z. 8) und war zu Unrecht der Betrag zu seinem Lasten gebucht worden. Der Bankier Python (vgl. P. L. Bat. 21, IX, *Prosopography*, s.v., Nr. 2) hat deshalb den Auftrag bekommen (Z. 7-8) diesen Betrag von der Rechnung des Eukles zu streichen (περιαιρεῖν, vgl. P. Lond. 7 1991, 11 et saepe; 1994, 236) und die Buchungen in Ordnung zu bringen.

18-23 In diesen Zeilen sieht man deutlich die Anwendung der so oft begegnenden Praxis-Klausel; vgl. z.B. P. Rein. 21 + P. Ross. Georg. 2 7: καὶ ἡ πρᾶξις ἔστω Ἀδύμωι καὶ τοῖς παρ' αὐτοῦ τῶν κατὰ τὴν συγγραφὴν ἔκ τε τῶν δεδανεισμένων καὶ παρ' ἑνὸς καὶ παρ' ἀμφοτέρων καὶ παρ' ὁποτέρου οὗ ἐὰν αὐτῶν αἵρηται καὶ ἐκ τῶν ὑπαρχόντων αὐτοῖς πάντων καθάπερ ἐγ δίκης.

21 Für Machimoi siehe P. Yale 1, S. 86-89. Die genaue Stellung des Lykophron ist nicht bekannt. Aus der Bezeichnung τῶν παρὰ Λυκόφρονος μαχίμων darf man nicht schliessen dass Lykophron einen Militärposten bekleidete, weil auch Zenon mit τῶν παρὰ σοῦ στρατιωτῶν bezeichnet wurde (P. Cairo Zen. 2 59.140, 15-16).

24a-29 Eukles hatte eine Forderung von 19 Drachmen und 4 Obolen, welche durch ein Pfand (διεγγύημα) gesichert war. Offenbar hat der Schuldner nicht gezahlt und ist das Pfand zum Eigentum des Gläubigers Eukles geworden; es handelt sich um ein Verfallpfand (vgl. E. Seidl, *Ptolemäische Rechtsgeschichte*, S. 141). Eukles fragt den Apollonios jetzt mit Erstaunen aus welchem Grund er noch das Geld einfordern konnte, da Apollonios selbst schon das zu Eigentum gewordene Pfand für ihn in die Buchhaltung eingetragen hatte.

W.

50

LETTER FROM THE PRIESTS OF APHRODITE TO APOLLONIOS

H. × W. = fr. *a* 16 × 12.5 cm.
fr. *b* 15.5 × 12 cm.

9 January, 257 B.C.

Biblioteca Medicea Laurenziana: two fragments published together as **PSI 4 328** (cf. PSI 4 p. xiii; PSI 6 p. x and p. xix); Sel. Pap. 2 411.

Few physical details of this papyrus are available. A vertical strip apparently is missing from the centre of the letter, and slight modifications in the length of some of the restorations here have been suggested since the first edition (see PSI 6 p. xix).

Contents In the notes below, the suggestion is put forward that the present letter was written because the Hesis-cow, the sacred animal of Hathor at Atfih, had recently died while she was away from Atfih in some other part of Egypt. Thus the priests of Aphrodite, that is, the priests of the temple of Hathor at Atfih, write to Apollonios the dioiketes, reminding him of his duty to provide 100 talents of myrrh, as granted by the king, for the entombment of the deceased Cow. They add, evidently to discourage Apollonios from attempting to delay the delivery of the myrrh, that it is not possible to bring the mummified Hesis back to the Aphroditopolite nome (no doubt with considerable pomp) until everything that will be needed for the burial ceremonies is ready, because, once the mummy has arrived, the entombment ritual must begin at once, on the same day.

When this letter was originally published, the evidence mentioned below for the name and cult of the sacred-cow of Atfih was not readily available to Greek papyrologists, and the text was at first interpreted in various ways that cannot now seriously be maintained, for example, as concerning a human burial, or ritual drowning. These interpretations (which can readily be traced in the bibliography given above and in U. WILCKEN, *Archiv für Papyrusforschung* 6 (1920), p. 386; cf. BL 1, pp. 395-6) will not be discussed further here. W. SPIEGELBERG showed in *Die Begräbnisstätte der heiligen Kühe von Aphroditopolis* (*Atfiḥ*), *OLZ* 23 (1920), col. 260, that the letter referred to the burial of the Hathor-cow of Atfih, whose name was Hesis (this was noted by WILCKEN, *Archiv für Papyrusforschung* 7 (1924), p. 86; cf. BL 2.2, pp. 138-9), but he did not discuss the text as a whole. The edition in *Select Papyri* 2 incorporated these improvements, but two aspects of the interpretation given there, which the editors themselves seem to have regarded as problematic, are not accepted here: that in *l.* 3 the text refers to the installation of a new Cow, and that in *l.* 5 the embalming of a Cow is meant. It is not quite clear if the *Select Papyri* editors took the view that the text stated or implied that the entire mummification process was accomplished in a single day, but this view also is rejected here. These and other detailed points are discussed in the notes to the text below, and only a brief general account of the Hesis is given here.

Our knowledge of the cult of the Hathor-cow at Atfih (in the 22nd Upper-Egyptian nome, the Aphroditopolite nome) is remarkably scanty. Little excavation has been done in this area, and little material — texts or objects — seems to have come from there (cf. B. Porter and R. L. B. Moss, *Topographical Bibliography* IV *Lower and Middle Egypt* (1934), pp. 75-6). It is difficult to say whether or not much is waiting to be found.

We can best proceed by working from the hypothesis that the cult at Atfih resembled that of the other famous bulls and cows of Egypt, and by then seeing how far our firm evidence bears this out. This is not, it may be thought, a very satisfactory way in which to approach the present letter, which has been supposed in the past to furnish some surprising information about the Hesis-cow. However, it appears to be written in fluent and well-spelt Greek (there is perhaps one odd phrase in *l.* 4), and we can ultimately ask whether or not the Greek clearly and naturally expresses the sense we wish to extract from it.

A great deal of practical information is known about the Apis-bull of Memphis, notably from the wealth of inscribed material found by Mariette at the Serapeum, a considerable amount is known about the Buchis-bull of Hermonthis, and recent excavations have revealed much information concerning the Mother of Apis burials at North Saqqâra. Brief accounts and bibliographies of these and other animal cults can conveniently be found in H. Bonnet, *Reallexikon der Ägyptischen Religionsgeschichte* (1952) s.v. *Apis, Buchis, Kuh, Mnevis,* and *Tierkult,* and under the corresponding articles in W. Helck and E. Otto, *Lexikon der Aegyptologie* (see also under *Atfih* and *Hesis*): See also recently P. L. Bat. 19, Appendix G.

It may be worth stating here briefly what our other evidence suggests is likely to have been the normal course of the Hesis-cow's life and funerary rites. We should expect that there would be only one Hesis-cow at any one time. We should expect her to be installed as a young calf (perhaps having been recognized by certain special markings) after the death and burial of her predecessor, to be kept near the temple of Hathor at Atfih, to die a natural death, and to be ritually embalmed, the process as a whole occupying 70 days: the mummy would be dragged up—perhaps several days might be required for this task—to the burial place near the desert edge not far from Atfih, and the ceremonies of entombment might then last four days.

The surviving evidence for the cult of the Hesis-cow is as follows. A single Cow-grave of Ptolemaic date was discovered, apparently in 1906, in the necropolis of Atfih. The significance of this find was first explained by W. Spiegelberg *Die Begräbnisstätte der heiligen Kühe von Aphroditopolis* (*Atfiḥ*), *OLZ* 23 (1920), col. 258-60. For bibliography and a short description, see *Top. Bib.* IV. 76. A stela from the reign of Ptolemy I Soter recording the death of a Cow had apparently reached the Cairo Museum before this grave was officially known, but Spiegelberg (*op. cit.,* col. 260) speculated that it might nevertheless have come from the same burial. The text was republished (with previous bibliography) by K. Sethe, *Urkunden des Ägyptischen Altertums* II, Heft I (1904) pp. 159-62.

Strabo, after discussing in their proper turn the Hathor-cow of the Momemphite nome (17.1.22 [803]), the Mnevis-bull (17.1.27 [805]), and the Apis-bull (17.1.31 [807]), singles out the Hesis-cow of Atfih as the one feature worthy of mention in the 22nd Upper-Egyptian nome: Εἶθ' ὁ 'Αφροδιτοπολίτης νομὸς καὶ ἡ ὁμώνυμος πόλις ἐν τῆι 'Αραβίᾳ, ἐν ᾗ λευκὴ βοῦς ἱερὰ τρέφεται (17.1.34 [809]). In all these passages, the verb τρέφειν is used. At 17.1.22, Strabo appears to draw a distinction between the Apis, the Mnevis, and the Momemphite cow on the one hand, which are regarded as gods (θεοί), and bulls and cows kept elsewhere, which are regarded as merely sacred (ἱεροί). This distinction, which seems to imply that the Hesis-cow was of a different kind or status from the three he mentions, is suspect. It is certainly not impossible to find in native Egyptian thought an appropriate type of distinction between major "gods" (or indeed animals like the Apis) and mere sacred animals (although the common Egyptian word *nṯr*, usually translated "god", and generally rendered by θεός in Greek, will not correspond precisely to Strabo's use of θεός here: for example, mummified sacred-animals of all kinds are frequently referred to as *nṯrw*, "gods"). However, any such distinction could not serve to mark off precisely the Apis, the Mnevis and Momemphite cow. In particular, it should be noted that Strabo has excluded the Buchis-bull, which, judging from the available evidence, might justly be placed alongside the Apis and the Mnevis. Yet he was perfectly well aware of the existence of the Buchis, as he mentions a bull kept at Hermonthis, without giving him a name, at the appropriate point in his text (17.1.47 [817]). In short, this comment of Strabo's may be disregarded in considering the nature of the Hesis-cow. He may have made it with some trivial, external criterion in mind, or it may be simply wrong, or carelessly expressed. The Apis and the Mnevis are of course sometimes mentioned as a pair by the Greeks, as being the most famous sacred-animals, or as representative of them. Strabo's inclusion of the Momemphite cow is perhaps more surprising than his exclusion of the Buchis: he may perhaps have recorded in Greek terms the feelings of the inhabitants of this particular part of Egypt.

The Hesis-cow appears in BGU 6 1216, a survey of temple land concerned with taxation, ascribed to 110 B.C. (see *l.* 64 with Schubart's note). The food (τροφή) is mentioned "of the ever-living Hesis, Isis, the greatest goddess", Ἔσειτος ἀειζωίου | Ἴσιος θεᾶς μεγίστης (*ll.* 32-3; cf. 55 and 113-4), and access to the land producing it is said to be prohibited to anyone except the priests and their subordinates (τῶν ἱερέων καὶ τῶν παρ' αὐτῶν—i.e. the lower ranks of the priesthood?) to avoid any pollution of the food of the goddess (*ll.* 33-7). It should be noted that the land of the goddess Hathor of Atfih herself is, as we should expect, mentioned quite separately: see ἐν τοῖς ἐδάφεσ[ι]ν [Ἀθερ]|νεβθφηι Ἴσιος θεᾶς μεγίστη[ς] (*ll.* 88-9), and Ἀθερνεβθφηι Ἴσει [θεᾶι] | μεγ[ί]στηι (*ll.* 100-1). Ἀθερνεβθφηι, plainly undeclined here, is equivalent, as pointed out by W. Spiegelberg, *Ägyptologische Beiträge, Archiv für Papyrusforschung* 7 (1924), pp. 183-5, to the Egyptian *Ḥw.t-Ḥr-nb.t-Tp-iḥw*, "Hathor, mistress of Atfih". It is in no way surprising that we should find elsewhere in this text many different temples and cults holding land in what is presumably a single area. Spiegelberg argued that the text was likely in fact to be concerned with the Aphroditopolite (22nd Upper-Egyptian) nome, the nome in which Atfih lay, and this is possible: certainly Schubart's assumption that it concerned land around Memphis cannot stand without qualification.

I am unable to give any satisfactory explanation of what may be an occurrence of the name of the Cow of Atfih in P. Lund. 3 10, col. 2, 20 = SB 5 8750, 26, a list of sacred-animals arranged by type (i.e. bulls, followed by cows), giving the town and the name of each animal. The SB prints as the name of the cow Σῶτις πεχις.

One further point requires separate discussion here. The identification of the "priests of Aphrodite" in the present letter with the priests of Hathor at Atfih, rather than with those of some other Hathor-temple, depends solely on the occurrence of the name Hesis. This is not in origin the specific name of the sacred cow at Atfih, but was the name of a mythical cow, not confined to any one locality. Thus by the normal workings of Egyptian mythical thought, we might expect that the name Hesis could in suitable contexts be applied to any sacred-cow, and in fact some examples of this are forthcoming. However, it is only in the case of the Hathor-cow of Atfih, originally called *Tp-iḥw* (whence the late-period Egyptian and the modern Arabic name of the town derive), that we find Hesis used as the actual name of the Cow. The name occurs in the grave discovered at Atfih in the form *ʾIs.t-Ḥs.t,* "the Isis, Hesis" (although the equation of Isis and Hathor at Atfih is of course well-attested, this particular expression obviously means "the deceased Hesis"), and the same expression is found on the stela *Urk.* II 159-62, which is proved to come from Atfih by the title *p3 ḥry-sšt3 n nb.t Tp-iḥw* (161.6), and there Hesis is also found without Isis preceding in the expression *ḥw.t-Ḥs.t* (161.8). The identification of the Hesis of BGU 6 1216 with the Cow of Atfih is virtually certain from the context. Thus, on our present evidence, the ascription of this letter to Atfih seems secure.

Οἱ ἱερεῖς τῆς Ἀφροδίτης Ἀπολλωνίωι [τῶι διοικητ]ῆι χαίρειν. Καθάπερ καὶ ὁ βασιλεὺς
γέγραφέν σοι δοῦναι εἰς τὴν ταφὴ̣[ν τῆς Ἕσιτος] ζμύρνης τάλαντα ἑκατόν,
καλῶς ἂν ποιήσαις συντάξας [δοθῆναι. Οὐ γὰ]ρ ἀγνοεῖς ὅτι οὐκ ἀνάγεται ἡ Ἕσεις
εἰς τὸν νομὸν ἐὰμ μὴ ἕτοιμα ἕ[χωμεν τὰ δέο]ντα ὅσα ποτὲ χρήαν ἔχουσιν
εἰς τὴν ταφήν, διὰ τὸ αὐθημερὸν [*c.* 10]. Γίνωσκε δὲ εἶναι τὴν Ἕσιν Εἶσιν·
αὐτὴ δέ σοι δοίη ἐπαφροδισίαν π̣ρ̣[ὸς τὸν βασι]λ̣έα. Ἔρρωσο. L κη Ἁθὺρ ιε̅.

1 [διοικητ]ῆι PSI 4 328, [τῶι διοικητ]ῆι M. Norsa, PSI 6, p. xix 2 ταφ[ὴν Ἄπιος?] PSI 4 328, ταφὴ̣[ν τῆς Εσιος] M. Norsa, PSI 6, p. xix (cf. p. x), ταφ[ὴν Ἕσιος] Spiegelberg, *OLZ* 23, ταφ[ὴν τῆς Ἕσιτος] Bilabel, BL 2.2, p. 138-9, ταφ[ὴν τῆς Ἕσιος] Edgar/Hunt, Sel. Pap. 2 3 [σὺ γὰρ οὐκ] PSI 4 328, [δοθῆναι· οὐ γὰ]ρ M. Norsa, PSI 6, p. xix 4 ἧ[ι . . . . . πά]ντα PSI 4 328, ἧ[ι τὰ καθή-κο]ντα Grenfell, PSI 6, p. x, ἕ[χωμεν ἅπα]ντα M. Norsa, PSI 6, p. xix, ἕ[χωμεν τὰ δέο]ντα Edgar/Hunt, Sel. Pap. 2; χρήαν, *l.* χρείαν 5 [ἐνταφιάζειν]? suppl. Edgar/Hunt, Sel. Pap. 2 in nota 6 π̣ρ̣[ὸς βασι]λ̣έα PSI 4, p. xiii, π̣ρ̣[ὸς τὸν βασι]λέα M. Norsa PSI 6, p. xix

Translation

The priests of Aphrodite to Apollonios [the dioiketes], greetings.

As the king has written to you that one hundred talents of myrrh should be granted for the burial [of the Hesis], please give orders for them [to be given. For you are not] unaware that the Hesis cannot be brought back to the nome unless [we have] ready absolutely everything that is needed for the burial, because [. . . . .] on the same day. Know that the Hesis is Isis: may she grant you favour [before the king.]

Fare well. Year 28, Hathur 15.

Notes

1 By οἱ ἱερεῖς τῆς Ἀφροδίτης the priests of the temple of Hathor at Atfih are meant, and not priests specifically of the cult of the sacred-cow. It is well established that, in the case of the Apis-bull, the priests of Ptah conducted the burial.

— The Greek might be understood to say "As the king *himself* has written", but this is probably not what is meant. For the royal commitment to pay for the burial of the sacred-animals, see especially the prostagma of P. Tebt. I 5, 77-9 [= C. Ord. Ptol. 53], and W. SPIEGELBERG, *Der demotische Text der Priesterdekrete von Kanopus und Memphis* (1922), Kanopus Gr. 9, Dem. A3 and B11, Hier. 5; Rosetta Gr. 31, Dem. 18 (Hier., K. SETHE *Urk.* II 185.2 ff.). The present text apparently refers to a particular letter written to Apollonios by the king, and not to a general ordinance.

2 In Egypt, the Greek word ταφή, like its Demotic equivalent *ḳs.t*, has a wide range of meanings. This point has recently been discussed and illustrated by R. L. VOS, P. L. Bat. 19, Appendix G, § 4. In the present letter, the word recurs in *l.* 5, obviously used in exactly the same sense as here in *l.* 2. The interpretation of the text as a whole and particularly of *l.* 5 demands that ταφή be ascribed the sense "burial". It will refer to the whole ceremony, probably lasting four days, in which the mummified Cow was laid to rest in her tomb.

— ζμύρνης τάλαντα ἑκατόν: myrrh is generally accepted to have been used chiefly for two purposes in ancient Egypt, for mummification and as incense. The evidence, textual and chemical, plainly shows that some use was or could be made of myrrh in mummification and burial, although there is no clear evidence for the use of massive quantities (see A. LUCAS, *Ancient Egyptian Materials and Industries*, 4th edition, ed. J. R. HARRIS (1962) pp. 299 ff., 312 ff., and 322 ff.; for the use as incense, see pp. 92 ff.). It is argued here that the actual process of mummification is not in question in this letter (see esp. n. *ll.* 3-4). There therefore seem to be three possible explanations of the large amount of myrrh mentioned here. First, that, although not used in the mummification, it was incorporated into the burial, no doubt packed into the sarcophagus. Secondly, that it was employed as incense during the burial ceremonies, which probably lasted four days (or, of course, it might be used *both* in the burial *and* for incense). The possibilities so far mentioned would clearly justify the priests in saying they needed to have the myrrh ready for the entombment. Thirdly, the hundred talents of myrrh may represent a payment made by the royal treasury for all the expenses of the funerary ceremonies. This seems clearly the correct explanation. There is no hint in our other sources that the king provided only one commodity for the burial of sacred-animals, and it would be odd if the priests wrote to demand only the myrrh: further, if the payment is in effect for all the expenses, the priests' comment, that they must have everything they could possibly need ready, follows far more naturally than if it must be taken as an involved way of saying that they need precisely the myrrh. Finally, it may be worth comparing the mention by Diodoros (I. 84.8) of a sum of one hundred talents:

> Μετὰ γὰρ τὴν Ἀλεξάνδρου τελευτήν, Πτολεμαίου τοῦ Λάγου παρειληφότος ἄρτι τὴν Αἴγυπτον, ἔτυχεν ἐν Μέμφει τελευτήσας ὁ Ἆπις γήρᾳ· ὁ δὲ τὴν ἐπιμέλειαν ἔχων αὐτοῦ τήν τε ἡτοιμασμένην χορηγίαν, οὖσαν πάνυ πολλήν, εἰς ταφὴν ἅπασαν ἐδαπάνησε καὶ παρὰ τοῦ Πτολεμαίου πεντήκοντα ἀργυρίου τάλαντα προσεδανείσατο. Καὶ καθ' ἡμᾶς δέ τινες τῶν τὰ ζῷα ταῦτα τρεφόντων εἰς τὰς ταφὰς αὐτῶν οὐκ ἔλαττον τῶν ἑκατὸν ταλάντων δεδαπανήκασιν.

> After the death of Alexander, when Ptolemy son of Lagos had just taken over control of Egypt, it happened that at Memphis the Apis died of old age. The man who had charge of him spent on the burial (ταφή) the entire allowance provided, which was quite substantial, and then borrowed in addition fifty talents of silver from Ptolemy. Even in our own time some of those who keep these animals have spent no less than one hundred talents on their burials.

That the king should wish to pay, and the temple be willing to receive a payment in the form of myrrh raises no difficulties. The present letter has been set in the context of the royal control of the trade in incense by C. PRÉAUX, *L'Économie royale des Lagides* (1939) p. 369; cf. *eadem*, *Les Grecs en Égypte* (1947) p. 73.

3 δοθῆναι is perhaps not the only possible restoration here, but the sense cannot be in doubt.

3-4 οὐκ ἀνάγεται ἡ Ἔσεις | εἰς τὸν νομόν. The verb ἀνάγειν here might have several senses, "to bring back", "to bring where something belongs", "to bring up", or "to bring up-stream". It seems quite certain that εἰς τὸν νομόν must mean "to the nome", that is, clearly, to the Aphroditopolite nome. One possible explanation is that suggested by EDGAR/HUNT in *Sel. Pap.* 2, that the phrase refers to the installation of a new Cow. In the case of the Apis-bull, we know that a calf with the correct markings was sought for throughout Egypt. In the present case, the priests may have assumed that the new Cow would be found in another nome; or more simply, she may already have been identified, and merely have been waiting to be "brought where she belonged", to the

Aphroditopolite nome. If so, the priests' argument must run that the Cow cannot be installed until everything is ready for her eventual mummification, because the process is carried out (or, more plausibly, begun) on the very day of her death. This was the view put forward, with due reserve, by Edgar/Hunt in *Sel. Pap.* 2: the problem of the restoration to be made in *l.* 5 had rather been avoided in previous discussions. Leaving aside minor difficulties, the reason why this interpretation cannot be correct is that the text simply does not say that whatever action or event is to be restored in the lacuna in *l.* 5 happens on the same day as her death. The natural interpretation of the Greek is that it happens on the same day as she is brought to the nome, and, if so, it is impossible to find any plausible explanation of the circumstances described in the letter. (It is perhaps just conceivable that "on the same day" might refer to the day, or the first day, of the ταφή; but this is unlikely, and would mean the priests' argument was a strange and unconvincing one).

The better interpretation is that the priests are referring to the bringing-back to Atfih of a deceased Hesis-cow who had died in another part of Egypt. In the case of the Mothers of Apis, we have evidence that two Cows died away from Memphis, one in 254 B.C., "in the north of the nome of Sais", and one, probably in 214 B.C., "in the nome of Thebes": see H. S. Smith, *Dates of the Obsequies of the Mothers of Apis, Revue d'Égyptologie* 24 (1972), p. 185 (Table 6). It may be noted that these dates, especially the first, are close enough to the date of the Zenon archive. Smith points out that in both cases there was a delay before the burial place was opened and the work on the vault started. It is impossible to speculate here why the Hesis-cow might have been away from Atfih, but clearly it seems plausible that she might have died in another nome, and have required bringing back in state to Atfih. The mummification would of course have been carried out in due course immediately after her death, and would not be awaiting her return. The priests contention is thus that they must have everything ready for the burial ceremonies, because, once the mummy has returned to Atfih, the rites must commence at once. This seems a reasonable kind of argument. Certainly our evidence for other sacred-animals suggests that the dragging of the mummy to the necropolis was followed immediately by the entombment ceremonies.

Several restorations might be possible in *l.* 5 to give this sense. Edgar/Hunt's ἐνταφιάζειν would not be very probable, but perhaps a phrase meaning "it (the ταφή) must begin/be begun on the same day" is likely.

The interpretation of the text just outlined seems, better than any other, to do justice to the precise way in which the Greek is expressed. It should, then, be pointed out that it is here assumed that the priests evidently expected that Apollonios would know what was meant by "bringing-back the Hesis to the nome". This does not seem to raise a difficulty. We might suppose that the priests notified the king of the death of the Hesis, and that the king accordingly wrote to the dioiketes (*ll.* 1-2), who thus presumably was aware of the circumstances. The purpose of the priests' present letter is to hasten the delivery of the myrrh, because, until they are sure of the expenses of the burial, they cannot bring back the mummy.

4-5 It is suggested above that the phrase [τὰ δέο]ντα (or M. Norsa's ἅπα]ντα) ὅσα ποτὲ χρῆαν ἔχουσιν | εἰς τὴν ταφὴν refers to all the requirements for an elaborate festival, and not just the mummification or burial equipment.

The phrase as Greek seems to be an odd compromise between the two uses of χρείαν ἔχειν, "to need" and "to be of use". It is perhaps best to understand ἔχουσιν as a translation of the common Demotic "periphrastic passive" or indefinite use of the 3rd pers. plur., "as many as one needs", "as many as are needed". The use of the strictly ungrammatical form ὅσα in such a phrase would not be surprising.

5 The kind of restoration needed here has been discussed above, especially n. *ll.* 3-4. Plainly the whole weight of the priests' argument rests on this αὐθημερόν phrase: the ceremonies must begin at once, hence the Cow-mummy cannot be brought back until the payment is made. Presumably the period of mourning would be continuous from the death of the Cow until her final laying to rest.

It seems quite clear from all the other examples of αὐθημερόν in the papyri that there is no warrant for taking the word in any sense other than literally "on the same day".

— The identification of Hathor of Atfih with Isis is well-attested. Thus there is nothing strange in the priests' statement here that "the Hesis is Isis". However, it is presumably in fact made to impress the foreigner Apollonios, who would be well-acquainted with Isis, but might care little about the Hesis-cow.

Nevertheless, we know from P. Cornell 1, 78-80 that on the 26th January, 257 B.C., a fortnight after this letter was written, lamp-oil was issued in connection with a dawn visit by Apollonios to the Serapeum, presumably the famous Memphite Serapeum, although it need not be assumed that he visited the subterranean galleries.

6 I do not know why previous editors have read αὔτη rather than αὐτή.

The phrase here αὐτὴ δέ σοι δοίη ἐπαφροδισίαν πρὸς τὸν βασιλέα translates a common Demotic phrase which has a long pedigree in Egyptian. It so happens that a longer form of it can be compared in a Demotic letter written by the priests of Soknopaios to the dioiketes Sarapion, E. Bresciani, *L'archivio demotico del tempio di Soknopaiu Nesos,* (P. Ox. Griffith) 1 13, 8 (presumably the letter is a draft, for translation into Greek?):

> . . . *ỉw=w dỉ n=k ḥs.t mr.t šw ⌜m-b3ḥ⌝ Pr-ʿ3 Sbk ⌜p3 nṯr ˋʿ3ˊ⌝ šʿ ḏt*
>
> . . . may they grant you favour, love, and respect before Pharaoh and Sobek the great god unto eternity.

Compare in Greek PSI 5 531, 2; UPZ 1 33, 8-10; 34, 5-6 (cf. *l.* 14); 35, 12-14 (cf. *l.* 28); 36, 10-12 (cf. *l.* 24). In Egyptian this kind of phrase follows on naturally as a pendant to the name of a god.

T.

51

BRIEF DES HIEROKLES AN ARTEMIDOROS

H. × Br. = 42 × 28 cm. Geschrieben 13. Dezember 257 v. Chr.
(10 × 14[a]; 9,5 × 13[b]; 32 × 28[c])

Jand. inv. 254[a] + Cairo JdE 22-4-33-1[b] + Biblioteca Medicea Laurenziana[c]: **P. Jand. 6 92**[a+b] (das Fragment *b* wurde auf Grund einer Photographie sowie der nicht veröffentlichten Umschriften von Edgar und Guéraud bearbeitet) und **PSI 4 340**[c] (nachträglich von Viereck und Norsa berichtigt, siehe PSI 8, S. XVI). Der gesamte Text wird hier zum ersten Mal gedruckt.

Der Anfang des Textes steht auf den Giessener (linke Hälfte, Zeilen 1-7) und Kairiner (rechte Hälfte, Zeilen 1-3) Fragmenten. Das Florentiner Stück setzt den gesamten Text fort. Die in P. Jand. 6 aufgenommene Tafel XVIII (Zeilen 1-9) zeigt deutlich, auf welche Weise der Text aus diesen drei Fragmenten zusammengestellt worden ist.

Der Text ist fast vollständig erhalten. Nur die Zeilen 5-7 sind schwer beschädigt, und durch die Mitte des Textes läuft eine senkrechte Lücke von 1-3 Buchstaben bis zur Z. 17. Auf der Rückseite des Florentiner Fragments (c) befindet sich die Anschrift, auf der Kairiner Papyrus (b) sind Schriftspuren erhalten, worin Edgar ἀπόδος erkennen zu können glaubte. Die Schrift läuft senkrecht zu der Faserrichtung.

Die elegante, geübte Schrift weist auf einen Berufsschreiber. Sie ist nicht dieselbe als in den anderen Briefen des Hierokles (vgl. P. Cairo Zen. 1 59.060, Taf. XVI, und 2 59.148, Taf. IV), die wohl von ihm selbst geschrieben wurden. In diesen andern Briefen ist auch das Fehlen von ἔρρωσο als Schlussformel charakteristisch (vgl. Skeat, P. Lond. 7 1941, Anm. zu Z. 12).

Inhalt In diesem Brief, den Hierokles an Artemidoros schreibt, ist Ptolemaios die Hauptperson. Er ist uns aus andern Briefen des Hierokles als ein Trainer in einer alexandrinischen Palästra bekannt; vgl. P. Lond. 7 1941 und die Anm. zu Z. 6 und siehe für die Palästra Rostovtzeff, *Large Estate*, S. 31-32 und 172-174. Offenbar haben einige Leute zugesagt Ptolemaios zu unterstützen; Artemidoros gehört wohl zu diesen Leuten, so dass Hierokles jetzt Artemidoros bittet sein Versprechen zu erfüllen, weil Ptolemaios sich in Schwierigkeiten befindet (Z. 8-10). Diese Schwierigkeiten hat der, Z. 10-11 erwähnte, Metrodoros verursacht, ein Mann mit einflussreichen Verbindungen bei Hofe (er gehörte vielleicht auch zum Haushalt von Apollonios; vgl. P. L. Bat. 21. IX, Metrodoros Nr. 2). Er hat ja, falls wir die schwierigen Zeilen 11-14 richtig deuten, sich geweigert Ptolemaios noch weiter Unterstützung zu gewähren, obgleich man ihn darum gebeten hat. Um seine Verweigerung zu begründen weist er auf „die Sache" (Z. 13) hin; warum es sich handelt, wissen wir nicht, aber selbstverständlich war es Artemidoros, dem Adressaten des Briefes, eindeutig, entweder aus diesem Brief (Z. 5-7) oder aus einem vorigen Brief (vgl. Z. 5).

Dann befindet auch Hierokles sich in Schwierigkeiten und beide Männer, welche er um Hilfe bitten konnte, sind nicht imstande ihm zu helfen: Apollonios nicht, weil er immer auf Reisen ist, und Amyntas nicht, weil er verheiratet ist und schon ein Kind hat, so dass er jetzt andere Sorgen hat (Z. 14-18).

Offenbar waren Probleme entstanden über die Eröffnung einer Palästra in der nächsten Nähe eines Hauses (des Apollonios?) in Alexandrien. Welche Probleme das gewesen sind, geht nicht deutlich aus dem Brief hervor, aber Hierokles will offenbar verhindern, dass der König die Ansicht hegen würde, dass er dafür verantwortlich war; Hierokles' Verantwortlichkeit würde nahe liegen, weil er im betreffenden Haus wohnt (Z. 18-19) und weil er sich immer für junge Athleten interessiert (Z. 20-21); er würde sich vor dieser Verantwortlichkeit nur sichern können, wenn er aus dem Haus wegziehen würde (Z. 23).

Hierokles sieht zwei Möglichkeiten die Schwierigkeiten zu überwinden: entweder die Palästra wird nicht eröffnet (das würden Amyntas oder Apollonios bewirken können [Z. 21-24], aber deren Hilfe kann, wie sich aus dem hervorgehenden Zeilen ergibt, kaum erwartet werden), oder die Palästra wird tatsächlich eröffnet, aber dann muss der vorher erwähnte Trainer Ptolemaios sie eröffnen; um das zu erreichen benötigt Hierokles aber die Hilfe des Artemidoros, der ja einer der Gönner des Ptolemaios ist. Deshalb wendet er sich mit diesem Brief zu ihm (Z. 24-27).

Welche Massnahmen Artemidoros getroffen hat, wissen wir nicht, aber es ist klar, dass er den Brief selbst an Zenon weitergeleitet hat, da der Brief aus dem Zenon-Archiv stammt; vielleicht hatte Hierokles dies auch beabsichtigt, da er ja so nachdrücklich in Z. 4 die Mitteilung macht dass Epharmostos, der Bruder Zenons, wohlauf ist. Zenon selber hatte triftige Gründe sich um Hierokles (der ja die Sorge für die Ausbildung seines Bruders übernommen hatte) zu bemühen und er kann entweder selber Massnahmen getroffen haben dem Hierokles zu helfen oder er kann die Sache an Apollonios weitergeleitet haben; keiner von beiden war zu dieser Zeit in Alexandrien, vermutlich befanden sie sich zusammen auf einer Reise im Delta.

Vorderseite:

῾Ιεροκλῆς ᾿Αρτεμιδώρωι χαί[ρε]ιν. Εἰ ἔρρωσαι καὶ ἐν τοῖς λοιπ[οῖς ἀπαλ]λάσσεις κατὰ νοῦν, εὖ ἂν ἔχοι. Αὐτὸς μὲγ γὰρ καταπλεύσας ἄνωθεν̣ [ἠν]ω̣χλήθην ἰσχυρῶς, νυνὶ δὲ πρὸς τῶι ἀναλαμβάνειν εἰμί. ῾Υγίαι[νε]ν δὲ καὶ ᾿Εφάρμοσ(τος) καὶ τὰ π̣[αρὰ σο]ῦ παιδάρια. Περὶ Πτολεμαίου καὶ πρότερομ μέν σοι ἔγραψα̣ [---]ν.[.].ε̣ισθ.[---] Ζήνωνος οἰόμενος ἔχειν τὴν [παλα]ίστραν π[---] σ̣α̣ι ἐ̣π̣ηνηνόχει τά τε ζω̣ι̣.[---]. [---] Νῦν οὖν συμβαίνει αὐτῶι ἀσχ̣[η]μ̣ονεῖν, ἂμ μὴ σὺ ἐνταθῆις περὶ αὐτοῦ, καθάπερ δίκαιό̣[ν] ἐ̣[στι]ν τοὺς ἐπ̣αγγειλαμένους συντελεῖν. ῎Εστι δέ σοι πάντωμ μὲν τῶν κακῶν αἴτιος Μητρόδωρος· ἀποκέκριται γὰρ τοῖς ἐντ̣[υ]γχάνουσι περὶ Πτολεμαίου ἐν αὐλῆι τοιαῦτα λέγων, ὅτι ἐ[γ]ὼ̣ πρότερομ μὲν ἐσπούδαζον περὶ Πτολεμαίου, ἐλάνθα̣ν[ε γ]ά̣ρ̣ με τὸ πρᾶγμα· νυνὶ δὲ ηἰσθημένος οἷόν ἐστιν ἀντιλέγω λέγων ταῦτα. ᾿Απολλώνιομ μὲν συμβαίνει τὸμ πλείω χρόνον [δια]τρίβειν ἐν τῆι χώραι, ᾿Αμύνταν δὲ ἔξω τε σκηνοῦντα [κ]α̣ὶ γεγαμηκότα καὶ τέκνον ὑπάρχον ἤδη αὐτῶι, ὥ[στε] μηδεμίαν ὑποψίαν ἐκείνωι γε προσπεσεῖν· λοιπὸν τὸ τόξον ἐ̣π' ἐμὲ τείνεται τῶι ἐν τῆι οἰκίαι σκηνοῦντι. Ἂγ γὰρ αἴσθητα[ι] ὁ βασιλεὺς τὴν παλαίστραν ἀνοιχθεῖσαν, ὑφοψίαν ἐγὼ πλείστην ἕξω δι' ἐμὲ ἀνοῖχθαι, ὅτι φιλόνειός εἰμι. Διὸ καὶ Ἀμύνταν ἀξιῶ συσπεύδειν ἡμῖν τοῦ μὴ ἀνοιχθῆναι τὴν παλαίστραν· ἂν δ' ἄρα καὶ ἐγβιασθῆι Ἀμύντας, συμβήσεταί μοι ἐκχωρεῖν ἐκ τῆς οἰκίας, ἐὰμ μὴ δύνωμαι Ἡγήμονα πεῖσαι τοῦ γράψαι Ἀπολλωνίωι. Σὲ οὖν καὶ ἀξιοῦμεν καὶ δεόμεθα πᾶσαν σπουδὴν ποιήσασθαι περὶ Πτολεμαίου τοῦ λαβεῖν τὴν παλαίστραν· πεπείσμεθα γὰρ σοῦ βουλομένου πάντ' ἔσεσθαι. Ἔτι δὲ κἀκεῖνο· οὐκ ἐττηθήσεσθε ὑπὸ ἀνθρώπου ἀνελευθέρου; Γράψον δὲ καὶ Ἀρτεμιδώρωι ἵνα τὸν γαυνάκην δῶι τοῖς παιδαρίοις· οὐ γὰρ δίδωσιν, ἂμ μὴ σὺ γράψηις. Ἀπόστειλον δ' ἡμῖν καὶ τὸ παιδάριον ὃ ἐδείκνυές μοι, ἵνα προσάγωμεν καὶ τοῦτον πρὸς τὰ μαθήματα.

Ἔρρωσο. L κθ Δίου $\overline{ιθ}$.

Rückseite:

33 Ἰατρῶι Ἀρτεμιδώρω[ι].

4 Ἐφαρμοσ: danach ein dicker Punkt als Abkürzungszeichen 10 πάντων ed. princ., πάντωμ BL 6, S. 174 14 Ἀπολλώνιον ed. princ., Ἀπολλώνιομ BL 6, S. 174 20 ὑφοψίαν, vgl. ὑποψίαν in Z. 17 21 *l.* φιλόνεος

Übersetzung

Hierokles grüsst Artemidoros.

Wenn Du gesund bist und es Dir sonst nach Deinem Sinn geht, ist es gut. Ich nämlich wurde heftig mitgenommen, als ich vom Süden heruntergefahren war; aber jetzt bin ich auf dem Wege der Besserung. Und auch Epharmostos und die von Dir gesandten Burschen sind gesund.

Über Ptolemaios schrieb ich Dir ja schon früher [--- --- ---]. Jetzt steht es schlimm mit ihm, falls Du Dich nicht für ihn anstrengst, so wie es richtig ist, dass diejenigen, die Zusagen getan haben, diesen auch (tatsächlich) nachkommen.

Und da ist eben Metrodoros an allem Übel schuld, denn er hat denjenigen, die sich mit Bezug auf Ptolemaios bei Hofe an ihn wandten, geantwortet mit etwa den folgenden Worten: „Was mich anbetrifft, ich habe mich früher öfters wegen Ptolemaios bemüht, denn ich wusste nichts von der Sache; jetzt aber, nachdem ich erfahren habe um was für eine Sache es sich handelt, bin ich dagegen, wobei ich dies vorbringe".

Apollonios verbringt ja die meiste Zeit in der Chora, und Amyntas verbleibt ausserhalb (des Hauses), ist verheiratet und hat schon ein Kind, so dass ihn kein Verdacht treffen kann; also wird der Bogen gegen mich gespannt, da ich ja im Hause verbleibe.

Denn wenn der König hört, dass die Palästra eröffnet worden ist, werde ich in den grössten Verdacht geraten, dass sie von mir eröffnet worden ist, weil ich ein Freund der Jugend bin. Deshalb bitte ich auch Amyntas, uns beizustehen, damit die Palästra nicht eröffnet wird. Ist nun aber auch Amyntas aus meiner Nähe verdrängt, werde ich das Haus verlassen müssen, es sei dann dass ich imstande bin Hegemon zu bewegen, dass er Apollonios schreibt.

Wir ersuchen also und bitten Dich, alle Bemühungen um Ptolemaios zu unternehmen, damit er die Palästra übernimmt. Denn wir sind überzeugt, dass alles gelingen wird, wenn Du es willst. Und auch noch das Folgende. Ihr werdet doch nicht von einem unfreien Menschen (Metrodoros) überwältigt werden?

Und schreibe auch an Artemidoros, dass er den Burschen den Mantel gibt, denn er will ihn nicht geben, wenn Du nicht schreibst.

Und sende uns auch den Burschen, den Du mir gezeigt hast, damit wir auch ihn unterrichten lassen.

Lebe wohl.
Im 29. Jahr, am 19. Dios.

Anschrift:

An den Arzt Artemidoros.

Anmerkungen

1 Für den Arzt Artemidoros siehe ROSTOVTZEFF, *Large Estate*, S. 31-32; C. GORTEMAN, *CdÉ* 32 (1957) 332-334 und FRASER, *Alexandria*, S. 370.

1-2 εἰ ἔρρωσαι καὶ ἐν τοῖς λοιποῖς ἀπαλλάσσεις κατὰ νοῦν, εὖ ἂν ἔχοι: diese lange Formel lesen wir öfter in anderen Briefen des Hierokles (vgl. P. Cairo Zen. 1 59.061; 2 59.148; P. Lond. 7 1941). Sie kommt aber auch sonst im Archiv vor.

2 Nach ἄνωθεν sieht man auf dem Teil des Blattes, der sich zwischen Z. 2 und 3 befindet, einen senkrechten Strich, der nach einer Biegung wieder aufwärts geht. Es könnte sich um den unteren Teil eines β handeln, aber dann ist das β von einer andern Hand geschrieben worden. Nach unserer Meinung gehören diese Spuren nicht zu dem hier herausgegebenen Text.

4 Ptolemaios, der in diesem Text öfter erwähnt wird, war ein Trainer. Einige Monate bevor er diesen Brief schrieb hat Hierokles sich in einem Brief an Zenon sehr günstig über Ptolemaios geäussert (P. Lond. 7 1941); vgl. P. L. Bat. 21. IX *Prosopography*, s.v. Nr. 17.

5-7 Die Lücken sind zu gross, um den Sinn dieser ganzen Stelle feststellen zu können. Bemerkenswert ist aber die Erwähnung des Zenon. Bekanntlich zeigte Zenon eine grosse Interesse an der Palästra; er vertraute sogar die Ausbildung seines Bruders Epharmostos (vgl. Z. 4) an Hierokles an; vgl. ŚWIDEREK, Eos 48.2 (1956) 136-137.

14 λέγων ταῦτα „indem ich das sage": ταῦτα weist auf οἷόν ἐστιν (τὸ πρᾶγμα) hin.

16-17 Amyntas verbleibt vielleicht in Kanopos (P. Ryl. 4 555, Einl.).

— σκηνοῦντα --- γεγαμηκότα --- ὑπάρχον: man erwartet hier infinitivi, von συμβαίνει abhängig; vielleicht hat Hierokles hier ein Verbum als οἶσθα anwenden wollen; vgl. MAYSER, *Grammatik*, II. 3, S. 200.

22 ἐγβιασθῇι: wenn Amyntas aus Hierokles' Nähe verdrängt ist (wegen der genannten privaten Verhältnisse?), kann er sich allein nicht mehr retten und dann muss er das Haus verlassen.

28 ἀνελεύθερος: ROSTOVTZEFF, *Large Estate*, S. 32, nimmt die Bedeutung "a man without culture", "a *parvenu*" an; diese Bedeutung ist aber sonst nicht bekannt. Es ist nach unserer Meinung möglich dass ἀνελεύθερος hier "geizig" oder "niederträchtich" bedeutet.

— Der hier erwähnte Artemidoros ist der Hausvorsteher des Apollonios, ὁ ἐπὶ τῆς οἰκίας; siehe P. L. Bat. 21. IX, *Prosopography*, s.v. Nr. 4.

W.

52

MEMORANDUM FROM ISOKRATES TO BION

H. × W. = 16.2 × 10.8 cm. Date unknown

A papyrus belonging to the Societas Archaeologica Atheniensis: **P. S. A. Athen. 4,** with plate.

The original size of this letter is preserved, although pieces are missing from the bottom left-hand corner, and there are various other holes. The surface of the papyrus appears to be worn towards the upper right-hand side. The text on the front is written along the fibres. There are narrow margins at left and right. The top margin measures a little over 1 cm., and that at the bottom about 1.5 cm. The back is presumably blank. Some minor changes have been made without comment in the transcription.

Contents Isokrates writes to Bion, requesting that fencing be installed in the vineyard for which he has responsibility, to protect the vines and the fruit. For two other texts from the archive concerned with viticulture, see text no. **26** above, and no. **64** below.

Ὑπόμνημα Βίωνι
παρὰ Ἰσοκράτους ο̣ἰ-
νο̣π̣ο̣ι̣οῦ. Περὶ τῆς
ὑφάμμου τῆς ἐν
τῆι ἐμῆι μερίδι
ῥῖποι ὅπω[ς] γένων-
ται καὶ περιφραχθῆι
κύκλωι τ[ὸ] κ̣τῆμα, ἵνα
μή[τε ὁ] βλαστὸς ὑπὸ
τῶν βοῶν κατέσθη-
ται μή⟦δε⟧\`τε {ἡ}' ἡ ὑπώρα
ὑπὸ τῶν ὑαινῶν
καὶ τῶ̣ν̣ ὄ̣γων κα-
τέσθηται [δ]ιὰ τὸ πρὸς
τῆ̣ι̣ κώμ[ηι] εἶναι. Ἐὰν
οὖν [περι]φραχθῆι ἡ ὑπ-
ώ̣ρα γένημα ἔστ[αι].

11, 16-17 *l.* ὀπωρα (?)   13 τῶ̣ν̣ ὄ̣γων Schubart, Wilcken (BL 3 p. 215); τῶ̣[ν κυ]νῶν Petropoulos

Translation

Memorandum to Bion from Isokrates, the winemaker.

In order that there should be hurdles around the sandy land which is in my part, and that the property should be fenced in a circle, so that neither the shoots should be eaten by the cattle, nor the fruit be eaten by the sows and the asses, because it is near to the village. So if it is fenced around, the fruit will become (*lit.* are) produce.

Notes

1 For Bion, see P. Cairo Zen. 3 59.366, 16-18, Εὐκλῆς Βίωνι τῶι μ̣ε̣τ̣α̣λ̣α̣βόν̣τ̣ι̣ | τὴν ἐπιστατείαν τῶν κ̣α̣τ̣ὰ̣ Φ̣ι̣|λαδέλφειαν; cf. *Prosopography*, P. L. Bat. 21. IX, Βίων (no. 1). For a discussion of the problems of the Eukles-archive, and Eukles' replacement by Bion, apparently in 241 B.C., see above p. 5, P. L. Bat. 21. VI (Fifth period), and E. SEIDL, *Ptolemäische Rechtsgeschichte* (1962), pp. 41-2. Thus a late date seems plausible for the present letter.

2 For Isokrates, who plainly does not occur elsewhere in the archive, see *Prosopography*, P. L. Bat. 21. IX, Ἰσοκράτης (no. 3).

2-3 The use of οἰνοποιός for "wine-maker" is a little surprising, and is only paralleled by a partly-restored instance at P. Mich. Zen. 62, 11-12. However, the reading here seems satisfactory (triangular forms of ο can be seen elsewhere in this letter), and no other restoration has suggested itself.

4 The sense of ὕφαμμος, "sandy (land)" is clear enough. It is common in the archive, always explicitly used in connection with the vineyards, except in P. Cairo Zen. 5 59.825, 20, where perhaps the vineyards are nevertheless meant. Vineyards are to be expected to be found on sandy soil (so Petropoulos, n. *ad loc.*), and it may be noted that the ὕφαμμος is never directly contrasted with any other kind of land. It perhaps simply describes the area where the vineyards were situated.

5 The μερίς here is presumably the "part" of the vineyards for which Isokrates had responsibility.

7 It is possible that Isokrates here is describing the same operation twice, the second time perhaps to emphasise that the enclosure must be complete. However, it is more probable that he first mentions the encircling of the vineyard, and then the enclosure of the house, where the fruit would be brought. Similar rush enclosures are used in modern Egypt to protect the date harvest spread out to ripen in villages—although it is not the intention to suggest here that Isokrates is necessarily referring to the *drying* of grapes. This interpretation makes sense of the distinction between the danger to the shoots from the cattle, and that to the fruit from the asses and the pigs "because it (the κτῆμα) is near to the village".

11 The scribe first wrote μήδε ἡ ὑπώρα, then cancelled the δέ, and then inserted τεη above the line: the ἡ thus inserted was not of course required.

— The word ὑπώρα here (cf. *ll.* 16-17) might be interpreted as a special form signifying unripe fruit, but it is plainly better to take it as equivalent to ὀπώρα, "fruit", and this suits the interpretation outlined in n. *l.* 7 very well. See BL 3 p. 215, H. CADELL, *La viticulture scientifique dans les archives de Zénon*: *PSI 624, Aegyptus* 49 (1969), p. 113, *LSJ*[9], s.v. ὀπώρα; cf. *Suppl.* s.v. ὑπώρα.

T.

53

LETTER FROM GLAUKOS TO DEMEAS

H. × W. = 12.5 × 9.5 cm.[a]; 12.5 × 6.5 cm.[b] Date unknown

Cairo JdE 48942[a+b]: **P. Cairo Zen. 3 59.413**[a]; P. Cairo Zen. 4 p. 288[b]

The text on the front is written across the fibres, presumably on the original recto surface. The address on the back is written parallel to the fibres, and the other way up in relation to the text on the front. A previous text stood on this piece of papyrus, and imperfectly erased traces can be seen on the front and at the top of the back. It is impossible to tell how much text is lost between the two fragments: no obvious very brief supplements suggest themselves.

Contents Glaukos writes to Demeas about various business matters. The general course of the letter is clear enough, as can perhaps be seen from the translation, but the nature of the transactions involved remains quite uncertain. If the letter is of a very late date (see n. *l.* 10), it is impossible to identify the recipient with Demeas the leader of the gymnasium (see *Prosopography*, P. L. Bat. 21 IX, Δημέας no. 1 and P. Lond. 7 2017 n. *l.* 3), as he died some 14 years before the Year 18 apparently mentioned in *l.* 5: however, the identification is plausible on other grounds, and the question of the date of the text should perhaps be left open. Edgar suggested (P. Cairo Zen. 3 59.413 n. *l.* 1) that Phanias might be the scribe Phanias: see text **D** in the supplement to this volume and *Prosopography* P. L. Bat. 21. IX, Φανίας (no. 1).

front [plate XXII]:

Γλαῦκος Δημέα[ι χαίρειν.	]ν ἡμῖν
παρὰ Φανία τοῦ δ̣[	]ται̣ τὰ
εἰς τὸ βασιλικὸν .[	]ε̣ι̣ν ἕως
[. . . .]. . φ̣εως το[	] L τοῦ πλείστου
Θεοκλέους L ιη τ[	ὀ]φείλημα
οὗ τὸ καθ' ἕν σοι δει̣[	ἐπὶ τὴν τ]ράπεζαν
καὶ τὸν σῖτον ἀπομε[τρ-	]ματος ὑπαρχέτω
παρὰ σοὶ ἕως τοῦ γραφ[ῆναι	ἐὰν] δ̣έ τι ἐπιζητῇς
ἐπίστειλον ἡμῖν ἵν̣[α	] *vacat*
vacat [	]ϛ̄.

back [plate XXII]:

11 Δη̣[μέαι.]

Translation

Glaukos to Demeas, [greetings.]

--- to us from Phanias the --- to the Crown --- until --- year at the most: of Theokles, Year 18 --- debt, of which the detailed specification [is set out] for you --- at the bank; and measure out the corn --- should be available with you until --- is written. --- If there is anything you need, write to us so that [we can *e.g.* arrange it for you.]

[Fare well. *Date.*]

Address:

To De[meas.]

Notes

3-4 It is very tempting to restore here for example ἕως | [τοῦ Φ]αωφέως το[ῦ *x* (ἔτους) ἢ τοῦ *month-name* τοῦ *y*] (ἔτους) τοῦ πλείστου, "until Phaophi of Year *x* or *month-name* of year *y* at the most". For the use of declined Egyptian month-names, see text no. **13**, p. 78, footnote 13 above. If this or something similar is correct, it is not clear how the name Θεοκλέους at the beginning of *l.* 5 is to be explained; but *l.* 5 of itself does not suggest any other plausible restoration in *l.* 4.

5 For L ιη here, see n. *l.* 10 below.

6 Clarysse suggests restoring part of δεικνύναι here, perhaps δεί[κνυται. Edgar printed δεῖ[, and not δεῖ [, and perhaps had δεῖγμα in mind.

7 Conceivably λόγος *etc.* τοῦ γενήμ]ατος?

10 The date of this letter is lost, except for the figure 6, indicating a day-date of the 6th, 16th, or 26th. In *l.* 5, there appears the expression L ιη, standing after the personal name Theokles, which is in the genitive case. It is conceivable that this expression gives Theokles' age, "Theokles, 18 years old", but it seems very difficult to explain why a man's age should be quoted here, and nothing else in the text suggests it is likely. Year-dates seem to be mentioned in *l.* 4 (see n. *ll.* 3-4 above), and this suggests that a year-date might be in place here in *l.* 5. However, it is not easy to explain the genitive Θεοκλέους: it seems more likely to begin a new clause, perhaps as a genitive absolute, or in the sense "(and) of Theokles, in Year 18", than to depend on some verb, or to agree with a participle, that stood in *l.* 3.

If the mention of Year 18 is accepted here, then the letter must be one of the latest in the archive, and relate to 230-229 B.C. See the chronological information in P. L. Bat. 21. VI (Sixth period) and VII.

T.

54

LETTER FROM NIKAIOS TO EUKLES

H. × W. = 34 × 8.8 cm.

Prob. 7 May, 246 B.C. (Financial year)
or 6 May, 245 B.C. (Egyptian year)

Sorb. inv. 283 recto + part of verso (see also no. **61**): P. JOUGUET, *Petit supplément aux archives de Zénon, Cinquantenaire de l'École Pratique des Hautes Études* (1921), pp. 228-31; **SB 3 6801**, recto.

The text is written along the fibres on the recto (a join between two sheets is visible at the right-hand edge) of a roll 34 cm. in height. It consists of two fragments which join between *ll.* 19 and 20. Only a small piece, the right-hand half of *ll.* 14-19, is missing.

The letter has been folded first three times from left to right, and then once from top to bottom. The docket on the back corresponds to the middle of the top of the recto and was visible when the letter was folded.

After the letter reached its destination, the back was used again for a draft of a letter, probably by Eukles. Since it is not certain that this letter has any connection with that on the recto, it has here been published separately as no. **61**. It gives us, however, an approximate date (Year 2, no doubt of Euergetes) for the whole papyrus.

The hand is identical with that of P. Cornell 3, which therefore was probably also sent by Nikaios. The subject-matter of the two letters, however, is not the same.

Contents This letter of Nikaios to Eukles seems to consist of a list of articles which the writer has received from different persons in order to transport them. Since Nikaios is called ξενιαγός in the docket, these articles could well be ξένια, gifts for the king or for some important official. One of the main points of interest in this text is the occurrence of several rare words, e.g. παράσιρον, διάρταβος, σίσαρον, ὀνικός, ξενιαγός.

front [plate XXIII]:

Νικαῖος Εὐ̣κ̣λεῖ χαίρειν.
Ἔχω παρὰ Θεοδώρου
ἀνθ' ὧν ἔδωκα Φυ̣ήρει
τῶι Ἄραβι εἰς καρτάλλους
χαλ(κοῦ) ⊦ β ⟦---⟧
⟦π̣α̣ρ̣α̣κ̣ ---------⟧
⟦κα̣ι̣------------⟧
Εὔστραν δὲ Νικαῖος ὁ γεωρ-
γὸς οὐκ ἔδωκεν.
Τὸ δὲ παράσιρον τὸ στυπ-
πέϊνον ἐν ὧι τὰς λ ἀρ(τάβας)
τῶν ἀλφίτων κ̣[α]τήγα-
γον αγω[......]το ε⟦ς⟧`ἰς´
Ἀλεξάνδρ[ειαν ...... Ἐπί-]
κουρος οὐχ̣[--------------]

τὰ ἄλφιτα̣[------------]
ἐμ Μέμφε[ι -----------]
καὶ τὰς εἰς τ[-----------]
καὶ τ̣ὰ̣ς κρι[θ------------]
[σ]φυρίδα̣ς̣ διαρτάβους ι
καὶ ⟦τῶν⟧ \`εἰς τὰ´ κάρυα ἄλλας
σφυρίδας γ καὶ εἰς τὰ
σίσαρα α τὰς πάσας
σφυρίδας διαρ(τάβους) κη.
Διὸ ἀπεχρησάμεθα τῆι
δέρρει \`⟦ἀνακομιῶ δέ σοι αὐτήν⟧´. Τὰ δὲ γ καρ-
τάλλια ἅ μοι συνέθηκας
καταλέλοιπα Θεοδώρωι
καὶ τὰ ὀ̣νικὰ μώστια δύο.
Ἔρρωσο. Φαμενὼθ ις.

back [plate XXIII]:

31 Παρὰ Νικαί-
ου ξενια-
γοῦ.

3 Φτηρει Jouguet, Φυ̣ήρει legimus 11 τάς corr. e ταε 13 ἄγω[ν καὶ αὐτ]ό Jouguet
26 ⟦ἀνακομι̣σ̣θ̣ῆ̣ν̣α̣ι̣ α̣ὐ̣τ̣ό̣ν̣⟧ Jouguet 29 ὠνικά Jouguet

Translation

Nikaios to Eukles, greetings.

I have received from Theodoros for what I have given to Phueris the Arab for baskets 2 copper drachmae. Nikaios the farmer has not given the roasted barley. The "parasiron" of tow in which I brought down the 30 artabae of groats --- (*l.* 20) 10 baskets of two artabae, and for the nuts 3 other baskets, and for the parsnip 1, together 28 baskets of two artabae. Therefore we have used the whole hide ⟦but I will bring it to you⟧. I have left for Theodoros the 3 small baskets which you have entrusted to me and the two jars for donkey-transport.

Farewell. Phamenoth 16.

Docket:

From Nikaios the xeniagos.

Notes

1 Whereas the xeniagos Nikaios cannot with any certainty be identified with any of the persons of that name elsewhere (except of course with the unnamed writer of P. Cornell 3: see above), Eukles is well-known in the later period, when he succeeded Zenon as the administrator of the dorea. See p. 5 above and text no. **49**.

3 Φυ̣ήρει τῶι Ἄραβι: The name Phtereus (so Jouguet and D. Foraboschi, *Onomasticon alterum*) is unexampled and hard to explain. We therefore prefer Φυήρει, the nominative being Φυῆρις. This is palaeographically possible (see photograph) and can be explained as a variant form of

Πγῆρις, Ποῆρις, Πουῆρις, Φοῆρις, Φουῆρις (for references see F. PREISIGKE, *Namenbuch* and D. FORABOSCHI, *Onomasticon alterum*). Many Arabs in the Zenon archive have Egyptian names e.g. Peteminis, Petechon, Portis, Pheros.

10 παράσιρον: listed in Liddell-Scott-Jones as a hapax of dubious sense, but no doubt Perdrizet (in a note in the edition of Jouguet) was right in connecting it with παράσειρον. The exact sense here remains however uncertain. It must have been quite a large receptacle to contain 30 artabae (some 1200 litres) of groats. The bulk of the freight suggests that it was transported by boat.

17 ἐμ Μέμφε[ι: cf. P. Cornell 3, 6 and 9, where it is written in exactly the same way.

20 διαρτάβους: a hapax in the sense of "containing two artabae" (included in the new *Supplement* to Liddell-Scott-Jones).

23 σίσαρα: see A. C. ANDREWS, *The Parsnip as a Food in the Classical Era, Classical Philology* 53 (1958), pp. 145-152. This is the only occurrence of the word in the papyri. Its appearance in Jand. inv. 249 *ll.* 7 and 17, recently published in the Mélanges Claire Préaux, pp. 591-593 is due to an error of reading, see *Chronique d'Égypte* 52 (1977), p. 121.

29 τὰ ὀνικὰ μώστια. The μώστιον (probably an Egyptian word) is a kind of jar which can be sealed (P. Grenf. I 14, 5). The word ὠνικός (so Jouguet and Liddell-Scott-Jones, *Supplement*) is a hapax and hardly makes sense (Jouguet translates: "les deux jarres à vendre"). The writer surely intended ὀνικά *i.e.* "fit for being carried by an ass", cf. PSI 5 527, 2, ὀνικὰ σάγματα. The first letter of the word can perhaps be read omikron (cf. γον in *l.* 13).

32-33 ξενιαγός. The word is included in Liddell-Scott-Jones but the reading is doubted there. The photograph makes clear that the reading is sure, but we cannot accept the equation of ξενιαγός and ξεναγός proposed by Liddell-Scott-Jones. Whereas the latter is a commander of mercenary troops, a ξενιαγός is "a man who brings ξένια", as was clearly seen by Jouguet.

C.

55

LETTRE DE PANAKESTÔR À KLEITARCHOS ET ANDRÔN

H. × L. = 10,5 × 4,5 cm. Novembre 257 a.C.

Biblioteca Medicea Laurenziana: **PSI 6 681**; T. C. Skeat, P. Lond. 7 1953 introd. Le texte est écrit parallèlement aux fibres. Il ne subsiste que le début d'une des deux moitiés d'un document double (cpr. P. Lond. 7 1953). J'ai pu collationner ce texte sur une photo qui a été aimablement mise à ma disposition par M. le professeur M. Manfredi.

Contenu Tout comme le P. Lond. 7 1953, qui date également de novembre 257, la présente lettre constitue un ordre, rédigé sous forme de document double, de donner du grain à un certain nombre de cultivateurs de la δωρεά, au titre de semences ou de prêts. Skeat a reconnu dans le P. Cairo Zen. 1 59.113 le reçu double remis par Stotoêtis, fils d'Oteüris, le premier bénéficiaire dans notre texte, à Kleitarchos et Andrôn, assistants de Panakestôr dans l'administration de la δωρεά.

[Πανακέσ]τωρ Κλει-
[τάρχωι Ἄ]νδρωνι χαί-
[ρειν. Μετ]ρήσατε Στο-
[τοῆτι Ὀτ]ẹύριος σπέρ-
[μα εἰς τὴν] γῆν ἣν ἔχει
[κριθῶν ἀρ(τ.)] γ καὶ δάνει-
[ον πυ(ρῶν) ἀρ(τ.) γ] *vacat*
[Καὶ c. 6].ωτου
[c. 8] πυ̣(ρῶν) ἀρ(τ.) α
[c. 8] ἀρ(τ.) γ
[c. 8] κριθῶν ἀρ(τ.) γ

1-6 suppl. Skeat 3 Μετρ]ήσατε ed. 4]υριος ed. 5]ην ἣν ἔχει ed. 6]. καὶ ed. 7]. ed. 8].ωτος ed. 7-8 ἀρ(τ.) γ καὶ Χ]ε|[σέρται Πα]σῶτος Skeat 9 ἀρ(τ.)  11 ἀρ(τ.) 

Traduction

Panakestôr salue Kleitarchos et Andrôn.

Mesurez à Stotoêtis, fils d'Oteüris, comme semence pour la terre qu'il détient, 3 artabes d'orge, et comme prêt 3 artabes de froment;

et à N, fils de [...]ôtês, ... 1 artabe de froment, ... 3 artabes, ... 3 artabes d'orge.

Note

8-11 Skeat a restitué aux *ll.* 7 et 8 Χεσέρται Πασῶτος et a vu dans ce fermier le second bénéficiaire mentionné dans notre texte; le P. Cairo Zen. I 59.114 aurait alors constitué le reçu délivré à la réception du grain. Notons toutefois que les dimensions réduites de la lacune, jointes au fait que s'est conservée la fin du nom du père, excluent la restitution proposée par Skeat; de plus, les quantités reçues ne correspondraient pas à celles que Panakestôr avait ordonné de donner.

À titre d'exemple, on pourrait restituer ainsi le texte des *ll.* 8-11: [καὶ Ὥρωι Ἁρ]ụώτου [δάνειον (ου σπέρμα)] πυ(ρῶν) ἀρ(τάβην) α [καὶ κριθῶν] ἀρ(τάβας) γ [καὶ σπέρμα (ου δάνειον)] κριθῶν ἀρ(τάβας) γ.

M.

56

BRIEF DES ZENON AN KLEITARCHOS

H. × Br. = 14 × 33 cm. Geschrieben 25. Oktober 251 v. Chr.

Nationalmuseum in Athen: der Papyrus wurde von S. B. KOUGEAS, Ἑλληνικά 9 (1936) 11-12 (mit zwei Tafeln) herausgegeben (= **SB 5 8244**) und ist von WILCKEN, *Archiv für Papyrusforschung* 13 (1939) 135-136 berichtigt. Die Zeilen A, 1-9 wurden in P. Lond. 7, S. 88-89 neugedruckt.

Das Papyrusblatt ist vollständig erhalten; rundum befindet sich ein freier Raum. Mit Ausnahme der Adresse sind beide Seiten senkrecht zu den Fasern geschrieben. Auf der Rückseite befindet sich auf der Adresse ein Siegel mit Resten der Verschnürung.

Der Text wurde in drei aufeinanderfolgenden Phasen geschrieben (vgl. ed. princ., S. 12; WILCKEN, *Archiv für Papyrusforschung* 13, 1939, 135). Zum ersten Mal wurde der Brief geschrieben auf die Weise, wie wir ihn unten als **A** abdrucken. So wurde der Brief adressiert und gesiegelt. Bevor der Brief aber abgesandt wurde, hat man das Siegel erbrochen und den Brief geöffnet um noch einige Änderungen vornehmen zu können (zwischen Z. 2-3 und 3-4). Schliesslich hat man die meisten Änderungen und einen grossen Teil des ursprünglichen Textes von A gestrichen und durch eine neue Fassung des Textes ersetzt, welche auf der Rückseite des Blattes geschrieben wurde. Deutlichkeitshalber drucken wir diese neue Fassung unten als **B** ab, zusammen mit den nicht gestrichenen Zeilen der Originalfassung A.

Selbstverständlich konnte man den Brief dann nicht mehr absenden. Allem Anschein nach hat man auf Grund der neuen Fassung eine Reinschrift ausgefertigt und das vorliegende Stück im Archiv gelassen.

A

Ursprüngliche Fassung

Herakleides war verantwortlich für den Ackerbau in der Dorea. Zu seinen Pflichten gehörten u.a. die Kornlieferungen für Saat, Futter und Löhne an die im Landgut des Apollonios angestellten Leute, sowie das Erheben des Kornes von der Dorea und dessen Lieferung an den Speicher in Philadelphia. Um das Letzte handelt es sich in unserem Brief: Herakleides hat weniger an den Speicher in Philadelphia geliefert als er in seinem Lieferscheinen verbucht hatte. (Für diese Diskrepanzen siehe P. Lond. 7 1991, 1993, 1994 und 1995). Die Tatsache hat Kleitarchos aufgedeckt, als er die Rechnungen von Herakleides erhalten hat. Als er das dem Zenon gemeldet hat, antwortet dieser dass er erstaunt ist dass Kleitarchos vorgibt nichts von der Sache zu wissen. Zenon hatte ihm ja selbst schon vorher von dem Defizit in den Buchungen des Herakleides Mitteilung gemacht. Darauf führt Zenon die Quanten Weizen, Mohn, Gerste, Rizinus und Olyra auf, welche, wie er sagt, noch fehlen; Kleitarchos kann diese Posten ruhig eintragen, da Herakleides zugesagt hat das Defizit auszugleichen.

Das Defizit ist ziemlich gross; auf welche Weise es entstanden ist, wissen wir nicht, aber es geht deutlich hervor, dass Herakleides dafür haftet und dass er das Defizit ausgleichen muss.

Z. 1-9 = SB 5 8244, 1-9: die erste Fassung des Textes (auf der Vorderseite des Papyrusblattes); Z. 10 = SB 5 8244, 20: die Adresse (auf der Rückseite):

A *Vorderseite*:

1 Ζήνων Κλειτάρχωι χαίρειν. Παραγενόμενος Σπινθὴρ ὁ παρὰ Ἡρακλείδου
2 ἀνήγγειλεν ἡμῖν ἀνειληφότα σε τοὺς λόγους εὑρίσκειν ἐν τῆι τοῦ λδ L
3 εἰσμετρήσει πλείω ἀνενηνοχότα αὐτόν. Θαυμάζω οὖν εἰ οὕτως
4 ἐπιλήσμων εἶ, καὶ ταῦτα προειρηκότων ἡμῶν ὅτι ἠξιωκὼς εἴη
5 ἡμᾶς Ἡρακλείδης κατὰ τὸν παρ' αὐτοῦ λόγον \`ἀνενεγκεῖν'. Καὶ ἔστιν ὧι πλείω
6 προστεθείμεθα· πυρῶν μὲν ἀρ(τάβαι) σμα, μήκωνος ἀρ(τάβαι) κϛ ∠ γ', κριθῶν ἀρ(τάβαι) ᾿Θχκη ∠ ι'β',
7 κροτῶνος ἀρ(τάβαι) ϛ ∠, ὀλυρῶν ἀρ(τάβαι) ρπη. Ἀνάφερε οὖν καὶ σὺ κατὰ ταῦτα,
8 ἐξωμολόγηται γὰρ Ἡρακλείδης ἀναπληρώσειν ταῦτα τὰ πλήθη.
9 Ἔρρωσο. L λε Θῶυθ ᾱ.

Rückseite:

(20 =) 10 Κλ[ει]τάρχωι.

3 ἀνενηνοχότα ..... ed. princ., ἀνενηνοχότας ἡμᾶς Wilcken, ἀνενηνοχότα αὐτόν Skeat 6 ᾿Θχκη ∠ γγ ed. princ., ᾿Θχκη ∠ ι'β' SB 10 Das Siegel befindet sich auf den Buchstaben ε und ι von Κλειτάρχωι

Übersetzung

Zenon grüsst Kleitarchos.

Als Spinther, der Mann des Herakleides, zu uns gekommen war, hat er uns mitgeteilt, dass Du, nachdem Du die Abrechnungen entgegengenommen hattest, gefunden hast, dass er (Herakleides) in der Kornlieferung des 34. Jahres zu viel gebucht hat.

Ich wundere mich doch, dass Du so vergesslich bist, während wir schon vorher gesagt haben, dass Herakleides uns gebeten hatte, auf Grund der von ihm gesandten Abrechnung zu buchen.

Und das Zuviel, das wir dazu verbucht haben, beträgt: 241 Artaben Weizen, $26\frac{5}{6}$ Artaben Mohn, $9628\frac{7}{12}$ Artaben Gerste, $6\frac{1}{2}$ Artaben Rizinus, 188 Artaben Olyra.

Buche also auch Du demgemäss, denn Herakleides ist einverstanden, diese Mengen zu ergänzen.

Lebe wohl.
Im 35. Jahre, am 1. Thoth.

Anschrift:

An Kleitarchos.

Anmerkungen

1 Für Kleitarchos siehe Einleitung zu Nr. **1** und P. Lond. 7 1953, Anm. zu Z. 1-2, und für Herakleides Grier, *Accounting in the Zenon Papyri*, S. 51.

5 \`ἀνενεγκεῖν' gehört sicherlich zur ersten Fassung, weil sonst der ganze Satz unverständlich wäre.

6-7 Vgl. den wahrscheinlich im Büro des Speichers ausgefertigten P. Lond. 7 1995, 127-129:

καὶ ὧι πλείω προστιθέμ[εθα]
αὐτῶι ἐν τῶι λδ L παρὰ τὴν
\`εἰσμέτρ[ησ]ιν' ἀξιώσα[ν]τος αὐτοῦ (= Herakleides).

Danach (Z. 130-134) folgen dieselben Posten wie in unserem Text (ähnlich P. Lond. 7 1994, 199-203). Nur für Olyra werden dort ρμη Artaben angegeben, dagegen ρπη in unserem Text. Die Vermutung Skeats (P. Lond. 7, S. 116, Anm. zu Z. 194-203; S. 129, Anm. zu Z. 127-134), dass es sich in unserem Text um eine falsche Lesung handelt, ist nicht richtig, da die Ziffer π sehr deutlich geschrieben wurde.

B

Verbesserte Fassung

Zunächst hat der Schreiber des Briefes versucht die erforderlichen Änderungen in A zwischen den Zeilen 2-3 und 3-4 anzubringen. Nach ἀνενηνοχότα αὐτόν in A 3 fügte er hinzu:

> | 3a κρ(ιθῶν) <ἀρ(τάβας)> ʼΘχκη ∠ ι′β′· εἰς γὰρ τοῦτο ὅσομ μὲν ἐν ταῖς κώμαις | 4a μέτρει· τὸν δὲ ἀπὸ τοῦ ⟦καὶ⟧ γινομένου κατέργου αὐτῶι οὗ ἕνεκεν καὶ τὸ σύμβολον ⟦εἰλήφαμεν⟧ παρ᾽ αὐτοῦ | 4b [ὅ]τι ἀπέχει καὶ εἰς τὸ λς L τὸ κάτεργον.

Nachher hat man den ganzen Zusatz (mit Ausnahme der Anfangsworte) gestrichen und auch Z. 4-8 der ursprünglichen Fassung (A); man hat dies durch eine neue Fassung auf der Rückseite ersetzt.

Da die Schrift auf der Rückseite stellenweise verblasst ist, sind nicht alle Einzelheiten der neuen Fassung klar, aber es geht deutlich hervor, dass die alte Fassung an einigen Punkten wesentlich geändert worden ist. Zenon spricht jetzt nur noch über einen Teil des Defizits, u. zw. nur über eine fehlende Quantität Gerste, den grössten Posten in der Fassung A (über den Weizen, den Mohn und die Olyra wird nicht mehr gesprochen). Über diese Gerste schreibt Zenon einige Einzelheiten welche er selbst offenbar erst gehört hat, als die erste Fassung des Briefes (A) schon geschrieben war. Zenon wirft dem Kleitarchos vor, dass er diese Einzelheiten hätte wissen müssen, wenn er der Sache gründlich nachgegangen wäre (παρηκολουθήκεις, B 4-5). Es geht hervor, dass Herakleides einen Teil der fehlenden Gerste schon von Kleruchen zusammengebracht hat, welche in Dörfern ausserhalb der Dorea wohnen. Auch hat Herakleides sich damit einverstanden erklärt, dass er den Rest des Defizits aus seinem Gehalt (κάτεργον) des nächsten Jahres zahlen wird. Zenon hat den Gehalt schon an Herakleides vorausbezahlt und dafür hat er von ihm ein Beweisstück (σύμβολον) erhalten, worin dieser den Empfang bestätigt.

Die Verbesserungen auf der Rückseite des Papyrusblattes sollten mit den nicht getilgten Zeilen der ersten Fassung A zusammengefügt werden, woraus ein neuer Brief (B) hervorgehen würde. Diesen Brief haben wir folgenderweise rekonstruiert: Z. 1-3 bestehen aus den Zeilen 1, 2 und dem Anfang von Z. 3 von A (SB 5 8244, 1-3) mitsamt dem Anfang der Korrektur über der 3. Zeile (SB 5 8244, 3a). Z. 4-13 enthalten den neuen Text auf der Rückseite (SB 5 8244, 10-19); Z. 14-15 enthalten die beiden letzten Zeilen von A (SB 5 8244, 9 und 20):

B

1 Ζήνων Κλειτάρχωι χαίρειν. Παραγενόμενος Σπινθὴρ ὁ παρὰ Ἡρακλείδου
2 ἀνήγγειλεν ἡμῖν ἀνειληφότα σε τοὺς λόγους εὑρίσκειν ἐν τῆι τοῦ λδ L
3 εἰσμετρήσει πλείω ἀνενηνοχότα αὐτὸν \`κρ(ιθῶν) <ἀρ(τάβας)> ʼΘχκη ∠ ι′β′.′
(10 =) 4 Θαυμά⟦.⟧ζω οὖ[ν, εἰ μ]ὴ παρηκολου-
(11 =) 5 θήκεις· εἰς γὰρ τὸ πλῆθος τοῦτο
(12 =) 6 τὸμ μὲν ἐν ταῖς \`πάσαις′ κώμαις συναγήοχεν
(13 =) 7 παρὰ τῶν κληρούχων, τὸν δὲ λοιπὸν
(14 =) 8 ἀπὸ τοῦ γινομένου αὐτῶι κατέργου
(15 =) 9 \`εἰς τὸ λς L′ αποδ..δ.... τούτου γὰρ χάριν
(16 =) 10 \`καὶ′ τὸ σύμβολον ἐλάβομεν παρ᾽ αὐτοῦ

(17 =) 11 ⟦ ⟧ ὅτι ἀπέχει ⟦ ⟧. Ἀνάφερε οὖν
(18 =) 12 τὰς Ἐθχκη ∠ ι'β' καὶ . . . . ἐπιμελές ἐστιν,
(19 =) 13 ὅπως τὸ πλῆθος τοῦτο ὑπάρχηι.
(9 =) 14 Ἔρρωσο. L λε Θῶυθ ᾱ.
(20 =) 15 Κλ[ει]τάρχωι.

3 κρ(ιθῶν) ἀρ(τάβας) χκη ed. princ., κρ(ιθῶν) Ἐθχκη Wilcken 9 ἀ̣π̣ὸ̣ δὲ (?) ⟦ ⟧δ. . σ. ed. princ. 11 Es ist nicht sicher, dass die jetzt gelöschten Worte derzeit absichtlich von dem Schreiber gelöscht wurden 12 κ̣α̣ὶ̣ ν. . . ed. princ.

Übersetzung

Zenon grüsst Kleitarchos.

Als Spinther, der Mann des Herakleides, zu uns gekommen war, hat er uns mitgeteilt, dass Du, nachdem Du die Abrechnungen entgegengenommen hattest, gefunden hast, dass er (Herakleides) in der Kornlieferung des 34. Jahres $9628\frac{7}{12}$ Artaben Gerste zu viel gebucht hat.

Ich wundere mich doch, dass Du der Sache nicht nachgegangen bist, denn für diese ganze Menge hat er einen Teil in allen Dörfern zusammengebracht von den Kleruchen, und den andren Teil [will er zahlen] aus dem ihm zukommenden Gehalt für das 36. Jahr; denn wir haben auch von ihm das Beweisstück erhalten, dass er (den Gehalt schon) empfangen hat.

Buche also die $9628\frac{7}{12}$ (Artaben) und es ist [seine?] Sache dass diese ganze Menge vorhanden ist.

Lebe wohl.
Im 35. Jahre, am 1. Thoth.

Anschrift:

An Kleitarchos.

Anmerkungen

7 Es scheint mir wenig wahrscheinlich, dass dieses Kleruchenland einen Teil der Dorea bildete, wie Cl. Préaux angenommen hat (*Chronique d'Égypte* 11, 1936, 122; *Économie royale*, S. 463; *Les Grecs en Égypte d'après les archives de Zénon*, S. 52).

Es ist möglich, dass die Gerste, welche Herakleides von den Kleruchen zusammengebracht hat, die (rückständigen?) Steuern bildeten, welche auf dem Kleruchenland ruhten, denn die Befugnisse von Apollonios' Leute haben sich, wohl auf Grund der mit der Dorea verbundenen Hoheitsrechte, auch über Philadelphia und einige Nachbardörfer erstreckt (vgl. Rostovtzeff, *Large Estate*, S. 49; Uebel, *Kleruchen*, S. 25).

Anderseits ist es auch möglich, dass die Gerste, welche Herakleides bei den Kleruchen eingetrieben hatte, der Ernte des Kleruchenlandes war, das Zenon gepachtet hatte.

9 αποδ. . δ. . . . : die Stelle ist verwischt und man kann nicht mehr lesen. Dem Sinne nach erwartet man hier eine Form von ἀποδίδωμι. Nach unserer Meinung muss hier ἀποδίδωσιν (viell. ἀποδείδωσιν geschrieben) stehen; das Subjekt ist dann Herakleides: dieser wird den Rest aus seinem Gehalt für das nächste Jahr zahlen. Deshalb hat Zenon dem Herakleides seinen Gehalt vorausgezahlt und dafür eine Quittung bekommen (Z. 9-11).

12 Vor ἐπιμελές stehen vier oder fünf Buchstaben, welche aber grösstenteils verwischt sind. Man erwartet hier αὐτῶι (d.h. Herakleides).

W.

57

LETTER FROM MARON TO PHANESIS

H. × W. = 8.5 × 19 cm. Date unknown

Sorb. inv. 284: P. Jouguet, *Petit supplément aux Archives de Zénon, Cinquantenaire de l'École Pratique des Hautes Études*, 1921, p. 232; **SB 3 6802**.

The letter is written across the fibres, no doubt on the recto as is the case with many letters in the archive. This enables us to estimate the length of the lacuna at about 10 cm., as the normal height of a roll was about 30 cm. For the two round holes in the papyrus, see the commentary of P. Jouguet: "La pièce a été pliée trois fois de bas en haut, et quand on se la représente en cet état, on voit que le dommage a été causé par une échancrure dans le bord du rouleau, provoquée peut-être, au début, par un fil qui le liait".

The hand, which looks quite ordinary at first sight, has the peculiarity of using linking strokes between the letters (e.g. *l.* 1, Φανη-σει, χ-α-ι-ρειν; *l.* 2, ευ-θεως, γινωσκ-ε). This feature may perhaps prove useful in searching for the missing right-hand portion.

Contents Owing to its fragmentary state, the content of Maron's letter largely escapes us. Lines 3 and 4 deal with a loan of corn and with corn that runs the risk of remaining unsold through the addressee's fault. The important point of this reedition is the photograph, which may help to find the missing right-hand portion.

front [plate XXIV]:

Μάρων Φανήσει χαίρειν. Ἐάμπερ ορθ[- - -]
εὐθέως παρέσει, εἰ δὲ μὴ γίνωσκε διότι οὐθ[- - -]
καταλιπὼν ἡμᾶς καὶ τὸν ἐγδανειζόμεν<ον> σῖτον απ[- - -]
ἡμῶν καὶ ὁ σῖτος κινδυνεύσει διὰ σὲ ἄπρατον γεν[έσθαι - - -]

back [plate XXIV]:

Χειριστῆι Φανήσει.

1 ὀρθ[ῶς? Jouguet 2 δύο[Jouguet; οὐθ[(vel οὐ θ[ ) legimus 4 ἄπρατον correctum (sic) ex ἄπρατος 5 χειριστῇ Jouguet, χειριστῆι legimus

Notes

1 Μάρων Φανήσει χαίρειν: both writer and addressee are well-known, see *Prosopography*, P. L. Bat. 21. IX Μάρων (no. 2) and Πανῆσις (no. 4). Maron had already been active in Philadelphia before Zenon's arrival (see PSI 5 500 and 501 from year 27). The last occasion on which we hear of him is in 249 B.C. (P. Mich. Zen. 53, year 37). Phanesis is attested as cheiristes (no. **12** note *g*) and sitometres between years 32 and 35 (for references, see Pros. Ptol. 1 142, 1448, 1454, and 1466). P. Mich. Zen. 52 shows that there were difficulties between the two men in year 35 (250 B.C.), and the rather harsh tone of the present letter concurs with this.

4 ὁ σῖτος κινδυνεύσει ἄπρατον γεν[έσθαι]: the scribe at first rightly wrote ἄπρατος, but changed this into the ungrammatical accusative ἄπρατον.

C.

58

LETTER TO PURON

H. × W. = 18 × 12 cm. Undated (251 B.C.?)

Jand. inv. 357: **P. Jand. 6 91** with plate.

The original size of this papyrus is preserved, but it has suffered much damage. A portion is missing from the right-hand side at the level of *ll.* 6-9, and towards the left-hand side the papyrus is badly shredded in *ll.* 1-2 and *ll.* 9-10. There is a margin of 2 cm. at the top, but virtually no left-hand margin. At the right-hand side, *ll.* 1-2 run right up to the edge of the sheet, but *ll.* 3-5 leave a margin of 2 cm. here. In *ll.* 6-9, where a piece of papyrus is missing, the text again seems to approach closer to the edge. There is no obvious explanation for this uneven arrangement of the line-ends. Below the ἔρρωσο in *l.* 11, there are 4 cm. of blank papyrus.

Contents In this letter a correspondent, whose name is damaged and cannot be read, warns Puron that he is likely to lose the earnest-money he has given in connection with a purchase of poppy, if he does not quickly complete the transaction. The nature of the "declaration" mentioned in *ll.* 8-10 poses a problem, chiefly because the present text is our only explicit evidence for the forfeiture of earnest-money: see R. Taubenschlag, *The Law of Greco-Roman Egypt*, second edition (1955), p. 409.

For Puron, a scribe, and an accountant in Zenon's service (cf. *Prosopography*, P. L. Bat. 21. IX, Πύρων for references), see Edgar's remarks in the introductions to P. Mich. Zen. 46 and 52. It seems plausible to suppose that the purchase mentioned in the present letter is the same as that involved in P. Mich. Zen. 46 and in PSI 6 571, letters that Edgar, in his introduction to P. Mich. Zen. 46, ascribed to 251 B.C. To judge from the contents of these two letters from Puron to Zenon, the author of the present letter cannot well have been Zenon.

front:

. . . . . Πύ̣ρ̣ωνι χαίρειν.
. . . . τ̣ὴν μήκω-
να οὐκέτι ἠγόρακας,
δοὺς τὸν ἀραβῶνα,
κινδυνεύσεις ἀπολέ-
σαι ⟦αὐ⟧τοὺς χαλκ̣[οῦς],
ἐ̣ὰμ μὴ ἐν ἡμέρ̣[αις]
τ̣ρισί. Ὁ γὰρ ἄν[θρω-]
π̣ος δ̣ιαμαρ[τ]ύ̣ρ̣[ε-]
τ̣α̣ι̣.
Ἔρρωσο.

back:

12 Πύρωνι.

2 [*vac.* 'Επειδή] Rosenberger, ["Ισθι ὅτι ἐπεί] Kalbfleisch apud P. Jand. 6 91 n. *l.* 2   4 *l.* ἀρραβῶνα   6 αὐτούς Rosenberger, ⟦αὐ⟧τούς Viereck (BL 3 p. 86)   9 διαμαρ[τ]ụρ̣[εῖ]|τ̣α̣ι̣ Rosenberger

Translation

..... to Puron, greetings.

[Since] you have not yet bought the poppy(-seed), although you have given the earnest-money, you will risk losing your money, if (you do) not (complete the purchase) within three days. For the fellow is making a solemn declaration.

Fare well.

Address:

To Puron.

Notes

1 The name of the sender of this letter contained 5 or possibly 4 letters. Rosenberger, in her introduction to the editio princeps, discussed the possibility that the letter might have come from Zenon. She suggested that the hand cannot be identified with that in any available photograph.

2 Many restorations might be possible here, but the sense is quite clear. The restoration of just 'Επειδή with a space preceding does not appear very probable, although of course no claim is made here to have identified traces of ink on the published photograph.

2-3 For μήκων see D. Crawford, *The Opium Poppy, A Study in Ptolemaic Agriculture*, in M. I. Finley, *Problèmes de la terre en Grèce ancienne* (1973), pp. 223-251.

4 The sense of what follows in the letter seems to demand that δοὺς τὸν ἀραβῶνα here signifies "although you *have* paid the earnest-money", and that it is not still governed by the negative word οὐκέτι. On this interpretation, τοὺς χαλκοὺς in *l.* 6 will refer to this earnest-money, which the purchaser risks forfeiting.

However, the possibility should be mentioned of understanding *ll.* 2-5 as "You have not made sure of the purchase *by* giving the earnest-money". In this case τοὺς χαλκοῦς in *l.* 6 would have to be interpreted in a very loose sense, "you risk losing money".

See F. Pringsheim, *The Greek Law of Sale* (1950), p. 384, who adopts the same view as that taken here.

6 It seems impossible to make good sense of αὐτοὺς χαλκοῦς here, and no doubt a rough attempt had been made to erase the αὐ. Perhaps the writer originally ended the clause with simply αὐτούς, and then realized that he had not mentioned χαλκοί previously.

7-8 Rosenberger's suggestion that a harsh ellipse has to be understood here, for example ἐαμ μὴ ἀγοράσῃς ἐν ἡμέραις τρισί, is plainly correct. The translation "... you risk losing your money, perhaps even in three days" is not plausible here. Pringsheim (*op. cit.*, p. 401, n. 4) supplements ἀποδιδοὺς τὸ λοιπὸν τῆς τιμῆς. Taubenschlag (*op. cit.*, p. 409) understands that this period of three days was a "fixed term" (perhaps he means "fixed by law") from the date of the payment of the earnest money, but it seems clear that the text is referring to three days that still remain for the completion of the sale.

9-10 The reading δ̣ιαμαρ[ ] is plainly correct here, and the only restorations that come into serious consideration are of parts of διαμαρτάνειν and of διαμαρτύρεσθαι. (The verb διαμαρτυρεῖν does not occur in the archive, and there seem to be no compelling grounds to restore it here: it is not to be expected in a Ptolemaic papyrus). It does not seem convincing to understand "For the fellow has made a mistake", and διαμαρτύρεσθαι, "to make a solemn declaration" is presumably to be restored. Elsewhere in the archive it is not used absolutely (it is generally followed by ὅτι). The sense is probably not "the fellow is protesting, complaining", for which there seems to be no parallel, but "the fellow is making a solemn declaration". Clearly the seller is meant, and he is protecting his rights by this affirmation.

Rosenberger n. *ad. loc.* cites a relevant passage in Theophrastos concerning Greek Law, where declarations concerned with disputed sales are mentioned, but there seems to be no close parallel in the papyri. PRINGSHEIM (*op. cit.*, p. 412) translates "For the receiver of the earnest-money will call in witnesses", but this does not seem plausible. Pringsheim's conclusion that the present transaction was oral, and not documented, will not, however, be affected by the interpretation followed here.

T.

59

LIST OF GREEKS AND SEMITES IN PALESTINE

H. × W. = 7.8 × 6.7 cm. Date unknown

Jand. inv. 413 (*verso*): **CPJ 1 3**.

F. Uebel, in *Die Giessener Zenonpapyri, Kurzberichte aus den Giessener Papyrussammlungen* 18 (1964), pp. 10-11, has indicated that Jand. inv. 413 belongs to the same roll as a number of other Giessen fragments, which bear the inventory nos. 412 and 414 (and probably also no. 415). V. A. Tcherikover made use of the evidence of the personal names preserved on *recto* and *verso* of Jand. inv. 413 in his study *Palestine under the Ptolemies, Mizraim* 4-5 (1937): see pp. 57-68. All the information on the text given there seems to be reproduced in CPJ 1 3. Tcherikover's publication of the text was based on a transcription made by T. C. Skeat in or before 1932. It seems best to retain here the terms *recto* and *verso* used by Tcherikover and Uebel. H. G. Gundel, in Katalog der literarischen Papyri in der Giessener Universitätsbibliothek, *Kurzberichte aus den Giessener Papyrussammlungen* 39 (1977), gives a short description (p. 41 no. 60) and a photograph (Abb. 14 b) of the *verso* of Jand. inv. no. 413.

Contents The contents of the *recto* of this fragment apparently show that it belongs to a list or account relating to Zenon's stay in Palestine, and may be compared with P. Cairo Zen. 1 59.004-8, P. Cairo Zen. 4 59.673, and P. Lond. 7 1930. Tcherikover's dating of the text to 259 B.C. seems to be based only on the fact that it belongs to the Palestine material, and, strictly speaking, part of 260 B.C. and part of 258 B.C. come into question. See the chronological information in P. L. Bat. 21. VIII, b. In CPJ Tcherikover gives notes on the Semitic names in the list on the *verso*, and see also the *Prosopography*, P. L. Bat. 21. IX. The list was obviously compiled for some practical purpose, and various checkmarks have been added.

The following persons occur in the course of the text on the *recto*:

Ἀγάθων, Δρίμυλος συν[ωριστής], and Κλεάναξ.

Verso:

•	Ἱππόστρατος	Hippostratos
•	Αὐαῆλος	Auaëlos
•	Παναβῆλος	Panabelos
•	Ζαβάλνος	Zabalnos
[•]	Φίλων	Philon
•	Μένων	Menon
.	Ζήνων	Zenon
•	Ὁσαῖος	Hosaios
	⟦Ἀνναῖος⟧	Annaios (cancelled)

•	Σανναῖος	Sannaios
•	Κο'υ'σνατᾶνος	Kousnatanos
/	Νικά̣νω[ρ]	Nikanor
/	Παρ.[ ]	Par.[ ]

2 perhaps Αυδηλος, Lipinski (possibility confirmed by Gundel) 4 perhaps Ζαβδανας (id.) 12 Νικά̣νω[ρ] Clarysse, Νίκων ed. princeps 13 Παρ.[Clarysse, Πρ.[ed. princeps

Notes

7 The checkmark, although damaged, is plainly different from the other marks in this text.

— In the texts relating to Zenon's stay in Palestine, Zenon's own name naturally occurs. There are also mentions at this period of persons called "Zenon" who are known not to be "Zenon son of Agreophon": see P. Cairo Zen. I 59.003, 20 (Zenon son of Timarkhos) and P. Cairo Zen. I 59.029, 2 and 4 (Zenon son of Herakleides: this text dates from November/December 258 B.C., but concerns a journey between Egypt and Caria). There are, of course, also other Zenons in the archive as a whole. In the Palestine documents, there are mentions of persons called "Zenon", where it is impossible to judge if "Zenon son of Agreophon" is in question (see P. Cairo Zen. I 59.006, 42; and 59.010, 12 and 20), and it is equally impossible in the present case. See further the *Prosopography*, P. L. Bat. 21. IX, Ζήνων.

8 Skeat noted that Ὁσαῖος had been "inserted later, presumably to replace the bracketed Ἀνναῖος".

T.

60

QUITTANCE

H. × L. = 8,1 × 5,9 cm.[b] 14 mars 256 a.C.

Jand. inv. 363[a] + Caire JdE 53733[b]. H. G. Gundel, *Verlorene Papyri Jandanae, Aegyptus* 41 (1961) p. 13 et F. Uebel, *Archiv für Papyrusforschung* 26 (1978) p. 30, n° 8 (transcription de Skeat, qui a reconnu en ce fragment la moitié manquante du fragment du Caire), reproduit dans **SB 8 9667**[a] (texte supérieur) et C. C. Edgar dans **P. Cairo Zen. 4 59.552**[b] (texte inférieur; collationné par moi sur l'original).

Le texte supérieur, autrefois conservé à Giessen, a disparu à la fin de la seconde guerre mondiale. Le texte inférieur est conservé au Caire. Ce texte est écrit parallèlement aux fibres, aucun κόλλημα n'est visible. Lors de la mise sous verre, certains morceaux de papyrus le long des bords sont restés repliés et cachent ainsi quelques signes: c'est le cas à la *l.* 6, où l'on ne voit que le pied du κ de κθ, et de ιω dans τριω- à la *l.* 10. Le verso est anépigraphe.

Contenu À la fin de l'an 29, Zénon succède à Panakestôr dans l'administration de la δωρεά d'Apollônios à Philadelphie pour assurer la mise en route définitive de l'exploitation des 10 000 aroures de terre. Le présent texte — qui est une quittance double pour $2\frac{1}{2}$ drachmes destinées à permettre la plantation de ricin sur une surface de 5 aroures, — date de cette année-là. Le 14 mars, c'est encore Panakestôr qui était en charge, et c'est donc vraisemblablement de lui que Théôn reçut les 2 drachmes et demie. Cela signifie aussi que le présent texte s'est introduit dans les archives de Zénon par le biais de celles de Panakestôr (voir p. 4).

Originaire de Canope,[1] Théôn fut employé par l'administration de la δωρεά pour la mise en culture d'une parcelle de terre et c'est à ce titre qu'il apparaît dans plusieurs reçus datés de l'an 29 (P. Cairo Zen. 1 59.119, 59.138, 59.139 et notre texte). Une fois la mise en culture assurée, il continua à cultiver la parcelle au moins jusqu'en l'an 35 (P. Cairo Zen. 2 59.292).

L κθ Τῦβι κ̣.
Ἔχει Θέων Πρωτάρ-
χου εἰς κίκιος φυ-
τείαν ἀρουρῶν πέντε
δραχμὰς δύο τριώβολο[ν].

[1] Un village du Fayoum (cpr. T. C. Skeat dans la note à P. Lond. 7 1953, *l.* 3) ou le faubourg d'Alexandrie (P. M. Fraser, *Ptolemaic Alexandria*, II, Oxford 1972, p. 127 n. 81).

[planche VIII]:

L κθ [Τ]ῦ̣β̣ι̣ κ̄.
Ἔχει Θέων Πρωτάρχου
εἰς κίκιος φυτ̣ε̣ί̣αν
ἀρουρῶν πέντε
δραχμὰς δύο τριώ-
βολον.

Traduction

An 29, 20 Tybi. Théôn, fils de Prôtarchos, a reçu pour la plantation de cinq aroures de ricin deux drachmes et trois oboles.

M.

61

DRAFT OF A LETTER TO THE GUARDS OF THE WATCH-POST

H. × W. = 34 × 8.8 cm. 23 May, 246 B.C. (Financial year)
or 22 May, 245 B.C. (Egyptian year)

Sorb. inv. 283 verso (part, see no. **54**): the text has been edited by P. JOUGUET, *Petit Supplément aux Archives de Zénon, Cinquantenaire de l'École Pratique des Hautes Études* (1921), p. 231, and is reprinted without modifications in **SB 3 6801**, verso.

The text is written across the fibres on the verso of no. **54** in a small, cursive hand different from that on the recto.

Contents Jouguet only commented that the text was very obscure. Thanks to a few new readings we can make a guess as to the contents of this draft. The writer (Eukles?) writes to Asklepiades (possibly the head of the phulakeion), that he has sent Philokrates with some goods from Memphis to Apollonios. He asks that Philokrates may pass unhindered.

[plate XXIII]:

L β Φαρμοῦθι $\overline{β}$.
Τοῖς ἐπὶ τοῦ φυ(λακείου). Ἀπεστάλκαμεν
\`ἐγ Μέμφεως΄ Ἀπολλωνίωι κατ̣[άγ]οντα
Φιλοκράτην̣ τ[. . . .]δι. . [. . .]
εξω̣ν. ια̣ς δει. . [. . . .]. φ̣η̣ν̣α̣ι̣.
Καλῶς οὖν ποιήσε̣τε
ἀπογραψάμεν[οι] καὶ ἀ[φ-]
έντες αὐτόν.
—
Ἀσκληπιάδηι.

2 φ(υλακείου) Jouguet 3 ἀπὸ λαῶν καὶ κα[τοίκ]ων τά Jouguet 4 Φιλοκράτου Jouguet 4-5 [Ἀλ]|εξανδρίας? Jouguet

Translation

Year 2, Pharmouthi 2.

To those in charge of the watch-post.

We have sent from Memphis to Apollonios Philokrates who brings down ---. Please, therefore, take notice of him and let him pass.

To Asklepiades.

Note

3 Although the palaeographical difference between Απολλων and απο λαων is very small indeed (cf. P. Cairo Zen. 5 59.836 *b*, 8, where Edgar cannot make a choice between them), the reading Ἀπολλωνίωι instead of ἀπὸ λαῶν καί is sure here, and so this text does not provide any information on λαοί or κάτοικοι. (This passage was cited as a reference to λαοί by Cl. Vandersleyen, *Chronique d'Égypte* 48, 1973, p. 339 no. 9).

Apollonios is apparently living north of Memphis (see κατ̣[άγ]οντα *l.* 3), most probably in Alexandria. If this text has anything to do with the recto (no. **54**), it looks as if the ξένια mentioned there are sent to Apollonios. In that case he is almost certainly the dioiketes and no. **61** would then be the latest source mentioning Apollonios the dioiketes as alive.

The chronology of Apollonios' last years has recently been studied by H. Hauben, *The date of P. Hibeh II 205 and the death of Apollonios the Dioicetes, Zeitschrift für Papyrologie und Epigraphik* 16 (1975), pp. 292-294. Following Edgar (P. Mich. Zen., introd., pp. 6-7) Hauben accepts that Apollonios could have left office already in Euergetes' second year. Edgar considers it "decidedly improbable" that Iason and Zenon, who in Year 2 and 3 respectively are formally described as παρεπίδημοι, would have been so entitled if Apollonios had still been in power. Since we know now, however, that Zenon left Apollonios' service at the end of Philadelphos' reign (see P. Cairo Zen. 5 59.832) this argument is no longer valid.

No. **61** suggests that Apollonios' career went on till at least 23 May 246 (2 Pharmouthi of Year 2). This is perhaps confirmed by a fragmentary letter in the Sorbonne collection, published by B. Boyaval, CRIPEL 1 (1973), pp. 276-279 (= SB 12 10872). During a recent visit to Paris I had the occasion of studying the original and I give here my slightly corrected version of *ll.* 6-8:

ταδε[. . . . .]ν ἔπεμψε .οι τὴν ταχίστην. L γ Παῦ[νι- - -]
Ἡφαισ[τίωνι. Τῆ]ς παρ' Ἀπο. .[. .]ίου τοῦ διοικητοῦ [- - -]
ἐπιστο[λῆς ὑπόκειτ]αί σοι τ̣ὸ [ἀντί]γραφον. Τήν τε δη[- - -]

The name of the dioiketes is so badly damaged that we dare not affirm Ἀπολ̣λ̣[ων]ίου as a reading. In fact, the traces after απο do not really suggest λλ, but they are very indistinct. The remaining letters, however, and the length of the gap, strongly favour an identification with the well-known Apollonios. If this is accepted, the Sorbonne papyrus gives us the latest terminus post quem for Apollonios' death or disgrace: July/August 245 B.C., Year 3 Pauni.

C.

62

STATEMENT CONCERNING A PLEDGE

H. × W. = 11 × 10 cm. After 254/44 B.C.

Biblioteca Medicea Laurenziana: **PSI 7 869**.

The text is written along the fibres. There are small margins on both sides, but the top and bottom are missing.

Contents This statement is perhaps part of a petition to an official against Zenodora. The subject matter is an embroidered chiton (lit. "adorned with figures") of considerable value which Zenodora was to procure. Since she did not deliver it in due time, she has to pay interest on the sum paid in advance by the plaintiff lest she should forfeit the pledge (ἀνθυπόθεμα?) she gave in security.

[plate XXVIII]:

- -

ἐν τῶι γ L τοῦ Φαμενὼθ γ
ἐπὶ ζω<ι>ωτῶι χιτῶνι (δραχμῶν) 'Ασο̣
ἐ̣πήνεγκα .... Ζηνο-
δώρας μοι πο[---]
ἀνθυπόθεμα [ἕως τοῦ]
[παρ' αὐ]τῆς αὐτὸν τὸν
ζωιωτὸν ἀποίσειν.
Οὕτως αὐτῇ ἐπίστευ-
σα. 'Επεὶ οὖν οὐδ' ἕως τοῦ
νῦν ἐνήνοχεν τὸν
ζωιωτόν, ὅ τε τόκος
ἀπὸ τοῦ προγεγραμ-
μέ[νου ἔ]τους [---

- -

2 ἐπιζωωτωιχ..ρωνι ⊦ 'A ed. princ., ἐπὶ ζω<ι> ωτῶι χείτωνι ⊦ 'A T. Reekmans (*Chronique d'Égypte* 43 (1968), p. 170) 3 ἐπήνεγκας ..ζ.ν Θ̣[εο-] ed. princ. 7 ..ιωτω̣ν ed. princ.; ζωιώτων T. Reekmans (*op. cit.*, p. 171) 9 ἐπεί corr. ex επη; οὐδὲ ὡς ed. princ. 11 ζω̣ντω̣ν ed. princ. 13 με[νο]υ του ε[ed. princ.

Translation

On the third of Phamenoth of year 3 I paid (in advance) for a chiton adorned with figures of 1270 drachmae [x drachmae], whereas Zenodora procured for me a pledge in exchange until I should duly receive from her the embroidered chiton. That is how I trusted her. Since she has not, up to the present, brought the embroidered chiton, and since the interest from the above-mentioned year [amounts to x drachmae ---].

Notes

2 ζωιωτὸς χίτων. Cloaks adorned with figures are mentioned by Polybius XXX, 25 in his description of the participants in the magnificent procession of Antiochos IV (πάντες --- εἶχον πορφυρᾶς ἐφαπτίδας, πολλοὶ δὲ καὶ διαχρύσους καὶ ζῳωτάς) and by Kallixenos in his famous account of the procession of Philadelphos (Athenaeus, Deipnosoph. V 197 e, about the Νῖκαι: ζῳωτοὺς ἐνδεδυκυῖαι χιτῶνας, αὐταὶ δὲ πολὺν κόσμον χρυσοῦν περικείμεναι). Both passages illustrate the exceptional circumstances in which this kind of luxury garment was worn.

This agrees with the high value of the chiton in the present papyrus: 1270 drachmae is quite a substantial sum, if one takes into account that the monthly wage of an Egyptian agricultural worker was about 5 drachmae, and that of a man like Panakestor, the manager of the dorea, 300 drachmae. For normal prices of garments, see for example P. Cairo Zen. 3 59.319 where mention is made of a himation of 25 drachmae (*l.* 4), a chiton of 40 (*l.* 3) and another one of 60 drachmae (*l.* 8).

4 πο[---]: e.g. πο[ριζούσης], or with a different construction πο[ικιλλούσης]?

5 ἀνθυπόθεμα: the word is apparently new, but regularly formed. The plaintiff's earnest-money (ἀρραβών) appears to have been protected by a *counter*-security on the part of Zenodora.

It is not impossible, however, that we must read ἀνθ' ὑποθέμα[τος] and that the lacunas in *ll.* 4-6 are to be supplied in a different way.

T. Reekmans

63

LIST OF PAYMENTS

H. × W. = 16 × 30 cm. Date unknown

Sorb. inv. 285: P. Jouguet, *Petit supplément aux Archives de Zénon, Cinquantenaire de l'École Pratique des Hautes Études*, 1921, pp. 232-6; **SB. 3 6803** (incorporating a few corrections, chiefly derived from U. Wilcken, *Archiv für Papyrusforschung* 7, 1924, p. 296).

The original top and bottom edges of the papyrus are preserved, and so, apparently, is the right-hand edge (as seen from the front); but the papyrus is broken at the left. The writing on the front is parallel to the fibres, and this surface is the original recto of the roll—a *kollema* between two sheets runs vertically between col. 1 and col. 2. The text occupies the front surface, and is continued on the back. The front preserves two columns, and it is evident that a preceding column is lost at the left (see below). A great deal of the text on the front was written over previous writing that had been washed out, although several letters are still legible. Some of the corrections to be found on this side of the papyrus were made by a rather crude second hand, which was also responsible for the totals in *ll.* 15 and 31. The text on the back (verso), although in a different (third) hand, undoubtedly forms a sequel to that on the front.

Contents The front contains a list of persons, both Greeks and Egyptians, the latter being in the majority, divided into five groups: all of them pay (?) small sums of money. The groups are headed

1 (*l.* 1) τὰ ἀπέναν<τι> τῶν καινῶν ᾱ
2 (*l.* 9) [... τ]ῶ̣ν καινῶν ᾱ
3 (*l.* 16) [τὰ .]. . ω τῶν Κρότο(υ) ᾱ
4 (*l.* 21) τὰ ὀπίσω τῶν Κρότου
5 (*l.* 26) τὰ ἐν τοῖς . . . . . οις

The prepositions (ἀπέναντι, ὀπίσω, ἐν) suggest that the groups are topographical in nature. It will be seen that some headings, but not all, contain an ᾱ. This might be understood as a numeral (cf. γ̄ in *l.* 10, ε̄ in *l.* 11, and ζ̄ in *l.* 12); or as an abbreviation, for which, unfortunately, many restorations might be possible. Thus the groups seem to be called τὰ --- ᾱ, or simply τὰ ---, although it is impossible to be sure how integral a part of the "name" the ᾱ might be.

It is, however, not improbable that the groups represent quarters of Philadelphia. τὰ καινά in *ll.* 1, 9, and 43 might refer to the new house of Apollonios, which is called τὰ καινὰ τοῦ Ἀπολλωνίου in P. Cairo Zen. 3 59.326, 189-90.

The payments are almost completely uniform within groups 4 (1 drachma, 4 obols) and 5 (1 drachma), but vary considerably in groups 1, 2, and 3. The reason why they are made is nowhere stated, but they may perhaps be connected with the beer monopoly. This is principally suggested by the occurrence on the back (col. 3) of ζυτοπ̣ω̣λ̣ί̣ου (*l.* 33) and of the abbreviation ζυτ( ) (*ll.* 40 and 42): and in fact by far the largest payment of the whole account (40 dr.) is made by the ζυτοπώλιον in *l.* 33. This might also account for the preponderance of Egyptian names (Egyptians, unlike the wine-loving Greeks, were beer-drinkers), and for the rather high number of women [1] in the list. If this is true, Aunchis in *l.* 19 could well be the female inn-keeper of P. Lond. 7 1976 (the name does not occur elsewhere in the archive). However, these suggestions as to the nature of the payments are rather speculative.

A second hand has provided the total for groups 1 and 2 in *l.* 15, and that for groups 3, 4, and 5 in *l.* 31. His arithmetic can be checked only for the first total. It proves correct, once we have changed Jouguet's reading Ἀντίπατρος -ϲ in *l.* 14 into Ἀντίπατρος η, and this is also palaeographically a preferable reading. The figures for the first total are

group 1		8 persons	19 dr.	1	ob.
group 2	left	4 persons	10 dr.	1½	ob.
	right	4 persons	15 dr.	3	ob.
total			44 dr.	5½	ob.

The lacunas in *l.* 26 and *l.* 30 prevent us from checking the second total. The grand total in *l.* 31 proves that a column is missing, evidently from the left of the first column preserved on the front. The figures are

grand total				117 dr.	1½	ob.
total for groups 1 + 2	44 dr.	5½	ob.			
total for groups 3 + 4 + 5	44 dr.	1½	ob.			
total for all 5 groups preserved	89 dr.	1	ob.	89 dr.	1	ob.
total for the missing column				28 dr.	½	ob.

No doubt the missing column possessed a heading, which would have provided much-needed information about the purpose of the text.

The back, which is written in a third hand, repeats in *l.* 32 the grand total from the front, 117 dr. 1½ ob., and attributes this to a certain Agathokles: Ἀγαθοκλῆς δὲ φέρει, "Agathokles records" (φέρω here and in *l.* 34 means "in einer Liste führen, buchmässig führen" (*Wörterbuch*), and not, as Jouguet takes it, "to contribute".

The following lines add supplementary payments, by the ζυτοπώλιον (40 dr.), and by various persons (9 dr. 5½ ob. + 3 ob.), the latter set recorded by Anosis. A new grand total is given in *l.* 44: 167 dr. 1 ob.

front [plate XXVI]:

Col. I

Τ̣ὰ ἀπέναν<τι> τῶν καινῶν ᾱ
 Ἁρσεμφθεῦς ⊢ γ ∠
 Ἁρχῶνς ⊢ β
 Ἁ̣ρκοννῶς β

[1] Dionusia (*l.* 9), Ammonia (*l.* 11), Theodote (*l.* 13), Tamein (*l.* 17), Aunchis (*l.* 19), Nophreis (*l.* 20), the hetaira Tateis (*l.* 24), Thatres (*l.* 26), Taesis (*l.* 27), Tabalis (*l.* 27), and Tamounis (*l.* 30).

῟Ωρος γραμματεύς ⊦ β ϟ
Π̣ετεθῦμις ⟦⊦ ε⟧ ⊦ ε
[Κ]α̣θῦθις ⊦ β ϟ
[῾Α]ροντώτης ⊦ α-
[᾿Απο]λλώνιος χαλκ[εύ]ς ϟ
[... τ]ῶ̣ν καινῶν α̅ Διονυσία ⊦ β ϟ
.[.]λαθις ⊦ γ γ̅ Διον̣ύσιος ⊦ α
᾿Αμμωνία ⊦ δ ε̅ ⟦Σ̣ε̣μφθ̣ε̣ῦ̣ς Σωτᾶς⟧
[.].θ̣ας ⊦ γ ζ̅ ⟦Λ̣α̣ο̣μ̣έ̣δ̣ω̣ν̣ Πάσεις⟧
⟦[.]... ⊦ ε⟧ 2nd hand Θ̣ευδότε δ
[.]αστιου Πετοσεῖρις -c 2nd hand ᾿Αντίπατρος η
2nd hand / μδ ϟ = c
[τ̣ὰ .]..ω τῶν Κρ⟦άτωνος⟧`ότο(υ)' α̅ Πάσεις ⊦ β ϟ-
.ουθαι̣ς ⊦ β = Ταμεῖν ⊦ ε

1 .ψα απεναν`ο̣'των Jouguet, τ̣ὰ ἀπέναν<τι> τῶν Wilcken 4 ⟦῾Αρ⟧κοννῶς Jouguet, ῾Α̣ρκοννῶς legimus 7 [.].θῦθις Jouguet, [Κ]α̣θῦθις legimus 8 [῾Α]ροντώτης supplevit Bilabel (SB VIII 3 6803) 13 ευδ̣οτε Jouguet, Θ̣ευδότε legimus 14 ᾿Αντίπατρος -c Jouguet, ᾿Αντίπατρος η legimus 16 [τὰ ὀπίσ]ω Wilcken 17 Ταλειν Jouguet, Ταμεῖν legimus

Col. II

Σεμφθεῦς ⊦ β Πάσεις ⊦ β
Πετῆσις ⊦ β ῾Αῦνχις ⊦ β
Πετεαρμῶτνις ϟ Ν̣ό̣φρεις ϟ
—
Τὰ ὀπίσω τῶν Κρότου ῾Αρμῶτνι̣ς ⊦ α ϟ-
Πεν.[.]σ̣ι̣ς ⊦ α ϟ- ἄλλ{λ}ος Πετεαρ-
μῶτνις ⊦ α ϟ- ῾Αρχῆβις ⊦ α ϟ-
Τάτ̣εις ἑταίρα ⊦ α ϟ- ὁ ἐπὶ τῆς ἕκτ̣ης ⊦ β
Πετο[σ]εῖρις ⊦ α ϟ-
Τὰ ἐν τοῖς .....οις Θατρῆς ⊦ α Π̣ε̣ρ..[.].ι̣ς [ ] ϟ [ ]
Ταῆσι̣ς ⊦ α Ταβάλις ⊦ α Νεχθῆσις ⊦̣ α
Πετοσῖρις ⊦ α Σαμῶυς ⊦ α ᾿Αχομνῆοις ⊦ α
Πάσεις ⊦ α ᾿Αμῶς ⊦ α Σεῶς ⊦ α
᾿Αμεννεῦς ⊦ α Ταμοῦνις ⊦ α ῾Αρμάι`ς' [..]
2nd hand / μδ -c / εἰς τὸ αὐτὸ ⊦ ριζ -c

19 Αυγ̣ιλις Jouguet, ῾Αῦνχις legimus 21 ῾Αρμῶτνος Jouguet, ῾Αρμῶτνι̣ς legimus 22 Πετο.σ̣ις Jouguet, Πεν.[.]σ̣ις legimus 23 in fine ⊦ α ϟ-, corr. ex ⊦ β 26 τοῖς ..μίοις Jouguet, τοῖς .....οις legimus

back [plate XXVII]:

Col. III (3rd hand)

᾿Αγαθοκλῆς δὲ φέρει ριζ -c
καὶ τοῦ ζυτοπ̣ω̣λ̣ίου μ / ρνζ -c
καὶ ὧι πλέω φέρει ῎Ανοσις

οὗ Ἀπολλώνιος ὁ χαλκεύς   α =
οὗ Βόηθος   ϟ -
οὗ Διονύσιος ὁ τὰ ἐλαικά   α
οὗ Ἀντίπατρος   ϟ
ο̣ῦ̣ Πετοσῖρις ϗ̣ο̣υρεύς   - c
Ἀμ̣ῶυς ζυτ(   ) . . . τοῦ πρὸς τῶι βαλα(νείωι)   ϟ
40a ο̣ῦ̣ .τοθοῆθ τοῦ πρὸς τῶι βαλανείωι   ϟ
οὗ πα<ν>τοπωλίου   β
οὗ α Κράτωνος ὑπὸ ζυτ(   )   ϟ -
καὶ τῶν ἐν τοῖς καινοῖς   γ / ⟦ . ϟ = c⟧ \` = c′
/ ρξζ ⟦c⟧\`-′ ⌒ ⟦.⟧\`γ′ ϟ ⟦c⟧

34 Κτηιλλέω Jouguet, καὶ ὧι πλέω legimus   37 ἀλικά Jouguet, ἐλαικά legimus   39 . . . ρεύς Jouguet, ϗ̣ο̣υρεύς dubitanter legimus   40a οὗ .τοθοῆθ Jouguet, valde incertum   43 κτυνενίοις Jouguet, καὶ τῶν ἐν τοῖς legimus

Notes

1 For τὰ καινά see in the *contents* above.

8a Ἀπολλώνιος χαλκεύς, whose name was added afterwards, reappears on the back in *l.* 35.

13 Θ̣ευδότε: Jouguet did not read the *theta*, of which only the upper part is preserved. Θευδότε is no doubt an orthographic variant for Θευδότη, *êta* and *epsilon* often being confused by Egyptians in the archive (see our commentary on no. **41**). It is surely not fortuitous that this error was made by the second scribe, whose hand is rather unskilled.

14 The first *iota* in Πετοσεῖρις is not visible on the photograph because of a fold in the papyrus.

17 Ταμεῖν: we prefer this reading to Ταλειν (Jouguet). It is true that the *mu* is not found written in the same cursive way elsewhere in the text, but the letter is not a clear-cut example of a *lambda* either. Ταμεῖν, a variant of Ταμῖνις, is a name of a regular theophoric form, whereas Ταλειν is unparalleled and unexplained.

19 Ἁΰνχις: the ghost-name Αὐνίλις must be deleted from the *Onomasticon*. For a possible identification of this person, see the *contents* above.

20-23 Πετεαρμῶτνις --- ἄλλ{λ}ος Πετεαρμῶτνις: the word ἄλλ{λ}ος was wrongly considered a personal name in SB 3 6803 and from there incorporated in FORABOSCHI, *Onomasticon alterum*, p. 26. The name Peteharmôtnis is typical of the Aphroditopolite nome, but also rather frequent in Philadelphia (cf. *Studia Hellenistica* 24, 1980, pp. 118-119). One of the two persons called Peteharmôtnis may be identical with the homonymous shop-keeper in P. Yale 1 39, *ll.* 8-9.

28 Ἀχομνῆοις: this is no doubt a variant of the more common Ἀχομνεῦις. The Egyptian labio-velar [ω] is represented in Greek by ου, υ, and ο (e.g. *'Is.t-wr.t* = Ἐσουῆρις, Ἐσυῆρις, Ἐσοῆρις); it often becomes a labialised velar [*g*ω] (e.g. *Ḥʿ-mr-wr* = Χαιεμνῆγοις); and even a velar [*g*] (e.g. *'Ip.t-wr.t* = Ἐφγῆρις). For the phonetic explanation, see J. VERGOTE, *Phonétique historique de l'Égyptien, Les Consonnes, Bibliothèque du Muséon* 19 (1945), pp. 11-12 and 16-17, who compares the Germanic [ω] taken over in Romance languages (e.g. war → guerra → guerre).

37 ὁ τὰ ἐλαικά: *scil.* ἐγλαβών or ἐξειληφώς. Jouguet's reading ὁ τὰ ἀλικά is clearly wrong.

43 τῶν ἐν τοῖς καινοῖς: for τὰ καινά cf. *l.* 1 and the *contents* above.

— The correct total of the amounts listed in *ll.* 35-43, including *l.* 40a, is 10 dr. 2½ ob., ι = c. If we assume that *l.* 40a with the sum of 3 ob. was added to the list subsequently, then the correct total before this addition was made would have been 9 dr. 5½ ob., θ ϟ = c.

In the total preserved in *l.* 43, the signs ϟ = c have plainly been crossed out, and = c has plainly been written above. The sign before ϟ = c might be taken as ι, or θ or θ corrected into a ι. The scribe may have crossed this sign out, perhaps in error, at the same time as the ϟ = c.

44 The total given in this line, in its corrected form of ρξζ-, 167 dr. 1 ob., would be the correct total of all the entries in col. 3 (including the balance brought forward from the front), before the addition of the 3 ob. in *l.* 40a There is no obvious explanation in the text for the "remainder" given in the same line.

C.

64

CALENDAR OF VINEYARD WORK

H. × W. = 19.5 × 9 cm. Date unknown

Biblioteca Medicea Laurenziana: **PSI 6 624**; H. Cadell, *La viticulture scientifique dans les archives de Zénon: PSI 624, Aegyptus* 49 (1969), pp. 105-20 (text on p. 118), with one plate (= SB 12 10768); cf. Pack², no. 1986.

The text is written along the fibres. The papyrus is in a poor state of preservation, being badly worn and frayed in places. The right-hand edge of the piece is well-preserved and has plainly been cut with a knife. It is impossible to judge from the photograph if the line of the cut has followed the contour of the line-ends, or if conversely the text has been written to fill the space up to an unevenly cut edge. Nothing that could be called a margin has been left at this side. Towards the left, the papyrus is poorly preserved, and only some 2.5 cm. of the original cut left-hand edge of the piece are preserved, at the level of *ll.* 11-15. The left-hand margin seems to be of about 0.75 cm. The bottom edge is torn, and some few projecting vertical fibres probably indicate that the piece was originally more extensive here. Disregarding these, 2 cm. of a bottom margin is still preserved, and Cadell (p. 119) suggests there is no text missing after *l.* 24. The top edge is apparently broken, and is very close to the first surviving line of the text. Judging from the contents, Cadell (p. 119) suggests that the amount of text lost before *l.* 1 roughly equals that which survives. She argues that the text does not come from a roll containing a substantial treatise, but was written on a single piece of papyrus. She continues "Sans doute faut-il voir dans ce coupon le revers d'un document officiel, dont les dimensions originelles (environ 40 cm. de large sur 10 cm. de haut) répondent bien au format des belles pièces de chancellerie du temps de Philadelphe. Le support a été peu soigneusement lavé: maintes traces d'encre restent ça et là visibles, souvent gênantes pour l'établissement du texte actuel".

G. Vitelli in the PSI edition suggested that the text was written in Zenon's own hand, and this is accepted by Cadell (p. 119).

The text has been thoroughly re-worked and discussed by Cadell in her *Aegyptus* article, and the present edition simply reproduces her readings and restorations, and reprints her translation. The apparatus criticus is here divided into two parts. The first records just the more important readings and restorations of the PSI edition that are rejected by Cadell. The second part gathers together for convenience some suggestions or alternatives given by Cadell in her notes. Finally the notes here have been added to clarify her reading and interpretation of the text wherever these may not be immediately apparent from the transcription and translation.

Contents This fragment preserves the latter half of a brief survey of the work needing to be done in tending vines throughout the year. The text employs the Egyptian month-names. Cadell points out that some of the mistakes in it indicate that it is a copy of a written original. She suggests that the text is a practical guide compiled by Zenon from a study of several treatises on viticulture, for the direction of the work on Apollonios' estate. The details, she suggests, have been adapted to local conditions. She finds no verbal correspondance with any of the surviving ancient texts that deal with the subject.

For two other texts from the archive concerned with viticulture, see texts nos. **26** and **52** above.

\- -

[*c*. 13]τομωτερον
[*c*. 13].ε τομὴν
[*c*. 7 τὸ ξ]ῠ̣λον καὶ τὴν
[*c*. 10] ἀ̣ρξάμενοι ἐν τῶι
[Χοιάκ, συντε]λ̣έσουσιν ⟦ἄχρι τοῦ⟧ \`ἔσχατον'
[τῶι Τῦβι. Τὴν δ]ὲ βλαστολογίαν ποι-
[ήσουσιν ἀ]κ̣ο̣λουθοῦντες ἀεὶ
[*c*. 10] βλαστῶι φανεροῦ-
τ̣α̣ι̣ κ̣αρ[*c*. 7] κ̣α̣ὶ̣ ἐγβ̣ά̣λλει
π[ολ]λ̣οὺς τοὺς βαρεῖς τῶν
[καρπῶ]ν̣, ἵνα μὴ ὑπ' ἀνέμου
[. . . . .]ωσι, ἕως τοῦ ὥραν γενέσθαι κατάγειν τὸν βλαστόν.
\`-Χαρακώσουσι δὲ τὸν βλαστόν,' ὅσαι ἂν δυναταὶ ὦσι τῶν ἀμ-
πέλων π̣[ρὸ το]ῦ̣ ἀπανθεῖν, τὰς
δ̣ὲ λοιπὰς πάσας ὡς ἂν ἄρξων-
ται ὀρ̣ί̣ζειν, καὶ συντελέσου-
σιν τήν τε χαράκωσιν τοῦ
βλαστ[οῦ] κ̣α̣ὶ̣ ⟦συντελέσουσιν⟧
[τὸν *c*. 6]μὸν τῶν ἀμ-
πέλων ἕως τοῦ Φαρμοῦθι.
Ὑποφυλλώσουσιν δὲ ὅσας
ἂν χρήσιμον ἦι ἐν τῶι
Παχ̣ῶ̣νς̣.

PSI 6 624: 3-4 [*c*. 9]. .ον καὶ τὴν | [ἄμπελον? ἐρ?]γασ̣άμενοι et in nota 'Forse τὸν βλα]σ̣τ̣ὸν καὶ etc.' 8-9 φανεροῦ-|σ̣θα̣ι̣ π̣αρα̣.[*c*. 6] 12 εκ̣π̣[. .]ω̣σ̣ι et in nota ἐκ̣π̣[έσ]ω̣σ̣ι? 14 χαραχώσουσι, *l*. χαρακώσουσι 20 [τὸν ἐγκεν]τρ̣ι̣σ̣μόν 22 in nota ὑποφυλάξ[ουσ]ιν et ὑπὸ φύλλα. . .ιν?

Cadell: 1 εὐτομώτερον, ὀψιτ., συντ.? 2 Τὴν] δ̣ὲ τομήν,] τ̣ε τομήν? 6-7 ποι-|[ήσουσιν] aut ποι-|[ήσονται] 8 e.g. ἅπαλος 9 e.g. καρποφόρος, καρπογόνος, καρποφορία, καρπογονία 17 ὀρίζειν: aut ὡρι<μά> ζειν, ut Edgar apud PSI 6 625, n. ad loc.; aut ὀ<πω> ρίζειν 20 [σκα-λισ]μόν aut [κοπρισ]μόν?

Translation

. . . la taille . . . on la commencera en Choiak et on l'achèvera au plus tard en Tybi. On fera l'épamprage en prêtant attention sans discontinuer à (tout) rameau (qui) se révèle (fructifère) et qui fait sortir en abondance des fruits qui seront lourds, afin qu'ils ne soient pas (endommagés) par le vent, jusqu'à ce que soit venu le moment d'incliner les rameaux. On palissera les rameaux, avant la défloraison pour tous les pieds de vigne pour lesquels ce sera possible, pour tous les autres dès qu'ils commenceront à (former le raisin?), et on achèvera le palissage des rameaux et (la fumure?) des vignes d'ici à Pharmouthi. On effeuillera à la base toutes celles pour lesquelles ce sera utile en Pachôn.

Notes

1-6 Lines 2-6, Cadell suggests, are devoted to "pruning" (τομή, *l.* 2), and ξύλον in *l.* 3 refers to dead wood. It is uncertain if *l.* 1 is also part of the account of pruning, or if this begins in *l.* 2.

5-6 The month-names Χοιάκ and Τῦβι (at this period, roughly late-January to late-February, and late-February to late-March respectively) are here restored by Cadell on the basis of various papyri in which actual dates of pruning are mentioned. From the archive she mentions P. Cairo Zen. 4 59.736 and 5 59.827, and compares P. Oxy. 14 1673 and P. Lond. 1 131 recto = SB 8 9699.

6 βλαστολογία: nipping off all but a few chosen shoots, to strengthen the growth of those left.

11 Cadell, p. 111: "La finale introduite par ἵνα dépend de ἀκολουθοῦντες; il faut suivre le rameau fructifère pour que les futurs fruits ne soient pas endommagés de façon quelconque par le vent. Enfin la surveillance ne doit pas se ralentir jusqu'au moment où le rameau, devenu plus robuste, pourra être incliné".

17 The translation follows Cadell's suggestion (p. 113) that ὀ<πω> ρίζειν should be read, and might here be used in an intransitive sense "to form fruit" (rather than the usual sense of "to gather fruit").

20 Cadell (pp. 113-16) puts forward strong arguments for refusing to restore here a reference to "grafting", ἐγκεντρισμός. She sees difficulties in restoring either σκαλισμός, "hoeing", or κοπρισμός, "manuring" ("mulching"?). The translation adopts the second of these possibilities (although her notes also speculate that a dressing of ashes or dust may be meant).

22 ὑποφυλλοῦν, not previously attested, is defended by Cadell (pp. 116-17) as signifying "to remove leaves" shading the grapes, from only the *lower* portions of the vine.

T.

65

FRAGMENT OF A LETTER

H. × W. = 4.2 × 8.5 cm. Date unknown

Berlin inv. 17278: **BGU 10 1997**; F. Uebel, *Neues über einen Gazellenjäger des Zenonarchivs, Archiv für Papyrusforschung* 21 (1971), p. 215.

The writing is parallel to the fibres. Margins are preserved on the right- and left-hand sides, but the papyrus is broken at top and bottom.

Contents This fragment, evidently from the middle of a letter, was published in BGU 10 by W. Müller, who suggested it might belong to the Zenon-archive, and further pointed out that the name he read as 'Α[.....] in *l.* 1, the name of a gazelle-hunter, might be identified with the gazelle-hunter of P. Cairo Zen. 4 59.744, 1, whose name is lost (*Pros. Ptol.* 4, no. 12426). Subsequently, Uebel (see above) showed that the name of the gazelle-hunter in the present text should be read Σεα[....] (the text certainly makes more plausible sense if the pronoun σέ is not read), and he identified him with the Σεαρτῶς/Σεωρτῶς known from the archive, who was already clearly identified as a hunter, although the evidence had not yet suggested that he was precisely a δορκαδοθήρας. See *Pros. Ptol.* 4, no. 12425 (cf. E. Van 't Dack, *Coniecturae Papyrologicae, Studien zur Papyrologie und antiken Wirtschaftsgeschichte Friedrich Oertel zum achtzigsten Geburtstag gewidmet* [1964] p. 62) and T. Reekmans, *La Sitométrie dans les Archives de Zénon* (1966) no. 133, p. 93. Uebel therefore proceeded to suggest that the title δορκαδοθήρας should be restored to follow Seortos' name in P. Cairo Zen. 2 59.294-5, and that Seortos' name should be restored to precede the title δορκαδοθήρας in P. Cairo Zen. 4 59.744.

Thus Uebel effectively identified the hunter in the present text, and both *Pros. Ptol.* 4, nos. 12425 and 12426, all as one person. Uebel finally suggested that Seortos, because of his association with Kuanos in P. Cairo Zen. 4 59.747, 16, might be a slave, although Reekmans, *loc. cit.*, had suggested he was probably free.

The word δορκαδοθήρας is not preserved in the archive anywhere other than in the texts mentioned above, and is not attested elsewhere in Greek.

γνώριζε Σεα[ρτῶν] τὸν δορκαδο-
θή[ρ]αν παραγεγονό[τ]α ἀπὸ κυνη-
[γίας τῆι --] τοῦ Χοιάχ
----

1 Σεα[ρτῶν] Uebel, σὲ 'Α[.....] Müller 3 τῆι supplevit Clarysse

Translation

--- Know that Sea[rtos] the gazelle-hunter has arrived (back) from hunting [on the ..th] of Khoiak --- T.

66

FRAGMENT OF A LETTER

H. × W. = 2.2 × 8.9 cm. 246 B.C.?

Berlin inv. 17281: **BGU 10 2010**.

Müller in his edition of this fragment in BGU 10 describes the hand as a small, elegant documentary hand. The writing is across the fibres. Parts of the margins are preserved to left and right, but the papyrus is broken above and below.

Contents This fragment, evidently from the middle of a letter, refers to the pouring-out of the new vintage of Year 2. The evident date of the hand, and the two place-names mentioned, strongly suggest that the letter belongs to the Zenon archive. The text is presumably to be dated to the Autumn of 246 B.C.

- -
εἰς Κερκὴν καὶ ἀποστελλομένου εἰς
Ταιτάρω ὥστε εἰς τὴν ἔγχυσιν τῶν οἰνικῶν
γενημ̣άτων τῶν εἰς τὸ β L [- - -]
- -

Translation

- - - to Kerke, and being sent to Taitaro, for the pouring-in of the wine-produce for Year 2 - - -

Notes

1 Kerke in the Memphite nome is frequently mentioned in the archive: see the study by J. Yoyotte, *Études géographiques II, Revue d'Égyptologie* 14 (1962), pp. 79-89.

2 Taitaro in the Memphite nome is otherwise attested in the archive only at PSI 5 486, 2, 4, and 17: see J. Yoyotte, *op. cit.*

The term ἔγχυσις does not occur elsewhere in the archive, and is only otherwise attested at P. Petrie 2 40, *b*, 7 (inserted above the line): the passage is καλῶς οὖν ποιήσεις ἀποστειλὰς τινὰ \`τῆι η̄', ὃς ἐπακολουθήσει \`τῆι ἐγχύσει' τοῦ γινομένου σοι γλευκοῦς, "Please, therefore, send someone on the 8th, who may supervise the pouring-in of the sweet-wine that is due to you". (The text is dated to the 4th Pauni.) Presumably ἔγχυσις τοῦ γλευκοῦς there refers to precisely the same operation as ἔγχυσις τῶν οἰνικῶν γενημάτων in the present letter.

T.

67

LETTER OF INTRODUCTION FROM ASKLEPIADES TO ZENON

H. × W. = 13 × 18.5 cm.[a]; 12.5 × 18.5 cm.[b]

Sent 20 November, 253 B.C.,
received 20 November, 253 B.C.

Col. inv. 240[a] + a fragment belonging to the Egyptian Papyrological Society—P. Cairo Fuad (no inventory no.)[b]: **P. Col. Zen. 1 48** and Zaki Aly, *New data from the Zenon papyri, Proceedings of the XIV International Congress of Papyrologists, 1974,* text no. 2, pp. 2-3 and plate 3; *idem, Additional notes on the Zenon papyri of the Egyptian Papyrological Society, Zeitschrift für Papyrologie und Epigraphik* 18 (1975), p. 314.

Professor Zaki Aly described the colour of the Cairo fragment as "light brown", and the photograph published in *Proc. XIV Congr.* shows that it is worn, with many loose fibres. The text of the front of the letter is apparently written along the fibres, and so is the address on the back. The hand is large, and written with a fine pen. Zaki Aly first suggested in *Proc. XIV Congr.* that the Columbia and Cairo fragments might belong to the same letter, and in *ZPE* 18 he announced that a photograph of P. Col. Zen. 1 48 had confirmed his suggestion (see our plate XXV).

The editors of P. Col. Zen. 1 48 pointed out that the torn edge at the bottom of the Columbia fragment ran through the *omega* of Ζήνωνι on the back. From this they concluded (no doubt because the letter was evidently folded and addressed in the usual manner, as, for example, discussed and illustrated by Edgar, P. Mich. Zen., pp. 58-9) that "somewhat more than one half of the sheet" was lost. In fact, unless there was some peculiarity about the folding of this letter, it is possible, and perhaps likely, that as much as roughly 18 cm. is lost from below the Columbia fragment. Zaki Aly does not state what kind of lacuna he assumes after *l.* 8 of the Columbia text. Precise calculation is impossible, but there may well have been room for up to seven lines.

Contents This letter of introduction from Asklepiades asks Zenon to assist Artemidoros, a soldier, in obtaining his land allotment.

front [plate XXV lines 1-8]:

Ἀσκληπιάδης ὁ πρὸς τῆι ἐλα-
ικῆι γενόμενος τῆι κατὰ
Μέμφιν Ζήνωνι χαίρειν.
Ἀρτεμί̣δωρος ὁ ἀποδιδούς σοι
τὴν ἐπιστολήν ἐστιν ἡμῶν
φίλος καὶ πολίτης. Ἀπεσταλ-
μένος δ̣ὲ μετ̣ὰ τῶν λοιπῶν
8 [στρατι]ωτῶ̣ν ἐπὶ τὰ γήιδια
--------- *c.* 7 lines ---------
16 σπουδάσας περ̣ὶ αὐτοῦ
πρὸς το̣ὺ̣ς κατα̣μετροῦντας.
Ἔρρωσ[ο.] L λγ Θῶυ̣θ κ̄ζ̄.

back [plate XXV]:

Ζήνω[νι.]
L λγ Θόυθ κζ. ’Ασκ̣λη-
πιάδης περὶ ’Αρτε̣μι-
δώ̣ρο̣υ.

15 [καλῶς ἂν οὖν ποιήσαις] rest. Zaki Aly, Proc. XIV Congr.

Translation

Asklepiades, formerly connected with the (state) oil(-trade) at Memphis, to Zenon, greetings.

Artemidoros, who gives you this letter, is a friend of ours and a fellow-citizen. He has been sent out with the rest of the soldiers for the plots of land [---]

[---] in taking some trouble on his behalf with those who are measuring out (the land).

Fare well. Year 33, Thoth 27.

Address:

To Zenon.

Docket:

Year 33, Thoth 27. Asklepiades about Artemidoros.

Notes

For other letters of introduction in the archive concerning, or presumed to concern cleruchs travelling to their allotments, see P. Cairo Zen. 2 59.284 (P. Cairo Zen. 2 59.283 is a letter of introduction, probably also concerning a cleruch, from the same writer as 59.284, but apparently not concerned with the taking up of an allotment); P. Lond. 7 1945-6, and 2027 (2026 is a letter of introduction from an Asklepiades who is presumably also the author of 2027, and probably the same man as the author of the present letter: see n. *ll.* 1-3 below. It does not mention a cleruchy. In his introduction, Skeat cites P. Col. Zen. 2 115*h* + P. Mich. Zen. 93 as a close parallel.); P. Mich. Zen. 33 (here the person recommended is the father of the cleruch); and PSI 4 415. P. Cairo Zen. 1 59.132 is a letter of a different kind, consulting Zenon about problems in the measuring out of an allotment.

It is a matter of speculation whether or not all these letters of introduction are to be understood as essentially being written in the hope that Zenon (or, in P. Lond. 7 1946, the Strategus) would use his influence in the actual measuring out of allotments. The present letter, as reconstructed by Zaki Aly, and P. Lond. 7 2027, both presumably written by the same Asklepiades (see *Prosopography*, P. L. Bat. 21. IX, ’Ασκληπιάδης (no. 11); cf. n. *ll.* 1-3 below), are the only ones actually to mention this.

1-3 This designation of Asklepiades as "formerly connected with the (state) oil(-trade) at Memphis" is discussed by the editors of P. Col. Zen. 1 48: they cite UPZ 1 29, 3, and suggest that Asklepiades may have been an official in charge of payments of oil from the state store-house.

It is probable that the Asklepiades in this letter (*Prosopography* P. L. Bat. 21. IX, ’Ασκληπιάδης (no. 4); *Pros. Ptol.* 1 1477 = 5 12558) is to be identified with the author of P. Lond. 7 2026-7 already mentioned (see introductory note). Skeat in his introduction to 2026 is more cautious: "it is possible, though of course not certain".

4 See *Prosopography*, P. L. Bat. 21. IX, ’Αρτεμίδωρος (no. 11). The Artemidoros in the present letter is plainly a στρατιώτης and a cleruch. *Pros. Ptol.* 2 3840 = 4259 = 4 9153 identifies him with the Artemidoros of PSI 6 627, 14 who is a πρεσβύτερος στρατιώτης and a cleruch, and the Artemidoros of P. Cairo Zen. 4 59.726, 6, who is presumably a cleruch. F. Uebel, *Die Kleruchen Ägyptens*, 1968, identifies the present Artemidoros with that in PSI 6 627, 14 as his no. 144, but rejects P. Cairo Zen. 4 59.726, 6, because of the size of the allotment: see his n. 2, p. 73, and his no. 232.

6 As the editors of P. Col. Zen. I 48 point out, both Asklepiades and Artemidoros are probably Carians, although perhaps not from Caunus, as Artemidoros is not specifically stated to be a fellow-citizen of Zenon.

20 The letter was received by Zenon on the same day as it was written. There is nothing impossible in this, but it is very surprising. We do not know where Asklepiades wrote the letter; it cannot, of course, be assumed that he was living at Memphis, where he had held office.

— For the military allotments distributed Nov./Dec. 253, see now *Studia Hellenistica* 24 (1980), pp. 84-89.

T.

68

FRAGMENT OF A LETTER

Dimensions unknown — Date unknown

Egyptian Papyrological Society (no inventory no.): ZAKI ALY, *New data from the Zenon papyri, Proceedings of the XIV International Congress of Papyrologists, 1974*, text no. 3, pp. 3-4 and plate 4; *idem, Additional notes on the Zenon papyri of the Egyptian Papyrological Society, Zeitschrift für Papyrologie und Epigraphik* 18 (1975), p. 314.

The right-hand and bottom edges of this fragment preserve the original cut edges of the piece of papyrus. Although, in its lower half, the left-hand edge also seems quite straight, clearly part of the letter is lost at the left. A portion of the top edge is similarly straight, and no trace seems to survive from any preceding line of text. Zaki Aly's transcription indicates that no lines are lost here. If *l.* 1 is the original first line, the lack of any sign of an address or opening formula suggests that a considerable amount of text may be lost to the left. If the writing ran across the fibres, this suggestion would receive some support, but the direction of the fibres is not known and it cannot be deduced from the photograph. Since the back is not mentioned in the edition, it may be presumed to be blank. This, together with the absence of any trace of a closing formula or docket at the end of what survives or in the bottom margin, may perhaps also suggest that the greater part of the width of the text is lost. Zaki Aly points out that there are traces on the papyrus that perhaps indicate that a former text has been washed away.

Contents Although nothing of the opening or closing formulae is preserved, this text is clearly from its contents a letter (in the widest sense of the word: it might, for example, technically be expressed as an ὑπόμνημα). The names of the sender and recipient are not preserved. Towards the end of the text, the writer seems to have cause to list numbers of pigs with the people to whom they have been, or are to be delivered, in one case specifying that they are for the festival of Isis. The letter may be furnishing an account of some pigs, and so might be written, for example, to Zenon by one of the men who rented pigs from him; but it may equally well be concerned with arrangements for the future delivery of pigs. The preceding parts of the letter cannot be devoted to precisely the same subject, and this must suggest that the document is not simply a report about or account of pigs.

]ντα περὶ δε
]ν̣ ἔ̣γ̣γραφον τὴν ἐπισ-
[τολὴν ---]οτερον ἐνέτυχον
]τομ παρ' ἡμῶν Θεόφιλον
]ην συντετρίφθαι
]η αὐτῶι λόγον εἶναι
]τηι ῑ ἵνα μὴ ἐμοὶ
]. ρ̣χιειον ᾱ Σεμφθεῖ
]. εἰς τὰ Εἰσιεῖα Εὐτυχίδηι γ̄
] τῶν ξ̄ τοκάδων
]α̣ ἔχωμεν φρόντισον

Textum et rest., nisi aliis adscriptae sunt, e Zaki Aly, Proc. XIV Congr. deprompsimus 1 ο]ντα, περὶ δέ Zaki Aly 3 ἐνέτυχον Clarysse, πρ]ότερον ἐνέτυχεν Zaki Aly 4 τόμ Zaki Aly 7 τῆι Zaki Aly 9 Εὐτυχίδηι Zaki Aly ZPE 18 11 [δὲ --- ἵν]α̣ ἔχωμεν φρόντισον. Zaki Aly ZPE 18

Translation

] . . . about . . .
] . . . I was writing this (?) letter
] . . . . . I met
] . . . from us Theophilos
] . . . to have been broken
] . . . his having (?) sense/an account
] . . . 10: so that not [- - -] to me
] . . . . . 1 to Semphtheus
] . . . for the festival of Isis, to Eutuchides, 3
] of the 5 sows
] . . . consider [- - -] we may have

Notes

4 For Theophilos: see *Prosopography*, P. L. Bat. 21. IX, Θεόφιλος.

8] . ρχιειον: no plausible reading has been found. The ε might possibly be read as σ, perhaps hardly as ρ or β. The rest of the text does not suggest that any extreme misspelling can be assumed here.

— For Semphtheus see *Prosopography*, P. L. Bat. 21. IX, Σεμφθεύς.

9 For Eutuchides see *Prosopography*, P. L. Bat. 21. IX, Εὐτυχίδης.

11 [. . . ἵν]α ἔχωμεν φρόντισον does not seem plausible as the close of a sentence, and the passages cited by Zaki Aly do not provide a real parallel. There are several other kinds of restoration possible here. Φρόντισον may or may not be the last word of the body of the letter. If it is not, then it may or may not govern ἔχωμεν. It seems most implausible that we should understand ἵνα ἔχωμεν as the phrase with no object expressed quoted by Zaki Aly from P. Lond. 7 1941, 12, if it is to be taken with φρόντισον.

It is perhaps simplest to take ἔχωμεν with φρόντισον, but not to read ἵνα immediately before ἔχωμεν.

T.

69

FRAGMENT OF A LETTER

H. × W. = 22 × 9.5 cm. Date unknown

Egyptian Papyrological Society (no inventory no.): ZAKI ALY, *New data from the Zenon Papyri, Proceedings of the XIV International Congress of Papyrologists, 1974,* text no. 4, p. 5 and plate 5.

The top and bottom margins of this document survive. At the right-hand edge, the papyrus has been badly damaged at each fold. In some places, a portion of the text is lost, while, in others, the original right-hand edge of the document is preserved. At the left-hand side, part of the text is lost. This edge is fairly straight, but does not follow the vertical fibres. It seems likely that the letter, when rolled up, has been sliced through, no doubt in modern times. The back is blank. A join between two sheets of papyrus can clearly be seen in the published photograph, just above *l.* 1, and there is another join near the bottom of the document. It is therefore apparent that the text is written on the recto surface of the roll, but, as indicated by Zaki Aly, across the fibres. This is not one of the usual ways of arranging a text. The direction of the writing along the height of the roll suggests that the document may have been of a considerable width, and much text may have been lost at the left. This, however, is only a possibility: the piece of papyrus could have been cut to any size desired, and the fact that the writing is not on the verso surface (as would be expected) might even suggest that it is likely that some odd remnant of papyrus had been used. The presence of the end of the date in *l.* 11 does not give any clue as to the original width. The date is frequently written towards the right on letters that are in the wide format: some typical examples in published photographs are P. Cairo Zen. 2 59.241 (plate 17); 59.245 and 59.251 (plate 20); and P. Cairo Zen. 3 59.314 (plate 2).

Contents The text is plainly a letter or report. If not very much is lost at the left-hand side of the text, then the dekatarkhoi are clearly to be understood as the authors. If the loss is substantial, this cannot be assumed to be the case. The text concerns the flight (anachoresis) probably of some of the agricultural workers on Apollonios' estates, although possibly of men engaged on building-works, dekatarkhoi being attested in both contexts within the archive.

]φ̣ι οἱ δεκάτα̣ρ̣[χοι]
ἐν Φι]λ̣αδελφείαι τῶν παρα. . .
τ]υγχάνουσι ἀνακεχωρη-
[κότες - - -]. Καλῶς οὖν ποιήσεις
]. . . τ̣[.].α η.[c. 7]
π]αραχρῆμα καὶ τῷ̣ι̣
]. ας μετ' ἀσφαλείας
ἀρ]γ̣ύριον οὐκ ἀποδιδ̣[ο]ν̣-
[τ - - - ʽΕρ?]ιεὺς Τε⟦σε⟧νοῦ̣φ̣[ιος?]
]. ηλιος.
Πα]χὼνς ῑ.

Textum et rest., nisi aliis adscriptae sunt, e Zaki Aly, *op. cit.*, deprompsimus 2 παρὰ σο̣ῦ̣ Zaki Aly; aut παρατ̣.., fortasse παρὰ τοῦ? 4]ς? 5]τ̣.τ̣[.].α υ̣π[Zaki Aly, η.[Clarysse 9]ρ̣ευς τε⟦ω⟧νος̣ φ̣[Zaki Aly; ʽΕρ]ιεύς Pestman

Translation

] . . . . . the dekatarkhoi
in] Philadelphia of those from . . . (?)
] It happens that they have fled
] . . . So, please
] . . . . [. . . . . . .]
] at once, and . . . . .
] . . . in safety
] not giving money
] Herieus (?) son of Tenouphis (?)
] . . . .
] Pachon 10

Notes

2 If σοῦ is the correct reading, the slightly obscure phrase τῶν παρὰ σοῦ στρατιωτῶν, P. Cairo Zen. 2 59.140, 15-16 (cf. Edgar, P. Mich. Zen., p. 43) might be mentioned. It is perhaps a little difficult to restore τῶν παρὰ σοῦ [ἐπιστολῶν].

8 ἀργύριον suits the context very well. It is disturbing that the υ is here made quite differently from any of the other examples in the text, but to suggest reading ἄγριον might perhaps be fanciful.

9 Ἑριεύς is a virtually certain restoration here, and he has been included in the *Prosopography* P. L. Bat. 21. IX Ἑριεύς (no. 6). Whatever precisely may be the reading of the following signs, if as seems very probable, they represent the name of his father, then he cannot be identified with any of the other Herieus who occur in texts that also mention δεκάταρχοι. See *Prosopography*, Ἑριεύς (no. 2) Ἑριεύς son of Ἑριεύς (himself probably a δεκάταρχος: see PSI 6 675, 2-3); (no. 3) Ἑ. son of Θοτμοῦις (for mention of a δεκάταρχος, see P. Cairo Zen. 4 59.745, 83); and (no. 4) Ἑ. son of Παροίτης etc. (for mention of δεκάταρχοι see P. Cairo Zen. 2 59.294 (see vol. 4, p. 287) *ll.* 5 and 18-19).

— The reading Τε⟦σε⟧νουφ[- suggested here has the advantage that it explains perfectly the shape and position of all the signs, and also accounts for the fact that two letters were written and then cancelled. Τεσενοῦφις is a well-attested masc. name; and Τενοῦφις exists, although perhaps only in P. Mich. 2 123, Recto 4, 29; 5, 6 (1st cent. A.D.)—SB 6 9418, 2, cited by Foraboschi, *Onomasticon*, apparently reads Τετνούφιος. The disadvantage of the reading is that these names are not attested in the archive. Conceivably we should read Τεσενούφ[ιος, taking the σε as blotted rather than cancelled, which would remove the problem of the questionable masc. name Τενοῦφις. The precise readings Τε(σε)νούφ[ιος may not be proven here, but what survives is difficult to understand as anything but an Egyptian name; and, granted this, it is almost certain to be the name of Herieus' father.

T.

70

FRAGMENT OF A LETTER FROM METRODOROS

H. × W. = 18 × 6.5 cm. Received 255/254 B.C.

Egyptian Papyrological Society (no inventory no.): ZAKI ALY, *New data from the Zenon papyri, Proceedings of the XIV International Congress of Papyrologists, 1974,* text no. 5, p. 6 and plate 6.

The original left-hand edge of the letter, and parts of the top and bottom edges are preserved, but the fragment is broken at the right-hand side. The text upon the front is written along the fibres, apparently upon the recto surface. This might suggest that the letter was arranged in a narrow format, and that not a great deal of text is missing at the right-hand side, but this is not certain. The fact that most of the date in the docket on the verso is preserved at any rate does not contradict this suggestion, although it does little to settle the question. Zaki Aly states that the docket on the verso occupies a position corresponding to that of the first line on the recto, and also that the papyrus was folded nine times.

Contents The papyrus is apparently a fragment of a letter from Metrodoros (see *Prosopography,* P. L. Bat. 21. IX, Μητρόδωρος), concerning seed for the sowing of a crop, although no indication of its nature is preserved.

front:

Μητ̣ρ̣[όδωρος ---
απ[
σπερμ[α
σφραγ[ι-
κομι.[
σπαρ[
ως δ.[
του[

back:

9 L λα Ἁθὺρ [

Textum, minimis mutatis, e Zaki Aly, *op. cit.*, deprompsimus 1 Μητ̣ρ[Zaki Aly; aut fortasse Μητ̣[ρ? 5 κομιζ[Zaki Aly 7 ὡς διδ̣[Zaki Aly; fortasse δρ̣[, δο̣[, δε̣[?

T.

71

FRAGMENT

H. × W. = 18 × 9.5 cm. Date unknown

Egyptian Papyrological Society (no inventory no.): ZAKI ALY, *New data from the Zenon papyri*, *Études de Papyrologie* 8 (1957), pp. 148-56, and plate 1 (p. 150); **SB 6 9580**.

The text on the front is written along the fibres. The papyrus is badly damaged at the left-hand side, where the vertical layer of papyrus on the back is mostly stripped away, and the horizontal layer is shredded and partly missing. Damage has also been caused by the horizontal folds, especially towards the top of the piece, and Zaki Aly suggests that the first line of the text has been entirely lost at one of these folds. The original cut edges of the piece are preserved, even at the left-hand side. The back of the papyrus apparently bears faint traces of writing, the nature of which is not clear.

Contents This document concerns a large quantity of wheat (the strikingly round figure of 1000 artabas); part is said to be in some sense in the hands of Khairigenes, and part in the hands of Hermon. The beginning of the text, which would have indicated its nature, is destroyed. In the notes below, it is tentatively suggested that the document relates to a purchase made by Zenon's agents, perhaps ultimately on behalf of Apollonios.

front:

[- - - - - - - - - - - - - - - - - - -]
. . . . . . 'Α ἀρ(τάβας) τῶν̣
π̣υρῶν ὧν τὸ
δ̣ε̣ῖ̣γμά σοι ἐδώκα-
μ̣εν· παρὰ Χαιριγέ-
[ν]ε̣ι̣ χ
π̣α̣ρὰ Ἕρμωνι υ

Textum, minimis mutatis, e Zaki Aly, *op. cit.*, deprompsimus 2 [χι]λ̣ίας 'Α Zaki Aly: v. notam

Translation

[*one line entirely lost*] . . . . 1000 artabas of the wheat, of which we gave you the sample: with Khairigenes, 600; with Hermon, 400.

Notes

1-2 The published photograph does not allow the probability of the reading [χι]λ̣ίας in *l.* 2 to be assessed, but a different reading (e.g. τάς) might suit the context better. From the contents, it does not seem probable that the text would be headed λόγος πυροῦ, "account of wheat". The text may have begun as a letter with a greeting-formula ("N. to N., greetings", *etc.*), and this might still leave room for a verb to be restored in *l.* 2 before 'Α ἀρ(τάβας); however, it is possible that the text had no heading. The resolution of ἀρ(τάβας) in the accusative is not of course certain, but seems very probable.

The text was clearly imparting information about some wheat, with which the recipient of the document was already familiar, at least because he had received a sample of it, if for no other reason. (It is also possible that the verb to be restored in *ll.* 1-2 was in the imperative, and that the document gave instructions rather than information: however, it is likely to be difficult to reconcile any such restoration with the mention of the sample (*ll.* 3-5) or with the contents of *ll.* 5-6, and this possibility is not pursued further here). There are two possible interpretations. Either the figures quoted are the important information—for example, we might translate "of the (kind of) wheat of which we sent you the sample, we have in store, *or* available, *etc.*, the 1000 artabas ...". Or the emphasis is upon the words missing at the beginning—for example, "We have now stored, *or* measured, *or* received, *etc.*, the 1000 artabas ...". Arguments might be brought forward to favour either view, and the question must be left open.

Similarly large quantities of grain feature for example in the long accounts P. Cairo Zen. 2 59.292 and P. Lond. 7 1994 and 1995 (see the editors' introductions), and, occasionally, round figures are involved.

3-5 The "sample" mentioned here might have been given to the recipient of this text as a sample of his own (or his employer's) produce: cf. P. Cairo Zen. 2 59.177, in which Apollonios asks Zenon for samples of various crops which are generally assumed to be crops grown on his own estate—the purpose of the request is not stated. Alternatively, it might have been given as a sample of grain that he was considering whether or not to buy, or possibly had just bought: cf. P. Col. Zen. 1 51; P. Col. Zen. 2 82; and P. Lond. 7 1999, which mention occasions when Zenon's subordinates had sent him samples of crops he intended to buy (perhaps as Apollonios' agent); cf. also P. Cairo Zen. 3 59.522, in which Philinos requests from Zenon samples of crops already purchased.

There is naturally a certain probability that this document was addressed to Zenon, and, if so, the parallels just quoted suggest that it may have been a brief note from a subordinate, reporting the progress made with a purchase of wheat.

It may be noted that the sample is here said to have been "given", not "sent"; it is not clear if this choice of word has any significance.

5-7 The quantities mentioned in *ll.* 6 and 7 are round figures, and might plausibly be taken to represent the cargoes of individual boats. The available evidence suggests that the Khairigenes and Hermon mentioned here were not themselves the captains of boats (see *Prosopography*, P. L. Bat. 21. IX, Χαιριγένης and Ἕρμων). Zaki Aly's conclusion that the Hermon in the present text was an agent employed by Zenon, and the special attention he draws to the Khairigenes of P. Mich. Zen. 87, 11, both seem well justified. The sample mentioned in *l.* 4 of the present text is plainly not the kind of sample regularly sent with shipments of grain (see the material collected by T. Reekmans and E. Van 't Dack, *A Bodleian archive on corn transport, Chronique d'Égypte* 27 (1952), esp. pp. 178-9).

T.

72

FRAGMENT OF A LETTER (?)

Dimensions unknown | Date unknown

Jand. inv. 362: H. G. Gundel, *Verlorene Papyri Jandanae, Aegyptus* 41 (1961), pp. 13-15; **SB 8 9666**.

This papyrus was lost at the end of the Second World War, and in 1961 Gundel published a "rough copy" made by Skeat in 1932 (see the introduction to text no. **35** above). No physical details are available, except that Gundel (p. 15) put forward a reason for supposing that the backs of all the Giessen Zenon papyri that are lost were blank.

Contents The nature of this text is uncertain. Three 1st pers. sing. verb forms occur, and the 2nd pers. sing. pronoun σέ, and it is natural to imagine that some kind of letter is in question. However, the contents remain somewhat puzzling.

ἐλήλυ]θα ἐκ τῆς αὐλῆς καὶ τῆς
] κ̣αὶ ἐλήλυθα εἰς τοὺς το-
κ]α̣τωικοδόμησα εἰς τὴν
]νου ἐνταῦθα πρὸς σὲ
]. ἐκ τούτων διδω-
- -

Notes

1 αὐλῆς: possibly the Royal Court, but equally the court of a temple etc. might be in question.
3 κ]α̣τωικοδόμησα: this is presumably a literal reference to building-works.

T.

73

FRAGMENT OF A DOCUMENT

H. × W. = 11.2 × 9.1 cm. Date unknown

Heid. inv. 1891 (verso): **P. Baden 6 176** verso (see p. 24). (Those who have subsequently discussed the literary recto text do not reprint this documentary text, nor do any of them do more than mention that its presence in the Zenon archive should provide a *terminus ante quem* for the literary hand. See for this text no. **16** above).

The hand of the verso documentary text edited here poses a problem. Some features suggest that it might possibly be of a later date than the Zenon archive. In particular, the writing of the two ξs in *l.* 2, especially the second one, where all three horizontal strokes are lightly ligatured together, seems to have no parallel in the material accessible to us, although it should be pointed out that this provides no infallible criterion, and that the basic form of the letter is precisely paralleled in several texts. The contents of course give no indication to confirm that the text belongs in the archive, but it cannot decisively be rejected.

Contents The phraseology and the hand both suggest that this is a document, and the words κατὰ τὸ διάγραμμα (*l.* 5) may indicate that it is a loan; cf. for example H. Kühnert, *Zum Kreditgeschäft*, 1965, pp. 73-4; and H.-A. Rupprecht, *Untersuchungen zum Darlehen*, 1967, p. 105. However, it might belong to another kind of contract,[1] or to a draft of a petition (cf. P. Col. Zen. 2 83, 16; and P. Mich. Zen. 71, 8). This last possibility seems the most likely, both because no other phrase suggestive of a contract can be recognized, and because two other fragments in this group of Heidelberg material concern petitions: see above nos. **17** and **19** (cf. no. **18**).

[plate XIV]:

] *vac.*? ἐ̣[ν Πτο]λ̣εμαίδι
]α̣ξα[. .] . ρυξαι
]φ. . . . [. . .]σασθαι
] . αιπα[.] . τισιν
]ι̣ κατὰ τὸ διάγραμμα

1 ἐ̣[ν (aut ἐ̣[μ) Πτο]λ̣εμαίδι Clarysse; Π̣[το]λ̣εμαίδι lacunam facile impleret, at haud post spatium expectaremus 2]ο̣ρυξαι? Clarysse 3]φων π̣[? aut]φουτ[? Clarysse 4] . αι πα[κ]τισιν? Clarysse: ι et π haud certae sunt, fortasse] . αριτ??

Transcriptio Gerhardi: ---] [. . .]εμ̣ο̣ι̣ δι |[2] ---]α̣τα κ̣ηρύξαι |[3] ---]ψωφπ̣[. .]σασθαι |[4] ---]λ̣οιπὰ[ἔκ]τισιν |[5] ---]ι κατὰ τὸ διάγραμμα

---

[1] Cf. P. Cairo Zen. 3 59.340, 16, a duplicate contract, lease of goats; P. Cairo Zen. 4 59.668, 5, a contract to cut wood; and P. Col. Zen. 1 54, 13 (cf. *l.* 50), a copy of a contract, lease of land.

Notes

1 Unless a restricted area of the papyrus has been abraded in an improbable fashion, a blank space stood before ἐν Πτολεμαΐδι. As the text shows no sign of being anything but a continuously written text (see the suggestions as to its nature made in the *contents* above), this is surprising. If the text were some kind of draft, this might explain why a space had been left. It is perhaps also conceivable that the five lines of which parts survive formed some kind of lengthy postscript or docket to a text of which no trace is preserved.

The text affords no clue as to which Ptolemais is in question here (see the geographical index, P. L. Bat. 21. XIII), although it is naturally likely to be Ptolemais in the Faiyûm.

5 See the remarks on the *contents* of this text above.

T.

75[1]

FRAGMENTS MENTIONED IN THE COMMENTARY ON OTHER TEXTS

a) Fragment of a letter

Strasb. inv. gr. 2491 *c*. This small fragment was briefly mentioned in the introduction to P. Strasb. 7 561 (see p. 85), where it is described as the upper left-hand corner of a papyrus. The following readings are given:

'Αντίγον[ος ---
χαίρειν [---

b) Fragment of a document

Brit. Mus. (now Brit. Library) inv. 2374 *e*. This fragment was mentioned by Skeat in his introduction to P. Lond. 7 2019, in order to point out the date in *l.* 1.[2] The fragment measures 5.0 cm. in height by 4.4 cm. in width, and is of rather a dark, greyish-brown shade. The text on the front is written along the fibres, but at the left-hand side of the fragment there is a band of vertical fibres visible on the front. This might perhaps be explained in several ways, but it seems likely it is part of the first sheet of a roll, a *protokollon*, the fibres of which run the "wrong" way. There is a margin of about 1 cm. above the text, and a similar margin at the left, consisting, in effect, of the band of vertical fibres. The back surface is blank, and all the fibres run vertically. Plainly the beginning of a column of a document is preserved, although it is impossible to be absolutely certain that it is the beginning of an individual document, rather than, say, the beginning of a column of an account. At any rate, there is every reason to accept that "Year 14" is the actual date of the text: 234-233 B.C.

L ιδ, μην[ός ---
—
ἀπὸ τ[
. . . . \`ου' . . . . [
εθ[
ε[
- -

---

[1] See p. XII note for no. **74**.
[2] We are most grateful for permission to give a longer description here.

c) Fragment of a letter

A Biblioteca Medicea Laurenziana fragment (mounted together with PSI 4 371). It is mentioned in PSI 4 371, n. *l*. 8, and contains the beginnings of 6 lines. The following readings are given:

1 Χοιρείνη Ζ[ήνωνι χαίρειν
3 ἐξαμήνου

d) Fragment of a letter

Presumably a Biblioteca Medicea Laurenziana fragment, although this is not entirely clear. It is mentioned in PSI 4 382, n. *l*. 21. The following readings are given:

front:

Σπονδάτης Ζήνωνι χαίρε[ιν ---
τῶν κεκομμένων δοκῶν .ν̣[---
βαλόμενος παρέσεσ̣θαι οὐκέτ[ι ---

back:

Ζήνωνι.
---] Χοιάκ
Σπονδάτης.

T.

76

DUPLICATE LETTER FROM EUDEMOS AND HERAKLEIDES TO HEGEMON AND ...PHILOS

H. × W. = **A**: 22.5 × 9.7 cm. 27 January 258 B.C.
B: 14.5 × 8 cm.

A: Cairo Museum 59803: **P. Cairo Zen. 5 59.803**. The text is written on the recto along the fibres; there is a kollema 3 cm. from the left-hand side. On the verso there are some blots, but no traces of writing.—**B**: Col. inv. 248: **P. Col. Zen. 2 73**. The text is written along the fibres. There is a spacious margin at the top and smaller ones to the left and at the foot. The address on the back is written upside down near the border.—Both texts are written in the same fluent, cursive hand.

Contents Official letter announcing the dispatch to the Emporion of Alexandria of cloths for wrapping mattresses. The letter was written in duplicate, both copies being written on the same day, probably one for each of the two addressees Hegemon and [...]philos. They were no doubt residing in Alexandria, and it is difficult to see how these letters came into Zenon's files, since he was still in Palestine at that time.

A

front [plate XXVIII]:

[Εὔδημος ὁ παρὰ Δημητ]ρίου τοῦ
[οἰκονόμου καὶ Ἡρα]κλείδης ὁ παρὰ
[Διονυσίου τοῦ ἀντιγρ]ạφ[έω]ς Ἡγή-
μ[ονι . . . . χαίρ]ειν. Κατάγει
ἐγ Νạυκράτẹω[ς εἰς Ἐ]μπ̣όριον Ἡρα-
[κλείδης . . . . τ]ạ̀ παραληφθέν-
τα παρὰ Ἑρμ[ο]δ̣ώ̣ρου τοῦ παρὰ
[Δη]μητ̣ρ[ίου οἰκο]ν[ό]μ̣ου (?) ὥστε εἰς
ἐνειλήματα τῶν στρωμάτων
σ̣ο̣ρ̣ω̣ίων ἱ̣σ̣τ̣(εῖα) θ̣.
Ἔρρωσ̣θẹ. L κζ Χοιὰχ γ̄.

5].ι̣τ̣οριον Edgar, Κλ]ε̣ι̣τ̣όριον Guéraud, Ἐ]μπ̣όριον legimus 7 Ἑρμ...ρου Edgar, Ἑρμ[ο]δ̣ώ̣ρου (?) Guéraud 10 ἱ̣σ̣(τεῖα) ε̣ Edgar 11 Ἔρρωσο Edgar

B

front [plate XXVIII]:

[Εὔ]δημος ὁ παρὰ Δημητρίου τοῦ
[οἰκο]ν̣όμου καὶ Ἡρακλείδης ὁ παρὰ Διο-
[νυσ]ίου τοῦ ἀντιγραφέως Ἡγήμονι
[. . .]φιλωι χαίρẹι̣ν̣. Κατάγει ἐγ Ναυ-

[κρά]τεως εἰ̣ς Ἐμπόριον Ἡρακλείδης
[. . . . . τὰ παρα]ληφθέντα παρὰ
[Ἑρμοδώρου τοῦ πα]ρ̣ὰ̣ Δημητρίου
[οἰκονόμου (?) ὥστε ε]ἰ̣ς ἐνειλήματα
[τῶν στρωμάτων] σ̣ο̣[ρ]ω̣ί̣ων ἱ̣σ̣τ̣(εῖα) θ.
[Ἔρρωσθε. L κ]ζ Χοιὰχ γ̄.

back:

[---] Ἡγήμονι.

4 [τῶι] φίλωι ed. princ. 4-5 κ̣α̣τάγει σὺν αὐ|[τῶι] Τεῶς ed. princ 5 Ἡρακλείδην ed. princ. 10 L λ]ζ ed. princ.; Χοιὰχ ϛ̄ ed. princ.

Translation

Eudemos, the agent of Demetrios the oikonomos, and Herakleides, the agent of Dionusios the antigrapheus, to Hegemon and . . . philos greetings.

Herakleides --- has brought down from Naukratis to the Emporion the 9 webs of soroia-cloth for the wrapping of mattresses that he received from Hermodoros, the agent of Demetrios [the oikonomos?].

Fare well, year 27, Choiach 3.

Notes

3-4 Ἡγήμονι [. . .]φιλωι (B): the editors supplied [τῶι] φίλωι. This is, however, most unlikely, both letters being part of an administrative correspondence in which the writers identify themselves by their function (this is unusual in Greek epistolography, even in official letters). There are some traces at this point also in the Cairo papyrus (A) but they do not correspond to the reading . . . φιλωι. We cannot explain this difficulty.

When one letter had to be sent to two persons, there were several possibilities.

Most obviously, when the two persons were in easy reach of each other, one copy was addressed to both of them together, e.g.:

PSI 4 390: letter from Theukles to Zenon and Herakleitos
PSI 4 410: letter from Keleesis to Zenon and Sostratos
PSI 6 594: letter from Nikanor to Zenon and Kriton.

When this was not the case, two letters with identical wording were dispatched separately.

— most commonly not only the address but also the greeting formula was different for each of them, e.g.:

PSI 4 324 (letter from Apollonios to Apollodotos) and *325* (identical letter from Apollonios to Hikesios).

P. Lond. 7 1945 (letter from Hierokles to Zenon, the address on the back wrongly gives "to Nikanor") and *1946* (letter from Hierokles to Nikanor, the address on the back wrongly gives "to Zenon").

— in some cases the greeting formulae were the same for both recipients, only the addresses being different. This was the way in which official ἐντολαί were distributed. In the Zenon archive we find this in *PSI 5 524*, a letter from Sostratos to Zenon and Xenophon: only the copy addressed to Xenophon survives.

In our opinion the latter method was also applied here: text no. **76 B** was the copy addressed to Hegemon, as is clear from the address on the back; **76 A** was no doubt similarly addressed to [. . .]philos (e.g. Theophilos, Pamphilos).

4-5 ἐγ Ναυκράτεως: this reading is made certain both by examination of the photograph of the Columbia papyrus (B), where the editors wrongly read σὺν αὐ[τῶι] Τεῶς [1] and by the separate fragment of the Cairo papyrus (A) which was correctly located by Guéraud.

5 There can be no doubt that the Ἐμπόριον mentioned here and in text no. **25**, 3 (see the commentary on this passage) is the great Emporion at Alexandria, as was already seen by Edgar (*Archiv* 11, 1935, p. 218). In both cases Hegemon is involved; this confirms Edgar's view that he was in charge of some warehouses at the docks.

5-6 Herakleides: no doubt a ship-captain. It is tempting to identify him with the kubernetes who transports goods between Palestine and Alexandria in May-June 259 and in September 258. After the early period he completely disappears from sight. See our *Prosopography*, (P. L. Bat. 21, IX) Herakleides no. 10.

8 It is very tempting to supply οἰκο]ν[ό]μ̣ου in A and to regard Hermodoros as a colleague of Eudemos. The supplement is, however, not assured, and one would expect that in that case Hermodoros would have written these letters himself.

10 σ̣ο̣ρ̣ωίων (A): according to the editors O. Guéraud and P. Jouguet the reading is very probable (comp. B, 9). The word occurs here for the second time. The editors of P. Hib. 1 67 and 68, where it is mentioned several times among cloths of various kinds, doubtfully connected it with σορός, translating "cloth used for burials". This meaning is however most unlikely in our text where the σορώια are used for the wrapping of mattresses. Probably the word is Egyptian.[2]

11 ἔρρωσ̣θ̣ε̣ (A): Edgar read ἔρρωσο but the papyrus clearly has the plural, as in other letters with more than one addressee e.g. PSI 4 410 and 5 524 (but ἔρρωσο in PSI 4 390).

— date (A; comp. B, 10): 27th of January 258.

The fragmentary state of both copies has led the editors astray. P. Cairo 5 59.803 (A) has preserved the date, but not the name of the addressee. Supposing that this was Zenon, Edgar commented: "If Zenon was really the addressee, we have here an indication that he was in Egypt, presumably in Alexandria, about the beginning of 258 B.C." This has been refuted by T. C. Skeat (P. Lond. 7 1931, introduction) and the argument has become worthless now, since we know that Zenon is not the addressee.[3]

On the other hand the editors of P. Col. Zen. 2 73 (B) supplied in *l.* 10 [(ἔτους) λ]ζ instead of [(ἔτους) κ]ζ, although they were aware that Hegemon is mainly known in the earlier period.

C.

---

[1] The reference to Teôs as a ship captain in Pros. Ptol. V 13969 must be deleted.

[2] Cfr. already H. Frisk, *Griechisches etymologisches Wörterbuch*, 1960, p. 754, s.v. σορός: "σορώϊον n. 'Mumienleinwand'. (Pap. III[a]; nach μνώϊον (*l.* μώϊον) ägypt. Bez. eines Behälters?)".

[3] For the dating of Zenon's return from Palestine to Egypt, see now text no. **32** and commentary.

III

SUPPLEMENT: RELATED TEXTS

EDITED BY

W. CLARYSSE, P. W. PESTMAN

A

PROGETTO DI DIGHE E CANALI PER LA DOREA DI APOLLONIOS

PREVENTIVO DELLE SPESE

A. × L. = 31 × 16 cm.

Progetto Nov./Dic. 259,
poscritto 1-5 Gennaio 258

Sorb. inv. 1: **P. Lille 1**, edito da P. Jouguet et J. Lesquier nel primo fascicolo (1907) p. 13-23 e corretto nel quarto fascicolo (1928) p. 265; tav. I-II. Cf. U. Wilcken, *Archiv für Papyrusforschung* 5 (1913) 218-221; BL 1 p. 199-200.

Il papiro è stato estratto da un cartone di mummie trovato nella necropoli di Ghorân. Il documento è in buon stato, la scrittura pure, salvo qualche parola sbiadita. Porta un disegno del latifondo di Apollonios con la leggenda in due lingue, e poi una serie di concisi appunti, pieni di correzioni e assai difficili da tradurre.

Contenuto Il documento è un memorandum che Stothoetis ha redatto per se stesso. La prima parte contiene il progetto del lavoro; Stothoetis vi elenca quante dighe propone di costruire — e dove — e quanto verranno a costare ad Apollonios. La seconda parte, aggiunta come poscritto, ricorda che Apollonios ha ben approvato la disposizione delle dighe ma ha deciso di farle meno massicce, quindi a un prezzo inferiore. In tutto Apollonios spenderà 8.600 dracme, ma quest'ammontare è basato su una valutazione assai sommaria della quantità di naubia da scavare (v. le incertezze a questo proposito § *f* e *g*). Per precisare questa valutazione Stothoetis ha bisogno, tra l'altro, di «scribi» e finisce il suo memorandum colla notizia sul viaggio che ha fatto per andare a cercarli.

Il terreno di cui si tratta misura 10.000 arure (*l.* 4) e appartiene ad Apollonios (§ *h*, comm.) — chiaramente solo da poco tempo — ed è situato nel Fayum, probabilmente nella Meris Herakleidou (§ *i*, comm.). Visto che Apollonios aveva nel Fayum soltanto una dorea (cf. ad es. Suppl. doc. **C**, 9) sono sicuro che il nostro documento concerne questa nota dorea di Apollonios vicino a Philadelphia.

Commentario

(a) *Intestazione*

Il progetto è stato fatto da Stothoetis in Novembre/Dicembre 259 per Apollonios e controllato (?) da Diodoros.

1 Stothoetis, che non si ritrova nell'archivio, ha scritto il testo greco e le parole demotiche (§ *b*).

— αν..γραφ: ed. princ. ἀντιγραφ(εύς).

— κα̣ὶ̣ Αἰ[γ]υπτίω̣ν̣ δέ: cf. P. Lille p. 265.

2 ο̣ἰκο̣νο̣μοῦντος .[.]νω̣νο̣ς: letto da Clarysse sull'originale; il nome dell'oikonomos potrebbe leggersi Ζ̣[ή]νω̣νο̣ς (in questo caso però è poco probabile che questo Zenon sia il nostro Zenon, che era in Palestina).

3 Diodoros: v. doc. **1**, introduzione.

(b) *Disegno*

Le linee semplici indicano le dighe ed i canali normali, le linee doppie i quattro acquedotti. A giudicare dalla direzione della scrittura greca e demotica, la carta è orientata verso Ovest per i Greci e verso Sud per gli Egizi.

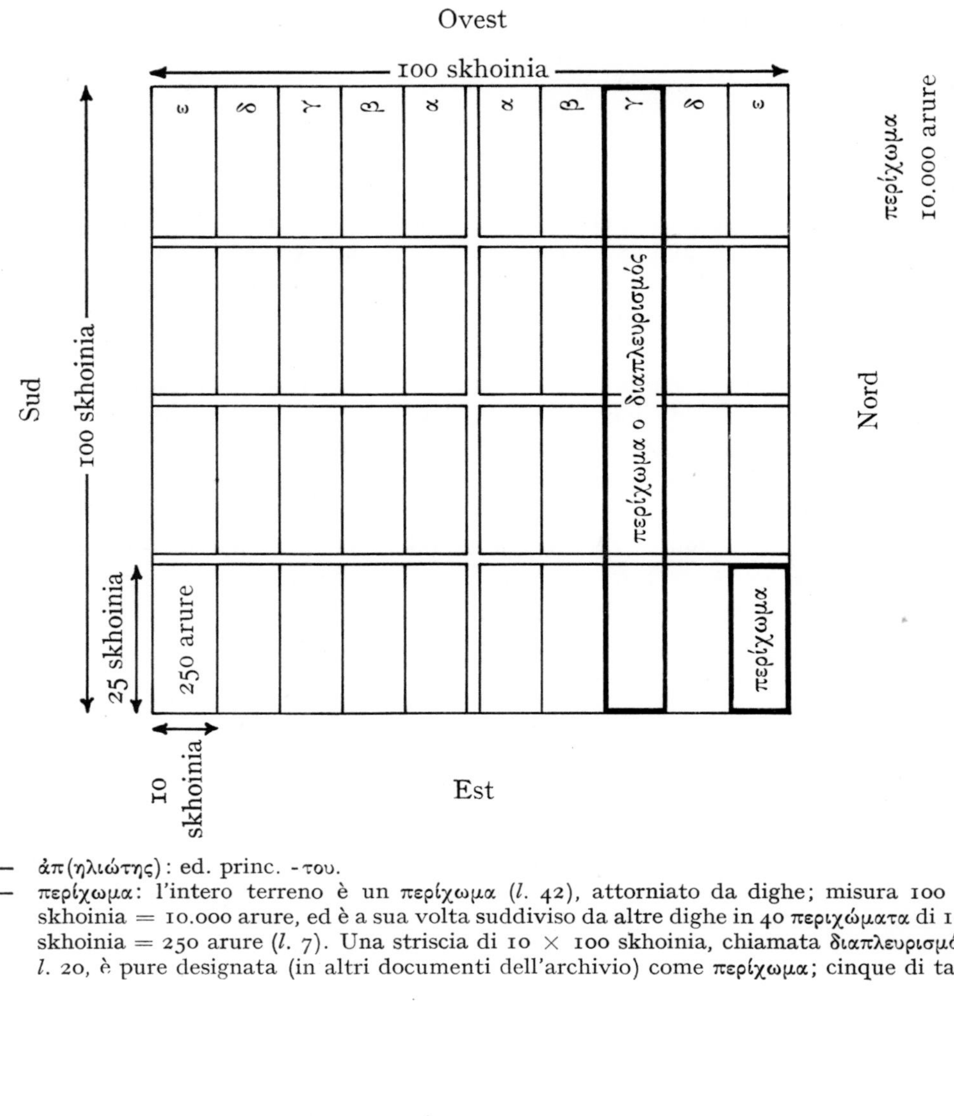

— ἀπ(ηλιώτης): ed. princ. -του.

— περίχωμα: l'intero terreno è un περίχωμα (*l.* 42), attorniato da dighe; misura 100 × 100 skhoinia = 10.000 arure, ed è a sua volta suddiviso da altre dighe in 40 περιχώματα di 10 × 25 skhoinia = 250 arure (*l.* 7). Una striscia di 10 × 100 skhoinia, chiamata διαπλευρισμός nella *l.* 20, è pure designata (in altri documenti dell'archivio) come περίχωμα; cinque di tali περι-

Testo

facciata anteriore [tavola XXIX]:

(a)

Σ̣τ̣οθοῆτ(ις) αν..γραφ Ἀ̣π̣ο̣λ̣λ̣ωνίωι. L κζ κ̣α̣ὶ̣ Αἰ[γ]υπτίω̣ν̣ δὲ
τὸ αὐτὸ μηνὸς Φαῶφι .. ο̣ἰκ̣ο̣ν̣ο̣μοῦντος .[.]νω̣ν̣ο̣ς
ἀντιγραφομένου Διοδώρου.

(b)

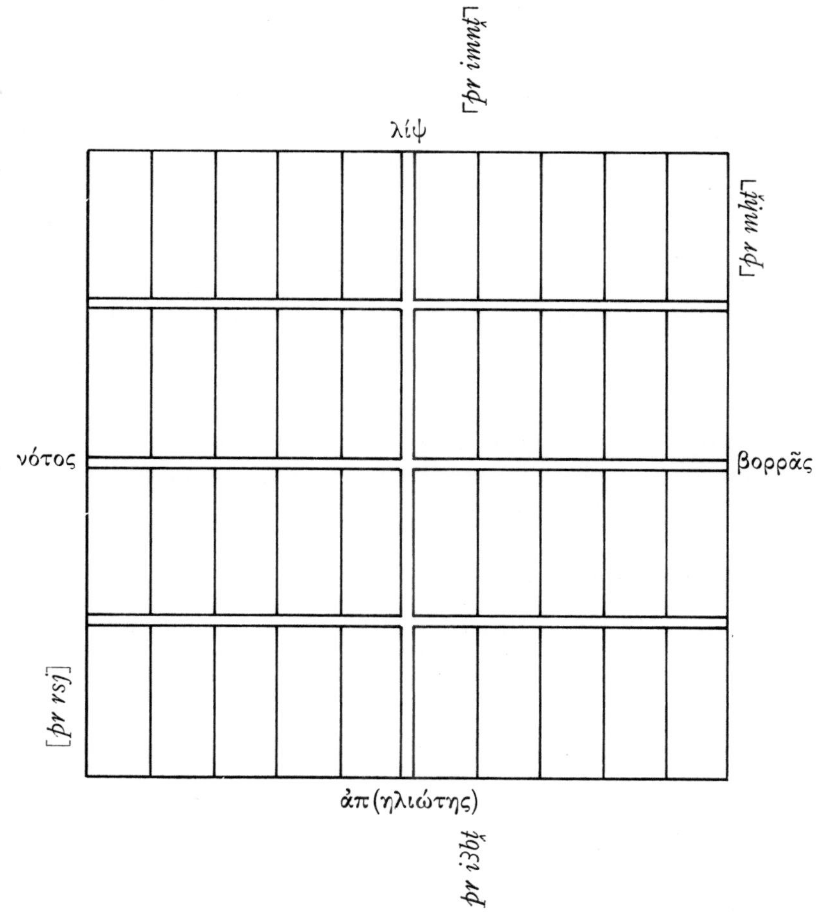

Commentario

χώματα si trovano a Nord (Skeat, P. Lond. 7 p. 256 n. *l.* 3) e altri cinque a Sud (P. Wisc. 2 77) della doppia linea centrale; erano numerati da α a ε (probabilmente nella maniera indicata nel disegno p. 254): v. ad esempio P. Cairo Zen. 4 59.745, 62 che tratta di un campo situato ἐν τῶι γ̄ περιχώματι τῶι πρὸς βορρᾶν (è il περίχωμα indicato nel disegno qui p. 254).

(c) *Dighe*

Sono progettate 16 dighe (o piuttosto paia di dighe con un canale in mezzo) di una lunghezza totale di 1.600 skhoinia = 84 km.

4 Il terreno è un quadrato attorniato da 4 (δ) dighe; il perimetro è 400 (υ) skhoinia.

5 ἀπέχον`τα': *l.* ἀπέχοντες.

— Da Sud a Nord sono progettate 3 (γ) dighe ad una distanza tra di loro di 25 (κε) skhoinia.

6 διαπλευρισμός «cross-dyke» (Liddell-Scott-Jones, s.v.), altrove nel testo semplicemente chiamato χῶμα; sono progettate nove (θ) di queste dighe. Nella *l.* 20 διαπλευρισμός indica probabilmente l'intera striscia di terreno che si trova tra due di queste dighe trasversali.

7 Stothoetis aveva scritto primo ὥστε εἶναι τὰ πάντα χώματα ις | ἀνὰ σχοι(νία) ρ, «cosicché ci saranno in tutto 16 dighe ...» Più tardi vi ha inserito il periodo sulle divisioni: le 10.000 ($\overset{\alpha}{M}$) arure saranno divise in 40 (μ) περιχώματα di 250 (σν) arure, larghi 25 (κε) per 10 (ι) skhoinia di profondità.

Per fare questo inserimento ha cancellato le parole ὥστε εἶναι τὰ πάντα χώματα, cancellando però, per isbaglio, le prime due parole ὥστε εἶναι. È possibile che abbia voluto rimediare a questo sbaglio poiché ha fatto iniziare l'inserimento solo sopra le parole susseguenti.

8 Ogni diga misura 100 (ρ) skhoinia, tutte messe insieme quindi 1.600 (͵Αχ).

(d) *Terra da scavare*

Per le 16 dighe bisogna ricavare 137.000 naubia di terra, e per gli acquedotti altri 34.400, cioè in tutto 172.000 naubia.

9 Il fosso progettato (accanto alle dighe) è largo 4 (δ) cubiti, profondo 2 (β) — e naturalmente (v. *l.* 10) lungo 1.600 skhoinia.

— ὅ: sta per διό o per ἐπεί (BL 1 p. 199), ma è anche possibile considerarlo come un tentativo di rendere in greco una proposizione relativa demotica col pronome relativo *ntj*; v. F. Daumas, *Les moyens d'expression du Grec et l'Égyptien* (1952) 72 sqq.

10-11 Da un tratto di 100 skhoinia del fosso, dalle dimensioni progettate, si ricavano 86 (πϛ) naubia di terra, e da 1.600 (͵Αχ) skhoinia quindi 13 × 10.000 ($\overset{\iota\gamma}{M}$) + 7.600 (͵Ζχ) = 137.000 naubia.

11-12 ⟦εἰς ṿ ṭῶṿ δ̣ ├̣⟧ | ⟦/ Τ̣̄ α̣ ├̣ Ἐ̣η⟧: al prezzo di 4 dracme per 50 naubia, cioè 1 talento e 5.008 dracme; le ultime parole della *l.* 11 sono state lavate e le prime della *l.* 12 cancellate: del prezzo si parlerà più a lungo nel § *e* (v. *l.* 25).

12 ὑδραγωγός: acquedotto, canale d'irrigazione.

13 Degli 8 acquedotti necessari, 4 (δ) ce n'erano già, cosicché solamente 4 sono ancora da scavare, lunghi 100 (ρ) skhoinia ciascuno, cioè in quattro 400 (υ) skhoinia. Un acquedotto ha le stesse dimensioni del fosso (*l.* 9), perché da un tratto di 100 skhoinia si ricavano ugualmente 86 (πϛ) naubia di terra. I 400 skhoinia rendono 400 × 86 = 30.000 ($\overset{\gamma}{M}$) + 4.400 (͵Δυ) = 34.400 naubia.

In tutto ci sono da scavare 137.000 (*l.* 10) e 34.400 naubia = 17 × 10.000 ($\overset{\iota\zeta}{M}$) + 2.000 (͵Β) naubia = 172.000.

(e) *Spese*

Secondo il progetto, Apollonios dovrà pagare 1 dracma all'arura se si riesce a finire il lavoro prima del raccolto in Giugno, e 1 dracma e 2¼ oboli in caso contrario.

15 εἰς ο τοῦ στατῆρος: 70 (naubia) costano uno stater (= 4 dracme) ed i 172.000 naubia 1 talento (Τ̄ α) + 3.834 dracme (├ ͵Γωλδ) = 9.834 dracme (in realtà costano 9.828 dracme e 3½ oboli). Per ciascuna delle 10.000 arure le spese sono fissate ad una dracma (├ α).

— Alla fine della linea tracce di c. 5 lettere: βλ̣ά̣β̣ο̣ς (ed. princ.), χαλκοῦ (P. Lille p. 265); subito sotto tracce di 3 lettere: δ̣ụọ (P. Lille p. 265), o forse διο, cioè Διό(δωρος), la firma di Diodoros (*l.* 3)?

Testo

(c)

Ἔστιν ἡ περίμετρος τῶν μυρίων ἀρουρῶν σχοινία υ, χώματα δὲ δ, καὶ ἐν μέσωι `ἀπὸ νότου εἰς βορρᾶν' χώματα γ ἀπέχον`τα' ἀπ' ἀλλήλων σχοινία κε, καὶ ἄλλοι διαπλευρισμοὶ ἀπὸ ἀπηλιώτου εἰς λίβα `θ', ἀπέχον(τες) ἀπ' ἀλλήλων σχοινία δέκα ⟦ὥστε εἶναι⟧ <ὥστε εἶναι> ⟦τὰ πάντα χώματα⟧ `ἐν ταῖς $\overset{\alpha}{\mathrm{M}}$ ἀρούραις περιχώματα μ ἀν(ὰ) ἀρού(ρας) σν, ὧν ἡ μέτρησις κε ἐπὶ ι, ὡς διαγέγραπται ἐν τῶι πλινθείωι / χώματα' ις ἀνὰ σχοι(νία) ρ / Ἀχ, ὧν δεῖ τὴν ἀνασκαφὴν γενέσθαι.

(d)

Πλάτος μὲν τοῦ ὀρύγματος πήχεις δ, βάθος δὲ β, ὃ ὑποτιθέμεθα ἐκ τοσούτου ἂν ὀρύγματος γενέσθαι τὰ ὑποκείμενα μέτρα τῶν χωμάτων· γίνεται οὖν εἰς τὸ σχοινίον ναύβια πς, εἰς δὲ τὰ Ἀχ ναυβίων $\overset{\iota\gamma}{\mathrm{M}}$ Ζ̓χ ⟦εἰς γ̣ τ̣ῶ̣ν̣ δ̣ ├̣⟧ ⟦/̣ ⊼̣ α̣ ├̣ Ἐ̣η⟧· καὶ ὑδραγωγῶν δ' ὧν δεῖ γενέσθαι πρὸς ταῖς ὑπαρχούσαις δ ἄλλας δ, ἀνὰ σχοινία ρ / σχοινία υ ἀν(ὰ) πς / ναύβια $\overset{\gamma}{\mathrm{M}}$ Δ̓ υ / $\overset{\iota\zeta}{\mathrm{M}}$ Β̓.

(e)

Ἐὰν μὲν κατὰ χειμῶνα συντελῆται τὰ ἔργα, τίθεμεν ἔσεσθαι εἰς ο τοῦ στατῆρος, ὥστε εἶναι ⊼ α ├ Γ̓ωλδ· ἐπιβάλλει τῆι ἀρού(ραι) ├ α . . . . .

. . .

Commentario

16-23 L'arco in margine indica che queste linee sono state cancellate; concernano l'oggetto che viene trattato nel § *f*. Per la traduzione v. p. 260 n. 1.

24 il secondo συντελῆται: *l.* συντελεῖται (ed. princ.).

25 Se il lavoro dura più a lungo, costerà di più: 50 (ν) naubia per uno stater, cioè in tutto 2 talenti ($\overline{\Lambda}$ β) + 1.760 dracme (⊢ Ἀψξ) = 13.760 dracme.

— ἀν(ὰ) α = 2— (P. Lille p. 265): 1 dracma e 2¼ oboli all'arura.

(f) *Spese per dighe e canali nei terreni bassi*

Le dighe di terreni in pendenza devono essere più alte per arrivare al livello delle dighe adiacenti: le spese in più verranno compensate da altre spese meno gravi.

27 τῆς μισθώσεως, cf. pure τοῖς γεωργοῖς (*l.* 32): l'ammontare delle spese che Apollonios deve pagare ai contadini per ogni arura è un ammontare medio, che può essere più alto o più basso secondo il caso: l'ammontare vero delle spese sarà fissato nei contratti individuali.

29 ἀρ(τάβας): *l.* ἀρούρας; alcuni terreni in pendenza si trovano in un bacino e formano un insieme di 1.000 arure senza dighe interne.

— περιχῶσαι (Skeat, P. Lond. 7 1955, 4 n.); περιχωσ<θῆν> αι (ed. princ.).

30 ἀνάλωμα, ma *l.* 19, 22 e 36 ἀνή-.

(g) *Spese per dighe e canali già esistenti*

Alcuni canali e dighe si trovano già nel terreno. Di questi bisogna usufruirne il più possibile affinché le spese siano più leggere per Apollonios che però dovrà pagare le spese per le solite riparazioni annuali.

33 ἀκολουθήσουσι: si deve cambiare il corso progettato delle nuove dighe per poter incorporare le dighe già esistenti.

35 Oppure ἐάν <τις> κατὰ φύσιν: ed. princ.

39-40 ἀρχιτεκτόνων «ingenieri» (cf. Kleon, Suppl. doc. **B** e **C**), βασιλικῶν γραμματέων «funzionari statali» (doc. **12** nota *e*): i primi devono stabilire quali siano le riparazioni da farsi, i secondi devono fare i calcoli e redigere un processo verbale.

41 Per la lettura della frase, v. P. Lille p. 265.

(h) *Decisione di Apollonios a proposito del progetto*

Alla fine della *l.* 41, dopo uno spazio bianco, inizia il poscritto colle parole ὕστερον δὲ ...

42 περίχωμα: l'intero terreno.

— συνέκρινεν: il soggetto dev'essere Apollonios, v. il principio del § *i*.

43 . . του . : P. Lille p. 265 αὐτοῦ.

— ναυβί(ων): *l.* πηχῶν (Wilcken, BL 1 p. 200).

— γ ἀν(τὶ) δ: P. Lille p. 265. Apollonios decide di far eseguire il progetto come proposto, fatta eccezione della larghezza dei canali che stabilisce di 3 invece di 4 cubiti; da uno skhoinion si ricaverà quindi 64½ (ξδ ∠) naubia.

44 εἰς ξ τῶν δ ⊢: il lavoro sarà effettuato al prezzo di 4 dracme (uno stater) per 60 naubia.

(i) *Ricerca degli scribi per iniziare il lavoro*

Apollonios e Stothoetis partano insieme il 7 Hathyr (1° Gennaio 258), ma poco dopo si separano. Stothoetis viaggia verso Sud (per cercare gli scribi) e quindi Apollonios, probabilmente, verso Ovest (visto che prosegue il viaggio in barca).

46 Σύρων κώμην: nella Meris Herakleidou (*Studia Hellenistica* 9, 1953, 69).

47 Λαβύρινθον: presso Hawara; ed. princ. -υνθον.

— τοὺς γραμματέας: saranno i funzionari statali menzionati *l.* 39-40. Sono necessari non solo per il lavoro indicato nel § *g*, ma probabilmente anche per fissare i dettagli dell'intero piano di lavoro; tanto vale per gli architetti, che non sono menzionati, forse perché già sul posto.

48 ἐπιστολήν: la lettera nella quale Apollonios ordina agli scribi di recarsi a Philadelphia e di eseguire là i lavori necessari.

— ἀπήλθομεν: Stothoetis e gli scribi.

Testo

facciata posteriore:

χωρὶς τῶν καταφερῶν πεδίων, ὧν δεῖ προσθεῖναι τὰ πλείω ἔργα τῶν χωμάτων, ἐπειδὴ συνεχῆ τὰ χώματα δεῖ γενέσθαι. Ταῦτ̣α μὲν οὖν ἐπὶ τῆς μισθώσεως ἐπισημανούμεθα τά τε πλήθ̣η̣ [τ]ῆς γῆς καὶ τὸ ἀνήλωμα τὸ πλείω ἐσόμενον. Τῶν δὲ προϋπαρχόντων χωμάτων ἐν τοῖς διαπλευρισμοῖς τούτοις, ὅσα ἂν ἐνπίπτηι χρηστ̣ὰ̣ ὄντα πρὸς τὴν ὑποκείμενην θέσιν τῶν χωμάτων, ὑπολογηθήσεται τοῖς μισθουμένοις εἰς τὸ ὑποκείμενον ἀνήλωμα· ὡσαύτως δὲ καὶ ἐάν τινες διώρυγες συνάπτωσιν τοῖς χώμασιν κατὰ ταὐτά.

Ἐὰν δὲ μὴ πρὸ τοῦ θερισμοῦ συντελῆται, συντελῆται εἰς τὸ ὑποκείμενον εἰς ν / ⊼ β ⊢ Ἀψξ / ἀν(ὰ) α = 2—.

(f)

Καὶ τῶν καταφερῶν τόπων δεήσει προσθεῖναι τὴν διαφορὰν τῶν σύνεγγυς χωμάτων· τοῦτο δὲ ἔσται ἐπὶ τῆς μισθώσεως, ἐπειδὰν εἰδήσωμεν τὰ πλήθη τῆς γῆς 'καὶ τὰ μήκη τῶν σχ̣οινίων' τῶν ἐν τοῖς χωρίοις τούτοις· ἔσονται δέ τινες τόποι τοιοῦτοι καὶ κοῖλοι ὥστε ἀν(ὰ) Ἀ ἀρ(τάβας) (*sic*) περιχῶσαι ὑπ' αὐτῆς τῆς ἀνάγκης τοῦ τόπου, εἰς ὃ ἔσται βραχὺ τὸ ἀνάλωμα, ὥστε ἀντ' ἐκείνου τοῦ πλεονάζοντος ἔργου ὧδε κομίζεσθαι.

(g)

Τῶν δὲ προϋπαρχόντων χωμάτων, ὅσα ἂν ἐνπίπτηι τοῖς γεωργοῖς, ὑπολογηθήσεται εἰς τὸ γινόμενον αὐτοῖς· ἀκολουθήσουσι δὲ τοῖς προϋπάρχουσι χώμασι, ὅπως ἂν μηθὲν αὐτῶν ἀχρεῖον ἦι· ὡσαύτως δὲ καὶ τῶν διωρύγων τῶν ἐνπιπτόντων εἰς τὰς περιχώσεις, ἐὰν κατὰ φύσιν τῶν χωμάτων κειμένη ἦι. Περὶ δ̣ὲ̣ τῶν ἀνηλ̣ωμάτων εἰς τὰς προϋπαρχούσας διώρυγας καὶ χωμάτων τῶν ἐν ἔθει ὄντων κατασκευάζεσθαι κατ' ἐνιαυτὸν δεήσει ἐπελθόντας ἐπισκέψασθαι μετὰ τῶν ἀρχιτεκτόνων καὶ τῶν βασιλικῶν γραμματέων καὶ ἀναγράψαντας δοῦναι· τὰ μὲν γὰρ αὐτῶν ἔστιν πρατα αποτακτ . . . . εθει ναυβίων λόγον.

(h)

Ὕστερον δὲ ἐπισκοπούμενος τὸ περίχωμα συνέκρινεν τὰ χώματα ποῆσαι . . του. πλάτος τοῦ ὀρύγματος ναυβί(ων) (*sic*) γ ἀν(τὶ) δ / εἰς τὸ σχοινίον ξδ ∠, εἰς ξ τῶν δ ⊢.

(i)

Ἀπεδήμησεν Ἀπολλώνιος Ἀθὺρ ζ, καὶ συνέπλευσα αὐτῶι ἕως Φυλακῆς κἀκεῖ ἐξέβην, τῆι δὲ η ἦλθον εἰς Τοῦφιν, τῆι θ̅ εἰς Σύρων κώμην, ι̅ εἰς Πτολεμαΐδα, ι̅α̅ εἰς τὸν Λαβύρινθον, καὶ ἐκεῖ εὗρον τοὺς γραμματέας καὶ ἐκομίσαντο τὴν ἐπιστολὴν καὶ ἀπήλθομεν εἰς πόλιν.

Traduzione

Progetto

(a) *Intestazione* (*l.* 1-3)

Stothoetis ... per Apollonios. L'anno 27 — e degli Egiziani lo stesso (anno) — il .. del mese Phaophi; .... mentre Diodoros contrassegna.

(b) *Disegno* [*ved.* p. 254]

(c) *Dighe* (*l.* 4-8)

Il perimetro delle 10.000 arure è 400 skhoinia, 4 dighe; e nell'interno (ci saranno) da Sud a Nord 3 dighe — distanti, l'una dall'altra, 25 skhoinia — e da Est ad Ovest 9 altre dighe trasversali — distanti, l'una dall'altra, 10 skhoinia —

cosicché ci saranno nel (latifondo di) 10.000 arure, 40 περιχώματα di 250 arure ciascuno e di una dimensione di 25 per 10 (skhoinia), come è disegnato nel quadrato [*ved.* § *b*];

in totale 16 dighe di 100 skhoinia caduna, cioè 1600 (skhoinia) per i quali bisogna fare lo scavamento.

(d) *Terra da scavare* (*l.* 8-13)

La larghezza del fosso (sarà) 4 cubiti, la profondità 2: supponiamo che da tale fosso si possa ricavare (la terra per) le dighe delle dimensioni progettate. Così si otterrà 86 naubia per uno skhoinion, cioè 137.600 naubia per le 1600 skhoinia;

e, quanto agli acquedotti, di cui si devono ancora costruire 4 — da aggiungere ai 4 già esistenti — di 100 skhoinia ciascuno, ossia 400 skhoinia, di 86 (naubia) ciascuno, cioè 34.400 naubia;

totale 172.000 (naubia).

(e) *Spese* (*l.* 14-15 e 24-25) [1]

Se i lavori vengono finiti durante l'inverno, supponiamo che le spese saranno: uno stater per 70 (naubia), cosicché saranno (in tutto) 1 talento e 3834 dracme. Per ogni arura si dà (quindi) una dracma ...

Se invece i lavori non vengono finiti prima del raccolto, saranno portati a termine per l'ammontare proposto (di uno stater) per 50 (naubia), cioè (in tutto) 2 talenti e 1760 dracme, cioè per (ogni arura) 1 dracma e $2\frac{1}{4}$ oboli.

(f) *Spese per dighe e canali nei terreni bassi* (*l.* 25-31)

E, quanto ai terreni in pendenza, sarà necessario aggiungere (nel calcolare le spese) la differenza d'altezza con le dighe adiacenti. Questo si farà allorché daremo (i terreni) in affitto, quando si saprà la larghezza della terra e la lunghezza degli skhoinia in quei posti.

---

[1] Le linee 16-23 sono state cancellate da Stothoetis e sostituite dalle linee 25-28 (§ *f*) e 31-36 (§ *g*): «Colla eccezione dei campi (πεδίων, *l.* 26 τόπων) in pendenza, a proposito dei quali bisogna aggiungere i lavori in più per le dighe, perché è necessario che (tutte) le dighe diventino della stessa altezza. Questo in più lo noteremo allorché daremo (i terreni) in affitto, cioè la quantità di terra (da scavare) e le spese che ci saranno in più».
«(Le spese) per le dighe già esistenti in quei διαπλευρισμοί (v. linea 6, nota), per quanto risultino utilizzabili per la progettata costruzione delle dighe, saranno dedotte per gli appaltatori dalle spese proposte (cioè dal denaro che loro spetta, v. *l.* 32-33)».
«E così pure, se vi sono dei canali che si uniscono alle dighe, nella stessa maniera».

Alcuni di tali posti però si troveranno inoltre in una depressione, cosicché si circonda in una volta sola 1.000 arure, per via della disposizione naturale del posto, e perciò le spese saranno leggere, cosicché (queste ultime) compenseranno in questo modo quel lavoro che ci sarà in più.

(g) *Spese per dighe e canali già esistenti* (*l.* 31-41)

(Le spese), per le dighe già esistenti che risultino (utili) ai contadini, saranno dedotte dal (denaro) che loro spetta: adatteranno le dighe già esistenti, affinché nessuna di queste rimanga inusata.

E nella stessa maniera, anche a riguardo dei canali che si trovano vicino ai recinti, almeno quando (il canale) si trova in una posizione che asseconda le dighe (progettate).

Per quanto riguarda le spese per i canali e le dighe già esistenti, che si sogliono riparare ogni anno, sarà necessario che andiamo ad ispezionarli con gli architetti e gli scribi del re, registrarli, e che daremo (le spese ai contadini) . . .

Poscritto

(h) *Decisione di Apollonios a proposito del progetto* (*l.* 41-44)

Più tardi. Apollonios, ispezionando il περίχωμα, decideva di fare le dighe . . . (la) larghezza del fosso di 3 invece di 4 cubiti, ossia 64½ (naubia) per uno skhoinion; (spese): 4 dracme per 60 (naubia).

(i) *Ricerca degli scribi per iniziare il lavoro* (*l.* 44-48)

Apollonios è andato via il 7 Hathyr ed io ho navigato con lui fino a Phylake. Là sono sceso dalla barca e l'8 sono andato a Touphis, il 9 a Syron kome, il 10 a Ptolemais, l'11 al Labyrinthos e là ho trovato gli scribi e loro hanno preso la lettera e siamo andati via, direzione città.

Leggenda

misure di lunghezza

1 cubito normale = 52½ cm. (7 palmi di 7½ cm.)
1 cubito grande = 55⅛ cm. (7 palmi di 7⅞ cm.) [2]
1 skhoinion = 100 cubiti normali = 52½ m.
100 skhoinia = 5¼ km.

misura di superficie

1 arura = 100 × 100 cubiti normali = 52½ × 52½ m. = 2756¼ m^2.
10.000 arure = 100 × 100 skhoinia = 5¼ × 5¼ km. = 27½ km^2.

misura di capacità (cf. p. 262 n. 3)

1 naubion = 2 × 2 × 2 cubiti grandi = 110¼ × 110¼ × 110¼ cm. = 1,34 m^3.
= 2,1 × 2,1 × 2,1 cubiti normali

[2] La larghezza di 7,875 (7⅞) è stata calcolata qui con l'aiuto dei dati forniti dal documento stesso (v. nota 3): è il palmo che si trova alla base della misura di capacità *hin* e che va da 7,802 a 8,041 (cf. R. A. Parker, *Demotic Mathematical Papyri*, p. 11).

monete
6 oboli = 1 dracma (simbolo ⊦)
4 dracme = 1 stater
6000 dracme = 1 talento (scritto ⊼, cioè τα)

Quadro esplicativo dei calcoli fatti nel testo

περίχωμα (v. § *b*, commentario)

περίχωμα = 10.000 arure = 100 × 100 skhoinia = 5250 × 5250 m.
περίχωμα = 1.000 arure = 10 × 100 skhoinia = 525 × 5250 m.
περίχωμα = 250 arure = 10 × 25 skhoinia = 525 × $1312\frac{1}{2}$ m. (*l.* 7)

dighe e acquedotti (v. qui sotto)

16 dighe = 16 × 100 skhoinia = 16 × $5\frac{1}{4}$ km. = 84 km. (*l.* 8)
4 acquedotti = 4 × 100 skhoinia = 4 × $5\frac{1}{4}$ km. = 21 km. (*l.* 13)
lunghezza totale: 2.000 skhoinia = 105 km.

Naubia: [3] la quantità di terra da scavare per i 2.000 skhoinia

— secondo il progetto (§ *d*): un fosso, lungo 2.000 skhoinia (di 100 cubiti normali), largo 4 cubiti normali, profondo 2 cubiti normali
= 2.000 × 100 × 4 × 2 cubiti normali
= 2.000 × 86 naubia = 172.000 naubia (cioè 137.600 per le dighe e 34.400 per gli acquedotti)

— secondo il piano definitivo (§ *h*): un fosso, lungo 2.000 skhoinia (di 100 cubiti normali), largo 3 cubiti normali, profondo 2 cubiti normali
= 2.000 × 100 × 3 × 2 cubiti normali
= 2.000 × $64\frac{1}{2}$ naubia = 129.000 naubia.

Spese che Apollonios dovrà pagare

— secondo il progetto (§ *e*)

1) se i lavori verranno finiti durante l'inverno: 4 dracme per ogni 70 naubia.
Spese per i 172.000 naubia, (172.000: 70) × 4 = $9.828\frac{1}{2}$ dracme (secondo il progetto, *l.* 15, 9.834), cioè per ciascuna delle 10.000 arure 0,98 dracma = c. $5\frac{7}{8}$ oboli (secondo il progetto, *l.* 15, 1 dracma);

2) se i lavori non verranno finiti prima del raccolto: 4 dracme per ogni 50 naubia.
Spese per i 172.000 naubia, (172.000 : 50) × 4 = 13.760 (progetto, *l.* 25, idem), cioè per ciascuna delle 10.000 arure 1,376 dracma = 1 dracma e $2\frac{1}{4}$ oboli (progetto, *l.* 25, idem);

— secondo il piano definitivo (§ *h*)

3) 4 dracme per ogni 60 naubia.
Spese per i 129.000 naubia, (129.000 : 60) × 4 = 8.600 dracme, cioè per ciascuna delle 10.000 arure 0,86 dracme = $5\frac{1}{5}$ oboli.

---

[3] Un naubion contiene 2 × 2 × 2 = 8 cubiti cubi, ma sono cubiti questi, più lunghi dei cubiti normali: secondo il progetto 100 × 4 × 2 cubiti normali = 86 naubia, e secondo il piano definitivo 100 × 3 × 2 cubiti normali = $64\frac{1}{2}$ naubia. Nei due casi un naubion contiene quindi 9,3 cubiti normali al cubo (800 : 86 = 9,3 e 600 : $64\frac{1}{2}$ = 9,3) cioè 2,1 × 2,1 × 2,1 cubiti normali.

Calcoli che si possono fare con i dati forniti

Numero dei giorni di lavoro

Visto che un operaio guadagna con questo tipo di lavoro un obolo al giorno,[4] si possono facilmente calcolare quanti sono i giorni necessari per fare il lavoro

1) progetto per l'inverno
172.000 naubia ai (4 dracme = 24 oboli =) 24 giorni di lavoro per 70 naubia = (172.000 : 70) × 24 = 58.971 giorni di lavoro;
2) progetto per il periodo fin dopo il raccolto
172.000 naubia ai (4 dracme = 24 oboli =) 24 giorni di lavoro per 50 naubia = (172.000 : 50) × 24 = 82.560 giorni di lavoro;
3) piano definitivo
129.000 naubia ai (4 dracme = 24 oboli =) 24 giorni di lavoro per 60 naubia = (129.000 : 60) × 24 = 51.600 giorni di lavoro.

Quantità di naubia che un operaio può scavare al giorno

1) progetto per l'inverno
172.000 (naubia) : 58.971 (giorni di lavoro) = 2,9 naubia al giorno;
2) progetto per il periodo fin dopo il raccolto
172.000 (naubia) : 82.560 (giorni di lavoro) = 2 naubia al giorno;
3) piano definitivo
129.000 (naubia) : 51.600 (giorni di lavoro) = 2,5 naubia al giorno.

A proposito dei risultati dei calcoli 1 e 2 conviene ricordarsi che il primo si rapporta all'ipotesi «se i lavori vengono finiti durante l'inverno» (*l.* 14) e il secondo all'ipotesi «se invece i lavori non vengono finiti prima del raccolto» (*l.* 24). Si vede che la diversa durata dei lavori dipende dalla difficoltà del lavoro da farsi; se il lavoro risulterà così difficile che un operaio non potrà scavare più di 2 naubia al giorno, i lavori non verranno finiti prima del raccolto.

Ipotesi a proposito del numero di operai impiegati

Il 1º Gennaio, dopo aver stabilito il piano, Apollonios parte accompagnato da Stothoetis, che va alla ricerca degli scribi necessari per elaborare il piano e li trova il 5 Gennaio. Penso che non si abbia potuto incominciare la maggior parte dei lavori prima di — diciamo — l'inizio di Febbraio. Dall'altra parte, nel «progetto per l'inverno» i lavori dovevano finire prima del raccolto in Giugno, cioè entro 4 mesi, allorché nel progetto alternativo i lavori dovevano finire, al più presto, in Giugno e durare quindi più di 4 mesi. Questi dati messi insieme mi fanno supporre che Apollonios avesse a sua disposizione, per questi lavori, 500-550 operai:[5]

1) progetto per l'inverno
58.971 (giorni di lavoro) : 500 (operai) = 118 (giorni di lavoro), cioè quasi 4 mesi; il lavoro sarà finito verso la fine di Maggio [per 550 operai saranno 107 giorni di lavoro, cioè $3\frac{1}{2}$ mesi: metà di Maggio]

[4] V. doc. **3**, introduzione nota 6.

[5] Può darsi che il numero degli operai sia stato un pó' più grande, perché ho fatto i calcoli in base a giorni lavorativi, senza tener conto di giorni festivi.

2) progetto per il periodo fin dopo il raccolto
82.560 (giorni di lavoro) : 500 (operai) = 165 (giorni di lavoro), cioè $5\frac{1}{2}$ mesi; il lavoro sarà finito verso la metà di Luglio [per 550 operai saranno 150 giorni di lavoro, cioè 5 mesi: fine Giugno].

Nel piano definitivo il lavoro si poteva fare in 51.600 (giorni di lavoro) : 500 = 103 giorni, cioè in $3\frac{1}{2}$ mesi, entro la metà di Maggio [per 550 operai saranno 93 giorni, cioè 3 mesi: fine Aprile].

Dighe, acquedotti e canali

Nonostante l'abbondanza d'informazioni non è facile immaginarsi la disposizione precisa della rete di dighe, acquedotti e canali progettati.

Dighe: sono progettate 16 dighe di $5\frac{1}{4}$ km. cioè, 4 ai lati esterni del terreno e 11 all'interno (§ *c*); alcune dighe che già si trovano sul terreno possono essere incorporate nelle dighe progettate (*l.* 19-21 e 32-33). Per la costruzione dei 84 km. di dighe bisogna scavare un fosso di 84 km., profondo 1,05 m. e largo 2,10 m. (*l.* 8-11).

Acquedotti: ci sono da scavare 4 acquedotti di $5\frac{1}{4}$ km., profondi 1,05 m. e larghi 2,10 m. Altri quattro acquedotti si trovano già da qualche parte sul terreno.

Canali: la parola «canale» viene usata solo più avanti nel testo, cioè là dove si parla di dighe e canali già esistenti (§ *g*; cf. le linee cancellate nel § *e*) e della necessità di usufruire di quei canali che si adattano alle dighe progettate.

Il primo problema che a noi si pone è quello di sapere a che cosa servono le *dighe interne*. Si direbbe a prima vista, leggendo la descrizione della loro disposizione (§ *c*), che servirebbero soltanto da separazione tra i 40 περιχώματα; però solo per questo le dighe sono troppo massicce (1,05 × 2,10 m.). Inoltre vi è il «fosso» con la stessa lunghezza delle dighe ed è difficile figurarsi questo «fosso» di 84 km. diversamente da un insieme di canali che raddoppiano le dighe. Tutto questo fa piuttosto pensare ad un sistema d'irrigazione e diffatti lo è, perché il rialzare l'altezza delle dighe dei terreni in pendenza per farle arrivare al livello delle dighe adiacenti (*l.* 17-18 e 25-26), non può che avere uno scopo, cioè quello idraulico. I 40 περιχώματα sono quindi altretanti «polder», circondati da dighe e canali. Adesso nasce però un altro problema: per contenere l'acqua di un canale ci vogliono due dighe e per i 40 περιχώματα ci vogliono 24 dighe interne invece delle 12 menzionate nel progetto; bisogna quindi considerarle come 12 *paia di dighe*. Questo significa che la quantità di terra scavata dal fosso deve servire per la costruzione di due dighe (probabilmente di mezza altezza), a destra e sinistra, e che ciò sia ben possibile dimostra a guisa d'esempio il disegno schematico sottostante:

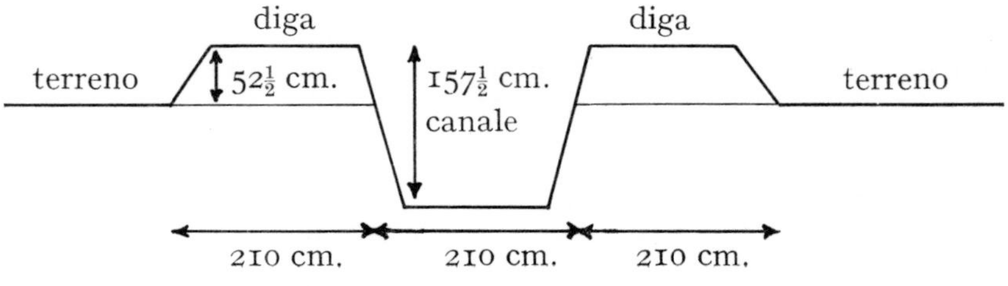

Nel piano definitivo la larghezza del canale (e quindi pure delle dighe) viene stabilita a 157½ cm. invece dei 210 cm. Oltre ad essere meno costoso (*l.* 44) da eseguire, il piano definitivo consuma anche meno terreno coltivabile: sul tracciato qui sopra tre volte 52½ cm. = 157½ cm.

I quattro *acquedotti* o fossi d'irrigazione sono progettati probabilmente là dove si vedono le doppie linee sul disegno (§ *b*), ed anche qui si posano alcuni problemi. Dapprima c'è da chiedersi quale sia la differenza tra un canale ed un acquedotto — visto che tutti e due servono a quanto pare per l'irrigazione — eppoi dove si lascia la terra scavata — visto che con questa non si costruivano altre dighe (gli acquedotti sono menzionati nel § *d* e non nel § *c*). Poi vi è il problema che, secondo quello che abbiamo visto qui sopra, al posto delle doppie linee del disegno, sono già progettati un paio di dighe ed un canale. Penso che si possa risolvere questi problemi assumendo che l'acquedotto venisse semplicemente aggiunto al canale in modo tale che il letto del canale venisse allargato secondo le dimensioni dell'acquedotto e che la terra scavata venisse aggiunta alle dighe, ad esempio, come segue:

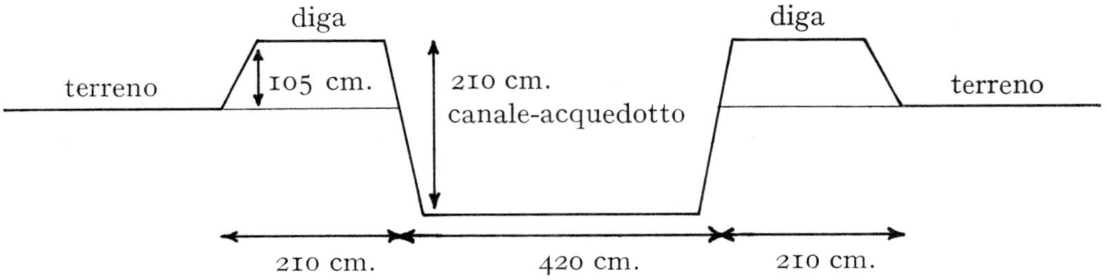

Si noti come queste dighe risulteranno più alte delle dighe «normali» e come il livello dell'acqua del canale-acquedotto, in conseguenza, potrà essere più alto, ciò che è utile per una buona distribuzione dell'acqua, che così scorre facilmente dai canali-acquedotti ai canali normali, che sono di 52½ cm. più bassi, e di là, attraverso canaletti (ὀχετοί: *CdÉ* 43, 1968, 162 n. 5), ai campi. Il disegno nel § *b* fa vedere il sistema di distribuzione.

Intorno al terreno intero corrono ovviamente, oltre alle *diga esterna* indicata nel progetto, un canale [6] ed un'altra diga. Quest'ultima serve al momento stesso ai vicini e si può anche immaginare qui una strada pubblica, ma di tutto questo il progetto non ne parla. Queste dighe esterne devono per forza essere alte come quelle interne che allungono i canali-acquedotti da costruire.

I quattro *acquedotti già esistenti* non sono indicati sul disegno § *b* ed il progetto non menziona la loro posizione. Si trovano forse intorno all'intero terreno? Comunque sia, la presenza di acquedotti dimostra chiaramente che la «dorea» non era interamente incolta quando Apollonios ne è entrato in possesso.

P.

[6] V. P. Cairo Zen. 2 59.220, 1-2: τὴν διώρυγα τὴν πρὸς λίβα τῶν μυρίων ἀρουρῶν.

B

LETTER FROM ZENON TO KLEON

H. × W. = 7.5 × 30 cm.

Sent on 14 October 258 B.C.,
received on 15 October 258 B.C.

Brit. Mus. (now Brit. Library) inv. 539: **P. Petrie II 13 (11)**; cf. P. Petrie III 42 A; C. C. Edgar, *Three Ptolemaic Papyri,* JEA 14 (1928) 288-289 (see BL 2.2, p. 108). The transcription and translation given below are Edgar's.

Zenon writes a letter to the architekton Kleon (see the text Suppl. **C** and the bibl. quoted in the note on line 1 of text no. **42**), concerning the irrigation of land. This land certainly lies in the dorea of Apollonios near Philadelphia, since we know that Zenon is staying there in October 258 (see P. L. Bat. 21. VIII, year 28), although not yet as manager of the dorea. It is remarkable that Zenon (or, perhaps more probably, one of Zenon's clerks) dates the letter to the *Egyptian month* Mesore; compare however the date in a docket of a letter which Zenon receives in this same month in Philadelphia: 14 Mesore, year 28 (PSI 6 559, see P. L. Bat. 21. IV s.v.). In both cases the year 28 is probably the *Macedonian year* (it is less likely that they are reckoning, as early as 258 B.C., according to Financial years).

The letter does not belong to the Zenon archive itself. Like the text Suppl. **C**, it was extracted from mummy cartonnage found by Petrie at Gurob, and doubtless belonged to the archive of the addressee Kleon.

front:

Ζήνων Κλέωνι χαίρειν. Τὸ ὕδωρ τὸ ἐ̣[ν τῆι διώρυγι οὐκ ἀνα]βέβη[κ]εν πλείω ἢ [πῆ]χυν
ὥστε μὴ δύνασθαι ἀπ' αὐτῆς ποτίζε[σθαι τὴν γῆν. Καλῶς ἂν ο]ὖ̣ν̣ π̣[ο]ήσαις ἀνοίξας
τὰς θύρας, ἵνα ποτίζηται ἡ γῆ.
Ἔρ[ρωσο. L] κη Μεσορὴ κγ.

back:

Κλέωνι.
Ḷ κ̣η Μ̣ε̣σ̣ο̣ρὴ κ̅δ̅.
. . . . ω̣ν̣ . . . . υ̣δ . . .
. . . [

Translation

Zenon to Kleon greeting.

The water in the canal has not risen more than a cubit, so that the land cannot be irrigated from it. Please then open the sluicegates in order that the land may be irrigated.

Fare well. Year 28, Mesore 23.

Address:

To Kleon.

Docket:

Year 28, Mesore 24. ---

C.

C

LETTER FROM PANAKESTOR TO KLEON

H. × W. = 12.5 × 30 cm. Sent on 11 October 257 B.C.

Brit. Mus. (now Brit. Library) inv. 534: **P. Petrie II 13 (5)**, plate VI; cf. P. Petrie III 42 B 2; E. Revillout, *Mélanges sur la métrologie, l'économie royale et l'histoire de l'ancienne Égypte*, Paris 1895, pp. 370-395, with translation (his reading and interpretation of the text is not very trustworthy); a new translation is given by A. Bouché-Leclercq, *L'ingénieur Cléon, Revue des Études Grecques* 21 (1908), p. 134. Our reedition of the text is partly based on an unpublished transcription by C. C. Edgar, which was put at our disposal by T. C. Skeat.

The text is nearly complete and written on the recto across the fibres. The verso is illegible. Edgar pointed out that P. Cairo Zen. 1 59.124 (a letter from Panakestor to Zenon) is written by the same hand.

Although this letter provides important evidence for the difficulties encountered by Panakestor in organising Apollonios' dorea in 257/256, it does not belong to the Zenon archive itself. Like the text Suppl. **B**, it was extracted from mummy cartonnage found by Petrie at Gurob, and doubtless belonged to the archive of the addressee, the architekton Kleon (see above text no. **42**, n. *l.* 1).

The word *Limne* "lake" (*l.* 9) designates the entire Arsinoïte nome, and *Mikra Limne* (*ll.* 3 and 5), the small lake, near the Northern border of the meris of Herakleides, see E. Van 't Dack, *Notes sur les Circonscriptions d'origine grecque en Egypte ptolémaïque, Studia Hellenistica* 7 (1951), p. 46 and n. 3.

Πανακέστωρ Κλέωνι χ[αί]ρειν. Ἀπεστείλαμέν σοι καὶ [τ]ῆι $\overline{\kappa\theta}$ ὅπως ἂν ἀποστε[ί]λ̣[ηι]ς π̣[λή]ρωμα ὃ κατασκ[ευ]ᾶι τοὺς ἀγκῶνας τῆς μικρᾶς διώρυγος. Σὺ δὲ φαίνει π̣α̣ρε̣λ̣ηλυθέναι εἰς τὴν μικρὰ[ν] λίμνην. Οὐ̣κ ἔδει μὲν οὖν σε π[α]ραπορεύεσθαι, ἀλλὰ καὶ πρὸς ἡμᾶς παραβαλεῖν ὥρ[α]ς μόρι̣ο̣ν καὶ τεθεα̣μένον σε μὴ βρεχομένην τὴ̣ν γ̣ῆν ἐπερωτῆσαι [δι]ὰ̣ τίν' αἰτίαν οὐ βρέχ[ομ]εν. Οὐ γὰ[ρ] μόνον τέταξαι τὴν μικρὰν λίμνην ἀρχιτεκτο̣νεῖν [ἀλλὰ] καὶ ταύτην. Ἔ̣τι ο̣ὖ̣ν κα̣[ὶ] ν̣ῦ[ν] σ̣υ̣νάντησον ἡμῖν αὔριον ἐπὶ τ̣ὴν ἄφεσιν καὶ ἀρχιτεκ<τ>ό[νη]σ̣ο̣[ν] ὡς δεῖ τὸ ὕδωρ ἀ̣γ̣κ̣ω̣[νίζειν· ἡμεῖς γὰρ] ἄπειροί ἐσμεν. Σώματ̣α̣ δ̣ὲ̣ κ̣α̣[ὶ] τὴν λοιπὴν [χ]ορηγίαν ἡμεῖς παρέξομέν σοι, ὅ[ση]ν ἂν συντάσσῃς. Ἐὰν δὲ μὴ παραγένηι, ἀναγκασθησόμεθα [γ]ράφειν Ἀπολλωνίωι ὅτι μονωτά̣τ̣η ἡ αὐτοῦ γῆ ἐν τῆι Λίμνηι ἄβροχός ἐστιν, ἡμῶν βουλομένων πᾶσαν χορηγίαν παρέχειν.

Ἔρρωσο. L κθ Μεσορὴ $\overline{\kappa\alpha}$.

1 ἀπέστειλα μέν Mahaffy, ἀπεστείλαμεν Wilcken (P. Petrie III p. xv); $\overline{\kappa\beta}$ Mahaffy, $\overline{\kappa\theta}$ Edgar (notes) 1-2 ἀπο|στείλῃς (?) [πλήρ]ωμα Mahaffy, ἀπο|στέλ[λ]ωμ[εν σ]ῶμα Wilcken, ἀπο|στε[ί]λ̣[ηι]ς π̣[λή]ρωμα Edgar (P. Cairo Zen. 2 p. 106) 2 κατασκ[...]αι Mahaffy, κατασκ[άψ]αι Wilcken, κατασκ[άψ]ηι̣ Edgar (Annales du service des Ant. 19, 1920, p. 14 n. 1), κατασκ[ευ]ᾶι Edgar (P. Cairo Zen. 2 p. 106), κατασκ[άψ]ε̣ι E. Mayser (Grammatik II. 1, p. 295) 5 ἀπ[ηρμ]ένον τε τάξαι Mahaffy, οὐ γὰ[ρ] μόνον τέταξαι Wilcken 6 [αἰ]τίαν κα[ταλύε]ιν Mahaffy, ἔ̣τι ο̣ὖ̣ν κα̣[ὶ] ν̣ῦ[ν] Edgar (Annales du Service des Ant. 19, 1920, p. 14); ἀντίασον Mahaffy, ἄντησον Wilcken, σ̣υ̣νάντησον Edgar (Annales du

Service des Ant. 19, 1920, p. 14) 7 τὸ ὕδωρ ἀπ[--] Mahaffy, τὸ ὕδωρ ἀ̣γ̣κ̣ω̣[νίζειν Edgar (P. Mich. Zen. p. 26, n. 1); [ἡμεῖς γάρ] supplevit Smyly (P. Petrie III 42 B 2); σώμ[ατα .... τ]ήν Mahaffy, σώματ̣α̣ [δὲ κα]ὶ [τ]ήν Smyly (P. Petrie III 42 B 2) 9 μονω[--] Mahaffy, μονω[θεῖσα] Rostovtzeff (A Large Estate, p. 67), μόνω[ι ἐπί σ]οι Wilcken (Archiv für Papyrusf. 8, 1927, p. 278), μονωτ̣ά̣τ̣η Edgar (P. Mich. Zen. p. 26 n. 1)

Translation

Panakestor to Kleon greeting.

We have sent you word already on the 29th (read 19th?) that you should send a group of workmen to construct the bends of the small canal. But you seem to have passed by, going to the *Mikra Limne*. You ought, indeed, not to have passed us by, but to have come over for a moment, and, having seen yourself that the land is not irrigated, you should have asked why we do not irrigate. For you are appointed not only to supervise the constructions in *Mikra Limne*, but in this lake as well. Now, then, at last come and meet us to-morrow at the sluice and give instructions as to how we must conduct the water, for we have no experience. We shall ourselves provide you with man-power and other facilities, as much as you order. If, however, you do not come, we shall be compelled to write to Apollonios that his land alone among all others in the *Limne* is not irrigated, although we were willing to provide every facility.

Fare well. Year 29, Mesore 21.

Notes

1 [τ]ῆι κ̅θ̅: this must be an error for ι̅θ̅.
2 For κατασκευᾶι, see E. MAYSER, *Grammatik* I. 1, pp. 128-129.

C.

D

LETTERA DI ZENON A PHANIAS

Dimensioni sconosciute 16 Novembre 248 a.C.

Berl. inv. 13.999: W. SCHUBART, **BGU 6 1297** e U. WILCKEN, *loc. cit.*, p. 192; W. SCHUBART, *Griechische Palaeographie* (1925) p. 29, Abb. 6; L. DELEKAT, *Katoche, Hierodulie und Adoptionsfreilassung* (1964) p. 71-74; BL 3, p. 20 e 5, p. 17.

Contenuto Si tratta del cavaliere ...akhos e di suo padre Nikandros, un ex sottocomandante. Il padre si trova in difficoltà — non sappiamo il perché, dato che né padre né figlio ci sono noti da altri documenti — e, per aiutarlo, il figlio si è deciso di rivolgersi ad Apollonios. Per questo deve però recarsi ad Alessandria, cioè lasciare il kleros che possiede nei dintorni di Philadelphia. A quanto pare non può andarsene senza il permesso di Phanias, il γραμματεὺς τῶν ἱππέων (P. Ryl. 4 562, 4-6) che ritroviamo assai sovente nell'archivio di Zenon (v. la prosopografia: P. L. Bat. 21. IX) e altrove (P. Tebt. 3.1 746 19 n. e P. Freib. 1 7 = EDGAR-HUNT, *Select Papyri*, 2 412). Benché la linea 7 (οὐ κρίνων) ci farebbe credere che si tratterebbe soltanto di una formalità, la realtà deve essere diversa: per ottenere il permesso il figlio fa notare (linea 5) che è suo dovere umano e divino di assistere suo padre, rinforzando la sua richiesta con una raccomandazione niente meno che di Zenon. È d'altronde tipico di Zenon di aver fatto tale raccomandazione.

Chi scrive (o fa scrivere) è senza dubbio il nostro Zenon; però la lettera non viene dal suo archivio, ma probabilmente dall'archivio di Phanias, il destinatario.

facciata anteriore:

[Ζή]νων Φανίαι χαίρειν. Εἰ ἔρρωσαι εὖ ἂν ἔχοι, ὑγιαίνομεν δὲ κα[ὐτοί]. [...]ạχος ὁ τὴν ἐπιστολήν σοι ἀποδιδούς ἐστιν τῶν περὶ Φιλα[δ]έλφ[ειαν] [κα]ταμεμετρημένων ἱππέων, υἱὸς δὲ Νικάνδρου τοῦ πρότερον ὑπὸ Ἱππ[ίαν ὑπο]στ̣ρ̣ατηγήσαντος ἐν Ὀξυρύγχοις. Ἠκλη[ρ]ηκότος δὲ τοῦ πατρὸς αὐτοῦ κα[ὶ ὄντος] ἐν κατοχῆι οἴεται δεῖν μὴ ἐγκαταλείπειν καθάπερ \`δίκαιον´ καὶ ὅσιόν ἐστιν, κα[τα]πλεύσαντα δὲ εἰς Ἀλεξάνδρειαν ἐντυχεῖν Ἀπολλωνίωι καὶ δεηθῆν[αι, ἵνα] παραιτηθῆι. Οὐ κρίνων *vacat* ἄνευ σοῦ ἐκ τοῦ τεταγμένου κινηθῆνα[ι] ἠξίωσεν ἡμᾶς γράψαι σοι. Καλῶς οὖν ποιήσεις ἐπιχωρήσας αὐτῶι.

Ἔρρωσο. L λη Θῶυθ κδ.

facciata posteriore:

Φανίαι.

Traduzione

Zenon saluta Phanias.

Se stai bene, mi farebbe piacere; anche noi siamo sani. [--]akhos, che ti dà questa lettera, è uno dei cavalieri a cui è stato assegnato un kleros nei dintorni di Philadelphia e figlio di Nikandros, che una volta era sottocomandante a Oxyrhynkha, sotto Hippias.

Siccome suo padre si trova in difficoltà ed è in detenzione, crede che è suo dovere — secondo ciò che è il diritto umano e divino — di non abbandonarlo alla sua sorte e di navigare verso nord, sino ad Alessandria, per supplicare Apollonios e scongiurarlo affinché (suo padre) sia lasciato in pace.

Poiché non trova corretto allontanarsi dal suo incarico senza te, ci ha chiesto di scriverti. Ti prego quindi di dargli il permesso.

Salute. Anno 38, il 24 Thoth.

Indirizzo:

A Phanias.

Note

2 [. . .]ạχος: ed. princ. e.g. [Λάμ]ạχος, ma è possibile integrare alcuni altri nomi che sono elencati dall'editore stesso e da UEBEL (*Die Kleruchen Ägyptens*, p. 103 n. 3).

3-4 ὑπὸ Ἱππ[ίαν ὑπο]|σ̣τ̣ρατηγήσαντος: così WILCKEN (*BGU* 6 p. 192).
Il nome del comandante non può essere altro che «Hippias»; la lacuna non permette una integrazione più lunga, come sarebbe Ἵππ[αλον o Ἱππ[ονίκον (v. ed. princ. e BL 3 p. 20).

4 ἀκληρεῖν: «subir un malheur», JOUGUET (Enteuxeis, p. 72 n. 3), «Unglück haben», DELEKAT (*Katoche*, p. 72).

5 κατοχή: «Haft», SCHUBART (ed. princ.). Diversamente, però, DELEKAT (*Katoche*, p. 71-74): «Tempelkatoche».

6 ἵνα] o ὡς]: SCHUBART (ed. princ.).

P.

E

LIST OF TAX ARREARS AND LETTER FROM ACHOAPIS TO PTOLEMAIOS

H. × W. = 17.9 × 13.6 cm. 14 February 229 B.C.

Corpus Christi College MS 541: A. S. Hunt, *A Zenon Papyrus at Corpus Christi College, Cambridge, JEA* 12 (1926) 113-115; **SB 3 7222**; comp. U. Wilcken, Archiv für Papyrusforschung 8 (1927) 285.

Contents The text concerns arrears of taxes on gardens, pigeon-houses, and pastures in several villages in the merides of Herakleides and Themistos. Etearchos (*l.* 33) is probably the well-known nomarches. A certain Zenon is mentioned in *l.* 40 as owing quite a large sum for the ἐννόμιον. Since we know that our Zenon was interested in animal-breeding even after he left the dorea, it seems likely that he is the person mentioned here. The amount of the tax that he has to pay is, in comparison with the other amounts, surprisingly high, but cf. PSI 4 386, 25-27 where he has to pay 343 dr. 5 ob. as arrears for the ἐννόμιον τῶν Ζήνωνος αἰγῶν of year 39 and year 2.

Therefore the text probably gives us a last glance at Zenon, who is apparently still active in 232/231 (Year 16); I do not believe that the text was part of his archive: the list is addressed, in a covering letter, to a certain Ptolemaios, no doubt a praktor or tax official, and must have been kept in his files. (See p. 6 and n. 11). Zenon is mentioned in it among more than ten other persons and the text was certainly not composed on his behalf.

There are no other compelling reasons to include the text in his archive: it was purchased in 1915 among a lot of Roman and Coptic papyri and belongs to a period which is hardly represented in Zenon's papers: no more than two or three texts dating from Years 18 and 19 are known to us.

[plate XXX]:

Col. I

['Οννιτ]ῶ̣ν Κοίτῃ
[. . .]στρατος ιͅα
[. . . .]α̣ς
[. . . .]χος β ϟ
[. . . .].
[καὶ τοῦ] ις L
[(ἕκτη) παραδ]είσων
8-15 ----------
16 [ ]ζ̣
[ ]
[ ]α ϟ-

Col. II

περιστερώνων γ´
Φιλαδελφείας
Ἄνδρων ζ
Νικόλαος (ἑκατοντάρουρος) ε
Ἡρακλείας
Δημήτριος ς
Καρανίδος
Θεόδοτος κ
[.]..ọμαχος ιη
Ἡφαιστ̣ί̣[ω]ν̣ ιε̣
/ οα
καὶ τοῦ ις L
Φιλαδελφείας
Ἀντήνωρ (ἑκατοντάρουρος) ιβ
Ἐτέαρχος ι
Ἀρσινόης Μενεσθεύς ιγ =
Ἡγήμων -C
Ἡρακλείας ις L
Δημήτριος η
[Ἱερᾶ]ς Νήσου

Col. III

ἐννόμιον
Ζήνων τοῦ ις L
ρξθ 𐅵-
Ἀχοᾶπις Πτολεμαίωι
χαίρειν. Κα(λῶς) πο(ήσεις)
πράξας τοὺς προ-
γε̣γραμμένο̣υ̣ς
τὸ ἐν αὐτοῖς ὀφίλημα.
L ιη Χοιὰχ κη.

27 Ν̣ι̣κ̣όμαχος ed. princ., [.]..ọμαχος legimus 39 ἐν ἡμῖν ed. princ., ἐννόμιον legimus 43 κα(τα)λο(γίζου) ed. princ., κα(λῶς) πο(ήσεις) legimus

Translation

(col. II and III)

The (tax of a) third on pigeon-houses
at *Philadelphia*: Andron 7 (drachmai), Nikolaos, holder of 100 arourai, 5 (drachmai); at *Herakleia*: Demetrios 6 (drachmai); at *Karanis*: Theodotos 20 (drachmai), ...omachos 18 (drachmai), Hephaistion 15 (drachmai).
Total: 71.
And for the 16th year
at *Philadelphia*: Antenor, holder of 100 arourai, 12 (drachmai), Etearchos 10 (drachmai); at *Arsinoe*: Menestheus 13 (drachmai) 2 obols, Hegemon 1½ obol; at *Herakleia*, for the 16th year: Demetrios 8 (drachmai); at *Hiera Nêsos*: ---
Pasture-tax
Zenon, for the 16th year, 169 (drachmai) 4 obols.
Achoapis to Ptolemaios, greeting.
Please collect from the persons above mentioned the sums due from them.

Year 18, Choiak 28.

C.

F

DÉDICACE À ANUBIS POUR APOLLÔNIOS ET ZÊNÔN

H. × L. = 52 × 15 cm. Milieu du IIIe siècle av. J.-C.

Stèle Caire JdE 44048: G. LEFEBVRE dans *Annales du Service des Antiquités* 13 (1914) pp. 93-96 et 226, édition reprise par **SB 1 5796**. Ce document vient d'être republié par É. BERNAND, *Recueil des inscriptions grecques du Fayoum*, I, Leiden 1975, pp. 200-202, pl. 76. À la bibliographie qui y est citée, on ajoutera P. M. FRASER dans *Opuscula Atheniensia* 3 (1960) p. 6 n. 7 et J.-C. GRENIER, *Anubis alexandrin et romain*, Leiden 1976 (*EPRO* 57), pp. 28-29.

Pour une description de cette stèle, qui provient de Philadelphie même ou de sa nécropole, voir LEFEBVRE, *o.c.*, p. 94 et BERNAND, *o.c.*, p. 200. Une excellente photographie en a été publiée dans G. GRIMM e.a., *Kunst der Ptolemäer- und Römerzeit im ägyptischen Museum Kairo*, Mayence 1975, pl. 12 (cp. p. 18).

A. Texte hiéroglyphique dans le champ:

«Anubis, maître des Deux-Terres, ...»

B. Texte grec au bas de la stèle:

῾Υπὲρ ᾿Απολλωνίου
καὶ Ζήνωνος
Πασῶς κυνοβοσκὸς
᾿Ανούβι εὐχήν.

«Pour Apollônios et Zênôn:
Pasôs l'éleveur de chiens sacrés,
à Anubis en ex-voto.»

Notes

A. Texte hiéroglyphique:

— L'épithète *nb tȝwy* «Maître du Double Pays», bien attestée pour le pharaon et pour certains dieux (cpr. *Wb* V 218, 11), m'est inconnue par ailleurs pour Anubis. Ce dernier est toutefois fréquemment qualifié de *ḫrp tȝwy* («Guide du Double Pays»),[1] de *sšm tȝwy* («Guide du Double Pays»),[2] de *nb tȝ-ḥḏ* («Maître de Ta-hedj») [3] ou encore de *nb tȝ-ḏsr* («Maître de la Nécropole»)[4] — ce dernier titre divin étant parfois mis au duel (*nb tȝwy-ḏsrw*),[5] — et il est parfois représenté avec la double couronne du roi de Haute- et de Basse-Égypte,[6] toutes choses qui ont pu causer une confusion dans l'esprit du rédacteur de notre texte.

— Le signe en bas à droite n'est pas un hiéroglyphe connu, et nous ne savons pas comment le rendre ni quel lien l'unit au 𓋴 (*ś*) en bas à gauche.

B. Texte grec:

1-2 ᾿Απολλωνίου καὶ Ζήνωνος: selon toute vraisemblance, il s'agit d'Apollônios le dioecète et de Zênôn fils d'Agréophôn, à l'étude des archives duquel le présent volume souhaite contribuer. Cpr. Bernand, *o.c.*, p. 201.

3 Πασῶς: correspond à l'égyptien *Pȝ-n-Šw* («Celui du dieu Chou»?); cpr. Ranke, *PN*, I 111, 10 et J. Quaegebeur, *Le dieu égyptien Shaï*, Louvain 1975 (Orientalia Lovaniensia Analecta 2) pp. 201-202 et 207-208.

— κυνοβοσκός: éleveur des chiens sacrés, animaux du dieu Anubis mentionné dans le texte hiéroglyphique et représenté sur la stèle, qui lui est consacrée. Ce texte est le seul document que nous possédons et qui suggère l'existence, à Philadelphie, d'un sanctuaire consacré à Anubis; cpr. W. J. R. Rübsam, *Götter und Kulte im Faijum*, Diss. Bonn 1974, p. 141 et Bernand, *o.c.*, p. 202.

M.

---

[1] A. M. Blackman and M. R. Apted, *The Rock Tombs of Meir*, VI, Londres 1953 (*Archaeol. Survey of Eg.* 29), p. 1.

[2] J. Vandier, dans *Mélanges Mariette*, Le Caire 1961 (*BE* 32), p. 115.

[3] J. Vandier, *Le papyrus Jumilhac*, Paris s.d., p. 158, n. 153.

[4] A. Kamal, *Stèles ptolémaïques et romaines*, Le Caire 1905 (Cat. gén. des ant. ég. du musée du Caire), passim (v. index).

[5] A. Kamal, *o.c.*, stèles 22123 (*l.* 3) et 22139 (*l.* 3).

[6] R. Holthauer and R. Ahlqvist, *The «Roman Temple» at Tehna el-Gebel*, dans *Studia Orientalia* 43, 7 (Helsinki 1974), p. 13, n. 2.

INDEXES TO PARTS TWO AND THREE

X. GREEK WORDS IN THE LITERARY TEXTS

ἄγγελος **15** 1175
αἰσχύνειν **15** 1172
ἀκούειν **15** 1170
ἀκτή **15** 1173, 1179, 1199
ἀλλά **14** 7
ἄλλοτε **16** I 9, 11
ἄλοχος **15** 1165
ἁμαρτῇ **15** 1195
ἀναστρέφειν **15** 1176
ἀπίσχειν **14** 5
ἄρα **15** 1169
ἀρά **15** 1167
ἀρᾶσθαι **15** 1168
Ἄργος **15** 1197
ἅρμα **15** 1166, 1195
αὐτός **15** 1166, 1172, 1178; **16** II 1

βαρύς **15** 1202
βία **15** 1165
βρόμος **15** 1202
βροντή **15** 1201

γάρ **15** 1175
γῆ **15** 1176, 1199
γιγνώσκειν **16** II 7

δάκρυον **15** 1178
δέ **14** 2, 3; **15** 1178, 1179, 1195, 1198, 1203, 1204; **16** I 6, 7
δέσποινα **16** I 8
δεσπότης **15** 1196
δίκη **15** 1171
διολλύναι **15** 1171

ἐγώ **15** 1172
εἶδος **16** I 3
εἴκελος **16** I 7
εἶναι **15** 1169, 1199, 1204
εἰς **15** 1194, 1203; **16** I 12
εἰσβάλλειν **15** 1198
ἐκ **15** 1177; **16** II 5
ἐμβάλλειν **14** 5
ἐμός **15** 1169, 1170

XI. DATING

a) *Rulers*

b) *Years*

c) *Double dates*

d) *Macedonian months*

e) *Egyptian months*

XII. PERSONAL NAMES

XIII. TITLES AND OCCUPATIONS

XIV. GEOGRAPHY

XV. RELIGION

XVI. MEASURES, WEIGHTS AND MONEY

a) *Measures and weights*

b) *Money*

XVII. GENERAL INDEX[1]

[1] Exclusive of καί, μέν, δέ, τε and the definite article.

βοῦς **52** 10
βραχύς **A** 30
βρέχειν **C** 4, 5

γαμεῖν **51** 16
γάρ **23** 3; **27** 12; **29** 2, 6, 7; **30** 12; **39** 18; **47** 4; **48** 4; **49** 28; **50** 3; **51** 2, 11, 13, 19, 26, 29; **56** *A* 8, *B* intr., 5, 9; **58** 8; **A** 40; **C** 5, 7
γαυνάκης **51** 28
γε **51** 17
γένημα **49** 27; **52** 17; **66** 3
γεύειν **30** 6
γεωμετρεῖν **38** 2, 4
γεωργός **54** 8; **A** 32
γῆ **38** 4, 13, 27; **55** 5; **A** 18, 28; **B** 2, 3; **C** 4, 9
γήιδιον **67** 8
γίγνεσθαι **17** 8; **20** 6; **27** 6, 11; **34** 1, 3; **41** 9; **46** 3; **52** 6; **56** *B* intr., 8; **57** 4; **64** 12; **67** 2; **A** 8, 10 (bis), 12, 17, 33; see also index XVIII *Symbols*
γιγνώσκειν **22** 5; **24** 1; **50** 5; **57** 2
γνωρίζειν **65** 1
γραμματεύς **18** 2; **63** 5; **A** 40, 47
γράφειν **20** 9; **22** 2, 7; **23** 1; **24** 4; **29** 7; **30** 2, 22; **31** 9; **32** 1; **36** 1, 3; **37** 1, 2; **39** 2; **40** 8; **42** 4; **43** 8; **44** 3; **49** 2, 5, 7, 12, 23, 26; **50** 2; **51** 5, 24, 28, 29; **53** 8; **68** 2; **C** 9; **D** 8

δάνειον **20** 3; **55** 6
δεῖγμα **71** 4
δεικνύναι **28** 2, 5; **51** 30; **53** 6
δεῖν **33** 22; **37** 2; **49** 3, 26; **50** 4; **A** 8, 12, 16, 17, 26, 38; **C** 3, 7; **D** 5
δεῖσθαι **17** 6; **19** 12; **29** 5; **51** 25; **D** 6
δέκα **33** 9; **A** 7
δεκάταρχος **69** 1
δέκατος **35** 21, 34
δεξιός **21** 1
δέρρις **54** 26
δέσμη **33** 24, 27
δεύτερος **35** 13
διά **17** 8; **27** 4, 8, 12; **30** 13; **31** 1, 7; **35** 12, 16; **37** 3; **49** 27, 29; **50** 5; **51** 20; **52** 14; **57** 4; **C** 5
διαγγέλλειν **24** 4
διάγραμμα **73** 5
διαγράφειν **A** 7
διαγραφή **48** 2
διακούειν **17** 7
διαμαρτύρεσθαι **58** 9
διαπλευρισμός **A** 6, 20
διάρταβος **54** 20, 24
διαστολή **38** 9, 13
διατηρεῖν **27** 11
διατιθέναι **32** 3
διατρίβειν **51** 15
διαφορά **A** 26
διαφωνεῖν **30** 5
διδάσκαλος **20** 9
διδόναι **17** 4; **30** 2; **31** 8, 10; **33** 22; **34** 1; **37** 1, 2; **39** 3, 7, 17, 22; **46** 3; **50** 2, 3, 6; **51** 29 (bis); **54** 3, 9; **58** 4; **71** 4; **72** 5; **A** 40
]διδόναι **19** 11
διεγγ[**19** 14
διεγγύημα **49** 29
διέρχεσθαι **41** 4
δίκαιος **17** 8; **19** 16; **51** 9; **D** 5
διό **29** 4; **51** 21; **54** 25
διοικεῖν **22** 8
διοικητής **20** 4; **50** 1
διορθοῦν **49** 8
διότι **57** 2
διῶρυξ **27** 5, 12; **38** 14, 16, 18, 20, 23, 25, 30; **A** 22, 35, 37; **B** 1; **C** 2
δοκεῖν **17** 6; **29** 2; **39** 11
δοκός **75** *d* 2
δορκαδοθήρας **65** 1
δραχμή **20** 5; **30** 7; **60** 5, 10; see also index XVIII *Symbols*
δρόμος **28** 5
δύνασθαι **29** 4; **41** 2, 5; **51** 23; **64** 14; **B** 2
δύο **33** 25, 27; **38** 27; **43** 3; **54** 29; **60** 5, 10
δωδέκατος **34** 4
δωρεά **28** 6

ἐάν **19** 13; **39** 4, 19; **42** 3; **50** 4; **51** 8, 19, 22, 23, 29; **52** 15; **53** 8; **58** 7; **A** 14, 22, 24, 35; **C** 8
ἐάνπερ **57** 1
ἕβδομος **35** 31
]εγγυᾶν **19** 12
ἐγγύη **33** 19
ἐγκαταλείπειν **D** 5
ἔγχυσις **66** 2
ἐγώ **18** 5; **19** 2; **21** 2; **22** 8; **23** 1; **28** 6; **30** 2; **31** 7, 9; **35** 16; **38** 2; **39** 2, 6, 12, 23; **41** 1, 3 (bis), 6, 8, 9, 10; **42** 4; **43** 3, 10; **44** 1; **45** 3; **49** 8 (bis), 26, 28; **51** 12, 13, 18, 20 (bis), 23, 30; **54** 27; **62** 4; **68** 7
ἔθος **A** 37, 41(?)
εἰ **17** 6; **23** 2, 4; **30** 8; **37** 2, 3; **40** 7; **42** 1; **51** 1; **56** *A* 3, *B* 4; **57** 2; **D** 1
εἰδέναι **22** 7; **30** 19; **36** 4; **40** 8; **44** 4; **48** 2; **A** 27
εἰκάς **35** 24
εἴκοσι **46** 3
εἶναι **21** 2; **24** 3, 5; **29** 6, 7; **30** 4, 8; **31** 2; **32** 6; **37** 3; **38** 7, 20 in margine; **39** 11, 12; **41** 7; **42** 2, 5; **47** 5; **48** 2; **49** 17; **50** 5; **51** 3, 9, 10, 14, 21, 27; **52** 15, 17; **56** *A* 4 (bis), 5, *B* 12; **64** 14, 23; **67** 5; **68** 6; **A** 4, 7 (bis), 14, 15, 19, 20, 27, 28, 30, 34, 36, 38, 41; **C** 7, 9; **D** 2, 4, 5
εἰς **20** 5, 6, 11; **21** 3; **23** 3; **24** 2; **25** 3; **26** 1; **27** 3, 5, 9, 13; **29** 4; **31** 8; **33** 12, 19; **35** 5, 11; **36** 2; **39** 16; **41** 4; **48** 4 (bis); **49** 12; **50** 2, 4, 5; **53** 3; **54** 4, 13, 18, 22; **55** 5; **56** *B* intr. (bis), 5, 9; **60** 3, 8; **63** 31; **66** 1 (bis),

XVIII. SYMBOLS

970127 171.00 (48.00) set